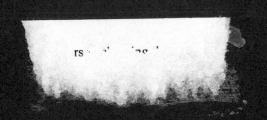

MARGARET MEAD
AND RUTH BENEDICT

# MARGARET MEAD AND RUTH BENEDICT

The Kinship of Women

Hilary Lapsley

UNIVERSITY OF MASSACHUSETTS PRESS   Amherst

LC 98-54185   ISBN 1-55849-181-3
Designed by Mary Mendell
Set in Quadraat by Keystone Typesetting, Inc.
Printed and bound by Sheridan Books

Library of Congress Cataloging-in-Publication Data
Lapsley, Hilary.
Margaret Mead and Ruth Benedict : the kinship of women /
IIilary Lapslcy.
p. cm.
Includes bibliographical references.
ISBN 1-55849-181-3 (cloth : alk. paper)
1. Mead, Margaret, 1901–1978. 2. Benedict, Ruth, 1887–1948.
3. Anthropologists—Biography. 4. Female friendship.
5. Lesbian anthropologists—Biography. I. Title.
GN21.M36L36  1999  301′.092′2—dc21  98-54185 CIP
British Library Cataloguing in Publication data are available

Acknowledgment is made to the following
individuals and organizations for permission to quote:
The Institute for Intercultural Studies: published and
unpublished writings of Margaret Mead; Ruth Benedict,
Patterns of Culture.
The Modern Poetry Association: Margaret Mead,
"Misericordia," Poetry, February 1930, © 1930 by the
Modern Poetry Association.
Excerpts from Derek Freeman, "Fa'apua'a Fa'amu and
Margaret Mead," American Anthropologist 91:4 (December
1989) reproduced by permission of the American
Anthropological Association; not for further reproduction.
Excerpts from Margaret Mead, An Anthropologist at Work:
Writings of Ruth Benedict, edited by Margaret Mead. Copyright ©
by Margaret Mead, renewed 1987 by Mary Catherine Bateson.
Reprinted by permission of Houghton Mifflin Company.
All rights reserved.
The lines from Poem XII of "Twenty-One Love Poems," from
The Fact of a Doorframe: Poems Selected and New, 1950–1984 by
Adrienne Rich. Copyright © 1984 by Adrienne Rich. Copyright
© 1975, 1978 by W. W. Norton & Company, Inc. Copyright ©
1981 by Adrienne Rich. Reprinted by permission of the author
and W. W. Norton & Company, Inc.

# CONTENTS

*Illustrations follow page 182*

## ACKNOWLEDGMENTS

 Much assistance, both in the United States and New Zealand, has been given to me in the writing of this book. In particular, I would like to thank the following people and institutions, as well as everyone else who contributed:

Mary Wolfskill, Manuscript Division, Library of Congress has been of invaluable assistance with the Margaret Mead Papers, as has Nancy McKechnie of Special Collections, Vassar College Libraries, which houses the Ruth Fulton Benedict Papers. I am grateful to Ruth Limmer for permission to quote from material in the Louise Bogan Papers, Amherst College Library Archives and Special Collections, Amherst, Massachusetts. Other useful collections are the Jane Howard Papers, Rare Book and Manuscript Library, Columbia University, New York; the Reo Franklin Fortune Papers, Alexander Turnbull Library, Wellington, New Zealand; and the Franz Boas Papers, American Philosophical Society, Philadelphia. I would also like to thank Ann Brownell Sloane, Mary Catherine Bateson, and the Institute for Intercultural Studies for permission to quote from Margaret Mead's unpublished works and for helpful responses to my numerous inquiries.

For permitting me to interview them, in person or by phone: Mary Catherine Bateson, Jean Houston, Philip Sapir (I owe a special debt of gratitude to him and other members of the Sapir family for making available correspondence from Edward Sapir to Ruth Benedict), Ann McLean, Deborah Gewertz, Evelyn Shritt, Nathalie and Richard Woodbury; and to other scholars in the same field, both for their helpful scholarly works and also for assistance on various points: Judith Modell, Margaret Caffrey, Desley Deacon, Virginia Yans-McLaughlin.

For thoughtful reading and editorial suggestions, I would like to thank my friends Heather McPherson and Anne Else, as well as Clark Dougan, Ella Kusnetz, and the anonymous reviewers at the University of Massachusetts Press. For indexing I thank Simon Cauchi.

Friends have also been patient and have often made helpful comments during conversations. They include Anna Whitehead, Margot Roth, Claire-Louise McCurdy, Daphne Hewson, Mairi Jay, Susan Cauchi, Aorewa McLeod, Paul Haines, and many others. I could not have completed the project without friends and colleagues in the United States who provided practical help, hospitality, and thoughtful conversation; here I would like to acknowledge Faye Crosby, Sandra Tangri, Bonnie Strickland, Esther Rothblum, Penny Dugan, Jackie Weinstock, Patricia Roberts, Harry Breger, Ruth Backes, Ellen Dickinson, Anne Mulvey, Donna O'Neill, Dee Breger, Joan Branwell, Peggy Shook, Gail Hornstein, Susan van Dyne, and Deb Gallagher.

Many of my colleagues at the University of Waikato have made helpful suggestions or at least listened patiently; they include Marion de Ras, Catherine Kingfisher, and Radhika Mohanram in Women's and Gender Studies, as well as Judith Macdonald, Tom Ryan, Wendy Cowling, and Raymond Richards. Secretarial assistance from Helen Baird and others must be acknowledged, too.

Funding and practical assistance for the project came from the School of Social Sciences, the University of Waikato/Te Whare Wananga o Waikato, which provided me with study leave and research grants; the N.Z.-U.S. Foundation, which awarded me a Fulbright Scholarship; the Center for Research on Women, Wellesley College, where I was a visiting scholar in 1992; and the Department of Psychology, Smith College, whose members made me welcome as a visitor in 1994.

Finally, a special tribute to Rosemary Barrett who has traveled with me on this journey.

**MARGARET MEAD
AND RUTH BENEDICT**

Works frequently cited have been identified by the following abbreviations:

| | |
|---|---|
| AW | *An Anthropologist at Work: Writings of Ruth Benedict*, ed. Margaret Mead |
| BW | Margaret Mead, *Blackberry Winter: My Earlier Years* |
| BW draft | Draft manuscript of BW, MM Papers |
| FB | Franz Boas Papers, American Philosophical Society, Philadelphia |
| GJ | Luther Cressman, *A Golden Journey* |
| Howard | Jane Howard Papers, Rare Books and Manuscript Library, Columbia University, New York. |
| JH | Jean Houston, interview with Margaret Mead, "The Mind of Margaret Mead," MM Papers |
| LF | Margaret Mead, *Letters from the Field, 1925–1975* |
| MM | Margaret Mead Papers, Library of Congress, Washington, D.C. |
| RFB | Ruth Fulton Benedict Papers, Special Collections, Vassar College Libraries, Poughkeepsie, N.Y. |
| RFF | Reo Franklin Fortune Papers, Alexander Turnbull Library, Wellington, New Zealand |
| SF | Sapir Family Papers |

## INTRODUCTION

This is the story of a lifelong friendship between two remarkable women, Margaret Mead and Ruth Benedict. In the forefront of their generation of anthropologists, Mead and Benedict fashioned unorthodox lives with intelligence and resourcefulness, creating freedom to love and work. The two first met at New York's Barnard College in 1922, Benedict the teacher and Mead, fifteen years younger, her student. They soon became mentor and protégée, then lovers. The friendship survived rough patches, outlasted Mead's three marriages and a love affair, and saw Benedict through the end of a marriage and two subsequent lesbian partnerships. All along it nurtured and influenced their scholarly work in anthropology, work of such significance that it has been part of a revolution in the way we think of ourselves.

Shared intellectual interests made fertile ground for companionship, although the two women were poles apart in temperament. Mead was energetic, optimistic, extroverted, and above all, a change-maker. She was "earthbound," to quote her poet friend, Louise Bogan, whereas Benedict was more of a dreamer. A reserved woman, prone to depression and acutely sensitive, Benedict felt herself an outsider, "a stranger in this land," as one of her biographers put it.[1] Out of their similarities and differences, Mead and Benedict forged a strong allegiance, a friendship characterized by both eros and agape, a bond incorporating sexuality and sisterly love. Between themselves they created a private myth for their relationship in an environment that did not readily uphold women's loyalties to each other. Their closeness lasted twenty-five years until Ruth's death in 1948.

With today's interest in exploring new forms of family, kinship and relationship, paying biographical attention to a friendship can be deeply rewarding. Mead and Benedict managed to sustain a significant relationship throughout their lives, successfully negotiating obstacles in the form of separations of long duration, the claims of their different partners, secrecy about lesbianism, the potential for professional rivalry, and, not the least, their own markedly different personalities. To use the words of Adrienne Rich, writing of the daily struggles of women to reinvent themselves, Mead and Benedict found ways to love one other as "two lovers of one gender, . . . two women of one generation."[2] The loyalty, commitment, and sheer inventiveness shown in their achievement give us food for thought on many questions. What is the role of sexuality in women's friendships? Do lesbian friendships lead to especially strong bonds between women? Does sexual expression between teacher and student have to be a harmful "power relationship"? Should "crushes" be dismissed as adolescent and immature? Have we focused on intellectual achievement as solitary in nature and neglected the synergistic nature of collaboration? What is the role of friendship communities in the production of knowledge? Might we be more intimate with a best friend than with a lover? Does loving men preclude loving women? Can relationships be loyal without being exclusive? How do marriage and children affect all of these areas? Though this was a friendship between women who lived their ideas at a moment in history, a cultural watershed, these questions persist.

Mead's and Benedict's era of anthropology was a classical period. In their day, anthropology became synonymous with fieldwork, its usual apprenticeship a lonely sojourn in a "primitive" society. Anthropologists saw their work as a race against time, for western influence was rapidly penetrating all corners of the globe, leaving few "unspoiled" societies. Ethnographic restudies of remote areas were seldom contemplated, as with meager funding and few to do the work, one anthropologist per culture proved the best strategy for harvesting quick dividends. This emphasis led to the "my people" syndrome, as historian George Stocking has termed it.[3] Returning from their quests, anthropologists laid claim to specialist knowledge of their territories, and though they often viewed colonials as crude, insensitive, and exploitive, many argued that anthropologists themselves were part of the colonial imperative, though they harvested intellectual rather than material spoils.

Though they were implicated in colonialism, the generation of American anthropologists coming of age after World War I contested the biological fundamentalism of their nineteenth-century predecessors, which they saw as a form of "racism," a term popularized by Ruth Benedict in the 1940s.[4] They embraced cultural relativism as a philosophy, believing that human races are equally endowed, that cultural differences arise from the circumstances of history rather than from biological destiny, and that westerners can profit from understanding the ingenuities of cultural arrangements different from our own. American scholars were at the cutting edge of the social sciences, contributing to a ferment of new ideas. Alongside progressive political thinkers, innovators in psychology, sociology, and psychoanalysis, and professionals in social work, child guidance, and psychotherapy, scholars created a singular vision of individual and society which gave rise to indelibly new forms of social understanding and has become part of the character of twentieth-century western thought.

Margaret Mead and Ruth Benedict were extraordinarily successful at popularizing this pathbreaking work, more so than any of their contemporaries in anthropology. Fieldwork was not, in fact, Benedict's forte, though she did spend several summers in the Southwest. Making her home at Columbia University, she earned a reputation as a great theorist, an insightful synthesizer of others' fieldwork, and not least, a gifted teacher and writer. For many years her 1934 classic, *Patterns of Culture*, was the best-selling anthropological work of all time, and her postwar exploration of Japanese culture, *The Chrysanthemum and the Sword*, was widely read and admired.

Though Benedict was renowned, Margaret Mead certainly eclipsed her. A celebrity by her mid-twenties, a daring young woman who had lived among "South Sea Islanders" and returned to give advice to Americans about their own sexual mores, Mead became the public face of anthropology. Her lifetime base was the American Museum of Natural History in New York, though before the Second World War drove anthropologists home Mead spent years in the field, emerging from time to time to publicize her work. After the war her popular writing, her tireless schedule of speaking engagements, and her refreshing enthusiasm for commenting with perspicacity on anything and everything kept her in the public eye. In her time, Mead's status as a woman in American public life was surely surpassed only by Eleanor Roosevelt. In her later years as a perpetual globetrotter, *Time* magazine went as far as calling Mead "the mother of the world."[5]

Despite their cultural relativism, anthropologists were not quick to acknowledge its implications for themselves. They sought the status of a scientific discipline, and with a modernist cast of mind they worshipped at the shrine of objectivity and scientific method. Yet inevitably they wove into their work concerns of their own, reflecting the preoccupations of intellectuals of their generation, as well as personal idiosyncrasies. With hindsight, we can see their work on "savage otherness" as revealing, in their representations of others, their own cultural worlds as much as the realities of "primitive" societies.[6] Though the core of Mead's and Benedict's life work genuinely lay in striving to make the world safe for difference by promoting understanding across cultures, they also promoted a vision of

America as a place where they could safely express their own differences. Their scholarly work mirrored questions they felt acutely in their own lives and in their friendship, questions about gender roles, homosexuality, deviance, temperament, tolerance, social change, and the role of the woman intellectual. Developing their ideas as New Women of the 1920s, they rejected the maternalist politics of an earlier generation of women's rights advocates, which sought to extend a womanly influence to the public sphere. Along with progressive women of their generation, Mead and Benedict wanted a world in which women could do anything and be anything.[7]

Although Mead and Benedict were not in the habit of joint authorship, their mutual influence was immense. They sparked off ideas in each other and went over work in minute detail, discussing it frequently and extensively in person or through correspondence. They encouraged each other, were unstinting with praise and at times with criticism. At the end of Ruth's life, Margaret was able to say truthfully, "When she died, I had read everything she had ever written, and she had read everything I had ever written. No one else had, and no one else has."[8] Yet their relationship has been largely neglected or underestimated in accounts of their life and work, especially in the case of Margaret Mead, whose personal life is often reduced to the fact that she had three husbands. Mead herself, to be sure, played down the importance of the friendship. In *Blackberry Winter: My Earlier Years*, now regarded as a classic of American autobiography, she deliberately presented a heterosexual face to her public. Mead did emphasize the importance of friendships with women, yet the reader would never guess the centrality of Ruth Benedict to her life. As her daughter, Mary Catherine Bateson, was to say, "Margaret's words are only a concealment to the reader who prefers to repose in a conventional mode of interpretation."[9]

The plain, everyday sexism of our culture, and its close cousin, homophobia, are largely responsible for women's friendships seldom being accorded their real worth. In most accounts of women's lives, their relationships with men are endlessly scrutinized for evidence of help or hindrance and for models to emulate or avoid. Sylvia Plath and Ted Hughes, Jean-Paul Sartre and Simone de Beauvoir, Virginia and Leonard Woolf, and Franklin and Eleanor Roosevelt are among the couples frequently discussed. The relationship between Beauvoir and Sartre makes for an interesting comparison with Mead and Benedict. Beauvoir promoted her way of living as a "life of freedom," and one might well ask why Mead and Benedict's friendship should not be subject to as much admiration and scrutiny. Beauvoir and Sartre made a commitment to a shared intellectual life and to a constancy of emotional support, which, as with Mead and Benedict, involved neither exclusiveness, nor sharing a household, nor any continuity of sexual relationship. Indeed, Beauvoir's adieu to Sartre begins in a remarkably similar manner to Mead's epitaph for Benedict: "This is the first of my books—the only one no doubt—that you will not have read. . . ."[10]

As a biographer, I have found that writing about Mead and Benedict has presented challenges and rewards. The nature of their friendship led to secrecy, although Mead's commitment to the preservation of both her own and Benedict's papers ensured that the story would emerge. Mead, in fact, did much to shape the image of Benedict's life. She was Benedict's biographer on two occasions, organizing the substantial *An Anthropologist at Work: Writings of Ruth Benedict* and writing a smaller volume, *Ruth Benedict*. Her own autobiography, *Blackberry Winter: My Earlier Years*, is a vivid account of her own life, though its flaws in dealing with the friendship have been noted. Mead had intended to write a sequel but never did, her chronology largely halting at the distressing period in her life when Ruth died and Gregory Bateson left her. It was Mead's daughter, Mary Catherine Bateson, who revealed in her loving memoir of her parents, *With a Daughter's Eye*, that Mead and Benedict had been lovers.[11]

A number of secondary sources have provided the groundwork for understanding the pair's relationship. I have been helped enormously by Jane Howard's *Margaret Mead: A Life*, with its extensive research involving hundreds of interviews with Mead's friends and associates, and by the two scholarly biographies of Benedict which add much to Mead's account, Judith Modell's *Ruth Benedict: Patterns of a Life* and Margaret Caffrey's *Ruth Benedict: Stranger in this Land*.[12]

The lifting of restrictions on some of Mead's and Benedict's personal papers has given me access to material previously denied to those outside the family circle and has made it possible for me to reconstruct the story of the friendship much more fully. I had access to Benedict's personal correspondence at Vassar College, which was helpful. The most crucial source has been the many letters between Mead and Benedict, housed in the voluminous Mead Archive at the Library of Congress. Much of their correspondence from the 1930s and 1940s, amounting to hundreds of closely typed pages, is now available, and this, more than any other source, displays the day-to-day texture of the friendship. A useful adjunct has been correspondence between Mead and her close friend, Marie Eichelberger. Eichelberger, always anxious for Mead's approval, provided many gossipy accounts of Benedict's domestic life, giving a level of detail often absent from Benedict's own letters.

Letters between Mead and Benedict from the Samoan period, and some letters from New Guinea, are still not available. Nevertheless, I have found revealing sources on that period. Mead herself published extensive extracts from the earlier correspondence, especially in *An Anthropologist at Work*. A Library of Congress folder, "Dream Research," provided a treasure trove, containing a compilation of dreams from the 1920s, both from Mead and from some of her friends, including Ruth Benedict. As a psychologist, I found the dreams fascinating, and with Mead's notes accompanying many of them, they act as a guide to her emotional concerns during that period. I was fortunate, too, in having access to Edward Sapir's letters to Ruth Benedict; sadly, hers have not survived, nor have letters between Margaret Mead and Sapir. Nevertheless, I have been able to uncover many of the details of the Sapir-Mead-Benedict triangle, a complex set of interactions, the fallout from which had a strong influence on the history of anthropology.

Many thousands of people who are still alive knew Mead, and some remember Benedict, but they are mostly of a younger generation. I interviewed several key informants, who helped me with firsthand knowledge and thoughtful interpretations, but on the whole I found the primary materials more informative, including Jean Houston's unpublished book-length interview with Mead. Among secondary materials, new sources in the history of anthropology, both scholarly writing and recollections, have been especially useful.

My interpretation of the friendship, both in its uniqueness and, to use a phrase loved by Mead and Benedict, in its cultural patterning, has been assisted by the new scholarship in women's studies, feminist psychology, and lesbian studies.[13] With so much writing about Mead and Benedict accepting uncritically the image of heterosexuality that they projected and focusing on the influence of the menfolk in their lives, I have taken a different stance, shifting the lens to emphasize the location of the relationship in a twentieth-century version of what historian Carroll Smith-Rosenberg called "the female world of love and ritual." The friendship was not conducted in isolation; it was framed by circles of friends, particularly women friends. I found that focusing on these friendship circles, which often involved affection, "crushes," and sometimes lesbian relationships, helped to provide a context for understanding Mead and Benedict.[14] The sexual aspect of the relationship has, of course, been difficult to investigate, and I hope I have not fallen too far into today's error of oversexualizing relationships. Although the many and varied sexual connections among Benedict, Mead, and their friends were important, perhaps these relationships depended even more on love and collegiality.

On a personal note, I would like to emphasize that the narrative is my own particular "take" on Mead and Benedict. I have researched it painstakingly and have tried to do justice to the complexities I have encountered, but the book is inevitably colored by my own point of view, just as I argue that Mead's and Benedict's work is colored by theirs. I am a psychologist, not an anthropologist, a position that leaves me free from troublesome loyalties but clearly identifies me as an outsider looking in. Mead and Benedict were, of course, psychologically oriented anthropologists, and in the process of writing about them I have come to an appreciation of their work, believing them to have been pioneers of an innovative form of "cultural psychology" underrated within my own discipline.

An outsider in another respect, I am not an American. In investigating Margaret Mead from the Pacific, perhaps I am returning the favor ("the Empire writes back"). As a Pakeha (white) New Zealander, much of my cultural heritage is, of course, shared with Mead and Benedict, but there are some differences that I have found strange or amusing and a few, no doubt, that I have failed to apprehend. One instance stands out. On my first visit to the American Museum of Natural History, feeling rather lost and homesick, I approached the Hall of the Pacific Peoples. When I came upon the display of Margaret Mead's well-known cape and cane I was very moved. Shortly afterward, noticing the shrunken head of a "native" from some Pacific island, I felt unexpectedly shocked, my mind flashing to my granddaughter, who has Maori ancestry. I was insulted on her behalf. It may not be possible—or perhaps it would take the skill of an anthropologist!—to unravel all the strands of thought and emotion arising from our differing *turangawaewae* (the Maori term for home or, literally, a place to stand), but that day I felt alien, sensing a gulf between my own and American sensibilities. I knew that New Zealand friends would easily understand what I was feeling, but I did not feel so sure about American friends.

Of course, it is not as if insults have not gone in the other direction. New Zealand-born Derek Freeman has done his best to bring Margaret Mead's work into disrepute, although he has dented her public image without having presented, in my opinion, an entirely convincing case.[15] This book does not have Mead's Samoan work as a central focus, but I will not hesitate to shed some light on the rather sour note introduced by my compatriot.

Another personal challenge has been in writing this book as a lesbian scholar. My initial feeling at embarking on the project was one of excitement at participating in sweeping skeletons out of the closets of history. The longer I worked at understanding Mead and Benedict's relationship, the less inclined I was to deliver too easy labels and the more I appreciated the subtleties of their own preferences and adaptations in a different cultural climate. I was also challenged by their sheer loyalty and the constancy of their mutual regard. Biography may well be "a scrofulous cottage industry," as Elizabeth Hardwick once scathingly termed it, but it does not inevitably make petty the lives of great people.[16] It can also enrich the lives of the less than great, and for that I thank Margaret Mead and Ruth Benedict. I have immensely enjoyed the time I spent unraveling the story of their friendship.

# 1

## The Punk

RUTH BENEDICT INITIALLY MADE a poor impression on Margaret Mead. They met in the fall of 1922 when Margaret, a psychology major in her senior year at Barnard, enrolled in an anthropology course offered by Prof. Franz Boas. Boas, a German Jew in his mid-sixties and the founding professor of anthropology at Columbia University, was a riveting presence. Passionate about his subject, he was single-handedly altering the course of anthropology in the United States.

With his unparalleled grasp of the history of human cultures, his progressive political views, and his experiences of fieldwork with the Eskimos of Baffinland and the Native Americans of the northwest coast, he was an intriguing man to Margaret and his other students. The professor's manner was forbidding, Margaret wrote, for "with his great head and slight frail body, his face scarred from an old duel and one eye drooping from a facial paralysis, [he] spoke with an authority and a distinction greater than I had ever met in a teacher." He would occasionally pause to put questions to the class, questions that were usually rhetorical, for the Barnard girls were too frightened to reply. Even Margaret, who could never have been described as a shrinking violet, wrote down her answers privately, "glow[ing] with pleasure" if she turned out to be right.[1] As the weeks went by, she became bold enough to speak up and stood out as a particularly enthusiastic student.

Ruth Benedict attended the Barnard class as Boas's teaching assistant. This was a new experience for the thirty-five-year-old doctoral candidate, although before her marriage she had taught in a girl's high school. Her duties included giving demonstrations for small groups of students at the nearby American Museum of Natural History, where she explained displays such as the model of the Sun Dance in the Plains Indian Hall. The Barnard girls found Benedict something of a puzzle, as she appeared entirely to lack confidence. She blushed easily and stammered a little; in fact, as Margaret Mead recalled in an interview with Jean Houston, she "could barely put one word after another in public." Her partial deafness gave her a strained air as she struggled to follow class discussions, and her appearance was unappealing: "We saw her as a very shy, almost distrait, middle-aged woman," said Mead. Her hair was "a drab, horrid half gray brown" which "fell down all the time," and her "hairpins fell all over the floor" (JH). Each week "she wore a very prosaic hat and the same drab dress" (RFB).

Appearances were deceptive, and Margaret soon realized that Benedict was worth listening to, whether she was comparing the Inca Empire to a communist state, describing the visions of Crow Indians, or explaining why it really was important to learn all the complex details of a kinship system. Along with her friend, Marie Bloomfield, Margaret began catching the bus with her teacher so that they could chat to and from the museum. One student in the class once dared to ask Benedict why she wore such dull clothes. The older woman's reply was not persuasive, though it was certainly feminist: "Men wore the same clothes every day. . . . Why shouldn't a woman, also?" (JH).

As her interest grew, Margaret noticed in Ruth a hidden beauty "misted over by uncertainty and awkwardness" (AW, 9) and further disguised by her disregard for appearance. Like many of her college friends, Margaret was not averse to forming crushes on teachers or older students. In one 1928 novel set at Barnard College they were called part of the "great human experience" in a girl's education, a natural and even desirable phase of growing up.[2] Margaret had her own stringent criteria. If she was to idolize someone, she had to be learned and she had to be good-looking: "I always picked out older girls, girls that were beautiful, yes, she [Ruth] was very beautiful," she later reminisced (JH). Yet Benedict's looks bothered her. The disappointment Margaret felt about a "plumed picture hat" that her teacher wore to a museum class was so intense that fifteen years later she reported to Ruth that she had dreamed about it up the Sepik River in New Guinea (MM, B14).

Who was Margaret Mead, and what had prepared her for so intense an interest in Ruth Benedict, Franz Boas, and the discipline of anthropology? In understanding her formative years, we rely heavily on her own accounts, most notably, *Blackberry Winter*, her autobiography.[3] The vividness, warmth, and charm with which she describes her family and childhood and the astuteness of her observations should not divert us from understanding that her reminiscences were organized to certain ends. Autobiographies, ultimately, are a defense of self. The dilemma for women writing autobiography, as Carolyn Heilbrun has argued so convincingly, is that femininity and achievement are uneasy bedfellows in our culture, so that the writer must account for herself in a way that does not tarnish her self-image, let alone her public image.[4] In writing about herself, Mead had to front up to a number of issues that had the potential to cast aspersions on her femininity: failures with husbands, intimate friendships with women, pursuit of career ahead of relationships, apparent neglect of children or domestic duties, and masculine interests or personality traits can be a public relations disaster for the successful woman. It is not surprising that women's autobiographies often show considerable ambivalence about success.

In contrast, men of achievement usually present autobiographical narratives of the heroic quest, describing their natural talents and early realization of lofty goals, the obstacles they overcame, and the mentors they learned from and surpassed. Mead's notable feature as an autobiographer is that though she tempered her accounts with an emphasis on femininity, she dared to produce an unapologetic narrative of success. Though she described family adversity, she had the happy knack of presenting it as happening around her rather than to her. Her ability to put a positive construction on unfavorable events was quite remarkable, and it is an attitude implicit in her title, for she describes "Blackberry winter" as "the time when the hoarfrost lies on the blackberry blossoms. . . . It is the forerunner of a rich harvest" (BW, frontispiece). Mead's self-presentations functioned to convey an image of herself as never discouraged, always capable of turning a situation to her own advantage. She portrayed herself as a resilient child who profited from a favorable temperament, above average abilities, and an unusual education.

Margaret Mead was born on 16 December 1901 in Philadelphia. An attention getter from her earliest moments, she was a first child who arrived to a warm welcome in a newly opened hospital. Emily Fogg Mead, Margaret's mother, was an intellectual woman with a passion for social reform. She had enjoyed studying in the all-female environment of Wellesley College until a reversal in the family fortunes necessitated her return home to the Mid-west, where she taught school and then, supported by a scholarship and the money she had saved, completed her degree at the University of Chicago and embarked on graduate study.[5] In Chicago she met and married Edward Mead, two and a half years her junior, and soon afterward their household expanded to accommodate her widowed mother-in-law, Martha, whose husband had died when Edward was six years old.

By the time the first baby was due, only a year after the marriage and a little too soon for Emily's liking, the trio moved east, where Edward took up a lifelong position as an economist with the Wharton School of Commerce at the University of Pennsylvania. Despite the imminent prospect of motherhood, Emily was not deterred from transferring her doctoral studies in sociology to Bryn Mawr College.

Edward nicknamed his baby daughter "the Punk," and Margaret received a full complement of love and attention from the three adults devoted to her welfare. As an aspiring social scientist, Emily showed a scholarly interest in the development of her baby and filled notebook after notebook with observations. She refused to be bamboozled by the "scientific motherhood" experts of her day who advocated a strict bottle-feeding regimen, and she breast-fed Margaret for her first nine months. When Margaret was two years old her brother, Richard, was born. To his father he became the "boy-punk," while Margaret was renamed "the original punk." As she pointed out later, this reversed "the usual pattern, according to which the girl is only a female version of the true human" (BW, 20).

Margaret was never to lose the advantage of being the first and the prototype. She never saw herself as the second sex and she was not aware until it was "too late to matter" that her arrival had not been gladly anticipated. In fact, in *Blackberry Winter* she referred to herself as a wanted child, excising a comment in the draft about her mother's "not wanting a baby yet" (BW, 243). But though she came too early, Margaret felt she had been exactly "the kind of child my parents wanted" and that "this sense of satisfying one's parents probably has a great deal to do with one's capacity to accept oneself . . ." (BW, 243).

The Meads were a couple of contrasts. Edward was six feet tall, loud, and extroverted, with a tendency toward crudeness. He would stride into the house at the end of the working day and demand attention. "The imperative mode was very congenial to him" (BW, 30), recalled Margaret. In the early years of their marriage, Edward seemed to adore his five-foot tall "Tiny Wife," as he called Emily, a name that Margaret ludicrously used as well. Emily was energetic, conscientious, and idealistic, seldom playful or overtly affectionate, and seemingly unconscious of her beauty. Her tastes ran to the high-minded in art, music, and literature, and she was an ardent feminist and a campaigner for women's suffrage. She had only contempt for the neurasthenic women of her generation stifled by their rigid roles, "the kind of woman who comes down at ten in the morning wearing a boudoir cap and who takes headache powders" (BW, 25).

Edward, however, liked to think of himself as a pragmatist. He was apt to conceal from his wife the sometimes inglorious details of his business schemes through which he indulged his fascination with inventions, industry, finance, and commerce. In his leisure time he enjoyed reading Westerns and socializing with business cronies, activities which met with Emily's disapproval. Margaret saw her father's personality as a mass of contradictions. He seemed hardheaded and very masculine, yet in many ways his masculinity was more mental than physical; although he was a risk-taker in business, he was also unathletic and lacking in physical courage (MM, A21). He was affectionate toward his children, fearful for their safety and even overprotective, yet he was always ready to use sarcasm and put-downs. He often broke promises, and Margaret claimed that she was the only one in her family who learned to cope with such behavior. She would play on his guilt to extract favors, whereas her mother and Richard always seemed surprised and hurt by his betrayals (JH).

Despite frictions, Edward Mead sincerely admired his wife and mother for their intelligence, culture, and accomplishments, expecting them to set civilized standards of behavior which he would then chafe against and try to subvert. The household they created was talkative, lively, and argumentative, enriched by the presence of Edward's colleagues and graduate students and Emily's feminist friends.

Margaret considered her grandmother, Martha Mead, "the most decisive influence" on her life (BW, 45). The two bore a striking resemblance to one another, judging from pictures of Martha Mead as a young woman. Martha was a college graduate who had resumed her teaching career after her husband died. All her life she was strongly interested in education, especially the progressive varieties. Martha and Emily had much in common, although Emily found she resented Martha's strong presence in the household, even though it gave her time to pursue doctoral research and social causes. Margaret described their joint influence in a section of her autobiography which told her readers in no uncertain terms that career women did not have to be masculine or feminist.

> I think it was my grandmother who gave me my ease in being a woman. She was unquestionably feminine—small and dainty and pretty and wholly without masculine protest or feminist aggrievement. She had gone to college when this was a very unusual thing for a girl to do, she had a firm grasp of anything she paid attention to, she had married and had a child, and she had a career of her own. All this was true of my mother, as well. But my mother was filled with passionate resentment about the condition of women, as perhaps my grandmother might have been had my grandfather lived and had she borne five children and had little opportunity to use her special gifts and training. As it was, the two women I knew best were mothers and had professional training. So I had no reason to doubt that brains were suitable for a woman. And as I had my father's kind of mind—which was also his mother's—I learned that the mind is not sex-typed. (BW, 53–54)

In all their residences, Martha Mead was given the best room and placed herself at the center of the household activities, though the more arduous chores devolved to cooks and housekeepers. Margaret spent most of her time following her grandmother around. A child could help with peeling apples or skinning tomatoes, learn the rudiments of embroidery and knitting, and chase chickens from the garden, though Margaret would be reprimanded if she messed her clothes and came inside looking like "the wild man of Borneo" (BW, 54). She took her earliest lessons at Martha Mead's cherry wood table. The old lady was entertaining company, with a fund of stories about the indomitable women and weak, self-indulgent men who had peopled her childhood. She was loving, but she set limits on her granddaughter's natural demonstrativeness: "I loved the feel of her soft skin, but she would never let me give her an extra kiss when I said good night" (BW, 54). Emotions were to be strictly contained. Grandmother set the example, which Margaret was never able to follow, buttoning up and holding her tongue when angered, though the fire that flashed through her eyes was a giveaway.

Moving house was an established pattern in the Mead family. The home they owned when Margaret was young was set on five acres in Hammonton, New Jersey, with its immigrant Italian community convenient for Emily's research. There the Meads would live during spring and fall. Each winter they would rent a house in Philadelphia, and every summer they would take a long vacation. Margaret adapted well to these moves, a trait which would prove indispensable to her future career. On first arriving somewhere, she would rush to "claim the most remote room at the top of the house, a room which combined the charms of godmothers and wicked fairies and was far enough away so that I could hear an adult coming and pretend to be asleep."[6]

From an early age, she showed evidence of a commanding personality, and her approving parents were often heard to say, "there's no one like Margaret!" (BW, 28). She had a loud voice, but not a tuneful one; to capitalize on its strength her father taught her public speaking, having her look him straight in the eye as she declaimed. She was noted for throwing very impressive "fits" of rage and was smarter than her little brother, though that was only to be expected of girls in the Mead household. She was also healthier and more outgoing than Richard. "Far from having any sense that I was being shut out of a male world," she wrote, "I felt that my little brother was always being kept indoors because he had a cold or an earache or a cough. My only feeling of deprivation was that I had to dress like a boy instead of as a frilly girl" (BW, 61). She recalled objecting to the sensible bloomers and beret inflicted by her enlightened mother, when other little girls wore fluffy petticoats and hats with ribbons.

When Margaret was four years old, a baby sister was born, and she was allowed to choose her name, Katherine. The newcomer was a happy little child, and her death at nine months of age cast a shadow over the household. Richard, too young to understand, searched for his sister disconsolately, but Margaret knew, at least in her conscious mind, that Katherine would not come back, though she figured in Margaret's imaginary life for years. A favorite daydream was that Margaret herself was stolen away from her family and returned triumphantly. The fact that she had a distinguishing feature, a scar on her wrist, convinced the little girl that she "could never be permanently lost or mislaid." Unlike her contemporaries, "I got my major identity crisis settled before the age of six," she remarked with characteristic aplomb.[7] Self-doubt was never to be a notable characteristic of the adult Margaret Mead.

Katherine's death deeply affected her parents. Edward, seemingly unable to express his sorrow, distanced himself emotionally from his wife and began to seek consolation with other women. Tensions grew in the household, and Margaret recalled having her long brown hair brushed and listening to her grandmother ruminating on the failings of "poor Emily" and "poor Eddie," speaking to her as if Margaret were "a full person, whose opinions were solicited and treated seriously." This gave the young girl "the confusing feeling that her parents were her children as much as she was theirs" (JH) and may have prompted a later remark that grandparents and grandchildren get along so well together because they share a common enemy. It was a statement made in jest, but the alliance forged between grandmother and granddaughter was a formative influence on Margaret's character. This early sense of responsibility persisted into her adult years in her sometimes confusing mixture of personal childlikeness and a tendency to treat other adults as children.

Margaret's schooling was unusual, closely supervised by her mother and grandmother, who had pronounced views on education. She was sent to kindergarten to learn manual skills but was kept out of elementary school to avoid having her brain harmed by rote learning. Grandma taught her algebra instead of arithmetic, instilled in her a delight in reading, and sent her off into the garden to botanize. Mother sought out opportunities for Margaret to learn from local artists, carpenters, potters, and musicians, sending her to the local school only for selected lessons. Social science was incorporated into her education. She sometimes accompanied her mother to events in the Italian community, including weddings where "most of the women were dabbing tears out of their eyes; my mother was always busy taking notes" (JH).

The next baby, Elizabeth, came into the family in an "atmosphere of estrangement through grief and doubt" (BW, 63). Emily was ill throughout the pregnancy, and Elizabeth was born a sickly child whose survival was not assured. Margaret believed that the new baby had been sent to replace Katherine and had "an abiding faith that what was lost would be found again" (BW, 63). Indeed, Elizabeth lived and supplanted Margaret in her grandmother's affections. There was a short interval before Priscilla arrived, the second of "the babies," as the little girls were known for many years. Martha Mead cleverly avoided a potential rivalry between Margaret and her younger sisters by enlisting her help in their care. Margaret was taught to observe them carefully, keeping notebooks on their development, just as her mother had done: "I knew she had filled thirteen notebooks on me and only four on Richard; now I was taking over for the younger children. In many ways I thought of the babies as my children, whom I could observe and teach and cultivate" (BW, 64). In this way, Margaret learned to think of the methodical observation of others not as intrusive, impolite, or overly inquisitive, but as "a friendly act, one that enhanced rather than diminished their uniqueness and identity."[8]

Margaret's assistance was needed for practical, not just educational, reasons. Weakened by successive pregnancies and strained by tensions with her husband, Emily developed postnatal depression after Priscilla's birth and was sent off to the country for some months when Margaret was about ten years old. Margaret by now had become "a sort of pivotal family confidant" and the person who got things done: "If we wanted the hired man to do something, somebody would get me to go and ask him" (JH). As if Emily's illness were not crisis enough, Edward's infidelities now threatened to rupture the family permanently. One mistress, a redheaded businesswoman, pressed him to divorce Emily and marry her, but Grandma Mead, who had a strong influence on her son, intervened on Emily's side. The two women put up a united front, and after Emily had told her husband just how much money she would require in maintenance if he left, he gave up his mistress, deciding, with characteristic irresponsibility, that "a woman who would try to persuade a man with four children to leave them wasn't any good" (BW, 35).

To appease his wife and mother, Edward agreed to buy a farm of 107 acres in Holicong, Buckingham County, Pennsylvania, which Emily had discovered during her convalescence in the countryside. Its farmhouse was enormous, with eighteen rooms all lit by kerosene lamps and no plumbing. Grandma Mead was not at all daunted by the prospect of living in such rugged conditions, arguing that "every child had a right to grow up on a farm" (BW, 74). In this environment, Edward Mead settled down, adding to his hobbies the pursuits of a gentleman farmer. He hired a real farmer to do the hard work and interfered as the impulse moved him. He named cows after any friends of Emily's he found pompous, and he "delighted in pointing out their names and milk yield on the chart in the dairy shed." When Emily grew exasperated with his antics, she would "grit her teeth and say that she knew—and hadn't forgotten—why the farm had been bought" (BW, 41).

The Mead children were free to roam widely, and in later life Margaret had fond memories of the place. It featured a ravine, fields of maize, oats, wheat and rye, a huge barn, a windmill, a dairy, farm and carriage horses, and, not least, plenty of people to amuse Margaret—the farmer's family, household servants and children, seasonal workers such as threshers, and any small children from the neighborhood schooled by Grandma when her own grandchildren were insufficiently challenging.

Tensions between Edward and Emily still rose to the surface from time to time, though the crisis that had brought the family to the farm at Holicong had been resolved. The young Margaret Mead must have been deeply affected by the separation from her mother and this period of conflicts and uncertainties about the future. Her autobiography, though giving some clues to her reactions, casts her more in the role of observer, the role her grandmother had encouraged.

In Mead's era early childhood was seen as the time of character formation. Influenced by psychoanalysis, Mead as a young woman must have wondered whether her early years were shaped by oedipal dramas. But she never adhered systematically to Freudianism and resisted being psychoanalyzed—which was perhaps just as well, since the new and fashionable therapies seemed to have little to offer women bent on careers. It is said that Edna St. Vincent Millay, whom Margaret greatly admired, described psychoanalysis as a Teutonic plot designed to keep women in the kitchen.

Feminist psychologies suggest that women's psychological development proceeds differently from men's, at least in our culture, and Mead, of course, helped us realize that childhood and adolescent development are culturally bound. Our notions of psychological health valorize the autonomous, ambitious, achievement-oriented individual who has a strongly developed sense of self. The socially necessary tasks of caregiving, housework, and emotional sustenance, all of which have been allocated to women, make public achievement difficult or impossible, while men are left free to cultivate their ideal human selves. During adolescence, when the developmental task is the formation of a strong and separate identity, social pressures bear down heavily on young women, for whom a culturally approved concern for the needs of others often threatens the development of a strong sense of self. Lyn Mikel Brown and Carol Gilligan argue that among girls the period of late childhood and early adolescence, rather than the early childhood years, are crucial to development. In listening to the voices of girls and women, they have detected a "relational crisis in women's psychology—a comparable crisis to that which boys experience in early childhood." Calling "the edge of adolescence" a hitherto uncharted territory in women's psychology, Brown and Gilligan see it as a time of disconnection and silencing when the characteristic courage, honesty, and openness of the young girl are lost and the pressure to please others may suffocate an awareness of her own needs and desires.[9]

The culture of Mead's growing years, though separated from our own by decades, was similar in its patterns and emphases. Indeed, the silencing of girls' voices was more pronounced in her time, when women's nurturing and relational capacities were more stultifyingly encouraged than they are now, and Mead's path through this developmental minefield was the exception that proves the rule. What is striking about Mead is that she was never silenced and her ego was seldom fragile. She did not have to struggle to keep hold of a sense of identity, and she was intellectually robust, adventurous, and truly an individual. Yet at the edge of adolescence she experienced her mother's breakdown and absence and the threat of abandonment from her father. What set her apart from many of her peers, I would argue, is the way she navigated this period.

During this unhappy time Margaret, at age ten, put on forty pounds and grew to her adult height of just over five feet. By the age of eleven she had developed breasts and begun to menstruate. Girls who mature early are often very self-conscious, but not so in Margaret's case. In return for free art lessons, she was quite happy to pose as a model for her painting teacher who illustrated stories for girls.

Margaret was warned that she might injure her breasts if she continued to participate in rough and tumble games, but rather than giving them up she "insisted on wearing corsets that girded me about like armor. . . . This is why, I suppose, I kept the movement style of an eleven-year-old and never acquired the staid walk and manner of girls who mature at a later age" (BW, 76). Indeed, Ruth Benedict once told Margaret as an adult that her girlish, confident stride tended to annoy people (JH). She readily broke into a run, but not being light on her feet and carrying extra weight as she grew older, she was subject to accidents and falls (JH). A test of body image that Mead once took in later life showed that she continued to imagine herself as an eleven-year-old girl.

Margaret was not kept in ignorance about sex. Unlike many of her peers, she knew from an early age where babies came from. Her mother, in a "real act of genius," referred to the vagina as Margaret's "little body." It was something that "the big body" protected, "because that's where you were going to have a baby" (JH). As a progressive parent Emily celebrated Margaret's signs of maturity, telling her daughter when she first menstruated that now she would be able to have babies. Nevertheless, Emily referred to periods as "the Curse" and Margaret did not avoid menstrual pain. She soon learned, though, that it was wise to avoid precipitating a scene with her mother, such as the one that occurred when she told her that another girl had accused Margaret of "going out behind the barn" with a farmer's son. So when a family friend "tried a little clumsy seduction, his hands exploring my breasts," she did not tell her mother, nor did she describe how she had "resisted him with all the fervor of every threatened maiden about whom I had ever read [and] lectured him with Biblical quotations. . . . He never knew quite what had happened to him" (BW draft). Further sex education came through the crudities of her rural schoolmates, who gossiped about a local rape, from her voracious reading, which taught her about abortion and the meaning of the word *illegitimacy*, and in her teens from reading about Freud.[10]

Though the family enjoyed their farm, the move resulted in new social pressures for Margaret. She started high school at Buckingham Friends School, where some of the pupils were as old as eighteen, city youths who had been fostered by a farming family, while others were graduates from a school for disturbed children. The mix was quite a trial "to small determined eleven year olds" like Margaret, who tried to prevent "their bullying, born of dullness, retardation and boredom." She made the best of things, finding someone close to her dream of a best friend in a girl who was something of an outsider. She was a farmer's daughter whom the other children called "Sally meat axe," though Margaret found her "intense, extraordinarily intelligent, exciting" (JH). She tried to develop a crush on the inherently uninspiring woman teacher, "because I knew this was the appropriate and rewarding attitude toward one's teachers."[11] There was also someone's older brother to worship, "simply to provide a necessary male star on the horizon" in order to realize her ideal of "a best friend, a childhood sweetheart and a favorite teacher," relationships in which she "should and could give my whole heart, life long commitments that would never fade" (BW draft).

At this age Margaret was beginning to strike out on her own. Fits of moodiness meant that sparks flew at times, especially between her and her father. She would storm off after an altercation and slam every door in the house on the way to her own room at the top. Her mother, whose life now seemed unenviable, had disappointed her, and Margaret was more than ready for a satisfying role model outside the family. Shortly after the move to Holicong, the rector and his daughter, the beautiful Miss Lucia, came to call, and "almost at once I felt that the rituals of the Episcopal church were the form of religious expression for which I had been seeking. . . . I also found a place for myself in the rectory. Miss Lucia was the loveliest, the most humanly sensitive person I had ever known. She took me into her life . . ." (JH). "The more I see her, the more I love her," Margaret wrote when she was twelve, and Miss Lucia was to remain a confidante and advisor for many years.[12] Margaret's new found Episcopalianism was a rebuff to her agnostic parents. When she chose to be baptized she bore the brunt of unkind teasing from Edward Mead, who threatened to have her unbaptized if ever she misbehaved.

Miss Lucia's decision to break off her engagement to a young man because he was "too dependent on his mother" was, Margaret maintained, one of the biggest upsets of these years. Margaret had been confided in at every step of the way, and "I can still feel the anguish that came over me as I looked at the lovely golden sunset on my way home. . . . I felt the world had no right to be beautiful when Miss Lucia was so unhappy" (BW, 77). Years later, when Mead had samples of her handwriting analyzed, the results showed dramatic changes around the age of twelve. It was suggested that something important had happened to her at that age, yet the only significant event she could remember was Miss Lucia's breaking her engagement. Perhaps this claim is evidence of selective memory, however, for Mead confessed that she always had trouble remembering her own personal catastrophes and had a tendency to project them onto others: "I early learned to expect that any disasters that occurred would happen to Dick and I even conveniently displaced onto him frightening memories, like being locked up in a dark cupboard by a German governess . . . and even today I have some difficulty in keeping in mind unpleasant things that have happened to me" (BW, 21–22).

So Margaret survived the onset of adolescence, though not without disruption. Her disappointment in her mother had been mitigated by finding a mentor in Miss Lucia, someone outside the family to love, admire, and confide in. Whatever the tensions in the Mead family, that trio of exceptional adults did not try to suppress or silence her. They did not make her feel ashamed of her body, nor did they force onto her any confining expectations of womanhood, what Brown and Gilligan have called the "tyranny of nice and kind."[13] She retained a childlike openness and directness in human relations, alongside an exceptionally empathic understanding of others which had been finely honed by her early training in observing human behavior. Though she was teased about the intellectual independence she expressed through her new religious convictions, she was expected to defend herself. The Meads had high expectations for their daughter and saw her as more promising material than her younger brother. Her sex would not prevent her from the intellectual achievement so valued in her family.

Margaret became more settled after moving to a larger school where she found more scope for her talents. She was a natural leader and took pleasure in organizing her schoolmates, her imagination fed by the school stories she enjoyed. She felt she "had a role to play and had to find actors to take the other parts. . . . And so I made a best friend out of the most likely candidate, fell sentimentally in love with one of the boys, attached myself to a teacher" (BW, 80), just as she had done in her previous school, though she neglected to mention that she also fell sentimentally in love with girls, picking out the older, good-looking ones. One of the objects of her devotion she later described as "beautiful and sweet and hadn't any brains in her head" (JH).

Though her family displayed few concerns about the conventions of femininity, and though her own affections seemed to be distributed just as readily toward females as toward males, Margaret decided by now that her course in life would definitely include marriage and many children. She met Luther Cressman while she was still in high school when he came to tea with his older brother, her teacher, on the night of the school prom. Luther was twenty years old, a college student who planned to train for the ministry. Margaret found him "a magnificent dancer," though that first evening with her future husband was marred when she was stricken with acute appendicitis. They began to correspond, and she spent Christmas 1917 with Luther and his brothers at the Cressman farm. Luther possessed the masculinity that Margaret felt her father never quite managed to achieve. He was "tall and slender and well built. He could drive a car and shoot a gun with great skill and he took beautiful photographs. . . . He had an engaging grin and a wry sense of humor, yet he took life seriously . . ." (BW, 83–84).

On a cold starry night that Christmas the two of them made declarations of love, became secretly engaged, and sealed their pact with a kiss. For Margaret, at just sixteen, dreams of the future were influenced by her disappointment at Miss Lucia's broken engagement. Luther seemed suitable in every respect, barring one detail—the Cressmans were Lutheran. But it did not take Margaret long to prevail upon Luther to train for the Episcopalian priesthood.

Wartime found the Mead family at the New Hope artists' colony, where the children attended the "frightfully idealistic, expensive" Holmquist school. The war had caused a labor shortage and Margaret took on the burden of keeping house and cooking meals for the large family, helped "only" by "a very small black girl and her mother."[14] Emily could not cook, and anyway, she was more interested in politics than housework. Margaret remembered that when her mother heard news of the Russian Revolution in 1917, she literally danced for joy in a most uncharacteristic outburst of demonstrativeness.

Margaret eagerly anticipated following in her mother's footsteps at Wellesley College. Edward Mead, however, had lost money in a business venture, and glossing over the catastrophe with his usual mixture of blustering and subterfuge, he produced out of nowhere the astonishing opinion that Margaret did not need a college education. Her only instructors there, he argued, would be "the same old-maid teachers" whom her mother had studied with years before. To lend weight to his case Edward called in his friend, the local physician, who said to Margaret, " 'Look at those useless little hands! Never did a day's work in their life and never will! You'd maybe make a good mistress, but a poor wife. You'd better study nursing!' " Margaret was incensed: "Hearing this, I exploded in one of the few fits of feminist rage I have ever had. At the moment I was not only carrying a heavy school program and making all the costumes for a play, but was also keeping house for the whole family. However, what really infuriated me was the totally contradictory notion that although I was not strong enough to study for a degree, I was strong enough to become a nurse" (BW, 85).

In fact, college was expensive and financial aid was uncommon. Tuition and room and board fees for Wellesley had cost $350 a year in Emily Mead's time, and students had personal budgets of at least the same amount and often more, about half the annual income of a college professor. Nevertheless, Margaret's expectation that she would receive a college education was not unreasonable—at least one in fifteen girls of her generation went to college, compared to less than 1 percent in her grandmother's day and only 2 percent in her mother's. In her case, the problem was that she had set her sights on the most expensive education money could buy.[15]

Emily intervened, this time using the feminine wiles she usually found disagreeable. She argued that Margaret should attend Edward's alma mater, DePauw University in Indiana, and Edward succumbed to this attempt to flatter him; after all, he was an advocate for education, he respected the intellectual capacity of his womenfolk, and DePauw was less expensive than Wellesley.

Margaret made the long journey to DePauw in 1919, beginning her freshman year burdened by an eastern accent, caseloads of books, a china tea set, portraits of Rabindrath Tagore and a heroine of the Russian revolution, a ludicrous evening dress she had designed herself with the theme of poppies in a wheatfield, and no taste for chewing gum. She failed to be invited into a sorority, and even decades later her account of college life at DePauw seethes with shame and indignation at the "snobbery and cruelty" of student life. Many of her fellow students came from uneducated families, and their parents "appeared at Class Day poorly dressed while their daughters wore the raccoon or muskrat coats that were appropriate to the sorority they had made. It was a college to which students had come for fraternity life, for football games, and for establishing the kind of rapport with other people that would make them good Rotarians in later life and their wives good members of the garden club" (BW, 90).

As an outcast for the first and perhaps only time in her life, Margaret made the best of the situation. She formed her own group of outsiders, "The Minority," comprising the only Jew, the only Catholic, Margaret the Episcopalian, and a few others averse to the Methodism that surrounded them. Though it was a hurtful time, she came to regard it as a broadening time as well. The college years were an "initiation into humiliation—through the experience of hardship in some petty caricature of the real world which, by its very pettiness, engages one's emotions and enlarges one's consciousness of the destructive effects of every kind of social injustice" (BW, 93).

In her dorm at DePauw Margaret met Katharine Rothenberger, a young woman a year ahead of her whose father was an Indiana undertaker. Katharine had transferred from another college because she could not afford the costs of joining a sorority, and as a Lutheran she was eligible for the outcast status of "The Minority." She was tall and slim and wore her long red hair pulled back. Margaret found her most appealing. Her name, of course, was evocative of Margaret's beloved baby sister.

Katharine remembered Margaret as "sweet and bright and quick, but so lonely, so lost, and she was different."[16] Margaret, she recalled, took her religious observances very seriously, kneeling by her bed every night to say her prayers. But piety did not necessarily preclude the expression of physical affection between young women, and it may well be that Katharine became Margaret's first lover. Mead's daughter, Mary Catherine Bateson, believes this was so because there was a certain coyness in her mother's tone whenever she spoke of Katharine. Bateson points out that the photographs of Katharine that Mead chose for Blackberry Winter give clues to the intimacy of their relationship.[17] One photograph shows the pair dressed for a May Day pageant which Margaret, her organizing talents triumphing over her unpopularity, had written and designed. She cast herself as queen and Katharine as king. In their lavender costumes, Katharine and Margaret stand arm in arm, Katharine a head taller and characteristically reserved in her demeanour with a sword sheathed at her side. Another photograph shows the pair sitting on the college lawn, Katharine smiling bashfully with Margaret's hand resting against her knee. The pageant was not their only triumph. Margaret ran a campaign in which, setting the sororities against each other, she managed to get Katharine elected vice-president of the student body, the first woman in the history of DePauw to hold this office.

Love affairs between girls like Margaret and Katharine were an expected part of college life, and the women's colleges even fostered them through the tradition of "smashing," an acceptable pattern of courting a desired girlfriend. Barbara Miller Solomon has argued that this was a time when adolescent peer cultures were becoming significant in American society, and in segregated dormitories, away from their families, "women's friend-ships became central to the undergraduate experience." In the late nine-teenth century such bonding was positively encouraged: "it was natural and desirable for a girl to have an intimate friend and to form with one or two others a 'bunch' or 'coterie,' the little crowd of peers who knew each other's deepest thoughts and feelings."[18] Though sororities were some-times curbed by college authorities, the objection was not that they pro-moted close ties between students, but that they introduced a sour note to college life with their exclusivity and discrimination. Crushes and intimate friendships were seen as a delightful part of a girl's growing up, teaching her to value the pleasure of women's company. Their intimacies were seen innocently as good preparation for the marriage relationship.

Whether overt sexuality was commonly expressed in such relationships has been a matter for debate among feminist historians. There is evidence to suggest that it was, at least some of the time. Kinsey's well-known surveys conducted in the 1940s showed that 21 percent of college-educated women said that by age twenty they had experienced arousal with another woman, and 12 percent had had overtly homosexual contact, 6 percent to the point of orgasm. By age thirty, 14 percent acknowledged homosexual contact with orgasm, and the proportions were higher among those who went to graduate school. Though generational differences were slight, Mead's was somewhat more familiar than later generations with love be-tween women.[19]

In a survey of sexual behavior conducted in the 1920s by Katharine Bement Davis, who would have been a contemporary of Margaret's mother as a graduate student at the University of Chicago at the turn of the century, half the middle-class women surveyed "admitted to intense emotional relations with other women and half of that number said that those experi-ences were either 'accompanied by sex or recognized as sexual in charac-ter.'"[20] Lillian Faderman, the historian of lesbian life, argues that though some love affairs led to full, genital sexual expression, it was strong romantic feelings that were central to most friendships, expressed through kisses, embraces, and sentimental declarations. She quotes the pioneering lesbian psychologist Charlotte Wolff, who claims that "it is not homosexuality but homoaffectionality which is at the center and the very essence of women's love for each other. . . . The sex act is always secondary with them."[21] Though many lesbians today might argue the point, Faderman endorses Wolff's interpretation of love between women in an earlier time, arguing that sexual intimacies that did occur may have been seen as anomalous, rather than as defining the nature of the friendship.

At any rate, women, by and large, were not seen as independently sexual, and so whatever they did together privately could hardly be named sexual. In England, when male homosexual activities were criminalized at the end of the nineteenth century, lesbian activities were not included in the new law. The reason for the omission, according to one story, was that Queen Victoria could not imagine what female homosexuality could possibly involve. With women's sexuality conceived of entirely in relation to men, women were free to invent it for themselves in private. By the time Mead went to college, however, the age of innocence was ending and the specter of homosexuality among women, fostered by the new science of sexology, loomed larger. The sexologists enthusiastically catalogued the variety of human sexual pleasures and perversions. Faderman quotes an article by "A College Graduate" in a 1913 Harper's Bazaar entitled, "Your Daughter: What Are Her Friendships?" It warned parents that one-tenth of college friendships were "morally degenerate."[22] As the climate of homophobia deepened, women were less likely to celebrate their college romances and many later destroyed letters and tokens of affection. Margaret Mead's "coy tone" in talking to her daughter of Katharine Rothenberger many years later was probably echoed in many American homes, women having learned to disguise the sexual elements in their college friendships. The gulf between these women and their nineteenth-century foremothers is demonstrated by the earlier example of M. Carey Thomas, later president of Bryn Mawr College, whose Quaker mother and aunt once wrote to reassure her about a girlish romance: "[We] guess thy feeling is quite natural. [We] used to have the same romantic love for our friends. It is a real pleasure."[23] But by Margaret Mead's time, women could no longer be so lacking in self-consciousness about their feelings toward other women, though no doubt there had always been some women who recognized their relationships as unabashedly sexual.

But what did Margaret Mead herself make of her close friendship with Katharine Rothenberger? Newly released archival materials give us some clues. It seems likely that she understood it as homosexual, though whether this occurred to her at the time or whether it was a realization that came with greater sophistication is hard to know. Dream records and accompanying interpretive notes from some years afterward, when Margaret was in her mid-twenties, indicate the strength of her attachment to Katharine and her anxieties about whether this attachment meant that she was homosexual (MM, A21). In one dream, the figure of a "beautiful young wife" is interpreted as representing Katharine, and Margaret, swimming naked, is "a perfectly natural person until brought clothes *by a woman*" (MM, A21). In another dream, which resonates with accusation, guilt, and loss, a young woman with long red hair hates Margaret, who is in some way culpable for the death of the woman's little sister (MM, A21). Red, the color of Katharine's hair, symbolized love to Margaret, and her analysis links Katharine with "first love" and with her baby sister Katherine, who died in infancy. The loss of love, in Margaret's interpretation, connects Katharine to death through Margaret's association between her old friend and the baby Katherine.

In another dream, Margaret's father is looking for a girl who works in a "low dive." The lost girl is also a Katharine figure, according to Margaret, and, recalling her father's peccadilloes, she interpreted the dream as alluding to illicit heterosexual activity, as well as her unresolved issues of sexual identity (MM, A21).

Dead or murdered babies were a common theme in the dreams, and Margaret later wrote that they stood for uncompleted tasks; they were "what I should have done" dreams (JH). But this was a revisionist remark, for in her analyses at the time she interpreted murdered babies as a "heterosexual attitude neglected and starved." In one such dream Margaret has kept a baby shut up in a box in her room and not looked at for days, and she noted that this was "an expression of a suppressed fear that I after all am primarily a homosexual person" (MM, A21). Mead does not comment further on the imagery of the baby in the box, but, given the widespread interest in dream symbolism at the time, it cannot have failed to escape her that boxes and their ilk might refer to women's sexual parts. In a linked dream, a young red-haired woman sits on a raised box.

Margaret's attachment to Katharine, however strongly felt at the time, did not prevent her from successfully persuading her father to allow her to transfer to Barnard College in New York. She said goodbye to DePauw, "sorry only to leave Katharine," and Katharine "minded terribly. . . . But I went to visit her, and she came back to visit me, and we kept in touch all the rest of our lives" (BW, 101). Katharine became a history teacher in her home state, and it seems likely that she never married as she still used her own name when Jane Howard interviewed her years later about her friendship with Margaret.[24] She was a guest at the wedding of Margaret's daughter, another Catherine, whose name Mead later confessed carried the "heavy weight . . . of all the Katherines who preceded [her]" (BW, 259).

Luther's being in New York may have been critical in Margaret's wishing to transfer to Barnard. Katharine's opinion was that Margaret was not "madly in love with Luther, but she figured she ought to marry someone and he was the one she was going to marry, and that was that."[25] Margaret sometimes gave heterosexuality a misleading weight in her autobiography; she suggested there that Luther was the main attraction, and after her undermining experience of the Mid-west, "I had had enough of the consolation of knowing that I was engaged, so that all the nonsense about having dates—or not having dates—was irrelevant. I wanted a life that demonstrated in a more real and dramatic form that I was not among the rejected and unchosen" (BW, 100).

Margaret arrived in New York in the fall of 1920, as part of a wave, for this was a historic year in which the percentage of women undergraduates in America reached 47.5 percent. Barnard was a women's college, less expensive than Wellesley and carrying an excellent reputation. It had begun as an annex to Columbia University, which excluded women as undergraduates, and had Columbia professors as well as its own very able professors teaching its courses. Barnard's location in Manhattan meant that students could participate freely in the life of the great city, a boon for Margaret after the isolation of her previous campus. Moreover, students were drawn from a more varied population, although Jewish students were still underrepresented and black students were rare. Sororities had been recently phased out, no doubt much to Margaret's relief, on account of their snobbishness and racial divisiveness.[26]

During her years at Barnard Margaret was to become a New Yorker, and although later she was known as a citizen of the world, it was New York that formed her in young adulthood and it was to New York that she always returned. The 1920s were ushering in an era of postwar prosperity, a time of optimism and extended horizons. Having fun became almost a religion; the stifling legacy of Puritanism was pushed aside by the jazz and dancing in Harlem nightclubs, the new dress codes, the attention to heterosexuality encouraged by the popularization of psychoanalysis, and the intellectual and artistic ferment of Greenwich Village. For young college women the ideal was the flapper, "a daring, even naughty tomboy, . . . high-spirited, flirtatious and often reckless in her search for fun and thrills."[27] Hemlines crept up and women bobbed once-cherished long hair.

Margaret found herself in her element in this vibrant city. At Barnard it was not necessary to live in a dorm. She became one of a group of young women who shared a cooperative apartment on West 116th Street. Friendships were founded here that lasted a lifetime. During their first year the roommates called themselves the "mental and moral muss," after an epithet thrown at them by their apartment supervisor. Next it was the "Communist morons," and then the name that stuck, the "Ash Can Cats." The Cats were a group of enormously talented young women, trend setters who sparked in each other limitless trains of ideas, who adored poetry and endless debates and took pride in their lack of athleticism. They included Margaret's closest friend, Léonie Adams, with her luminous poetic talent and her endless procrastination when it came to writing term papers for which, maddeningly, she always seemed to receive As; Lee Josephson Hanna, sophisticated yet sympathetic; Deborah Kaplan, "normal, as unsophisticated, as biological as a roan stallion" whose joyful heterosexuality would later act as a trigger for the murdered baby dream (MM, 211, A21); Viola Corrigan, conservative, Catholic, and permanently mystified by the other Cats; and Mary Ann McColl, otherwise known as Bunny, "the perfect flapper" (BW, 105).

The Ash Can Cats were organized according to a kinship system which Margaret, evincing a natural talent for anthropology, liked to think she invented. This was a sore point with Léonie Adams, who once told an interviewer that the system had been in place the year before Margaret came; they had designated one of their group the "father" because "she was the least determined." She also remarked, somewhat uncharitably, that "Margaret could never accept the fact that this 'family' had existed before she came along. When I told her that it had, she was too taken aback to acknowledge that I might be right."[28]

Whatever the origins of the group, it was clear that Margaret had a flair for organizing. Like Léonie, also an oldest child, she was comfortable in a maternal role and in the following years grandchildren were added, including Louise Rosenblatt, also to become a close friend, and a great-grandchild, Hannah Kahn, who was nicknamed "David" for her resemblance to Michelangelo's David (BW draft).

Luther was hardly an overwhelming presence in Margaret's life at Barnard except as a continual excuse for not dating. They went out together twice weekly and she set up dates between his seminarian friends and her fellow students in need. She found her own milieu totally absorbing and exciting and could hardly fail to be fascinated by all that was opening up before her eyes. She and Léonie adored Edna St. Vincent Millay, the daring poet of Greenwich Village who around that time wrote "The Lamp and the Bell," with its motif of romantic friendships among college women.[29] The Cats took as a motto her verse about burning the candle at both ends, though Margaret herself dressed plainly, went to bed promptly at ten o'clock, and refused to take off her glasses at dances. "There was always a choice between keeping your glasses on and relating to what happened, or else taking them off" (JH), she said, and left no doubts as to her preference. She was in no way the stereotypical Barnard girl. She was an intellectual, never a flapper, her relationship with Luther remained chaste, and unlike some of her classmates who contributed to the reputation of Barnard students as "nymphomaniacs," she did not have affairs with men.[30] Among their group she was one of the last to have her hair bobbed.

The Cats engaged themselves in radical political causes of the day, enjoying thumbing their noses at authority and received opinions. On one occasion they all donned red dresses and appeared in the college dining hall with red flags, flowers, and candles at their table to celebrate the fifth anniversary of the Russian Revolution. Together they sang the "Internationale" and incurred the wrath of some of their fellow students, one of whom wrote to the college newspaper calling their demonstration "out of place, highly uncalled for and in poor taste."[31] Vice President Coolidge had recently written an article with the alarmist title, "Are the 'Reds' Stalking Our College Women?", and the Ash Can Cats were happy to fan the flames of the "Red scare." Margaret was following her mother and carrying on a family tradition as well as affiliating with New Women of the twenties who have been underestimated by the "flapper" stereotype. In this postsuffrage era, women at the forefront worked on political and economic change as well as for freedoms in their personal lives.[32] Other causes Margaret involved herself in at Barnard included protesting the executions of Sacco and Vanzetti and supporting the Amalgamated Clothing Workers' strike.

Toward the end of the first year at Barnard, Margaret suffered a setback. She developed severe muscular pains and lost all the strength in her right hand. She had to wear her arm in a sling, learn to write with her left hand, and take her examinations orally. It was most peculiar that her sister Elizabeth and her grandmother developed exactly the same problem at the same time. With three women in the family suffering, Edward Mead, in another episode of skinflintedness, tried to prevent Margaret from returning to Barnard. She was terribly upset and "considered running away and taking a job as a cook. [It was] my only fully developed skill" (BW, 37).

The causes of this family epidemic of neuritis were never found. Repetitive strain injury, now much better understood than in those days, suggests itself as a likely candidate. Margaret had learned typing at a young age and applied herself strenuously to her work. But how her grandmother and sister fell ill at the same time remains a mystery. Margaret discounted the suggestion of a virus, since she was in New York when the problem first occurred. To her it "looked very much like a contagious little bit of hysteria. . . . Someone was imitating someone." Perhaps none of them wanted to do the chores Emily had opted out of. A Freudian-minded classmate thought it must have been Margaret who was hysterical because of her repressed relationship with Luther (BW, 104). The neuritis was to remain with Margaret, and for months at a time her right arm "was never free from pain" (JH). Continuing to work despite pain became second nature and may have built into her maturing personality a heightened ability to dissociate herself from unpleasant internal sensations or emotions and an enhanced tendency toward outwardness and extroversion. Certainly, her continuing pain was at times to cause others concern about her health, mental as well as physical.

Returning to Barnard for her junior year, Margaret now shared a bedroom with Léonie Adams. The largest in the apartment, it became the center of gossipy conversations and passionate debates. Léonie was finding her own emotional interests troublesome as it became clear to her that she more readily fell in love with women than men. Later in life, after she had married and traded in her communism for Catholicism, Léonie took great pains to cover any traces of her youthful homosexuality and further pains to ensure that Margaret did, too. In *Blackberry Winter* Margaret describes her friends from the Barnard years as a mixture of sophistication and innocence in matters of sexuality. She wrote: "We learned about homosexuality, too, mainly from the covert stories that drifted down to us through our more sophisticated alumnae friends, through the Coop group [from the year preceding Margaret], and through Léonie's older sister, who was close to some members of the faculty. Allegations were made against faculty members [Dean Gildersleeve, the President of Barnard, was a strong feminist and 'generally assumed to be homosexual'[33]] and we worried and thought over affectionate episodes in our past relationships with girls and wondered whether they had been incipient examples" (BW, 103–4). Even so many years later, Léonie was annoyed at being implicated in Margaret's brief remarks about homosexuality, if only by association with her older sister. She wrote sternly to her friend, and although Margaret defended her version of events, replying to Léonie that "I can give chapter and verse for all this," she agreed to make alterations, and in the paperback edition of *Blackberry Winter* the passage is softened to: "We learned about *the existence of* homosexuality, too, mainly from the *occasional* covert stories that drifted down to us through our more sophisticated alumnae friends and through *upperclassmen who were* close to some members of the faculty" (emphasis added) (111).

In fact, the Cats were thought by some of their contemporaries to be a lesbian group, one of them later recounting the story that "once, someone asked all of us Ash Can Cats as a group to go to tea and we wondered why, until we figured that they must have thought we were lesbians. But we weren't, of course, at all."[34] Despite this disclaimer, who or what was a lesbian depended on one's point of view. Affectionate feelings, having a crush, or even engaging in sexual activities with women did not necessarily result in the label "lesbian," yet women, in achieving more freedom, could no longer pretend innocence. As they came to be seen as capable of sexual pleasure in their own right, in other words, as active sexual agents, lesbianism had become a sexual category, a perversion, a sin, or at best a psychological deviation. During the twenties some sophisticated women (of whom Ruth Benedict's childhood heroine Mabel Dodge Luhan was an example, as was Edna St. Vincent Millay) flaunted their lesbianism or bisexuality, and lesbian cultures began to flourish in the largest cities in Europe and the United States.[35]

Margaret Mead, although avoiding explicit reference to love between women in her closest circle, summed up the spirit of the times when she said, "We belonged to a generation of young women who felt extraordinarily free—free from the demand to marry unless we chose to do so, free to postpone marriage while we did other things, free from the need to bargain and hedge that had burdened and restricted women of earlier generations. We laughed at the idea that a woman could be an old maid at the age of twenty-five, and we rejoiced at the new medical care that made it possible for a woman to have a child at forty" (BW, 108).

Margaret, anyway, had Luther to vouch for her heterosexuality. She did not need to display any sexual or romantic interest in him; it was enough that she had marriage plans. She did not even have to approve of heterosexuality in her friends to demonstrate her own. One of them recalled that Margaret "couldn't stand it if I was out with a man," and they all decided when discussing categories of sexual type that Margaret was "castrating."

It seems that at this time women alone stirred Margaret's imagination, to paraphrase historian Blanche Wiesen Cook in her writing about love between women.[36] Her sexual drive may have been in good working order but her passions, such as they were, were not essentially heterosexual. One of her contemporaries noted that Margaret "fell for my mother, and my mother in turn admired her very much."[37] And there were other romances, or at least young women who admired Margaret, such as Lee Newton, who created a lively world of fantasy between herself as "Peter" and Margaret as "Euphemia" (MM, Q11, C1). Marie Eichelberger, an older student whose college education had been delayed because of tuberculosis, was never to dislodge Margaret from a central place in her heart. "You just looked at me across a room and fell in love with me," Margaret recalled later, and though she never returned the feeling, exactly, Marie went on to arrange her whole life to be of service to her friend.[38]

Reflecting on the Barnard years, Margaret would emphasize the importance of friendships between women in her group:

"Never break a date with a girl for a man" was one of our mottoes in a period when women's loyalty to women usually was—as it usually still is—subordinated to their possible relationships to men. We learned loyalty to women, pleasure in conversation with women, and enjoyment of the way in which we complemented one another in terms of our differences in temperament, which we found as interesting as the complementarity that is produced by the difference of sex. Throughout extraordinarily different career lines we have continued to enjoy one another, and although meeting becomes more difficult as we scatter in retirement, we continue to meet and take delight in one another's minds. (BW, 109)

Her feminist sentiments were genuinely felt, but they would be tested in time as they went against the grain of the wider culture. It was in her burgeoning friendship with Ruth Benedict that the strongest test of her loyalties would arise.

# 2

*Two Worlds*

"NEGATIVE PEOPLE LIKE ME . . . I GET picked up by depressives," Margaret Mead once announced, referring to Ruth Benedict. "It would have been very easy to say that when I entered anthropology and [Benedict] was a teaching assistant, I became interested in her." But it was Ruth who had noticed Margaret first, riding the subway two years earlier. "She watched me with a group of girls coming back from a lecture, but she only knew my name was Margaret. . . . How do you say who picked who? because she'd known who I was for two years and she was new to me." In fact, Margaret claimed that she had never been the instigator of any important relationship in her life (JH).

Whoever started it—and there have been such arguments as long as there have been love affairs—Ruth must have been flattered by Margaret's interest in her teaching. She recalled affectionately, "I used to meet her on the campus with dictionary-sized monographs under her arm that were almost as big as she was."[1] But shyness was a problem. Once when Margaret asked Ruth to elaborate on a point that had come up in class,

> She replied hurriedly, in a manner which I first perceived as brushing me aside, that she would give me something later. What troubled her was diffidence about mentioning her own work, as I realized when the next week she gave me the small, bright blue reprint of her first publication. "The Vision in Plains Culture."[2]

Ruth managed to invite Margaret and Marie to listen to her present a graduate seminar at Columbia. They turned up but "found her combination of shyness and inarticulateness devastating" (AW, 4–5). Nevertheless, Margaret continued to attend the course every week, and Professor Boas never challenged her right to be there though she was still an undergraduate.

Ruth was something of a puzzle, her dowdiness masking physical beauty, her intellectual brilliance dimmed by communication difficulties, and her reserved manner masking a deep unhappiness. If Margaret's autobiography told the story of the education of an anthropologist growing up in an environment full of opportunities she was always ready to grasp, the organizing theme of Ruth's life story is division and the search for wholeness.

Benedict never wrote an autobiography for public consumption. She found even profiling herself for a book jacket a difficult exercise and once asked Mead to do it for her.[3] "The Story of My Life" is a short and incomplete account of Ruth's childhood, written at Mead's instigation and for Mead's eyes only when Ruth was in her forties (AW, 97–112). Not being the story of her career, it does not grapple with the dilemmas of femininity and achievement; rather, it explores the foundations of her adult self. Along with some journal entries and fragmentary writings also reproduced by Mead in *An Anthropologist at Work*, it is the main source of insight into her inner life.

Ruth Benedict was born in New York City, thirty-five years before she and Margaret met, but grew up on her grandfather's farm in New York State. The fertile hundred acres of Shattuck Farm were nestled in a valley surrounded by wooded hills in Chenango County, three miles from Norwich down the Oxford Road. The area had been opened up late in the eighteenth century by Yankee pioneers pushing westward from New England. Norwich, the hub of the county, was now a bustling market town of six thousand inhabitants, located about halfway between Binghamton and Utica.

The Shattucks could trace their history back to the *Mayflower* and were fond of recounting their family's epic journey out of Massachusetts, traveling on a bobsled through the winter snow with a cow to provide milk for the babies bringing up the rear. They became respected citizens of Norwich, God fearing, hard-working Baptists who believed in education for their four girls. Bertrice, Ruth's mother, went to Vassar downstate in Poughkeepsie and graduated Phi Beta Kappa in 1885. At graduation she was already engaged to Frederick Fulton and her parents may well have been relieved, as around half the graduates of women's colleges never married. Having enjoyed a few liberating years in a women-oriented environment, many went on to pursue careers closed to married women, though some graduates who did not marry, like Bertrice's older sister, Hetty, remained at home in the traditional manner.[4]

Frederick Fulton was also a Norwich Baptist and, like his father, a homeopathic physician. In those times homeopathy was a respectable profession, not yet sabotaged by the competing tradition of allopathic medicine with its leeches, poultices, and purges. When he married Fulton was busy establishing a new practice in New York City and at the same time writing a book on tumors, for which he drew all the detailed illustrations. Ruth was born less than a year afterward, on 5 June 1887. Like Margaret Mead, she was a first child. Her parents had already chosen the name Robert in the expectation of a son, and Ruth was later to become acutely aware of the disadvantages that arose from her arrival in the world in a female body, seemingly an arbitrary trick of nature (MM, A21).

Tragedy struck the Fulton household when Ruth's father acquired a mysterious illness and was forced to close his practice; with Bertrice pregnant again, the family moved back to Norwich and onto Shattuck Farm. Margery, Ruth's sister, was born there in 1888, and three months later, shortly after his return from Trinidad where he had gone to escape the harsh winter, Frederick Fulton died.

Ruth Benedict believed that her father's death was the formative event of her life. In "The Story of My Life" she summoned up shadowy memories of its impact on her as a child less than two years old. From these and an aunt's reminiscences about Fulton's death, Ruth was struck forcefully by the contrast between her childish reactions and her mother's. Bertrice Fulton, overwhelmed by grief, "wanted desperately to have me remember my father. She took me into the room where he lay in his coffin, and in an hysteria of weeping implored me to remember." Ruth faintly recollected that her father had "a worn face illuminated with the translucence of illness" and looked "very beautiful," though she could not recall the scene with any vividness. But traces of the memory did remain, and she believed they must have become a powerful unconscious force. As a young woman, she could not understand why she was drawn repeatedly to an El Greco in Boston's Museum of Fine Arts until her mother told her that the painting exactly captured her father's appearance just before he died. Benedict argued that this incoherent memory of her father in his coffin—as opposed to any Freudian-style screen memories of parental sexuality—had created her " 'primal scene,' the forgotten hour when my mother had implored me to remember, and loving my father's face, I had violently repudiated her and her grief" (AW, 98–99).

Bertrice's grief did not give way with the passing of time. In the late nineteenth century long periods of mourning accompanied by public outbursts of emotion were unremarkable, and she "made a cult of grief out of my father's death, and every March [the anniversary of her loss] she wept in church and in bed at night." The young child, lying awake in bed unable to shut out the sounds, was repelled by her mother's bouts of weeping. She experienced "an excruciating misery" of her own, accompanied by "physical trembling of a peculiar involuntary kind which culminated periodically in rigidity like an orgasm. It was not an expression of love for my mother, though I often pitied her. The affect was devastating" (AW, 98–99).

For Benedict, this trauma at two years of age marked the beginning of a divided self. Her childhood had two worlds, "the world of my father, which was the world of death and which was beautiful, and the world of confusion and explosive weeping which I repudiated. I did not love my mother; I resented her cult of grief, and her worry and concern about little things. But I could always retire to my other world, and to this world my father belonged. I identified him with everything calm and beautiful that came my way" (AW, 98–99).

Ruth became solitary and inward looking, keeping her feelings to herself as she participated in the daily round of farmhouse activities. No one was emotionally close to her, though she did admire her grandfather and she enjoyed her grandmother's affectionate ways. Her younger sister, Margery, who had been blessed with a sunny, untroubled temperament, became the family favorite. Margery was a beautiful child who drew admiring comments, but Ruth did not remember experiencing feelings of envy or rivalry toward her. Though they were constant companions, Ruth felt her sister had been surprisingly unimportant to her: "Nothing seems to me more striking in my whole childhood than this small role that warm human relations played. I can't remember any longing to have any person love me . . ." (AW, 109–10). Nevertheless, Ruth did describe herself as a "warm little girl," protective toward her mother and sister. Bertrice Shattuck's obsession with her dead husband must have made her children feel that their affection was an unworthy substitute. Her emotional withdrawal had its impact on Margery, too—some years after Ruth's death she told Margaret Mead that she had never loved their mother either (MM, Q23).

Though reserving her strongest allegiance to the dead, Bertrice by no means neglected her duties toward the living. In the Shattuck household there were usually twelve or thirteen at table, including grandparents, assorted servants and farmhands, and the aunts. Hetty was in her late thirties, clever, capable, pious, and fond of reading, and Mamie and Myra were lively young women. Bertrice made sure that her household duties did not interfere with the moral and intellectual education of her daughters, family values that her Vassar education had reinforced. There was time to attend to them, since her own mother still supervised domestic affairs, which in those days included sewing, mending, preserving food, tending the barnyard animals, keeping the fire going, trimming the lamps, caring for the kitchen garden, and churning butter, in addition to the regular round of cooking and cleaning. There was plenty for even a small child to help with, chores such as picking blackberries, feeding animals, and hunting for eggs in hidden nests in bushes and the hay barn.

Ruth had a sensual and imaginative nature, delighting in the natural world and in worlds of her own creation. She found it difficult to share her pleasures: "Happiness was a world I lived in all by myself, and for precious moments. These moments were my pearls of great price. . . . I associated them especially with holding a sleeping kitten on my lap on the woodhouse steps looking out over the east hills, and with shelling peas for the family . . . at peace on the front porch while everyone else was busy in the kitchen" (AW, 100). Moreover, "I was quite conscious as a child that nobody around me lived for the things that I did. . . . Among a religious family no one loved praying and processions with candles, both of which filled me with bliss. They did not want to put on their best dresses and watch the evening come on. They did not watch for the four black crows that flapped westward every sunset. It was of course all quite ridiculous and I was a moony child. But I learned well the technique of keeping all this to myself, and in this secret world I had one resource, my father. . . . I could picture him as completely understanding and I aligned myself with him and his world against an alien one" (MM, A21).

Ruth would escape from the bustle of the household to a retreat in the haybarn: "Under a big beam one could make a cavern in the hay completely concealed in the dark. . . . I used to go there alone and lie in the hot dark, the hayseeds sticking to my wet skin. The family could always understand jumping in the hay, but they could never have understood lying in the dark in the hay if there wasn't a hide-and-seek game going on. (I suppose I liked my hiding place because it was my 'grave', and they certainly would have disapproved if they'd known that)" (AW, 101–2). In her daydreams she escaped into the world of the dead and allowed no living persons a role in them: "People always moved as in a pageant . . . and they were never worried or querulous. My father used to stand welcoming me when I came, much in the attitude of Christ before Pilate [in the picture] that hung in the sitting room," which Ruth believed was her father until she was old enough to realize her mistake (MM, A21).

Early on, Ruth formulated principles of living that would carry her into adulthood. Central to these was the value she set on privacy. One day, "it came to me with a brilliant flash of illumination that I could always without fail have myself for company, and that if I didn't talk to anybody about the things that mattered to me no one could ever take them away" (AW, 102). Like many children, she invented an imaginary playmate, a girl who was one of seven little sisters in a beautiful country over the hill, with a warm and friendly family who lived "without recriminations and brawls" (AW, 100). This favorite daydream was ruined one day when Ruth climbed up through the woods and saw over the brow of the hill a familiar sight, the farm belonging to her uncle George.

The beauty of death was reinforced for Ruth at the age of four when her grandmother took her to one of the tenant's houses where a baby had just died, "and we saw the dead child as a matter of course. She was laid out in the stiff parlor, and I remember vividly her transparent beauty. She seemed to me the loveliest thing I had ever seen, and I remember contrasting her with the ragamuffin brothers and sisters and the bedraggled mother. If they had died, mightn't they have been beautiful like that?" (AW, 99).

It was a family joke that Ruth shrank from physical contact, hiding under the sewing machine and refusing to kiss a "cocksure" uncle (AW, 109), but some aspects of Ruth's behavior caused her mother concern. At five she sprained her ankle jumping from a height in the barn. It hurt so terribly that she fainted, but she remained in hiding, since her self-imposed emotional isolation meant that she could not cry in front of others or tell anyone if she was in pain. If she was suddenly dislodged from her private world by everyday demands, she would throw temper tantrums and lash out, hurting herself, Margery, or anyone else who was in the way. These emotional storms were so overwhelming that they sometimes ended with vomiting, and from an early age Ruth developed a pattern of bilious attacks that lasted for several days and recurred every six weeks.

Ruth could not reveal her inner world to her mother. Once as a punishment for not owning up to some misdeed, "Mother took me into the downstairs bedroom and said that I must stay there without anything to eat till I'd told. I remember very well my efforts all that day. The family ate dinner at noon, and the afternoon wore on. They ate supper and the lights were lighted. Mother sat with me most of the day waiting. At last I got it out. My relief was like physical drunkenness. I had achieved one of the most difficult tasks I've ever been set. Mother took me out to the dining room and we ate together alone by the lamplight" (AW, 101).

Ruth often did not answer when spoken to and it was not until she started school that it was discovered that she was partially deaf, most likely from a bout of measles during infancy. Deafness is a disability that cuts away at the heart of the child's social world. Children with an undiagnosed hearing problem are often seen as willful, refractory, and inexplicably withdrawn. Instructions may not be heard, communication is an effort requiring great concentration, and social contacts are rarely carefree and spontaneous. Loud noises may be grating, and "it was a particular grievance of mine that my family stomped on their heels" (MM, A21). Ruth was not a talkative child, and the hesitancy of speech that later dogged her may have been linked to her hearing disorder. In fact, the characteristics that Ruth as an adult attributed to the "primal scene" of her father's death could also be attributed to her deafness.

Once she learned to read, Ruth devoured everything she could lay her hands on, her favorite reading place a hammock strewn with pillows on the vine-covered porch. Her vivid imagination was fed on tales from the Bible, whose imagery permeated her mental world. Later, she read the classics, but still "the story of Ruth was better than Ramona, and the poetry of Job was better than Longfellow" (AW, III).[5] From an early age she formed her own ideas about religion, and by the time she was six she had stubbornly refused to ask for forgiveness while reciting the Lord's Prayer at bedtime, since it seemed wrong for the slate to be wiped clean every evening. Her sex education came largely from religious sources: "I learned most of what I knew about life from the Bible. I can't remember when I did not know about position in intercourse and about semen—I think I knew almost everything except menstruation, for I learned it all in the Bible stories . . ." (AW, 107–8).

When Ruth was seven, Bertrice left the farm at Norwich accompanied by her children and Aunt Hetty as housekeeper to take up teaching positions, first in Missouri and then in Minnesota where she became the "Lady Principal" of the Pillsbury Academy. Ruth found school lessons "a world apart from our eager, hurrying, investigating life outside" school, her teachers operating at "a dead-level of incurious indifference."[6] Yet she began to make friends with schoolmates, and "for the first time people began to play some real part in my life—not very real, but at least occupying. At school I was the leader of the little group of the élite, and curiously all the professors' children were girls and those we took in were also girls. Boys did not figure at all." She did like the janitor, though, who was "the warmest person I knew." He used to stroke her hair and was later dismissed for "soliciting young girls" (AW, 107).

When Ruth was nearing adolescence, the Fultons moved to Buffalo, New York. Bertrice had taken a low-paying but more secure position as superintendent of circulation at the library. They took up residence as poor relations on the top floor of a house belonging to her younger sister Mamie, who was married to a lawyer and comfortably off. Now it was easier to return to the farm at Norwich every summer, a pilgrimage Ruth would continue to make throughout her life except for the years of her marriage. In Buffalo, Ruth and Margery secured a good education by winning scholarships to the exclusive St. Margaret's School, where they were surrounded by girls from wealthy families.

Ruth did not recall feeling at a disadvantage. Popularity was not important to her, and she said that she "was never conscious of my clothes or of poverty." However, she did remember "the momentous occasion of spending one dollar and fifty cents for a hat" and that "each year in rotation one of us could have a new coat" (AW, 110). The girls were expected to sew their own shirtwaists and underwear, and this task was a torture for Ruth, who, as she said, was not at all "handy."

Like Margaret Mead, Ruth matured early. A preadolescent growth spurt meant that by age eleven she had become an awkward five foot eight. Her menstrual periods came every six weeks, supplanting the bilious attacks she had suffered as a child. But she did not grow out of her tantrums as she matured; instead, they grew more frequent, and now that she was of adult height, her mother worried that Ruth might really hurt Margery in one of her rages. "I was having a seizure every day or so," she remembered. "After an especially bad week Mother summoned all her forces. I had had one going to bed. It was late and I was crying myself to exhaustion after one had passed. Mother talked to me solemnly and dictated a promise, which I repeated after her, never to have another tantrum. She went out of the room and brought back a Bible and a candle, and gave it to me to read at a verse which invoked the aid of Jehovah. Afterwards I slept the sleep of utter exhaustion. I never had another tantrum. Not that I was strengthened to repel them; I have never from that day to this had the familiar impulse" (AW, 109).

The tantrum cure may have bordered on the miraculous, but it was not without consequence for the eleven-year-old girl. The rage that used to spill over shamefully, despite her best efforts, was now turned inward, fueling the depressions that troubled Ruth for much of her adult life and at times put her life at risk. She called these persistently black moods her "devils," the name she used to give her tantrums. "Both of them were protests against alienation from my Delectable Mountains [of her imaginary world], and both of them thrust me further from them and were therefore sins. I don't think during all these years I've ever loved and luxuriated in my fits of depression. They were always set over against my beautiful country, but they were more acceptable than unwanted participation in the 'other' world that was not 'mine' " (AW, 108).

In forcing underground her strong emotions, Ruth in many ways resembled other girls who, according to feminist psychologists, begin to silence their inner selves as they approach adolescence.[7] It is interesting to compare the adaptations that Ruth and Margaret Mead made to the arrival of womanhood. Mead was not punished for childish ways—she could slam doors and get away with it—yet she was practiced at adult roles, having been encouraged by her grandmother. This upbringing helped her later to negotiate a better deal. She refused to vanquish her child-self, though the result was that her adult personality sometimes bordered on eccentricity, with its forthrightness, quick temper, and lack of constraint. Ruth, in contrast, was brought up to perform the classic maneuvers of womanhood. Within the two worlds of her childhood she had long practiced the dissociation between public and private self often forced on women by the requirement that they put others' needs before their own. Yet if her self was silenced, at least it was not negated, for it existed in her rich, imaginative life. Her depressions arose from the collision and conflict between the inner life and the outer world which seemed to offer no room for what she really valued. Self-realization seems to have been disallowed at birth by virtue of her having been born female, and it was challenged further by the death of her father at age two, which forced her into an imaginary world that went deeper underground as the child became a woman. It was not until years later, after having experienced unhappiness and battles against thoughts of suicide, that Ruth was to find the conditions that would lead to a resolution of these dualities and a sense of wholeness.

Margery must have proved a mystifying contrast since she negotiated the social demands of young womanhood without apparently being troubled by any of the painful questioning that dogged her sister. Both outstanding students, they shared classes through high school and mixed with the same girls, though few made any impression on Ruth. One exception was an older girl, Mabel Dodge, who was to become the celebrity, Mabel Dodge Luhan, the Greenwich Village bohemian known for her scintillating parties and lesbian exploits. Years later, married to a Native American from Taos, New Mexico, she crossed paths with Ruth again. But back then, according to Ruth, "I remember knowing that she lived for something I recognized, something different from those things for which most people around me lived. I am sure she never knew I existed, but I carried a very vivid image of her in my mind without being attracted to her emotionally at all" (AW, 109).[8] Others were attracted to Mabel, who even then enjoyed the pleasures of seducing young women, whether or not she cared for them.

The generosity of a private benefactor gave the girls, whose top-of-the-class grades were virtually identical, full four-year scholarships to Vassar. Higher education for girls was no longer as remarkable as it had been in Bertrice's day, though in antifeminist quarters the claim had been made that excessive studying in adolescence could impair the development of women's reproductive organs and cause infertility. Concerns about the low marriage rate of college graduates had come to be linked with the specter of racial degeneration haunting the popular imagination. It seems unlikely that the Fultons took any of this nonsense seriously, and Bertrice must have felt satisfied that her girls would follow in her footsteps and repay her dedication to their education.[9]

Broadsides against education for girls would have been the last thing on Ruth's and Margery's minds when in the spring of 1905 they took the train to Poughkeepsie, a commercial town an hour or so north of New York on the banks of the Hudson river. The tree-lined campus of Vassar College lies on the edge of town, by the lush farmland of the river valley. Matthew Vassar, the beer baron who endowed the college, had created secure and pleasant surroundings where young women of the wealthier classes could receive an education equal to that of their brothers. The faculty of men and women professors were chosen for their exceptional ability. One of the first professors at Vassar had been Maria Mitchell, the doughty astronomer from Nantucket who, as a young woman, became world famous for her discovery of a comet. Though long gone by Ruth's and Margery's time, she had left as one of her legacies a splendidly equipped observatory and an unapologetically strong program in the teaching of science. In the tradition of Maria Mitchell, the women faculty were devoted to their careers and, not infrequently, to each other. The "Boston marriage" was well established here, since heterosexual marriage usually put an end to the career of a woman academic. Partnerships between single women caused little comment in the late nineteenth century, though after the turn of the century the specter of homosexuality began to affect the public perception of these relationships. The Bostonians, Henry James's 1886 novel on this theme, was omitted from the Scribner edition of his works issued in the early twentieth century because its topic was considered unacceptable. Though increasingly discreet, Boston marriages among the professors offered to the students models of women living independently, affection between women, and lives dedicated to scholarship.

At Vassar, Ruth received a liberal education, choosing English literature as her specialty. She and Margery were happy there and Ruth made several lasting friends. It seems she was immune to the college "smash," in that she did not pursue any romances with other girls, although sometimes she was herself the object of devotion.[10] Ruth derived no great pleasure from being the inspiration for crushes, but from high school years onward there were girls and later women who found her irresistible and declared themselves to be in love with her. Her shyness and aloofness no doubt gave her an air of mystery. What Margaret Mead was later to call her "castor oil face" seems to have been behind her classmates' portrait in the college almanac: "A salad, for in him [sic] we see, Oil, vinegar, pepper and saltness agree."[11]

Margery became class president in their final year at Vassar and graduated second in her class, with Ruth just one place behind. More important than grades was the fact that during the Vassar years Ruth began to formulate questions that would shape her intellectual life. She gravitated toward the romantic traditions of literature and philosophy, and her heroes were various: Walter Pater, with his prescription for living, "to burn always with this hard, gem-like flame, to maintain this ecstasy"; Nietzsche, flamboyantly rejecting bourgeois morality and calling for the creation of heroic new values; the New England transcendentalists, Emerson and Thoreau, with their nature worship; and Walt Whitman, whose poetry was suffused with an underlying gay sensibility.[12]

Suffrage was a burning issue at Vassar. "Votes for women" was the cry of the day, and some professors were openly feminist. Ruth's inclinations were intellectual rather than activist and she seems to have refrained from joining in marches or rallies. A classmate was Inez Milholland, who began her career as a feminist by holding meetings in the graveyard beyond the boundary of the campus since the college president had forbidden such seditious activities on the grounds. Ruth may have heard Charlotte Perkins Gilman speak at the college; her plea for women's economic independence struck a chord.

Upon Ruth's graduation a Vassar patron offered her an all-expenses paid one-year tour of Europe. In the spring of 1909 she set out for Europe in the company of two young Californian women, first traveling to Chicago, where a friend took her to visit Hull House, the settlement house founded by Jane Addams as part of a movement that inspired some of the brightest young college women of her day to work on issues of poverty and social justice. The visit seemed to make little impression on Ruth, who did not feel that her talents lay in the direction of social service. Nor was she distracted by shipboard flirtations. Her mind was set on Europe with its cultural treasures, and it proved the delight she had hoped for.

Living with families in Rome, Dresden, and London, she and her companions visited art galleries and museums, made an unchaperoned walking tour in Switzerland, and spent time in Paris. It was a glorious way to embark on adult life, though Ruth was acutely aware of the uncertainties that lay ahead of her. At the National Portrait Gallery in London she paused before the painting of Mary Wollstonecraft. Later in life she was to reflect on the thoughts that went through her mind at the time, when she was "haunted by the terror of youth before experience. I wanted so desperately to know how other women had saved their souls alive. And the woman in the little frame arrested me, this woman with the auburn hair, and the sad, steady, light-brown eyes, and the gallant poise of the head" (AW, 519). Although Wollstonecraft looked at peace, Ruth knew that her life had not been easy. In laying the groundwork of modern feminism, she had paid a price for her independence of mind and action. But her great achievement, in Ruth's view, was that she had succeeded in being herself. Here was a role model, even if the path ahead did not promise to be easy.

Ruth returned to Buffalo and life with her mother in the fall of 1910. Grandmother Shattuck had died during her absence, her grandfather was growing frail, and Aunty My, who remained single, was increasingly responsible for the farm. Margery was now married to a local minister, Robert Freeman; they had an infant son and were planning to move out west.

Ruth considered her options. Suitable occupations for a young woman with a college education and without means were few. Teaching was the obvious one, though social work, as she had seen from her visit to Hull House, was becoming a new profession for women. Both professions, Ruth felt, drew on the stereotypical qualities of womanhood: caring for the young or sick or needy and requiring their practitioners to set a good moral example.

She chose social work as the lesser of two evils, becoming a district visitor for the Charity Organization Society in Buffalo. Her work took her to immigrant Polish families who were down on their luck. Her job was to assess their needs, put them in touch with helping agencies, write reports, and act as a model of the behavior proper to a middle-class American. As a shy, intellectual young woman, hampered by a hearing disability and hesitant speech and with no experience of cultures other than gleanings from her grand tour, Ruth was unlikely to become a competent social worker. She did not. Moreover, she rapidly became skeptical about the utility of the profession. Although it had moved from the charitable traditions of alms giving and now emphasized the scientific investigation of social problems, its fundamental aim was to instill in the poor and unfortunate and in recently arrived immigrants the values of the dominant culture. The Poles she visited strongly resisted such attempts at acculturation. Most of them were doing quite well in their new land and saw no reason for not keeping alive their language and culture. Ruth soon grew weary of her incompetent, bungling interference with people who did not always want the kind of help she was authorized to offer. At home, she was not happy either. Life with her mother was "impossible" now that she had tasted freedom, and she turned to writing for solace, hoping perhaps that this might provide the financial means for escape (AW, 126).[13]

After a year of misery, Ruth switched to teaching and made the more radical change of moving to California, following in Margery's footsteps. She taught English, first in Los Angeles at the Westlake School for Girls and then at the Orton School in Pasadena, where Margery and Robert welcomed her into their family. She enjoyed being an aunt, but teaching made her no happier than social work had, even though she found that if she made sufficient effort, the girls enjoyed their schoolwork and liked her as well. But the strain of the work wearied her, the lack of direction in her personal life was disturbing, and she was troubled by thoughts of suicide. A journal entry made at the end of the first year in California is revealing:

> I've just come through a year in which I have not dared to think; I seemed to keep my grip only by setting my teeth and playing up to the mask I had chosen. I have not dared to be honest, not even with myself. I could only try to live through day after day, day after day, and not dishonor them overmuch. In spite of myself bitterness at having

lived at all obsessed me: it seemed cruel that I had been born, cruel that, as my family taught me, I must go on living *forever*. Life was a labyrinth of petty turns and there was no Ariadne who held the clue.

I tried, oh very hard, to believe that our own characters are the justification of it all. Bob believes it, and I think Margery would if she ever felt it mattered. But the boredom had gone too deep; I had not a flicker of interest in my character. What was my character anyway? My real *me* was a creature I dared not look upon—it was terrorized by loneliness, frozen by a sense of futility, obsessed by a longing to *stop*. No one had ever heard of that Me. If they had, they would have thought it an interesting pose. The mask was tightly adjusted.

I could see no way out. All my cheerfulness, my gaiety were part and parcel of the mask—the Me remained behind. I longed to be old— sixty or seventy—when I fancied the Me might have been strangled by the long-continued tight-lacing of the mask. I only wanted my feelings dulled—I wanted to be just placidly contented when I saw the full moon hang low over the ocean. And the weary years seemed unendurable. I am not afraid of pain, nor of sorrow. But this loneliness, this futility, this emptiness—I dare not face them. (AW, 119)

In commenting on this passage from Ruth's journal, Richard Handler, a historian of anthropology, discusses the values of the era in which Ruth came to young adulthood and the Puritan notions of character, which Ruth felt were a sham. In searching for the "real Me" she was evincing, according to Handler, a modernist attitude in an era that had lost the religious emphasis of Puritanism, which had given meaning to the struggles of individuals. The modern era saw "character" replaced by "personality," and from that would develop "a new 'therapeutic' morality of personal health and self-development, in which the secular self became an ultimate value, an end in itself which people systematically cultivated in order to achieve fuller lives and true experiences."[14] Ruth, in rejecting "character" as a goal, could not see how she could cultivate a valued self. She wrote in her journal about how much she envied Walt Whitman and other male writers in the romantic tradition who developed the concept of self, with their "unwavering, ringing belief that the Me within them is of untold worth and importance." She asked herself, "Does this sense of personal worth, this enthusiasm for one's own personality, belong only to great self-expressive souls? or to a mature period of life I have not yet attained? or may I perhaps be shut from it by eternal law because I am a woman and lonely?" (AW, 123).

Benedict herself would eventually become one of those who helped create the new culture of "personality," her personal struggles as a young woman influencing her later work with its searching for the real, the true, and the authentic. But that was years ahead, and for now, merely surviving was the best she could do. As a woman, she felt that liberating the "frozen Me" was a task too great for her. She felt trapped, and she was horrified at the chronic loneliness she saw in her older colleagues, often women who had spent the best part of their lives teaching. Bob and Margery joked about her "course in old maids," and there seemed to be no models of love between women that had any appeal to Ruth. She had grown up in a household of women, and with her mother as example, she doubted that a woman on her own might lead a satisfying life: "We have not the motive to prepare ourselves for a 'life-work' of teaching, of social work—we know that we would lay it down with hallelujah in the height of our success, to make a home for the right man. . . . And all the time in the background of our consciousness rings the warning that perhaps the right man will never come. A great love is given to the very few." It was so unfair that men could marry, raise a family, be themselves, and make an impact on the world, whereas women had to choose. Despite her discontent, feminism as a social movement still failed to engage Ruth, although a lively suffrage campaign had succeeded in California in the year of her arrival: "To me it seems a very terrible thing to be a woman. . . . It is all so cruelly wasteful." At times the only solution that she could imagine, without a trace of cynicism in those pre-Freudian times, was to fulfill herself through a son: "of all blessings on earth I would choose to have a man-child who possessed [a] sense of personal worth" (AW, 120, 123).

One man was interested in her, though Ruth thought he was unlikely to qualify as the "great love" she believed in so sincerely. Back east she had met Stanley Benedict, a young scientist and the brother of one of her Vassar classmates, and they had kept in touch by letter. At New Year 1913, Stanley made the long trip by rail to California with the prospect of spending only two days with Ruth before returning home. They spent an enjoyable time together hiking on a canyon trail, but Ruth was not swept off her feet. For his part, Stanley found Ruth's mixture of idealism and despair irritating and unrealistic. She should not have expected any miracles in the short time they had spent with each other: "I fancy neither of us are easy to get really acquainted with. If you didn't see your own sister for three years you'd find you were partial strangers for a day or two." What Stanley did not realize was that Ruth felt estranged from everyone, including her sister, whom she saw every day. He continued with persistence:

> Why worry Ruth, about what you can give, or what I can give? It's been too much of that looking forward which has kept our getting really acquainted back. . . . You're willing to give up the person who'se

tried so hard to understand you—and who may have succeeded better than most other people. And Ruth—your mask is getting thicker and thicker—I could see that it is—and that's all wrong. You belong somehow where you never have to wear it . . . and it's so wrong for *you* Ruth. . . . (AW, 539–40)

This approach did not work, and Ruth noted in her journal that "Stanley's ruled out" (AW,126). As she prepared to return to Norwich for the summer of 1913 she wondered if she could bear to come back after the four-month break. Miss Orton, the principal, seemed to understand her feelings, and Ruth was quite overwhelmed to have someone take her seriously instead of saying, like Mother, that "life isn't all cake." Ruth felt valued, and "then and there I would have done anything for that woman; coming back next year seemed too small a test" (AW,127). At the farm her resolve weakened and she wondered about staying on the farm and earning her keep off the garden and the orchard, though she worried about being seen as a "quitter" (AW, 129).

Stanley came to visit Ruth for a week in July. She wrote in her journal that it was "a glorious week of tramping and rowing and reading, of lying on the hilltops and dreaming over the valleys. But I let him go again." He came back in August for a brief stay, and this time, the miraculous happened—she realized that she had fallen in love:

> Oh I was so glad to see him! I think I knew it that night. But he did not see it. We went down to the Collins' Woods in the boat, and still he did not see. It was afternoon when I told him—I had hoped he would see for himself. But it had happened, and I'd rather be with him than anywhere else in God's universe.
>
> He had been lying on the ground. He sat up and moved toward me, and said with a tenderness and awe I had never heard before, "Oh, Ruth, is it true?" And then he put his arms around me, and rested his head against me. In the long minute we sat there, he asked in the same hushed voice, "Ruth, will you marry me?" And I answered him, "Yes, Stanley." After that we did not speak. Later it was I who told him first that I loved him.—And so the whole world changed. (AW, 128–29)

Buoyed up by her newly discovered feelings, Ruth went back to California and saw out another year of the hated teaching. Soon after her departure, Grandfather Shattuck died. There is no record of Ruth's reactions to his death, though she wrote in "The Story of My Life" that in her childhood he was "the one person who stood out for me above all others" (AW, 102). Perhaps Stanley would take the place of the father and grandfather she had lost. Ruth sent him her father's medical writings and his response was gratifying: "I've been reading your father's papers,—and I do so wish he could have gone on. Your mother needed him, you needed him, and I think the whole world needed him. . . . I am glad that I am doing some work along the line he took up—even though it's a different aspect of it, and the problem is so terrible that I can't keep so closely to it as he did . . ." (AW, 537).

In the year of their engagement Stanley became a full professor at the Cornell University medical school where he conducted pioneering research in chemotherapy. He was three years older than Ruth, just as her father had been three years older than her mother. His self-confidence and his strong sense of the importance of his work impressed itself upon Ruth at a time when she felt unsure of her own direction. The marriage took place at Shattuck Farm in the summer of 1914 and the two of them set up house in suburban New York City.

At first Ruth seems to have been very happy. Her sexuality blossomed, with journal entries referring to "passionate love," "ecstacies," "this satisfying comradeship, this ardent delight, this transforming love" with "its strength and depth and power of healing." Seemingly without regret, she had given away what there was of her independence, deciding that to find "our whole world in the love of a man" was a praiseworthy solution to her problems, even though others (and she remembered Charlotte Perkins Gilman) regarded such a womanly role as "parasitism." Nevertheless, "do we care whether Beatrice formed clubs or wrote a sonnet? In the quiet self-fulfilling love of Wordsworth's home, do we ask that Mary Wordsworth should have achieved individual self-expression? In general,—a woman has one supreme power—to love" (AW, 132–33, 130).

But it was hard to give up all personal ambition, and Ruth proposed to occupy the time left over from her undemanding household duties in writing a book on "the lives of restless and highly enslaved women of past generations . . . from the standpoint of the 'new woman.' " If ever an idea had within itself the seeds of discontent, this was it. But Ruth planned to show that her heroines—Mary Wollstonecraft, the pioneer of women's rights, Margaret Fuller, the New England transcendentalist philosopher, and the South African writer Olive Schreiner—illustrated, not a feminist argument, but that "restlessness and groping are inherent in the nature of women . . . [and] that nature lays a compelling and very distressing hand upon woman, and she struggles in vain who tries to deny it or escape it" (AW, 132–33).

Ruth's heroines are celebrated by feminists today for their adventurous attempts to refashion women's worlds; they do not constitute a good advertisement for the joys of conventional marriage. Mary Wollstonecraft's first love was Fanny Blood; next, she negotiated a *ménage à trois* with the artist and pornographer Henry Fuseli; she was seduced and abandoned by an American soldier of fortune and eventually married philosopher William Godwin only to die in childbirth. Margaret Fuller advocated passionate love between women, became emotionally entangled with Ralph Waldo Emerson, who was married at the time, and in her late thirties married an Italian nobleman considerably younger than she was. Olive Schreiner had an emotionally tortured and probably nonsexual involvement with Havelock Ellis, the founder of modern sexology, who avoided putting what he knew into practice; then she married and spent most of her life in separate households from those of her husband.[15]

Not surprisingly, given her naiveté, Ruth found it difficult to motivate herself to keep at her writing. For several years she occupied herself with the project, more off than on, and there is an extant manuscript for the Mary Wollstonecraft section. She was unable to interest a publisher, which was the final discouragement. She thought she might turn her hand to detective stories, with Stanley supplying scientific plots, but that project also made little headway. She amused herself with rhythmic dancing classes and taught Sunday school until she was asked to leave after advising her pupils, in a moment of cynicism, to look up Jesus Christ in the *Encyclopaedia Britannica*. Above all, she was bored, and the more she read about her restless and enslaved women, the more restless and enslaved she felt.

The material on Mary Wollstonecraft says quite a lot about Ruth herself. What must she have been thinking when she wrote, "The idea with which she shocked her contemporaries was only that women are more than men's playthings, that they have lives and understandings of their own, and that anything short of a full development of their powers is a duty left undone. . . . She never flinched before the hazard of shaping forth a personality not duly authorized and accepted. . . . [In her life story] we can measure that passionate attitude toward living out of which all the restlessness of modern womankind has grown" (AW, 493–94). In a personal touch, Ruth told her own story of gazing at the Wollstonecraft portrait in London. But although Ruth valued the way in which her heroine had, against all odds, carved out a life suited to her gifts, her own portrayal of Wollstonecraft's love for Godwin as the crowning achievement of a tormented life showed her continued attachment to the "great love" as a solution.

Ruth's discontent and Stanley's dullness soon caused tensions in the marriage. Her husband liked a quiet and orderly life. After a year or two they moved to Bedford Hills, an outlying suburb of the city, so that Stanley could sleep peacefully at night. He enjoyed hobbies as a relaxation from work, spending his spare time tinkering with engines or photography. The couple bought a cottage on Winnepesaukee Lake in New Hampshire, but despite Ruth's fondness for the peaceful surroundings, summers there came to seem endless. Occasional quarrels underscored Stanley's disapproval of what he saw as Ruth's inability to stick to anything, which was part of her continued search for meaning. She wrote soulfully of "the deepest cry of my heart: 'Oh God let me be awake'—awake in my lifetime" and how much she longed for "anything to live! To have done with this numbness that will not let me feel" (AW, 135, 137).

Pushing back the feelings that threatened to overwhelm her, Ruth fantasized about "planning actual suicides . . . in very considerable detail," even in happy moments when a reverie about death seemed a "fitting conclusion" to an achievement, a sense of " 'if only I didn't have to go on with it again', it being conceived as a dull row that has to be hoed to the end, but which has excellent interludes." She would imagine how everyone she loved best would be happy in remembering her if she were dead and she would "lay great emphasis on the fact that I haven't hurt them drastically so far." Such fantasies, she recalled, were not expressions of desperation, but "more in the spirit of a Buddhist ascetic contemplating consummation in Nirvana" (MM, A21).

However she regarded these fantasies of death, her battles with depression were real. She invented techniques to get her through each day. She would imagine as she did each task that she was doing it for the last time, for tomorrow she would be dead. That thought inspired her to do things with "a dash of zest." One such technique to give the daily grind "a fictitious importance" was "wonderfully effective. . . . It's very simple: this is my daughter's life that's posing as mine. It's my daughter's love life which shall be perfect; it's my daughter's abilities which shall find scope; it's my daughter's insight that shall be true and valid; it is she who owes it to speak out her beliefs. It is she who shall not miss the big things of life" (AW, 141).

A rising source of tension in the marriage, in fact, was Ruth's desire to have children and failure to become pregnant. She had enjoyed the company of Margery's children and longed for her own, even though she knew at heart that motherhood would not still her restlessness any more than romantic love had, despite its sensuous satisfactions. She wrote: "There is no misreading of life that avenges itself so piteously on men and women as the notion that in their children they can bring to fruition their own seedling dreams." Yet she also accepted the crudely biological ideas of her day, believing that women inevitably prepared themselves for motherhood, drawing on "a great battery charged by the accumulated instincts of uncounted generations. When there are no children, unless the instinct is somehow employed, the battery either becomes an explosive danger or at best the current rapidly falls off, with its consequent loss of power" (AW, 136, 141).

Stanley accused Ruth of weakness of character, saying that she could not hold onto anything and that if she did have children they would only save her from herself for a year or two. He had wearied of her search for personality and authenticity. It was not until some years later, nearing the end of their marriage, that Ruth learned she had a blocked fallopian tube that might be corrected with some complicated surgery. Despite the marital problems, Ruth's desire to have children was still strong and she was willing to undergo surgery, but Stanley, exercising his male prerogative, would not give his consent to the operation. There was little she could do but submit to his decision.[16]

Ruth's childlessness has played a central role in some accounts of her life. Jessie Bernard has argued that Benedict's distinguished career was an unsatisfactory substitute for a child, a disappointing claim from a feminist sociologist, who would not be expected to portray childlessness as the motivating force for intellectual achievement.[17] Judith Modell, one of Benedict's biographers, made a similar claim, arguing that by bearing a child Ruth hoped to prove her heterosexuality and her womanhood and put to rest a fear of sexual frigidity.[18] These interpretations, though, fail to do justice to Ruth's very real disappointment. Given cultural preoccupations, infertility may well have called into question her image of herself as a woman, but the evidence is that this was not Ruth's biggest concern. Her dilemma was that her life as a woman contradicted the life of the mind and the self that she strove for. Womanhood itself was problematic, not whether she was "womanly." As far as frigidity goes, her journal from the early years of the marriage clearly celebrates the sensuality she found with Stanley and only later mourns its loss. Ruth wanted a child as an investment in living, not to demonstrate some mystical quality of womanhood. And she grieved that her body had let her down. As a later poem, "For Seedbearing," expressed these feelings:

> Blossomtime shall flaw
> To arid seed-bearing, and the hard alien pips
> Be weary consummation of the ecstacy
> She knew on summer mornings. All her scope shall be
> Maturing of their sapless entity for ends
> Unloved and hidden. (AW, 71)

Ruth's reactions to her infertility were not static and her grief faded over time. She had wanted children and hoped that becoming a mother would help her get a grip on her life. Influenced by the social thought of her time, she believed that women were at the mercy of their maternal instincts. At the same time, she knew that her bleakness would not be so easily cured. Childlessness added to the problems of the marriage, which was strained, but having a child, she realized now, would not have solved those problems. Continuing to wrestle with herself, Ruth as a mother would have found it almost impossible to use her exceptional intellectual and literary talents, even though she undoubtedly would have loved, cherished, and enjoyed her children. The greater cause for grief is those exceptional women of her time who have remained unsung: who never found fulfillment, who lived behind their masks, who were suffocated by the expectations of womanhood in their time, and who sometimes went mad. Margaret Mead's analysis of Ruth's condition was more accurate than that of many others. She recognized the strength of Ruth's desires for children, but she did not reduce Ruth's life work to a frustrated desire for children. As she put it, quoting Ruth's journal, "Facing empty years in a childless marriage, she recognized that she must commit herself to her 'own individual world of effort and creation.' "[19]

As time passed, tensions within the marriage moved from the occasional to the corrosive. Even though after two years Ruth still wrote of the "ecstacy" and "quiet satisfaction of Stanley's presence" which "is like a great sweet light around me," estrangement became a theme of occasional journal entries: "So we grow more and more strangers to the other," she wrote, "united only by gusts of feelings that grow to seem more and more emptiness in our lives, not part and parcel of them; and by an intolerable pity for each other as human beings cruelly tortured" (AW, 137, 143).

By 1917, with America involved in the First World War, Ruth, demoralized by struggling with her manuscript on the lives of women "that nobody believes in," turned again to the "meddling of social work," joining in the war effort with a project she coordinated to set up day nurseries for working women. This time she found the challenge invigorating and judged the work she did useful, even though it was not "the self I love" (AW, 142).

In 1918, at age 31, she went back to school, studying educational philosophy at Columbia University with the progressive thinker John Dewey. In 1919 she enrolled in the first session of the innovative liberal adult education venture, the New School for Social Research. Here she received her first taste of anthropology, a course on sex and ethnology taught by Elsie Clews Parsons, a well-known free thinker and a feminist.[20] Parsons was wealthy, unconventional, and married to a Republican politician to whom she was devoted in spite of her poor opinion of the institution of marriage and her independent way of life. She belonged to Heterodoxy, the radical women's discussion group which met in Greenwich Village, and she wrote for The Masses and the New Republic. She had been a pacifist during the war, refusing to let her husband in the house when he was in uniform, and her books on women's issues and the family advocated sex education, birth control, and trial marriage. Disillusioned with radical groups after the war, she increasingly turned away from her original discipline, sociology, and concentrated with almost fanatical commitment on ethnographic work. She was known for returning from expeditions to her exclusive Manhattan residence in a disreputable state, wearing khaki clothes, an old felt hat, her hair tied up in a bandanna, and carrying saddlebags full of manuscripts. In winter she sometimes went to lunches wearing two moth-eaten fur coats, one on top of the other.

Ruth did not warm to Elsie Parsons, a woman unbending in her principles, somewhat aloof, high-minded, and not always easy in her social manner. Anthropology, however, proved interesting, and Ruth enrolled for a further course with Alexander Goldenweiser, a teacher who took a great interest in his students and engaged with them in animated conversation outside classes. Conversation was not all he engaged in; in fact, he had a reputation as a "womanizer" and was later dismissed from Columbia on some pretext. But Ruth found him inspiring anyway, and his flirtatious manner seems not to have irked her and may even have been flattering.

Ruth was captivated by anthropology as presented by "Goldie." It offered an outsider's view of life which accorded with her own sense of isolation. It pulled the rug out from under social conventions, displaying them as arbitrary rather than God given, offered a tolerant approach to different ways of life, and had a social purpose, both to put on record vanishing cultures and also to provide, through comparison, an understanding of contemporary society. Ruth was swept up in this challenge, which fascinated her intellectually and, in contrast to her solitary writing, brought her into contact with other lively and unconventional people with a shared sense of purpose.

It was Goldenweiser who first recognized Ruth's potential as a scholar and persuaded her to pursue her studies seriously. He suggested that she enroll for graduate studies with Franz Boas at Columbia, and along with Elsie Clews Parsons, he recommended her for the program. In 1921, at the mature age of 33, Ruth entered Columbia as a doctoral student.

# 3

## Companions in Harness

DURING THE 1920S, according to one feminist historian, women who wanted to succeed in the professions usually survived by means of "deliberate overqualification and personal stoicism."[1] Yet whatever tactics they adopted, few women did succeed, and equality was still a vision rather than a reality. Universities were increasingly willing to provide graduate education for women, but this broadening of opportunities was not matched by a growth in jobs.

The New Women of the 1920s wanted to work alongside men. They rejected the tactics of feminist foremothers who had adapted to the Victorian doctrine of separate spheres by carving out opportunities while at the same time exercising caution lest their femininity be seen as compromised. The New Women, especially in the social sciences, had begun to argue that women were the same as men, not different, though they found that obstacles to women's succeeding did not melt away in the face of their logic. Most of the professions had been opened up, yet highly qualified women still tended to be corralled off to teach at undergraduate women's colleges, given research opportunities on "soft" or no money, or sidelined into certain professional areas judged suitable for women's talents. Others were lost to marriage. There were always a few eccentrics and wealthy women "amateurs" who tried to rock the boat, but the reality was that there were few woman in positions of institutional power in graduate schools or professions to provide mentoring and patronage. For the most part, women in the twenties relied on older men of liberal leanings to help them get ahead, even though these same men were liable to treat them as potential wives, probable dilettantes, and sources of free labor.

It was Columbia University that made anthropologists of Margaret Mead and Ruth Benedict. Founded as a college in the middle of the eighteenth century, Columbia had become a university in 1896, and by 1920 it was a prestigious educational institution.[2] From 1901 until 1945—nearly the entirety of Benedict's career—Columbia was presided over by Nicholas Murray Butler, a man who has been described as the archetype of the modern, managerial university leader. Butler understood intuitively that in the twentieth century education would lead to power. He aimed to train a new elite of middle-class professionals and took care that this elite would be recruited from traditional sources—middle-class young men of Anglo-Saxon heritage.

New York's cosmopolitanism was created by its immigrants. Early in the century, 40 percent of New York public high school graduates were Jewish, many of them first-generation Americans wanting to better themselves through education. In an atmosphere of racial tension and hostility toward immigrants, Butler introduced, with some sleight of hand, a quota system. New admission policies deliberately favored applications from outside the city, and the proportion of Jewish students at Columbia was nearly halved in just four years.

Those in the university who cherished ideals of Columbia as a democratic institution serving the city were further upset when, on the eve of America's entry to World War I, Butler made a declaration of loyalty and mobilized the university, reorganizing faculties—social sciences were absurdly retitled the "Economic and Social Service Corp"—and declaring pacifism treasonous. He immediately fired two prominent professors for their public statements of opposition to the war.

Butler's emphasis on the university as the source of professionalism and expertise rather than as critic and conscience of society, along with his isolation of Columbia from the larger life of New York City, alienated many of the city's intellectuals. By the twenties Greenwich Village had developed a lively culture of independent inquiry, functioning as an alternative to the university, a place of heady debates on social, political, literary, and artistic issues with a character that was cosmopolitan and radical rather than exclusive. Columbia's position also resulted in the development of alternative educational institutions and opportunities. The New School for Social Research, which Ruth Benedict attended in its first semester, was founded in 1919 by disillusioned liberal academics specifically as an alternative to Columbia.

It is hardly surprising that Franz Boas, a Jew, a pacifist, and a socialist was unpopular with the Columbia administration. It was always a battle for him to obtain resources for the anthropology department, which was squeezed onto the seventh floor of the Journalism building. Despite his prestige, he came close to being fired in 1917 after he criticized fellow anthropologists for spying for the government as part of the war effort. For this action Boas was also censured by his peers in the American Anthropological Association and ejected from the influential National Research Council, the main source of funding for field trips and other projects.

Boas had immigrated to the United States from Germany late in the nineteenth century, taking a position with the Bureau of American Ethnology in Washington, D.C., then the American Museum of Natural History in New York. In 1899 he became the first Professor of Anthropology at Columbia.[3] Trained in the natural sciences, he was a rigorous scholar as well as a man of principle, his commitment to scientific progress and social freedom exemplifying the liberal values of the nineteenth century. His initial optimism about the opportunities for a freer and more equal society in the New World was dented by his exposure to the crass materialism associated with late nineteenth-century capitalism. He was unpleasantly surprised, too, by the xenophobia of American society as it was manifested in the destruction of Native American cultures, the poverty and powerlessness of blacks in the postemancipation era, and growing calls to restrict immigration to Northern Europeans.

Racism became a lifelong preoccupation for Boas, who had won the duelling scars that disfigured his face in a skirmish over anti-Semitism when he was a university student in Germany. At the time Ruth Benedict began her studies in anthropology, he was already involved in a running battle with apologists for the "white race" who misused the scientific data of anthropology in their campaigns against immigration. And Columbia's quota system was, of course, a running sore.

Though he actively involved himself with issues of race, Boas saw himself as a "scientist-citizen" rather than a policy researcher. His stance toward his former colleagues, the Washington anthropologists of the Bureau of American Ethnology, was often confrontational, since the Bureau concentrated on setting policy that would contribute to a "rational management" of Native American reservations.[4] In contrast, Boas had a vision of anthropology as an academic discipline based on sound scientific principles, its research program the careful documentation of "primitive" cultures and its theorizing cautious and skeptical. This rational science would foster tolerance and demonstrate the shallow foundations of racial prejudice.

The Boasian method consisted of examining cultures in depth, establishing their history through language, art, myth, and ritual and studying the influences that shaped them in their distinctive environments and in contacts with neighboring cultures. His theory of "cultural diffusionism," as it came to be called, also set itself in opposition to the ideas of nineteenth-century evolutionists who constructed grand universal charts of human progress showing the development of "mankind" from savagery to civilization. Their empirical basis, Boas argued, was a motley collection of tales from travelers and missionaries chosen to illustrate outlandish marriage customs or superstitious myths.

For Boas, cultures could not be explained in terms of the native endowments of particular races. His work led inevitably to cultural relativism; he argued that anthropologists needed to bring to their work the fearless vision of the outsider and the capacity to see another culture unblinkered by one's own. Under his influence anthropology became the study of culture, not race, moving away from its biological determinist roots toward a more genuinely historical understanding of the relationship between ethnicity, culture, and society.

Boas was a polymath, deeply knowledgeable in physical and natural sciences, mathematics, and linguistics, as well as anthropology. The brilliance of his scholarship and the strength of his commitment to the task of understanding culture meant that he attracted clever, enthusiastic graduate students to a field that had little to offer in the way of material reward, not even to men. As a teacher he had high expectations. He was what one historian has called "a pedagogue of the sink-or-swim school"[5] and graduate students found his manner forbidding and his lectures difficult to follow. Yet he engaged with them intellectually and insisted they learn to function at the highest levels of scholarship, advising them to work with "icy enthusiasm."[6] As Margaret Mead recalled,

> In his lectures Boas referred to tribes all over the world without placing them in time or space or by author, and even when one sat 'on the right side of his mouth' his very German pronunciation was hard to understand. He always gave references first in German and only then in English, and there were rumors that, on two weeks notice, he would demand seminar reports based on sources in such languages as Dutch or Danish. The student struggled with the clear, higher-level abstractions and the unintelligible details in lectures and with reading, most of which was specialized, technical, and not organized to any point of current interest. The few students in the department took courses more than once because each time they were completely different. For in spite of the intolerable load of teaching, which he combined with the direction of great bodies of research in folklore and linguistics, Boas always prepared each lecture as if it were to be given for an audience of a hundred of his peers. (AW, 10)

Boas was committed to training students to go out into the field with the gargantuan and urgent task of recording rapidly vanishing cultures. For many years he was the only tenured staff member in anthropology and single-handedly taught the program, administered the department, continued his own research, and fostered the careers of promising young anthropologists, organizing projects for them, finding snippets of funding here and there, and prodding them into publication.

In his work Boas relied heavily on the generosity of Elsie Clews Parsons, his first woman protégée.[7] They had met in 1907 when she was already a well-known sociologist, her popular book on the family causing a furor with its advocacy of trial marriage. Ironically, for an advocate of women's rights, Parsons had been expected to resign her Barnard position when she married, and so for most of her career she worked outside the framework of formal institutions. By 1915 she had converted to anthropology, and after the war, when as a pacifist she had lost most of her friends, she turned increasingly to fieldwork and to collecting minutiae of empirical fact, projects that helped allay the disappointment she felt in radical causes. In her early forties, a mother of four with a tolerant husband and a private fortune, Parsons would make lasting changes to the field of anthropology with this redirection of her scholarly interests.

In her role as patron and independent scholar, Parsons had an influence on anthropology that has been underestimated by historians. She encouraged Boas to return to the field at a time when he was disheartened, and she financed his trips, on several occasions traveling with him. For years she paid the salary of the departmental secretary and funded many publications for Boas and his students. She and Boas became friends, though they were respectful rather than intimate ones. Closer alliances developed between Elsie and several of Boas's male protégés who formed "the gang" of Columbia anthropologists. Both Pliny Earle Goddard and Alfred Kroeber were romantically interested in her, leading to some competitiveness between them. As time went on, Parsons became a mentor and patron to a number of anthropologists starting their careers, particularly women.

Anthropology at Columbia was especially appealing to those who felt excluded from the mainstream of American society because of their sex, their ethnicity, or their personal feelings of alienation. They learned that cultures are constructed from human activities over the course of time, rather than determined by nature. This meant that the parameters of society were not fixed but open to challenge. Boas was hardly surprised at having many Jewish students, but he did not expect that women would flock to his graduate program, many from Barnard. As early as 1900 he had one class in which women outnumbered men, and in 1920 he wrote, "I have had a rather curious experience in graduate work during the past few years—All my best students were women."[8]

There were a number of factors beside the almost de rigueur "outsider" status which made the study of anthropology, and Columbia anthropology in particular, welcoming to women.[9] First, there was the vast increase in the numbers of women entering higher education. In 1920 women composed 47 percent of all students, a figure not to be matched again until the late 1970s. College education for women had flourished since its inception and growing institutions eagerly recruited students. But as higher education became an accepted part of American life, the enrollment of male students increased and they soon outdistanced women. Young men now recognized the importance of college as providing entry to the professions and government. The difference was especially marked at graduate level, where women's participation remained unusual.[10]

In fact, for women at Columbia and elsewhere in graduate school there was a danger of becoming overqualified for their future work, since universities increasingly accepted them as students but provided no comparable follow-through in terms of jobs, either in the academy or elsewhere. Margaret Rossiter's thorough examination of the careers of women scientists in the United States shows that the only likely source of work after graduate school was the women's colleges, although a few other occupations seen as particularly suited to women opened up, such as work in observatories and museums. In a relatively new science like anthropology, a woman could rapidly gain expertise, make recognized contributions, and generally gain intellectual status, but she would be unlikely to receive material benefits. Not even women's colleges would be open to her, as few offered anthropology. In 1921 there were only eight women anthropologists listed in *American Men of Science*. Five of these were employed, four at research institutes where they would have been on "soft" rather than having tenure. Only two women held doctorates compared to fifty-four men. By 1938 the discrepancy was still large, though the ratio of twenty women with doctorates to one hundred men was an improvement; however, only three women were employed at major universities.[11]

Boas attracted women students and encouraged them in their work. In fact, when he fell out with the Columbia administration, he stopped offering undergraduate courses at Columbia College, the men's undergraduate college. He was disgusted at the anti-intellectualism of the university and was welcomed at Barnard which was developing an excellent undergraduate social science program.[12] The result was that for a number of years around half of the women doctorates in the country were trained at Columbia and almost half of the Ph.D. recipients from Columbia were women. It has also been suggested that Boas's reputation for political radicalism meant that men planning a career in anthropology often preferred to study at Harvard, Chicago, or Berkeley.[13]

With their numbers reaching a comfortable level, women felt increasingly at home at Columbia. Boas, who had been famously hard on his earliest male students, perhaps softened a little under their influence. George

Stocking, a historian of anthropology, has portrayed Boas as a Victorian paterfamilias, his "family" of aspiring anthropologists characterized by "the oedipal rebellion of certain older male offspring, the rejected sons, the sibling rivalries, the generational and sexual differentiations—most notable in the softening of the patriarch toward the younger generation of daughters, who called him 'Papa Franz' and accepted the sometimes ambiguous benevolence of a man who facilitated the entry of many women into the discipline. . . ."[14]

However much Boas encouraged his women students, he was to some extent a man of his time in his attitude toward their work. He favored men when making recommendations for jobs and relied on women's willingness to work for little or no remuneration. His desire to advance anthropology meant that he exploited any source of available labor. Having a male mentor might be wonderful for women who generally lacked recognition from men, but it could also mean forming a daughterly attachment that continued unbroken far beyond young adulthood, since independence in a protégé was less likely to be encouraged among women than men.

At Columbia Ruth found an intellectual home. Boas's mentoring was crucially important in her decision to advance in anthropology. This was a critical juncture in her life and one where she could not have tolerated discouragement. She had failed as a social worker, as a teacher, and as a writer, her marriage was failing, and she had been denied the opportunity of motherhood. Goldenweiser and Boas represented an anthropology that could prove an outlet for her literary imagination. It offered a route to different worlds and provided a relief from her own. It engaged her wry humor and philosophical acumen. Goldenweiser had drawn her out and delivered her to "Papa Franz," who recognized a light hiding under a bushel and had the wit to appreciate Ruth's talents, notwithstanding her shyness, her deafness, her sex, her age, and her married state, all disadvantages to a conventional scholarly career. He shepherded her through her doctoral studies in only three semesters, giving recognition to the work that she had already completed at the New School.

Aware that as a married woman Ruth did not feel able to undertake prolonged fieldwork, Boas organized for her doctorate a library-based project centering on her interest in religion. Using an approach that Goldenweiser had pioneered in his study of totemism, Benedict made a thorough study of guardian spirit practices among Native Americans who made use of self-torture, fasting, and prayer in their arduous searches for a vision.[15]

For Ruth, Boas functioned as a guardian spirit. In a sense she had called him up, not through the ancient means but nevertheless through a long and painful period of self-doubt and questioning. Boas was more truly the inheritor of her father's mantle than Stanley Benedict ever proved to be. Ruth was to develop an affectionate and daughterly relationship with Boas and he, in turn, liked and respected her and relied on her increasingly over the years. In anthropology Ruth found her future, though at times in the early years she was not convinced that she would be able to continue. Like the best of protégées, she was to master the discipline and go beyond her mentor to make her own distinctive imprint.

After her first year of graduate study, Ruth became the teaching assistant for the Barnard course in which Margaret Mead was a student. Ruth had just returned from a first brief taste of fieldwork. Going west for the summer, she had studied the Serrano people under the direction of Alfred Kroeber, now at Berkeley. On day visits to a reservation in the Morongo Valley she had taken her mother along for company. Tame as this project was compared to the work of more adventurous contemporaries, firsthand experience of a Native American culture brought anthropological texts to life and gave her some authority with the Barnard students when she took them to the Museum of Natural History to study displays of Indian culture.

Ruth had found one experience with the Serrano particularly memorable. Ramon, an old man who spoke to her with sadness of his disintegrating world, told her a fable: " 'In the beginning,' " he said, " 'God gave to every people a cup, a cup of clay, and from this cup they drank their life. . . . They all dipped in the water . . . but their cups were different. Our cup is broken now. It has passed away' " (AW, 38–39).

Here was the Boasian imperative in its real life setting. The accumulated wisdom of cultures like the Serrano's were fast disappearing, impoverishing the store of human knowledge through the loss of myriad inventive solutions that had been found for the problems of living. Though Ramon's people might survive, "the whole fabric of [their] standards and beliefs had disappeared," and "with them, the shape and meaning of their life" (AW, 39). "Cups of clay" was to remain, for Ruth, a central metaphor which she was to rework in her classic *Patterns of Culture* to demonstrate her vision of cultures as unitary wholes.[16]

At the time Ruth met Margaret Mead she was close to finishing her doctoral thesis. She enjoyed the work, and the world of anthropology, which valued her talents, contrasted so strongly with the bleakness of her marriage that a crisis was building. If she could not remain in the marriage she would need to be financially self-supporting, yet Boas seemed to feel no obligation to provide for her. For him, Ruth's married state was useful, as she was someone who could be yoked to the cause and supported by her scientist-husband who would surely recognize the importance of the work and willingly subsidize it. Other promising anthropologists more desperately needed an income and there was no telling whether Ruth might be merely a dilettante, easily diverted by family matters.

So when a full-time job for a woman came up, he did not offer Ruth his support. Barnard was to establish the first anthropology department in a woman's college, replacing Ruth's teaching assistantship with a more permanent position which, if we are able to believe Margaret Mead, must have arisen partly as a result of her enthusiastic proselytizing for the course. Boas endorsed the candidacy of another Columbia doctoral student, Gladys Reichard, who had been his assistant before Benedict and was not married, which undoubtedly made her more acceptable to the college. Unsupported, Reichard might be a lost cause to anthropology, and that year she had been doing useful fieldwork, writing her dissertation on the grammar of the Wiyot of northeastern California.[17]

Ruth's disappointment was intense. Her teaching assistantship would disappear, and she had enjoyed becoming closer to Boas while they worked together. Through it, she was achieving a measure of recognition in her new profession and the chance to overcome the handicap of her shyness. Above all, Ruth smarted at her status as a wife; as Charlotte Perkins Gilman had warned, it condemned her to being an economic parasite. The situation harked back to earlier years when she wrote bitterly in her journal, "To me it seems a very terrible thing to be a woman" (AW, 120).

Boas recognized her disappointment. He turned to the "soft" money solution, suggesting to Elsie Clews Parsons that she employ Ruth through the Southwest Society she funded. The reply was favorable. Parsons told him she could create an opportunity for work collecting information about southwestern mythology with the eventual aim of producing a concordance.[18] Perhaps surprisingly, Ruth was far from delighted. The offer set off an intense personal conflict. She had never warmed to Parsons, and Reichard's winning the Barnard position had wounded her pride. After Boas told her of the suggestion, Ruth reported in her diary the "worst sick headache I've had in years. I know my subconscious staged it—But really I suppose it's hanging on to the idea that I can teach at Barnard—which my conscious self has known I couldn't do, always" (AW, 63).

Two days later she lunched with Parsons but could not bring herself to raise the matter, and her potential sponsor said nothing of it either. The next day she wrote, "Couldn't," crossed it out, noted "Wrote Mrs. Parsons I'd take the job," crossed this out again, and finally, "Wrote Mrs. Parsons I was interested" (AW, 65).

She then lunched with Pliny Earle Goddard, curator at the natural history museum, barely managing to say anything nice about Gladys Reichard, who would now be the one to show the Barnard students around the exhibits. They went on to talk about Ruth's position. Goddard told her that "Boas supposed there'd always be these driblets of research but that was all he could see ahead for me." Ruth was extremely offended: "I feel some capacity for making a place for myself, thank you!" she wrote in her diary. On the way out in the elevator, "I was weary, and plain wept with vexation."

A couple of days later there was a letter in the mail from Parsons with a firm offer of one thousand dollars for the study of southwest mythology, leaving room for at least some work on problems of Ruth's own choice. There would also be the opportunity for a field trip to the Southwest. There was really very little choice: "Wrote Mrs. Parsons I'd take the job" (AW, 65–66). The necessity for her capitulation was underscored when several months later her application for a National Research Council fellowship was turned down, as it was again the following year. She was just over the age limit of thirty-five, and when Elsie Clews Parsons protested on Ruth's behalf, the reply was that someone of that age "is not very promising material for development."[19]

Crisis built throughout the early months of 1923. On 20 February she told Parsons she would accept the job, and the following weekend Stanley was threatening divorce: "It's as if we inhabited the opposing poles—He kept talking about a job for him at California or for me at Wellesley. S[tanley]—'It isn't any laws people need [for divorce]; just the nerve'—He has a fixed idea, and he'll drive me to it—maybe."

By now Ruth was spending weekdays in a room she rented near Columbia, away from the stifling atmosphere of suburban life. On weekends she returned to Bedford Hills to take up her separate existence with Stanley, who had little interest in her anthropology friends and remained a shadowy figure to them since Ruth, with her aptitude for a divided life, hardly ever introduced them. Once, when Ruth invited Columbia colleagues to a picnic at Bedford Hills, Stanley remained "barricaded in his dark-room, ostensibly developing pictures" for the entire day.[20] Stanley may not have actively opposed Ruth's taking a room or discouraged her involvement in anthropology, but her new social circle was not part of their shared life. Ruth seems to have felt that she should at least earn enough to pay her professional expenses. Virginia Woolf's dictum that the creative woman needs a room of her own and five hundred pounds a year certainly applied to her, and if divorce really was on the horizon, Ruth, with no assurance of Stanley's continuing financial support, faced the possibility of losing both her marriage and her career.

It seems to have been Ruth's increasing independence of mind rather than her physical absence on weekdays that Stanley found abhorrent. For the most part, of course, she stayed behind the mask, from which he once thought he could release her. Looking back on that time, she recalled, "I loved Stanley, and to him love is identity; anything in me that was not in him was betrayal of love, and wounded him as desperately as malice could have. Therefore . . . I tried to show him less and less of myself. I thought that if he were not pressed by the interchanges he counted as betrayals, I could give him peace. And at the end it was not peace—it was indifference" (RFB, Box 106).

Keeping the mask tightly adjusted was a survival strategy that put Ruth's mental stability at risk. Her diary from 1923 (one of a handful of personal records that have survived) records her battle against depression. Two weeks after her conversation with Stanley about divorce, Ruth seems to have been close to breaking down. She finished her thesis, put it in the mail, went to an anthropology lunch, and then stopped off at the museum to talk over the Peruvian materials with Goddard. She then surprised herself by going downtown and buying a suit, perhaps inspired by her Barnard students, but exhaustion set in:

> Weary—too weary to stay for theater. Home and read Many Marriages and Faint Perfume. Quickening of the spirit is pain almost to madness. And in spite of all I say, pain is not indifferent to me! I can't exclude the knowledge of pain from my choices. I dread intense awareness.—And yet it comes with ghastly frequency. I had one today, buying stamps at the underground Library post office—inconceivable that such a thing as life existed—such a thing as my power to look out and be conscious of these other people. The whole thing an arrangement of lines and dots in a kaleidoscope. . . . And then it seems to me terrible that life is passing, that my program is to fill the twenty-four hours each day with obliviousness, with work—And oh, I am lonely. . . . (AW, 67)

The experience of depersonalization such as the one Ruth describes here as "intense awareness" reflects the severity of the stress she was under. Ruth may well have worried about her own sanity, as people often do when they feel that their experience has become "colored by a frightening sense of strangeness and unreality."[21] This phenomenon is often linked to dissociative disorders, although in its milder forms it is not an uncommon occurrence and is not necessarily accompanied by the lack of insight characteristic of full-blown dissociative states. Ruth's habit since childhood of seeking refuge in the imaginative world of her father may have been at the root of her tendency to react to extreme stress in this manner.

Stanley's rejection, coming on top of her disappointment about the anthropology job and undoubtedly her fatigue at completing the thesis, had driven her to the brink of psychological disintegration. As she later recalled, "He rejected me—all of myself I valued—and however calmly my outward self agreed and resigned itself to a course of action, it cut the roots of my life at their source. Months and years were just a routine to keep suicide from becoming too strong for me in an unguarded moment" (RFB, Box 106). Ruth's poem, "She Speaks to the Sea," written around this time, shows her perception of death as a state of release and peacefulness. Imagining the sea as a bridegroom, she longs for death in words that resonate with desire:

> Now would I lay aside the garment of my body
> Lay quite aside its slavery of breath
> For I am smitten to my knees with longing
> Desolate utterly. . . . Will you have minstrels, Ocean
> when I come, bride to eternal bridegroom
> And save one jeweled chamber for our eternity?[22]

Ruth later said of this time with Stanley, "the only motive that drove me was dread, and all my hope was to be able to circumvent some moment of unbearable reckoning" (RFB, Box 106). The reckoning really lay with herself. She had arrived at a crossroads, just as she had when she reached the end of her tether with teaching and tricked herself into falling in love with Stanley. Now she had to ask whether she could sacrifice herself and her career for the sake of her marriage. Just as Ruth needed Boas's mentoring to find her way into anthropology, she could not have weathered this personal crisis alone. Through her developing relationships that year with two very different people, she began to build the foundations for a new approach to her life, though with no immediate respite from despair.

Nineteen twenty-two had been an auspicious year. It marked Ruth's entry into teaching and her meeting Margaret Mead, and she also met Boas's gifted protégé, Edward Sapir, a brilliant linguist who since 1910 had been in exile in Ottawa as head of the division of anthropology in the Geological Survey of Canada. Most likely Boas introduced them, and Edward began what was to become a voluminous correspondence when he wrote to congratulate Ruth warmly on her first published article.

Sapir was married with three children. Both he and his wife, Florence, came from Jewish families who had emigrated from Lithuania. Sapir was born in Poland, growing up with Yiddish as his native tongue.[23] His father was a cantor who finally gave up his ambition to sing with the Berlin Opera when he was reduced to selling peanuts on Hester Street on the Lower East Side of New York City. As a sober and studious fourteen-year-old, Edward had won a citywide competition identifying him as the brightest boy in New York, and his scholarly career confirmed this early promise.

At this time Sapir was beset by family problems. Florence, who as a young woman had been noted for her gaiety and fondness for music and dancing, began to suffer from mental health problems early in the marriage which worsened with the birth of each child. She found Ottawa dull, cold, and distant from family and friends, but when Edward's mother came to help with domestic duties the two women only quarrelled. In 1921 Florence had her worst breakdown, becoming severely depressed and exhibiting symptoms of psychosis.

She entered a hospital in New York and then moved with her oldest son, Michael, to a room near Columbia where she could convalesce. Sapir visited as often as he could, sometimes bringing the younger children. It was during these visits, harried as they were, that he and Ruth got to know each other better.

Ruth's 1923 diary contains frequent references to Sapir. It is clear she had something of a crush on him, though there is no evidence of an affair. In addition to their shared interest in anthropology, the two had aloof and melancholy temperaments and wrote poetry, though at that time Ruth was quite secretive about her literary ambitions. She had been dogged by failure and, always a private person, wrote under the pseudonym "Anne Singleton," a name that certainly suggested her need for independence.

It must have been clear to Ruth that Edward was romantically unavailable, preoccupied as he was with anxieties about his unstable wife and the needs of his children. She proved to be an excellent confidante and was willing to help Florence amuse the children. In a January 1923 diary entry she wrote, "Anthrop. lunch—ES there, and walked to Museum with him. His wife mentally cured, physically very ill. Talked of Esther [Goldfrank, Boas's secretary] and Mrs. Parsons; relationship terms [i.e., technical anthropology]. Bought jam and cards! I must remember afterwards how simple happiness is—I don't want anything more or different at such times—I'm just at ease" (RFB, Box 37).

The succeeding entries record more such interactions before Sapir went back to Ottawa. He returned in March, Florence having been in the hospital yet again, where she had all her teeth removed and her lungs drained for an abscess. On 12 March Ruth wrote: "Dr. Sapir, with Michael, in hall—'At least there's something else to think of besides life and death', he said when I said how glad I was his wife was well again. She doesn't 'want' to go back to Ottawa and he's looking for a place for her." Two days later: "Dr. Sapir came to ask about country boarding places. He wanted me to come to see his wife today—and I went at three—sordid ugly surroundings—a furnished room on Broadway—she with her teeth out and an ill-fitting large dress. O horrible! Only one double bed for three of them; how could he commit such an error of judgment after all this separation? All she's willing to do is fend for herself in this city—and she not able to walk a block" (RFB, Box 37).

Next day: "Anthropology lunch, and I stayed afterwards to talk to Dr. Sapir who came very late. I spoke of Miss R[eichard?]'s paranoic trend, and he said, 'It's very easy for me to understand that type of person. It comes naturally.'" And the following day: "Saw Dr. Sapir ahead of me at noon, but suddenly I didn't care whether he looked up or not. He didn't, and I went on to the train" (RFB, Box 37).

That was a Friday evening and Stanley's birthday. Ruth went to Bedford Hills as usual. Stanley was intrigued with a new lens for his camera, but Ruth felt very low. It was "the cliff tonight. Nothing could bring life to it." The following Monday she worked all day and "No word from Dr. Sapir, though I know he's still here." Better luck on Tuesday: "Tonight message from Dr. Sapir to me through Michael. He's been ill with grip [*sic*] and he'd like to have me come to see them. The room is just across from mine now. A much less depressing cell than the first one; the room's much better and quieter. He looks dreadful. How do we ever escape the upper and the nether millstones? Anyway he's between them . . ." (RFB, Box 37).

Despite his personal concerns Edward was unfailingly encouraging toward Ruth in her work. He thought she was the "logical writer" of a general book on culture representing the Boasian point of view, and when she replied that she was now more interested in writing a book on mythology he responded, "we are going to get a really fruitful treatment . . . from you. I wish I knew enough about it to discuss it intelligently" (SF, 10 Sept. 1923). In Sapir Ruth found a different kind of mentor than Boas was, someone just as affirming, at least initially, but also someone she could confide in, for they were closer to one another in age and Sapir had no immediate power over her work prospects. Also, Ruth was half in love with him.

The suicide of Margaret Mead's friend Marie Bloomfield in February 1923 brought Ruth and Margaret closer together. Marie, whose brother Leonard became the well-known linguist, had spent six weeks in the hospital over the winter break with a bad case of measles. Her parents were no longer alive and there was no one to look after her when she was well enough to be discharged, so Margaret helped settle her back in the Barnard dormitory, which was deserted for the weekend. Leaving on another mission to help a girl who had emerged from a college examination stricken with hysterical blindness, Margaret decided to spend the weekend with the latter friend. When Marie did not come down to dinner the following Monday, Margaret, with the help of others, broke into her room and discovered her dead from a dose of cyanide. The suicide was an immense shock. Margaret felt that had she not left the girl to her own devices, she might have prevented the suicide. She had not found Marie "especially congenial," describing her as "an awkward girl, intellectually eager but stiff and unresponsive to any kind of physical affection" (BW, 114). But she had been aware of Marie's loneliness.

Suicides are public as well as private events, as Margaret soon found. "Marie's death was spread all over the newspapers," she wrote in *Blackberry Winter.* "Her face stared up at us from trampled newspapers on the subway floor. Understandably, the college administration was frantic and was determined to convince me—so that I would convince others—that Marie had been insane. I resisted this, feeling very much embattled against the adult world of doctors and deans who cared nothing at all about Marie Bloomfield's plight, but only about keeping the college community quiet" (BW, 114).

Ruth read the reports of Marie's death and immediately wrote: "My dear Margaret, You will be needed by the other girls to the limit of your strength, and if there is anything in the world I can do to leave you freer, send me word. . . . Or if you can get away, come yourself. I've nothing all day that can't be put off. I shall be thinking of you today—and wishing people could be of more use to each other in difficult times. Affectionately, Ruth Benedict" (MM, B14).

"It's unbearable that life should be so hard for them," Ruth confided in her diary. "I know it's all wrapped up with my wish for children—and dread that they might not want the gift.—It bowls me over completely. Wrote M. Mead—She came to my room before bed time" (RFB, Box 37).

Margaret found Ruth a sympathetic listener. "She was the one person who understood that suicide might be a noble and conscious choice," she wrote in *An Anthropologist at Work* (83). Ruth spoke to the younger woman of her own puzzlement as a child when a servant on a neighboring farm killed herself. Her grandparents said that the girl had done something wicked, yet Ruth knew of the honorable suicides of Romans who readily fell upon their swords. As Margaret put it, "It did not make sense to her that suicide should be applauded among the ancient Romans and at the same time be execrated in northern New York State" (AW, 83).

Whether Ruth spoke to Margaret of her own suicidal feelings on this occasion is not known, but she was certainly able to empathize with Margaret's anger and confusion at the manipulativeness of the authorities. "From that time," said Margaret, "I began to know her not only as a teacher but also as a friend" (BW, 124).

By March 1923 the two were seeing each other frequently. A true mentor-protégée relationship was developing, with all the sparkle that occurs in the early stages, quite similar really to a romance.[24] Ruth was flourishing, thanks to the encouragement of Boas and Sapir, and she was now able to give of herself, despite the difficulties of her personal life. Good mentoring often occurs when there is not a wide gulf in status between mentor and protégé. Though there was a fifteen-year age difference between the pair, the gap was not an unbridgeable one. Margaret, in her final year at Barnard, was not far behind Ruth, who was in her third and final semester of graduate study. Ruth possessed all the qualities that Margaret was ready to admire, and as Ruth wrote in her diary, "She rests me like a padded chair and a fire place. I say it's the zest of youth I believe in when I see it in her. Or is it that I respond understandably to admiration?" (RFB, Box 37).

Together they discussed Margaret's career plans. She had briefly harbored literary ambitions, but now realized through contrasting herself with Léonie Adams that her talents were slight. She had also considered politics, what with her abilities as a public speaker, her capacity for argumentation, and her social concerns. But given her family background, a career in social science was almost inevitable. She had chosen psychology as her major at Barnard and now hoped to take a master's degree in that field the following year at Columbia with the intention of becoming a school psychologist. But she disliked the racism, sexism, and narrow-mindedness of psychology at that time, particularly in the field of mental testing. The army intelligence testing program of the war years had brought in conservative male psychologists and deflected attention away from feminist pioneers like Leta Hollingworth, the wife of Margaret's psychology teacher Harry Hollingworth, who had been busily demonstrating that men and women were not so different from one another after all.[25]

Also, psychology lacked adventure. It did not seem to offer as compelling a mixture of urgent work and social radicalism as anthropology did. An educational psychology course Mead took at Columbia's Teachers College in her final year completely put her off. She complained that all the other students were men who aspired to be or already were high school principals and that both they and the class were exceptionally dull. Anthropology seemed increasingly attractive, and Margaret was pleased to be able to attend graduate seminars, especially since there was a rumor that Boas might retire the following year.

So it was hardly surprising when Ruth noted in her diary in March 1923: "Lunch with M. Mead—discussed her going into anthropology. I hope she does it. I need a companion in harness" (RFB, Box 37). What tipped the balance, apparently, was Ruth's saying, "Professor Boas and I have nothing to offer but an opportunity to do work that matters." "That settled it for me," Margaret recalled, although she spent a sleepless night mulling over her decision.[26] "Anthropology had to be done *now*," she decided. "Other things could wait" (BW, 123). It was a field in which she might succeed by dint of sheer hard work. Excitedly, she informed Boas that she wanted to enroll for a Ph.D. in anthropology following her master's year. "He poured cold water but she arose," Ruth noted in her diary (RFB, Box 37). In fact, he advised Mead to study at Harvard, not Columbia, but she was not to be deterred, and he excused her from taking the final exam.

When Ruth told Margaret that she had nothing to offer but work that mattered, she was, of course, speaking the literal truth. As a school psychologist Margaret could have expected to find a job at the end of her studies. For an anthropologist there could be no such assurance. At the end of her senior year at Barnard, Margaret graduated with honors and was elected to Phi Beta Kappa, matching Ruth's achievements fifteen years earlier. She just missed out on the graduate fellowship awarded to the best student of the year; this meant she had to ask for continued support from her father.

Edward Mead was proud of his daughter's achievements. Conveniently forgetting the obstacles he had put in her way, "he grasped the key that was hanging around my neck, and said, 'That cost me ten thousand dollars and it's worth it!' " (BW, 36). He even agreed to provide her with further support, but in line with his belief that "he who pays the piper calls the tune," his offer came with a condition. Margaret could go to graduate school and also take a trip around the world with a very generous allowance—provided she break her engagement to Luther Cressman. Grandmother Mead had apparently expressed her concern that Margaret was marrying just because marriage was the appropriate step to take on completing college. Edward Mead may well have shared her concern, but equally telling may have been his dislike of Luther, as Margaret understood: "Unquestionably, he sensed how much I valued in Luther exactly those abilities in which I felt my father was lacking—his precise physical skills and his sensitivity to other human beings" (BW, 39). Margaret, used to outmaneuvering her father in his fitful attempts to lay down the law, stood firm, but this time so did he. Support for her graduate study was withdrawn.

Margaret's career as an anthropologist seemed threatened. But Ruth Benedict was not about to lose her companion in harness. She dipped into her own pocket and Margaret received a note from her, accompanied by a check announcing the "First Award No Red Tape Fellowship, $300." Margaret found another sponsor in her Barnard professor, William Fielding Ogburn, who asked how much she needed for living expenses and then offered her that amount as a teaching and editorial assistant. She accepted with alacrity and her graduate work was now assured; so was her marriage to Luther.

"I continued to call [Ruth] 'Mrs. Benedict' until I got my degree," Margaret said, but by the time her graduate work commenced they were on more familiar terms (BW, 124). They saw each other almost daily. Ruth offered her protégée knowledge of her discipline, a useful standing with Boas, and contacts with other anthropologists. Margaret usually sat by her in the graduate seminar and "acquired a very useful speed . . . by . . . writing down the parts of the discussion which [Ruth] was unable to hear" (AW, 9). She and her fellow students relied on Ruth to act as an intermediary with Boas as they continued to be apprehensive of the "great man." Legends circulated about his famously demanding treatment of an earlier generation of students, men like Goldenweiser, Kroeber, and Sapir, and still he taught "in dreadful concentration and with no quarter to beginners or those with a defective background. In the biometrics course," Mead remembered, Boas said one day, " 'I am embarrassed. Some of you do not know the calculus. I will teach you the calculus.' In the twenty minutes left of the hour he did!" (AW, 10).

Boas himself seemed to take little interest in Margaret's group: "[He] had a keen eye for the capabilities of his students, although he confounded them by devoting his time to those whom he found least promising. As long as a student was doing well, he paid almost no attention to him at all" (BW, 138). Early in the first year she wondered what she might choose for a thesis topic. She consulted Boas, and in one of the few interviews they ever had together ("lasting all of three minutes") the professor suggested that she do a comparative study. He gave her three choices: Siberia (she must learn Chinese and Russian), the Low Countries (Dutch, German, and Medieval Latin), or Polynesia ("which you could do with only French or German"). "I chose Polynesia" (BW, 138).

Ruth was not always easy to comprehend either. For her first seminar Margaret chose tattooing as a topic. Wanting to impress the group with her flair, she decorated the seminar room with "beautiful, enlarged reproductions" of Polynesian designs. At the end of the seminar, instead of offering the praise Margaret expected, Ruth merely said "with one of her strange, distant smiles, 'I learned a lot' " (BW, 131). Upset by this cool response, Margaret decided that Ruth must be very disappointed in her. She grew more and more distressed and that evening Luther had to visit Ruth to ask if the performance had really been as bad as she feared. Ruth reassured him that Margaret had no reason at all to be upset. The episode was merely a storm in a teacup.

Ruth and Margaret often spent time together at the Kingscote in Ruth's rented room. It was not a place that expressed her personality or tastes, containing nothing of her own, not even a picture, as the furniture belonged to the permanent tenant, a schoolteacher who used the place at the weekend. They also went on outings to the theater, no doubt financed by Ruth, enjoying such plays as Pirandello's *Henri IV*. But their lives revolved around anthropology. Once when they were lunching together in the Bandbox, a restaurant on Amsterdam Avenue near Columbia, a friend of Ruth's interrupted their conversation to say, "When I hear the word *culture*, I know it must be an anthropologist speaking" (BW draft).

In the early days of the friendship Margaret sometimes felt a little out of her depth, as the incident in her graduate seminar showed. A poem she wrote for Ruth several years later, "Your Gift," includes the lines,

> For you have given me speech!
> No more I'll sit, an anxious child
> Awed by articulate elders
> Dumb in envy of the melodies
> That fall from human lips, while mine
> Can only give straight, formal kisses
> And the slight, unfreighted syllables of infancy.

Is this the ever-confident Margaret Mead? Perhaps her emotions were getting in the way of her usual directness, for she concluded:

> No more I'll fear that love
> Will strangle in his two swift hands
> A speechless heart . . .
> All travelled and untravelled ways
> Are for me now.
> For all encountered beauty I may press
> Upon your lips of loveliness. (MM, Q15)

Perhaps Margaret did feel overawed, and at times admiration may have "strangled" her words, but there is no suggestion she was ever struck dumb. She did wonder, though, if she really could sustain a friendship with someone so much older than she. In later life, Margaret told Jean Houston, "Ruth Benedict's attitude to me was that I was the child she hadn't had. . . . I had all the things she would have wanted for a child. The joy in living which she didn't have. The positive assumption [about] life which she never had." Although the fifteen-year age difference was not quite large enough for them to resemble mother and daughter, those fifteen years always worried Margaret: "Sooner or later it's going to catch [up]. . . . She's read fifteen years of books that I haven't read. She's experienced fifteen years of life and sooner or later she's going to run out of being interested in me because I haven't got enough to meet the knowledge and experience that she had. . . ." Margaret was "haunted by two or three conversations," including one in which she had expressed an opinion that was not really her own and Ruth had disagreed: "I said Edna Millay's 'Renascence' was the best poem she'd written . . . [because] somebody had said it the day before . . . and she said, Oh, *she* didn't think so at all, and I didn't go on with it. . . . I was just deeply embarrassed that I had said something that a) wasn't my real feeling and b) she didn't approve of, and . . . [I feared] these discrepancies were going to mount" (JH). As she put it on another occasion, "I always felt the fifteen years between us hanging over me like a Damocles sword that would someday somehow turn into a dividing line that I could not cross" (BW draft).

Margaret recalled, nevertheless, that in these early days of the friendship the two women luxuriated in conversation; Ruth "loved the minutiae of real life, and we spent hours telling each other stories about people whom the other had never met, wondering and speculating why they had done or felt or thought what they seemed to have." They must have particularly enjoyed telling stories of their families. Ruth would have shared vivid impressions of her rural childhood, Margaret her acute observations of the people who dominated her earliest landscapes. They both had affectionate memories of grandparents, and they could compare difficult relationships with mothers. Ruth's idealized absent father and Margaret's very present and egotistical father must have provided fruitful material for discussions of oedipal influence. Margaret was fascinated with child development, fueled by her interest in the differences in personality between herself and her brother and sisters. Ruth shared her feelings of alienation from her family, tracing them back to her childhood pattern of hiding out from the tumults of farmhouse life. But as Mead noted, "in all the stories she told there was no one whom she had really hated or feared. Her own feeling of being different she saw as a threat to the happiness and the incomprehensible contentment and involvement of the people around her. Her inappropriate gay laughter at some incongruity which no one else recognized was read by her sister as 'liking to see people put on a griddle' . . ." (AW, 84).

They discussed the friends they had in common, poets and anthropologists, and amused themselves with gossip about their affairs, same sex and opposite sex. Margaret probably talked to Ruth about Katherine Rothenberger and their mutual affection, about Marie's attitude toward her, and about love affairs between Barnard friends. Feminism and other burning issues of the day were also grist for the conversational mill. Margaret thought her mother's feminism might have arisen from a deep-seated envy of men (BW, 15). Ruth spoke of her despair as a young woman at the lack of choices she faced. They would have talked about the feminists and socialists whose milieu was Greenwich Village, and Ruth no doubt told Margaret of her mixed feelings about Elsie Clews Parsons and Gladys Reichard.

But Margaret remained sensitive to the difference in their ages. On a dark windy night in the middle of winter, she had a minor accident on Broadway when the wheel of a taxi ran over her foot as she was chasing her hat through traffic. The next morning she phoned Ruth from the emergency room where Luther had taken her to have some broken bones set, and fifty years later she recalled with indignation Ruth's response: "You miserable child. What have you done to yourself now?" (BW draft).

Despite the lack of a salary, Ruth maintained her affiliation with Columbia. She worked on the project funded by Parsons, and from 1923 until the early thirties she was Lecturer in Anthropology, a title which recognized her participation in the life of the department. She enjoyed the "anthropology lunches" that took place each Tuesday at the Hotel Endicott on Columbus Avenue and Eighty-first Street with the departmental regulars, as well as any "irregulars," Boasian-trained anthropologists such as Alfred Kroeber, Elsie Clews Parsons, and Edward Sapir and foreign visitors. Her position allowed for occasional paid lecturing at summer schools or university extension classes. As time went by her professional stature grew and she was appointed editor of the *Journal of American Folklore.* She worked on a manuscript on the anthropology of religion, and she and William Ogburn considered collaborating on a text about the family, for which a publisher offered them an advance of $2,400. But the project came to nothing, and financial independence still seemed out of reach (SF, 21 March 1924).

Ruth's daily pattern was to work in the seminar room near Boas's office. Graduate students like Margaret often worked there, too, and many would ask her advice rather than approaching Boas directly. In this way her role as a go-between developed, laying the foundation for her mentoring of the next generation of anthropology students, or "the children," as they came to be known, in a kinship system that resembled the Ash Can Cats and may, in fact, have been introduced by Margaret.

Boas, or "Papa Franz" as he was coming to be called, began to lean on Ruth more and more. She became his "left hand," as Mead put it, taking on some of his more irksome duties (AW, 341). Lacking formal power, she nevertheless established herself in her discipline like many women of her time—valuable and highly regarded, though potentially dispensable, with considerable informal influence. This was not the sort of role that Margaret foresaw for herself, but she had the confidence of youth.

# 4

## I Shall Lie Once With Beauty Breast to Breast

SOME TIME IN 1923 OR 1924, after Margaret graduated from college, she and Ruth became lovers. "Almost imperceptibly, our relationship became one of colleagues and close friends," Margaret recalled, omitting to mention, in the interests of secrecy, this other transition (BW, 124).

The love relationship presented more difficulties for Ruth than for Margaret. With her marriage in crisis and her future in anthropology uncertain, Ruth was particularly vulnerable. The intimacies with Margaret affected her deeply, leading to turbulent emotions which she expressed in poetry. She came alive to the pleasures of the senses, her verses celebrating loving a woman and alternating between joy and despair as she wrestled with the difficulties of incorporating the profoundly transformative experience of a great love into the established framework of her life. Same-sex love as an issue that needed addressing was crowded out in those early days by her onslaughts of feeling. Her poetry, though, was not just an expressive outlet but also a vehicle for self-transformation. Ruth's literary imagination forged the data of experience into emotional truths and ideals to live for. As Edward Sapir told Margaret, Ruth had once confided to him that she thought experience, contrary to common belief, *was* mostly imagination (MM, Q11).

Of Margaret's reactions we know less. At twenty-two, she was just beginning to explore adult relationships. Her emotional engagement with Ruth was strong, but as in her friendship with Katharine Rothenberger and other young women, she may have thought sexual expression anomalous rather than central. To feel affection toward a woman and to give that affection physical expression was nothing out of the ordinary; Margaret was later to imagine a society that approved "easy physical intimacy" between women, one in which women "would embrace each other, caress each other's hair, arrange each other's clothes, sleep in the same bed, comfortably and without embarrassment."[1] This was her preferred model of love between women; if sexual desire sometimes developed, why should that be a matter of concern?

Although the Freudianism of her day had alerted her to the power of the unconscious mind and its fundamental sexual imperatives, Margaret's outlook had been formed in an earlier era when erotic exchanges between women were not seen as sexual and were therefore not worrisome. Younger than Ruth and still in awe of her mentor, she may have been more dismayed by the older woman's vulnerabilities than by the sexual components of their love. Not that she was a stranger to adult frailties, with her early training in parenting her parents.

For Ruth, passionate love was not a state she could regard as transient. This was a potentially divisive issue, and as they found their way through it, the two women invented a unique, shared mythology which was to provide a creative foundation for their relationship across a lifetime. They would sustain a loyalty to each another—at least most of the time—in an era that increasingly devalued women's friendships and became overtly hostile toward lesbianism.

Charting the dynamics of the early period of the Mead-Benedict friendship demands caution, as the evidence is fragmentary. Both women were circumspect; that they were lovers was known only to close friends. When the secret was made public by Margaret's daughter, Mary Catherine Bateson, in her memoir about her parents, she was revealing knowledge she had come by only indirectly.[2] It was after Mead's death, when she had access to her mother's private papers, that she learned about Mead's bisexuality and the nature of her relationship with Benedict. This discovery was supplemented by information from her "aunt," Marie Eichelberger, who, apart from keeping tabs on Margaret's private life, had spent years cataloguing and organizing both Mead's and Benedict's papers.[3]

Bateson's observation that "Margaret's words are only a concealment to the reader" is a good warning, as Mead's published writings provide only hints and indirect references to the relationship. Benedict's poetry and some of her journal entries reveal more clearly her emotional landscape and help date the commencement of the affair. In addition, there are unpublished materials, many of which have been only recently released. Letters between the two and Margaret's dream records from the twenties are especially helpful, both for understanding the friendship as well as its place within a circle of women friends, many of whom also struggled with issues of same-sex love.

Margaret was inclined to secrecy, but she would not allow her relationship with Ruth to be entirely misconstrued. When she was an elderly woman she once made herself very clear when an interviewer assumed the friendship to be less important than her marriages. In talking about relationships with men and women, Margaret had contrasted her mother and grandmother with her father, commenting that her connections with the women in her family were the most satisfying but that she had found her father more interesting. The interviewer responded, "Could you say that your relationship to some of your female friends, like Ruth Benedict, may have been more comforting and soulfully satisfying, but your relationship to your husbands was more interesting?" Margaret came right back: "No, I put my relationship to Ruth and my relationship to my husbands in the same box—whole relationships to adults" (JH).

In the summer of 1923 everyone associated with anthropology at Columbia had gone their separate ways. Boas sailed for Europe on a family visit. Gladys Reichard, who had won the Barnard position over Ruth, caused ripples of gossip by making a field trip to the Southwest with the museum curator, Pliny Earle Goddard, a married man.

Ruth and Stanley Benedict spent the summer at their cabin at West Alton on Winnepesaukee Lake. Ruth occupied herself with the mythology of the Southwest, learning Spanish so that she could translate tales recorded centuries earlier, and Stanley tinkered with his photography. Sometimes the two of them climbed in the mountains, hiked, or drove to the ocean. Ruth enjoyed the solitude and peacefulness of her canoe, where she would drift for hours on the lake, reading and taking notes.

Margaret was at home with the family in Pennsylvania, gathering data for her master's thesis in psychology. She administered the Otis intelligence test to nearly three hundred children of Italian immigrants in the community her mother had studied, her idea being to assess the amount of English spoken in the home as a factor in the children's intellectual development. Margaret's topic had been suggested by Boas, who had once demonstrated that the average head size of the Italian child was larger in the generations following immigration. As head size was widely thought to be a fixed racial characteristic correlating with intelligence, Boas's findings, which demonstrated the benefits of a favorable environment, had undermined one of the fundamental tenets of racialist science. Margaret's study did indeed show that IQ was related to exposure to English, challenging the assumption that IQ tests measured native intelligence. This discovery also provided counterevidence to arguments about Northern European superiority used by psychologists who advocated racist immigration policies, though because hers was only a small study and a master's thesis it seems to have had little impact.[4]

Margaret's other task for the summer was to prepare for her wedding to

Luther Cressman. If she had private misgivings about the wisdom of her decision, she left no record. It is unclear, too, whether her relationship with Ruth became overtly sexual before or after her marriage.

Margaret may also have felt some regrets about leaving her vibrant household of Barnard fellow students. What did her friends think? On the whole, they assumed the inevitability of marriage in general and of this marriage in particular, though one friend expressed amazement to Marie Eichelberger that Margaret was going ahead with it (MM, TR1). Léonie Adams, though not particularly inclined toward heterosexual relations, accepted Margaret's invitation to be the bridesmaid.

Lee Newton, who had once sent Margaret a post card declaring, "Dear— I am holding you very closely—before my altar of Beauty" (MM, Q11), light-heartedly tried to discourage her: "Euphemia—I have always trusted you implicitly but now suspicion begins to filter in—to poison my mind— people are coupling your name with that of one Luther—this must stop at once—But there, little innocent girl, I didn't mean to scold, it is undoubt-edly all his fault and he shall hear from me—the beastly wretch to take advantage of a child's inexperience—if he dare to taint your pure white soul—For the sake of our children let me hear from you—Peter" (MM, C1).

Whether jealousy lay behind this ribbing is hard to say, but it is instruc-tive to compare the remarkably similar, though more literary, letter Virginia Woolf wrote to her sister on the eve of Vanessa's marriage more than a decade earlier. Virginia, as her biographer makes clear, really did feel jealous and betrayed when she wrote, "We have been your humble Beasts since we first left our Isles, which is before we can remember, and during that time we have wooed you and sung many songs of winter and summer and autumn in the hope that thus enchanted you would condescend one day to marry us. But as we no longer expect this honour we entreat that you keep us still for your lovers."[5]

Marie Eichelberger was never able to disguise her feelings. Her role in Margaret's life as admirer, spectator, and helper when she could manage it was just becoming established. In the South with her family during this time, she took an eager interest in the wedding, approving of the groom because he seemed considerate of Margaret's health, Marie's preeminent concern (she herself was often unwell, a legacy of tuberculosis). Letters to her "Dearie" are an affectionate, sometimes tiresome babble: "If only I could manicure your hands for your wedding day"; and, "I am praying you won't have neuritis and a headache on your wedding day" (the novelist Willa Cather only a few years earlier had developed neuritis when the woman she loved was married).[6]

Marie evidently shared Margaret's interest in Ruth, perhaps as the usual sort of teacherly crush: "I like your letters to be all about yourself. I only want to know about one other person—do you hear from Mrs. Benedict?" Waiting eagerly for letters from Margaret, Marie could not contain her disappointment if they did not arrive when expected. "I haven't yet discovered the word in any language which describes you," she once announced to her heroine in a mystified tone. "There's no one like Margaret," Mead's parents habitually exclaimed, and this was a sentiment Marie would continue to endorse (MM, B14).

Usually eager to offer approval, Marie was not at all sure that she liked the "At Home" cards announcing Margaret and Luther's future address; they looked "a little queer—a trifle immoral as Vee would say." This remark referred to Margaret's decision to keep her own name rather than becoming Mrs. Luther Cressman. Edward Mead was annoyed at Margaret's bumptiousness; Luther, with his usual mildness, merely wondered how this would affect her passport. Margaret had this to say: "I'm going to be famous some day and I'm going to be known by my own name." Her break with convention excited comment in newspapers across the nation, bringing her an early taste of notoriety (BW, 126).

Margaret married Luther Cressman in early September 1923. The night before the wedding Luther slept at a nearby hotel. His parents and five brothers, driving to pick him up next morning, stopped at the Meads to ask for directions, looking dusty and disreputable in their open car. The moment they left Margaret phoned Luther, frantic that they might turn up at the church in that state. Margaret had always arranged ceremonies and was not about to see this one escape her direction.

The wedding mass was Episcopalian. "Everyone came, by train and by car," Margaret remembered, though it is not clear that "everyone" included Ruth, sequestered up at the lake with Stanley (BW, 116). Luther, now an ordained priest, had asked a professor from his divinity school to say a nuptial mass, and Margaret's parish priest presided at the later service where Margaret promised to love, honor, and obey eternally. The reception was held at home and Margaret, sensitive about her appearance that day, could hardly contain her annoyance when her father's friend spilled coffee on her wedding gown. Before the pair set off on their honeymoon in the Meads' Studebaker, she stopped to brush the confetti away with a broom. She was not pleased, according to Luther, when they gave a ride to a policeman whose eye fell on some confetti that had escaped her notice and commented on their newly wedded state (BW, 125–26).

The honeymoon was spent in a cottage on Cape Cod.[7] Luther recalled that they were both virgins, a term which to him must have denoted heterosexual rather than sexual inexperience, and that sexually "there was nothing doing" at first (GJ, 93). Margaret told him that her hymen had been broken in an operation to remove an ovarian cyst.

She also announced, "We are going to use separate bedrooms; I have a seminar paper, a book report, to prepare for right after our return and I have to do some skull-splitting thinking" (GJ, 93). Luther was irritated at what he regarded as her defensiveness: "the book she had to review was one of those stupid publications spawned by the Army Intelligence Tests and written by a psychologist who wanted to be in the swim of things. I read it subsequently, only to find it required little effort to see the fallacies of the author's argument. Margaret, as she so often did, was dramatizing a situation and, I think, seeking to avoid an experience and a possible emotional commitment she preferred not to have. . . . Her tightly barred gates were a sign of both psychological fear and hostility to the commitment of marriage" (GJ, 92). Perhaps a friend's later insight that for Margaret "pleasure was always an interruption of cerebration" would have been helpful to him (Howard, Box 50).

After several days at the Cape, Luther said "she got very eager to fondle me while I was driving, and I had to tell her, 'Watch what you're doing, or we'll end up in a ditch.'" The marriage was soon consummated, and afterward "we went to a movie called Branded. I remember her snuggling and asking, 'Have you put your brand on me?'"[8] The plan was to avoid having children until after graduate school and Luther took responsibility for birth control, which in those days meant condoms. The pair, "although sophisticated intellectually and verbally," according to Luther, were "both physically and emotionally immature" and were disappointed in each other: "We both, I think, had a sense, an awareness we could not quite conceal that something expected, hoped for, was lacking" (GJ, 92).

Margaret, more charitable than Luther in her recollections of the honeymoon, admitted that she lacked finesse in her early explorations of heterosexuality. But she found it irritating that the woman's role in a sexual exchange involved boosting the male ego: "Our enjoyment of these long lazy hours did not mean that even after an engagement of five years there were not moments of strangeness and disappointment to overcome. We had read so many books written by the kind santa clauses [changed to 'the sex specialists' when published] of the 1920s, who believed that sex was a matter of proper technique—that men should learn to play on women's bodies as if they were musical instruments, but without including in their calculations a demand that women be such good musical instruments that they would flatter the men who attempted to play on them" (BW draft). Margaret had read the works of Havelock Ellis, who had used the "musical instrument" analogy in his writings.[9] She used the same imagery in the introduction to her 1949 book, Male and Female, and one could well read that passage as a comment on her early experience of marriage: "In the 1920s an attempt to change the position of women was accompanied by an insistence on women's need for sexual climaxes comparable to men's, and the demand that women respond to men became a burdensome demand on them to behave like musical instruments rather than full human beings."[10]

Feminist historians have discussed the companionate marriages of the twenties as a reaction to nineteenth-century feminism, which encouraged women to form loyalties to each other within the separate sphere to which they were confined. Now women were to be the equals of men and the sexes expected to enjoy each other's company. The sexual brute of the nineteenth century who sullied his refined and asexual wife with unbridled masculine lust had become the sexual blunderer, whose masculinity depended on satisfying his wife. But either way, men were assumed to be in charge.[11]

Margaret and Luther, though they shared Christian ideals, did not believe in marriage as a lifetime commitment. As Luther put it, "love is the only justification for marriage, and when that foundation no longer exists, dissolution is called for or else the pair prostitutes the marriage bond" (GJ, 88). Margaret recalled that they saw themselves as having an open marriage, meaning a marriage free of jealousy. Freedom in love was not sexual license, she said, but an idealistic belief espoused as a "sort of religious . . . highly ethical position" (JH). But with hindsight, Margaret knew that she had never been "in love" with Luther. That had "nothing to do with [it]," she asserted categorically many years later (JH).

With the honeymoon over, perhaps to the relief of both, it was back to New York to embark upon a busy year. For Margaret there was the degree in psychology to complete as well as graduate study in anthropology. As a married woman student, she would be in a minority, since American college women, though increasingly career oriented, could rarely envision combining marriage and a career. (Of course, this point of view did not merely reflect limited aspirations, but also showed their realistic appraisal of barriers to married women.) A study of women doctoral students in the 1920s showed that few married while studying, and of those who did, only half continued with their studies.[12]

Margaret had taken on a heavy load, planning to finish her doctorate only two years after her graduation from Barnard so that she would catch up with Luther, who had already finished his theological studies and was to enroll for a doctorate in sociology at Columbia. Income for their first year derived from the Ruth Benedict "no red tape fellowship," Margaret's work for Ogburn, and Luther's part-time position as minister to a small parish in New Jersey.

They pooled their money and shared the housework in the small apartment Luther had found at 419 West 119th Street. Overlooking a courtyard, it was furnished with an assortment of pieces, including bookcases Margaret had assembled "in a last tribute to the days when Mother had made us learn carpentry [and] a filing cabinet left over from the Consumers Cooperative that Father had tried to start." Luther's desk and screen came from the seminary, there were old Dutch chairs that Margaret's mother had bought for twenty-five cents each, a "strange, Gothic-style mission chair" that had belonged to Marie Bloomfield, and two new single beds with Appalachian woven covers (BW, 117).

Their hard work was punctuated by plenty of entertaining, especially among Margaret's circle of friends. There were the Ash Can Cats of course—particularly Léonie Adams, Pelham Kortheuer, and Louise Rosenblatt—other Barnard friends such as Marie Eichelberger, new friends from more sophisticated literary circles, such as poet Louise Bogan and her lover, Raymond Holden, and fellow graduate students Dorothy Swaine Thomas, Mel Herskovits, and Otto Klineberg. Luther was president of the sociology students' club, and they feted prominent sociologists like Lewis Mumford and W. I. Thomas, who told them the family was on its way out. And, not least, there was Ruth Benedict, who introduced them to anthropologists, including her friend Edward Sapir. They are mostly hamburger at their "formal dinners," a phrase of Margaret's whose pretentiousness irritated Ruth. Few of Margaret's college friends had their own apartments, most of them living in "some odd arrangement" or in dormitories, so the Mead-Cressman establishment became a drop-in center and rarely a week went by without someone's sleeping on the couch (BW, 119).

Most of Margaret's college friends threw themselves into their newly found independence with gusto. Well educated and unmarried, they earned their own income, established themselves in shared apartments, drank, smoked, and had affairs with men and women. They took emotional risks rather than opting for older securities and often found themselves in situations laden with drama. Margaret introduced Ruth to her friends, and it was a period when they gathered around them a mutually supportive circle that provided sustenance and context for their own friendship.

Perhaps the most vibrant was the literary set. Léonie Adams had become coeditor of a small, literary journal, *The Measure*, pleased to be working in the company of her seniors, especially Louise Bogan. The magazine hardly provided enough financial support, however, and both women were grateful when Margaret found paid employment for them in Professor Ogburn's office at Barnard, working alongside her on his academic journal. The office became something of a hub for the poets and writers associated with *The Measure*, a development that Ogburn treated with amused tolerance.

Louise Bogan, several years older and considerably more sophisticated than Margaret and Léonie, had no profession except for her writing, and scraped together a living from part-time jobs, including clerking in Brentano's bookstore. Her daughter, Maidie, the child of an early and unsuccessful marriage, lived with Louise's parents in upstate New York, her existence apparently a secret Louise kept from her friends until Margaret, puzzled by the dedication in Louise's first volume of verse, The Body of this Death, asked who Maidie was. "Louise, stop hiding your child!" was Margaret's outraged response, which perhaps helped Louise realize that she could manage parenting and poetry, for not long after Maidie came to live with her mother again.[13]

Brilliant, impulsive, passionate, and inclined toward mental instability and depression, Louise had led a turbulent life. She was in analysis with Samuel Tannenbaum, a specialist in treating artists. It was widely rumored that she had once been a "gangster's moll"; one story had her aiding and abetting her lover in shoplifting a fur coat. She was now involved with Raymond Holden, a young man with a private income and literary interests. Ruth Benedict, closer in age to Louise than to Margaret, found she liked Louise immensely and the two became good friends.

Edmund Wilson was one of this talented circle, though he would later claim that the twenties, with all the conviviality and "wild parties," were a dreadful waste of time.[14] It was the era of Prohibition, speakeasies, and bootleg alcohol. Raymond Holden was famous for making drinkable gin in his bathtub. Louise Bogan claimed that she "should go down in history as the heartiest drinker among the female poets," though she acknowledged that Léonie, who was well known for "downing pony after pony of brandy, and staying cold sober" was a worthy rival for that accolade.[15] Added to the drinking, gossiping, and amateur psychoanalysis that took place at these parties were frequent games of bouts rimés, in which players were challenged to construct a poem out of given rhymes—"feather-ooze-booze-weather, together-choose-moos-leather" was one typical example.[16] Perhaps they also tried to understand one another's "pattern," for this was the buzz word in their circle. Introduced by the anthropologists, it referred to the organizing principles underlying behavior in culture. The women especially got into the habit of seeing patterns everywhere as they examined themselves and their surroundings. Louise worried on one occasion that Margaret must have seen in her a paranoid streak because she became so adept at this way of thinking. Amy Lowell's well-known poem of that era, "Patterns," used this concept in describing its female protagonist as, variously, "held rigid to the pattern" and breaking the pattern.

Love affairs and emotional entanglements were certainly a favorite topic of conversation among the group, though Ruth's reticence may have put her on the outside, at least when it came to discussing her own. She was a good listener and delighted in hearing about the joys and miseries of the others. Léonie had fallen helplessly in love with Louise, while being pursued by Edmund Wilson, who was puzzled by her determination to remain a virgin. She characterized her female contemporaries as the "oh-God-the-pain-girls," since they "plaintively descanted on the self-destructive elements common to their erotic lives as women."[17] Louise, in her widely anthologized poem "Women," scorned her own sex for their softness and masochism.[18] At least they had erotic lives, something women from the previous generation had often not managed to achieve.

Luther liked women's company and was, according to Margaret, a "marvelous listener" (JH), enjoying the liveliness of Margaret's friends, "especially the freedom with which they sat at our breakfast table and explored the intricacies of their disturbing love affairs" (BW, 133). He may not have appreciated, though, Margaret's throwing him out of his home on one occasion when Katharine Rothenberger came to stay.[19] Margaret sometimes lent their apartment for assignations, and he once came home to find a condom in the bathroom and a couple making love in the bedroom—not what one might expect in the household of an ordained priest. Although it had been Margaret's girlhood ambition to marry a minister, when faced with the reality, she was completely uninterested. In Barnard days she had taught Sunday school with Luther, but later, as she put it bluntly, she did "not have time to be a minister's wife in the depths of Brooklyn, and so it was decided that I would not take any responsibility" (JH). "It was decided" no doubt meant that Margaret decided; she only once made an appearance at a church function, and Luther came to realize that her "dream of a future as the wife of an Episcopal minister in a peaceful country parish clearly belonged to the past" (GJ, 193).

Luther himself was losing his faith, and he found Margaret unsympathetic and uninterested in his "acute personal problems of belief" (GJ, 194). But though he was disappointed in her, Luther did not appear to begrudge Margaret her way of life. She was a free agent, and she recalled gratefully, "We never quarreled and never had a misunderstanding even of the kind roommates often have over leaving the light on or keeping the bathroom tidy." Luther agreed, though he saw their relationship as having been on too tenuous a footing to afford the luxury of quarreling. Margaret's summary of those times was that, untroubled by "the pressures of mate-seeking . . . I had what I thought I wanted—a marriage that contrasted sharply with my mother's, a marriage in which there seemed to be no obstacles to being myself" (BW, 133).

Being Margaret Mead involved taking a direction that would leave Luther wondering whether he had any role at all in her life. In her autobiography,

Margaret characterized theirs as a "student marriage" (BW, 125), a choice of words that distressed him since his analysis was that it was a genuine but "ill-starred" marriage (GJ, 191). Margaret's grandmother had been right after all. Margaret had rushed into marriage only because she wanted to *be* married. Since her emotional and sexual leanings, though she may have been reluctant to admit it, were perhaps more toward women, marriage to an unthreatening man who would encourage her career and respect her freedom made a certain sense. But it could be only a temporary solution; the relationship with Luther, convenient and even pleasant, was not emotionally fulfilling.

Margaret's literary efforts expressed her psychic conflicts in the way that her conscious life did not. They were "curiously contrapuntal to my expressed contentment," she said later (BW, 133). Poetic images such as "Throttled by sullen weeds I lie" suggested to her years later that perhaps "I had accepted a too easy felicity" (BW, 133). A graphologist named Rose Wolfson whose opinion Margaret valued highly said that her handwriting in 1923 revealed "at times an almost hysterical disintegration of feeling content," and that around this time Margaret's inner world showed "insecurity and a good deal of fright" which, despite her sexual interest, inhibited her relationships with men. Wolfson also suggested "an unresolved adolescent or homosexual component that may have a part in predisposing her to her own sex at this stage" (MM, Q35).

Sharing literary aspirations is one route toward intimacy. Margaret was the first to confess to writing poetry; Ruth was slower to show her verse. Always a private person, Ruth would not consider publishing poetry under her own name (though she once told Margaret that she regarded her married name, Benedict, as a nom de plume). An early pseudonym was Ruth Stanhope, which of course emphasised her tie to Stanley, but by the time Margaret knew her she was already writing under the name Anne Singleton. Her difficult, even obscure, poetry allowed her to reveal herself indirectly to Margaret. It must have disturbed the younger woman with its themes of marital desperation and suicidal impulses, yet at the same time flattered her with its charting of her role in the emergence of a woman who loved women.

Dismantling the barriers she had relied on for protection since childhood was a difficult task for Ruth. While she may not have spoken freely to Margaret about the ups and downs of her life with Stanley—as Margaret said, Ruth kept people in separate rooms—Ruth did begin to display more of her private self (AW, 3). She told Margaret of her infertility and the disappointment she felt at not being able to have a child. Ruth had always trusted in keeping things to herself; if she avoided talking about the things that mattered, no one could take them away from her. She feared that disclosing her personal life might hurt people or lead them to interfere, "a dangerous thing for a child to learn," she once remarked.[20]

Stanley was a case in point. He did not want to know about Ruth's interior life and responded critically to any revelations as if threatened by her independence of mind. But at the age of thirty-five, in the first year of her friendship with Margaret, Ruth realized that "being oneself was too big a job to keep the seal of secrecy on always, and other people could take it or leave it" (AW, 102).

Margaret later identified Ruth's turnabout as happening when she commenced a series of important relationships, "chief among these" the one with Edward Sapir (AW, 87). Sapir was certainly important to Ruth, but Margaret deceived her readers in neglecting to mention her own role. It was Margaret, not Edward, who was brash and fearless, who did not avoid topics for reasons of discomfort or resistance. Edward, given his traditional attitudes toward women, was more respectful of boundaries.

Ruth overcame another emotional block around this time. During her childhood she had developed a strong taboo against crying in front of anyone; she had found her childhood tantrums humiliating and devastating. As an adult she had "exposure dreams"; in minute detail, she dreamed of "bursting into tears in a room filled with attentive well-known faces. This tabu continued in full force until long after I was married." But in an episode described in "The Story of My Life" she tells of a " 'daydream' . . . more actual than any dream" that had a permanent effect on her. "I was alone on a great desert that was dominated by a magnificent Egyptian sphinx. Nothing can describe the wisdom and irony of that sphinx's face, and I went to it and buried my face on its paws and wept and wept—happily and with confidence. And the paws of the sphinx were soft and furry like a kitten's." Benedict concluded, "I had wept before 'my' world, and the tabu was never so compulsive after that" (AW, 106).

In contrast, Margaret cried easily and lost her temper readily. Her forthrightness and exceptional talent for empathic listening, noted by many, must have contributed to freeing up Ruth emotionally. These qualities deepened the relationship, although Margaret, in becoming aware of Ruth's "strain of almost unmanageable depression" (AW, 86), may sometimes have felt burdened beyond her years. Marie Bloomfield's death had made her aware of the possibility of suicide among people she knew.[21]

Along with Ruth's sensitivity, powerful intellect, and melancholy strain, Margaret often saw a woman who took "a sensuous delight in life—in swimming and dancing, in the heat and sting of the changing seasons, in startlingly sharp kinesthetic perceptions" (AW, 86), who was "tall and strong, with large capable hands," who enjoyed walking and who "sometimes sought catharsis in chopping up logs for firewood."[22] The contrasts between the two were so marked that the friendship must often have seemed unlikely, to themselves and to those who knew them. Apart from the fifteen-year age gap, their physical differences were striking. Margaret was short—five foot, two and one-half—rather dumpy, clumsy with her hands, never taking exercise when she could avoid it. She was indefatigably sociable and her optimism was infectious. Theirs was a classic match of introvert and extrovert, and despite, or because of, their differences, they rejoiced in each other's company. In becoming lovers, they took a step into a shared private world.

Ruth's efforts as a poet were intense and serious and she used her verse as a vehicle for personal transformation. She saw herself in the lyric tradition popular among the women poets achieving recognition around that time. Through Margaret she got to know some of them—Louise Bogan and Léonie Adams—and there were the better known Edna St. Vincent Millay and Amy Lowell. Lyric poetry, its exponents believed, should not be read *directly* as autobiography, though it was revelatory. Louise Bogan, for example, gave expression in her exceptionally fine poetry to the emotional truths of her own life, inventing as she did so a more powerful, contemporary, and evocative manner of expression than most of her peers, including Ruth. Speaking of poetry and autobiographical truth, Bogan once said: "The poet represses the outright narrative of his life. He absorbs it, along with life itself. The repressed becomes the poem. Actually, I have written down my experience in the closest detail. But the rough and vulgar facts are not there." As Bogan's biographer commented on this passage: "To read the poems as autobiography violates their privacy, yet completes their sense."[23] Much the same could be said of Benedict's poetry.

Something of a mystery surrounds Ruth's developing lesbian orientation. Her biographer, Judith Modell, was warned emphatically by Margaret Mead to be discreet about Benedict's private life. Exactly wherein such discretion should lie was unspecified. Modell asserts that Benedict was already "expanding the expression of her own sensuality" when she met Mead.[24] The implication seems to be that Ruth may have already loved a woman, but the only clue available is the evocative imagery about women's bodies in two early poems, which seem to predate the growing intimacy with Margaret. To further complicate matters, at the time of writing them Ruth harbored romantic feelings toward Edward Sapir, and her personal anguish about career and marriage had so intensified that she was near to a breakdown.

Ruth had a number of women friends; her closest seems to have been Marguerite Israel Arnold, an old friend from Vassar days who shared her interest in poetry and whom Marie Eichelberger once described as "beautiful and strange Marguerite who used to lock herself in her room and refuse to communicate" (MM, TR1). Marguerite figures prominently in Ruth's 1923 diary, which covers the first months of the year when she could hardly have known Margaret Mead well. On 3 January she recorded having walked home in a "thick wet snowfall" in a mood of "Depression. Edge of cliff; sensation of falling; vacuum" (AW, 57). Later in the evening and for several days afterward she met up with Marguerite, once to go to the theater to see Somerset Maugham's *Rain*, which was set in Samoa. That weekend, home with Stanley in Bedford Hills, Ruth recorded in her diary a poem expressing her belief that the marriage could not be salvaged: "We'll have no crumb in common / In all our days . . ." (AW, 58). The following week she and Marguerite again met frequently, with Ruth's state of mind varying from "remarkably undistraught" to feelings of weariness and exhaustion (AW, 59).

A week later Ruth found Marguerite "increasingly impossible at breakfast" and was informed that Dr S. (most likely Marguerite's analyst) thought his patient let people walk all over her (AW, 60–61). After the impossible breakfast, Marguerite left New York for a while and Ruth received a note from a mutual acquaintance saying that Marguerite "doesn't want you [to] come down here. She thinks you'd be shocked. . . . Yes she thinks you're part of all that background she's trying to break away from" (AW, 62). Three exclamation marks following indicate that Ruth thought Marguerite's claim extraordinary.

Then there was "a long and egotistic but reassuring letter" from Marguerite, and finally her return (AW, 62). The two women had dinner together and went to Ruth's room afterward: "An undiscussed reconciliation. Walked an hour at 9:30—cold night with moon; peculiar blue sky" (AW, 63). A couple of days later Ruth saw Chekhov's *Three Sisters* and was "repelled by Masha's lack of reserve, her childishness in her love affair" (AW, 64). Yet overcoming her own reserve, Ruth once confessed to Marguerite her feelings for Edward Sapir; Marguerite responded that the reason Ruth had fallen in love with Edward was precisely because he was unavailable (MM, A21).

It could be argued that Marguerite was the inspiration for the earliest of Ruth's woman-centered poems, "New Year." This striking poem, written in the back of the 1923 diary, was dated 12 December 1922, "on buying this diary":

I shall lie once with beauty,
Breast to breast;
Take toll of you, year;
Once be blessed—

I'll walk your desert quite
Self-possessed;
Nor once cry pity
At any jest;

All thousands of hours, year,
Be undistressed—
When I lie once with beauty
Breast to breast. (AW, 56)

Along with "Release" (AW, 64), a poem written in a similar vein, this one suggests that something important was going on. Mary Catherine Bateson believes "New Year" to have been written about her mother, although this seems unlikely, the poem being dated two months before Marie Bloom-field's suicide, the event Margaret said marked their getting to know one another better. Mead, who reprinted the diary and its poems in her book on Benedict, gives no hints.[25] Whatever relationship, real or imaginary, lay behind "I shall lie once with beauty," Ruth's prediction—that intense feelings arising outside her marriage would eventually offer her a respite from the deteriorating relationship with Stanley—was an accurate one.

As well as writing poetry, Ruth grappled intellectually with personal issues. She wrote, for her own eyes only, fragments of essays on the marriage bond, adultery, divorce, and free love—but not specifically, at least according to the evidence that remains, on homosexuality. She had come to reject the conventional moralities of her upbringing: "We have never trusted love," she wrote in her journal. "How should we? Born of a Puritan distrust of the senses, of its disgust at the basic manifestations of life, brought up from our youth to think sacred and indispensable the perpetual lock and key of marriage—how should we have faith in love?" (AW, 147–48).

Would the world be deluged with immorality if divorce laws were broad-ened so that "loveless cohabitation" could be done away with, she won-dered? Surely not. Ruth railed against the moralists. Could they really have known "love's dear dream of permanence, could they ever have seen that only in this dream love attains dignity? . . . Could they have known love's passion to give itself new and new and new, never as something promised and expected, as a glorious free-willed flood tide in the morn-ing?" (AW, 148).

She still believed in "the loyalty of one woman and one man. . . . I can't believe that 'free love' is a way out—it seems to me that every chance love's got for dignity and distinction depends on a belief in its permanency. It is repulsive to me to think of blunting its possibilities by casual shiftings" (AW, 148). But she was troubled by sexual frustration, "this other hunger" rising without letup from the strongly sensual side of her nature. The expression of sexuality held out the possibility of personal strength and transformation, but perhaps sexual desire was a snare and a delusion, a physical need which once slaked ceases its torments: "it's an end in itself, and it's culmination is—sleep. Oh, I know that's enough—these tortured years don't ask for any more." Sexual cravings have to be satisfied, she concluded, "SO THAT *we'll be free to go on to something else*" (RFB, Box 107).

Masturbation was a possible solution, and Ruth decided that, despite the moralists' disapproval of "self abuse," she could not "make out any verdict against" this simple means of pleasure and release (AW, 149). The effect of sexual frustration on women has hardly been investigated, she complained. What are its effects on health and sanity? Unprejudiced research might show that "conventional purity has bred more bitterness and disgust of life than prostitution" (AW, 149).

But to reject the "perpetual lock and key" of marriage in the abstract was one thing; to face up to the cruel reality of a loveless marriage and the practicalities of supporting oneself was another matter. Looking back, Ruth wrote in a journal entry from around 1935 that "in those long years" with Stanley she always felt guilty because his disapproval and harshness made her lose faith in the transformative power of love, the state of grace that conquered depression and negativity, the love she had kept in the secret and imaginary world of her father since childhood. "God knows, I didn't want to be set on a pedestal or handed candies. But the kind of love I had in mind couldn't live in that dislike" (RFB, Box 107).

It was important to Ruth that her relationship with Margaret move beyond the inequalities of mentor and protégée. Margaret, however, found it difficult to respond as an equal, though she realized she was playing out the "culturally standard idea" of devotion to one's teacher (BW draft). Her admiration was generous, but Ruth did not want the distance that admiration inevitably brings. Ruth's 1924 poem, "This Gabriel," written expressly for Margaret, conveys her unease about the younger woman's adoration. Ruth is Gabriel, the lonely angel wandering the universe, having been exiled through mortal admiration and separated by divinity from any human intercourse:

What comfort had he had in praise
That makes of him this Gabriel
Walking the stars, his even pace
Shaped to a crystal citadel.[26]

Mead commented that what lay behind the poem was her estimation of Ruth as "specially gifted," while Ruth was "repudiating such a role" (BW draft). Once, in 1938, when Margaret remarked that her work in anthropology was a tribute—a flower for Ruth's hair—Ruth reminded her of "This Gabriel." Someone else might have seen the remark as an extraordinary compliment, but it grated on Ruth: "It was an echo of our old cross-purposes when I wrote 'This Gabriel,' do you remember? Your obsessional self is always looking for a creature from the upper realms at whose feet you can lay an offering. And I always look for an equal denizen. Well, you are the equal denizen, and the only one there's ever going to be. So when you feel I don't take your work with a gesture as if it were a tribute, remember it's only because I need so much to take it as between equals. It's so much more appropriate, too!" (MM, B14).

This interchange is evidence of the private myth Ruth and Margaret developed which became foundational to their friendship. Based on a sharing of their private "obsessional selves," a term they seem to have used to describe the unconscious, their myth had Ruth in her "Gabriel" persona wandering the stars in her other world, the world of her father, the world of love, peacefulness, and death to which as a child she had retreated. Margaret, who looked for "a creature from the upper realms," was the only person ever admitted to Ruth's "far country," not merely because of her empathy, her intelligence, and her forthrightness, but preeminently for her "effortless" happiness which facilitated Ruth's entry. As Margaret wrote to Ruth, "it is of the journeying thither that I am a symbol. I do not live in that country itself, except as I see it through your eyes. In that sense I have been a proper denizen" (MM, B14). As Ruth put it, "You are one of the blest for whom things do work together for the good. It's a patent you took out in heaven; everybody had always been looking for it, and always will be; but it's yours" (MM, B14).

But in Margaret's eyes, it was Ruth who was one of the blessed. The analogy she sometimes used was that of Martha and Mary. The "Martha" aspects of Margaret's character—hard working, reliable, conscientious, and earthbound—readily admired the "Mary" side of Ruth, the fragility and hypersensitivity, the mixture of gaiety and spirituality. Ruth was one of those "gifted ones" who are "stain[ed] glass windows into heaven, through which a light is shone, which I would otherwise never see" (BW draft).

Jean Houston, a later friend of Margaret's, has offered an analysis of the Mead-Benedict friendship which seems to fit with the evidence—to an extent. Houston, too, emphasizes a mythic quality to the relationship; Mead and Benedict may well have been at the back of her mind when she wrote The Search for the Beloved, an essay in "sacred psychology" which describes "the deep yearning for the Beloved of the soul." This yearning for the other, the missing twin, Houston maintains, is central to "all the great spiritual and mystery traditions . . . a profound longing, which transcends the desire for romantic love. . . ."[27] It is best described by the Greek word pothos, that element of eros that longs for the unattainable, for sleep, death, or eternal bliss, a state of spiritual union with something or someone, perhaps the "oceanic" sense Freud found so mysterious. The "Beloved" can be sensed through a human relationship, though the relationship may also pose danger since no human can match the lover's ideal.

Mead talked to Jean Houston about her friendship with Benedict on a number of occasions. Houston uses the myth of Demeter and Persephone as a metaphor to describe her understanding of it.[28] The young Margaret Mead, she argues, was immensely intelligent, very quick, and utterly empathic. Benedict, challenged and engaged by her energy, saw Margaret as representing life itself—Persephone, daughter, youth, the season of spring, offering renewal by calling forth the mother/Demeter figure from her despair, the dark underground of the soul.

Mother-daughter resonances did not exist for Ruth alone. With her expressiveness, her mothering qualities, and her ability to take care of others, Margaret was completely affirming, releasing Ruth from her spiritual burdens. Margaret was apparently fond of quoting the English ballad phrase, "the new moon with the old moon in her arm," an image suggesting her ability to care for someone older than herself. Ruth, in turn, was a mystic, according to Houston, "a Hildegard of Bingen type," able to project her intense sense of longing into her poetry, her anthropology, and her relationship with Margaret.

Houston believes that the lesbian element in the Ruth and Margaret's relationship was not central, arguing that such intimacies were the fashion in the 1920s as in ancient Greece, and that though the erotic element was present, especially early on, it was never the mainspring. Had the two met in an era when lesbian relationships were heavily proscribed, the friendship would have been just as strong and evocative but its erotic elements would not have been overtly expressed. Sexuality was not central to its intensity, she argues, calling it a "transformational" friendship, a "co-creative relationship" in which each evoked "the essential genius" in the other. She believes that Ruth could not possibly have hoped to enter any kind of practical or domestic partnership with Margaret, such a relationship for both seeming outside the bounds of possibility.

Although convincing in its own way, Houston's judgment misses the mark a little. To reduce Mead's and Benedict's sexual interchanges merely to conformity with the fashionable behavior of the smart set in the twenties is to underestimate the power of eros between women. One could argue, instead, that the climate of the time made it possible for Mead and Benedict to express their love for one another sexually, but was not affirming enough to make a permanent place for lesbian love. Sexual passions are often at the heart of a transformational relationship between women. True, they may not be expressed, especially since our culture has difficulty accepting love between women. The passion that can occur between mentor and protégée, often central to the development of intellectual and spiritual aspirations in women, may be smiled on dismissively as a youthful "crush." Yet between men and women such "crushes" often have led to a more permanent partnership; of course, one may query the wisdom of marriage to one's mentor, a step which, as many women have found, sets a seal on the inequity inherent in the relationship.

On a practical level, Margaret's primary loyalty was to her career, and she soon realized that she had no intention of marooning herself in one relationship, nor did she wish to identify with a sexual minority. For Ruth it would be some years before she had the courage to step outside her marriage and enter into domestic partnerships with women, and it was not Margaret who occasioned that step.

We have little in the way of details to describe the development of Ruth and Margaret's love affair. Their friends may not have known much more; to most in their circle their relationship would have been seen as a friendship, though its emotional dynamics may have been obvious. But whatever details they may have shared with close friends, the relationship fitted into the established framework of their lives. There seems to have been no gossip among colleagues at Columbia. Camaraderie was part of life around the anthropology department, where sharing books, offices, food, and apartments was a common practice among the group that studied with Boas, and close friendships were not out of the ordinary.[29]

Apparently, the two women experienced conflict as well as love in their relationship, differences which arose because of different needs and values. Margaret found Ruth captivating, but she had her whole life before her and a place of temporary safety in her marriage. With Luther she could try intimacy in a domestic setting without stifling herself and risking her career; she certainly did not want to be curtailed by any other relationship.

A personality analysis from later decades, which examined Margaret's earlier life, suggested that she showed evidence of both homosexual and heterosexual interests and that in 1923, "where the intense emotional situation must be taken into account," there was "an unresolved adolescent or homosexual component that may have a part in predisposing her to her own sex at this stage." She also, according to the evidence, existed in "an emotionally ambivalent state, in which her attitude towards her own and the other sex [were] likely to go through mercurial changes . . ." (MM, Q35).

Ruth experienced all the pain that awakening feelings brought, ricocheting from rapture to desolation. She had found love again and was haunted by her longing for permanence, surely the only worthy outcome of such intense feeling. Anything else would be a cheap mockery. But then, the literary traditions in which she was immersed always portrayed love as partly tragic. It was a misfortune to be struck down by an emotion whose intensity was irrelevant to the mundane details of daily life.

Margaret, interviewed in later years, explained that her more prosaic attitude to relationships usually brought her into conflict with those she loved. Early on, she had decided that she could not commit herself to exclusivity, even though others wanted it from her. The people she found herself loving were, like herself, "the most complex and intense people," and on the whole, beautiful as well. The experience of being in love made Margaret feel intensely alive. She would see the face of the beloved constantly before her eyes: "Your awareness of yourself is enormously enhanced. . . . Any experience you've ever had or any poem you hear, any music that you hear is more attractive or . . . more enthralling. The whole of life changes its character."

Margaret's is a conventional description of romantic love. What was unconventional was the determination with which she held out for nonexclusivity. She said, "The very funny problem with me is that people I am in love with are wine. But to them I'm always bread. I've never been wine to anybody [but] they are wine to me. Exciting, wonderful, lovely, and not necessary. And not exclusive, you know, because you drink good wine with one dish and drink another good wine [with] another, and you don't live on wine for breakfast, and the people that I want to be wine always decide that I am bread they want for every meal" (JH).

For Ruth, Margaret was bread, manna from heaven—a phrase she used more than once in the letters she wrote (MM, B14). She felt consumed by passion, by a "bonfire of the blood" (RFB, Box 45). But she could not entirely throw off her Puritan heritage; nor was she able to adopt the mores of Margaret's generation.[30] Poetry was the outlet for the feelings she must have been too restrained and ultimately too sensible to burden Margaret with.

"Discourse on Prayer" evokes a physical aching for contact:

> Beauty has blown
> Her fever through me
> and every kiss that died
> On passionate flesh been flame intensified
> Upon the quick in nights I lay alone.

It also expresses the satisfaction that comes after loving:

> And I have peace. The moon at harvest is
> Round jocund laughter on the sky,—no more;
> And I have sleepy comfort in your kiss
> That is a wind-blown flame to you. (AW, 160–61)

The affair brought to the fore all her suppressed sensuality, the physical side of herself that Stanley had rejected. Now she found that she could love a woman completely, with sensual abandonment and the investment of all her emotions. She wrote of the physical satisfactions of love, "Here only bliss/Is for our taking,"[31] and she asked how anything could "compete/ With sleep begotten of a woman's kiss."[32] In an unpublished poem, "For Faithfulness," she wrote, "I lie so in quiet at your breast. . . . I am so safe with you, so blindly blest" (RFB, Box 45).

The body of a woman—and there is no doubt that here Margaret was the inspiration—is portrayed with striking eroticism throughout Ruth's poetry. She sang "songs of her great loveliness," her "beauty sudden-fluttering," "the milk-white fairness of her body / the quiet of her brooding fingertips," the "thousand dancing laughters of her lips," and the "slim white hands upon their naked flesh."[33]

Ruth's poetry also wrestled with the doomed nature of the liaison. How could she honor her feelings yet remain realistic? If only she could seize and enjoy the moment: "Our Task is Laughter," she argued to herself, not altogether convincingly, and she wondered, "Who cannot know the folly of a kiss?"[34] Love surely made the old taboos absurd. "Dear God! those weeks in which they saw we sinned," she wrote in "At Last" (RFB, Box 44). Yet its rewards were great: "I have content more in your loveliness / than all the honor good men ever earned." Even chocolate-box poetry was possible, as in the valentine Ruth sent to Margaret, telling her how "in icy winter's time . . . roses glow, lilies chime."[35]

In those gray moments when she was likely to commit her feelings to poetry, Ruth railed against her circumstances. The poem "Sight," clearly based on Stanley and herself, has a man and woman arguing, he the conservative, down-to-earth pragmatist who accuses the woman of ignoring reality and asks, "Is it not anything to you that this roof/Will last our life-time, and will keep us warm/On every winter night?", while she "could only wonder at his sight/That made of these four walls reality/The equal of her dreaming." The woman could not see these walls, the rock-solid reality of convention, for obstructing her vision was "the urgency/Of tortured promises that starred her night/With their implacable transplendency."[36]

Ruth was tormented in "Unicorns at Sunrise" (AW, 481) by "nights of long loneliness" when she could not be with Margaret, and in "Spiritus Tyrannus" by flesh that "cries out for flesh."[37] She longed to go to her lover for comfort, to "escape from walls and safety" to relax into "your lazy flag/Unfolding to the fling and caress of the wind/That so shall be in beauty naked to my sight" (unpublished fragment, RFB, Box 44). But dreams were not only foolish because they could not be realized in the practicalities of the safe world, but also because they gave an illusion of eternity. The harsh reality, she wrote in "For the Hour after Love," was that "all our fires go out in nothingness" (AW, 480). Depression was never far behind the celebrations of sensuality and its short-lived satisfactions. "Withdrawal" expresses the loneliness and acute feelings of loss that were their natural heir:

> At dusk the wind fell to a whispering,
> And rain withdrawn left all the air a clear
> And bitter loneliness, wherein I hear
> Down all its firmament no echoing
> Of that but now so dear. (AW, 482)

Several verses that Margaret wrote about the relationship do not have the sensuality of Ruth's. They convey, instead, some anxiety about the intensity of Ruth's feelings. "Absolute Benison," which she explicitly acknowledged as having been written for Ruth, presents contrasts between Ruth's needing love to be permanent and Margaret's refusing to mourn its impermanence.[38] Wanting things always to be the same is seen as a nostalgic attitude, not in accord with Margaret's delight in life's changes. Why not be pleased to "measure the larkspur head-higher than the rose" instead of regretting differences? Margaret had the insouciance of a younger woman, and although she was conflicted in her feelings about sexuality, she held a confident expectation that her own needs would be met.

# 5

*I Hear the Wind at Your Heart*

THE AGE DIFFERENCE BETWEEN Margaret Mead and Ruth Benedict meant that there was a "generation gap" between them, to use a term Mead popularized later. The 1920s, she recalled, was a time characterized by "our struggles to relate ourselves to men and women in the next older generation who were close to us in mind but far removed in practice."[1]

The First World War had put an end to the Progressive Era in the United States, an age marked by a spirit of optimism and reform. Many intellectuals who had readily assumed personal responsibility for participating in civic life were now overtaken by cynicism. Politics seemed hopeless— internationalism was a dream that had become a nightmare, the feminist movement had faltered, and there was a widespread distrust of radical solutions. Big business seemed to have taken over the country, and everywhere selfishness and materialism were in evidence. Modern life seemed increasingly isolating, soulless, and mechanized.

Ruth Benedict had stepped diffidently into adulthood in the prewar world. The landscape of her upper New York State childhood had been imprinted on her for a lifetime, but she rejected the moral and emotional territory that went with it. She had felt terribly alone in her attempt to find meanings other than the absolutist values of the Puritan heritage, although her intellectual contemporaries experienced similar struggles.[2]

Edward Sapir was Ruth's closest friend of her own generation. Despite his immigrant Jewishness and her native Protestantism they had much in common, sharing musings on poetry, anthropology, and society. Sapir had flirted with socialism as a young man, but after the war he became infected with the cynicism of his era, which found echoes in his own temperament and the difficult circumstances of his life. He deplored the character of modern America, especially its lack of cultural vigor and its devaluation of the arts. Through their literary aspirations, Sapir and Benedict joined the quest among the cultured people of their generation to discover the real, the authentic, and the genuine and to counter the crass values of the machine age. The endeavor required intellectual rigor and commitment, and Sapir, flatteringly, judged Benedict equal to the task, with her "sincerity" and her "high and passionate seriousness."[3]

The scientific and rationalist values of the emerging social sciences were not fundamentally disrupted by the war in the way that aspects of American artistic and intellectual life had been. Anthropology provided continuities and commonalities for Benedict, Mead, and Sapir, but Margaret was coming of age in a generation determined to be frivolous. The security of her "student marriage" and the ideals of her childhood, centering on a loved teacher and a best friend, had carried her forward into adult life and allowed her to devote her energies to preparing herself for a career. Intellectually, though, her outlook was changing. She once announced confidently to Ruth that she had dismissed Puritanism as "a rather puerile accent to Paganism," a bogey her generation had no need to battle with (AW, 285).

It was in the development of a triangular relationship between Ruth, Edward, and Margaret that generational differences began to play themselves out. At the same time, both Ruth and Margaret were taking steps, through the initiation rite of fieldwork, toward becoming full-fledged anthropologists.

After a meeting in New York in early 1924, Ruth told Edward Sapir that he should stop addressing her as Mrs. Benedict. He replied, "Florence is quite right when she says of me that with all my Bolshevistic fanfare, I am really a most hide-bound and conventional fellow. I accept the privilege—call it not too obvious!—with an important reservation. I don't have to say Gladys, do I? Let me continue blindly with Miss Reichard!" (SF).[4] Life was not going well for Sapir as he discontentedly continued his career in Ottawa with his wife still unwell: "I seem to be in very poor trim psychologically and none too good physically either. Forty is a dangerous age, is it not?" (SF).

Edward now sent poems to Ruth for comment, and after some months as his critic, she risked sending hers. He was unreservedly encouraging: "I feel it in my bones that you have much to say. And you can say it, if you'll only take the trouble to spend time learning a few technical tricks. It is incredible that one so sensitive to imagery, feeling, idea, rhythm as you and with so rich a nature should not be writing distinguished verse. Of course you can" (SF).

The first batch included "New Year," with its lesbian overtones. Edward thought the verse needed "a more careless defiance." Another was "Pool," which hinted of the self Ruth was used to concealing: "I know this pool / For I am secret."[5] Lack of confidence weakened her style, Edward felt, and he urged her to overcome the "apologetic, conditional style of utterance. It is in your speech and letters, but eschew it in verse. You have more defiance than you allow yourself to express. . . . If you are not careful, you will become mincing, like Henry James" (SF).

What did Edward, Ruth's closest male friend, make of the lesbian aspects of her poetry? Was he aware of her love affair with Margaret? How would he have understood it, given that he may well have known that Ruth had also been attracted to him? Edward was no stranger to writing by women who loved women, though he may not have been attuned to the veiled homoerotic experience underlying their work.[6] Ruth had already sent him Léonie Adams's work, which he told her he admired, though finding something in it that faintly repelled him, perhaps its "exceeding richness" (SF). He had read Katherine Mansfield with enjoyment, Willa Cather with dislike, Emily Dickinson with puzzlement ("it is hard to know what really happened to her"), and admitted to having been influenced himself by H.D.'s poetry (SF).

Edward may have been able to enjoy the work of women who wrote about love between women by paying attention to their art, but not to their lives. Any deficits in understanding on his part were matched by a lack of clarity in those writers, who often adopted a male persona in portraying desire for women. Without the protection of a literary mask, many simply would have been unable to write; and after all, speaking in the masculine voice was a convention of poetry.

So the homoerotic resonances running through Benedict's work may have not struck Sapir as noteworthy. Later that same year, 1924, he judged "This Gabriel," a poem dedicated to Margaret, as having "wonderful passages" which "take one's breath away" in their "majestic originality," but he also found it difficult to understand. He continued to insist that Ruth's emotional reticence inhibited her poetry: "You must take this business of writing verse far more seriously than you do or pretend to do, Ruth. . . . I should not waste too much time on the sonnet but go clean into the barer and stronger forms, which best suit your temperament and genius" (SF). Yet his urging Ruth to let down her barriers and use her poetic voice with clarity and directness did not mean he was on intimate terms with her private emotional world. He did praise "Moth Wing" as "exquisite, Sapphic," but by Sapphic he may have referred to its lyrical qualities as much as to its expression of lesbian desire (SF). He seems to have been particularly lacking in insight, since this poem, too, was written for Margaret.

In fact, though Edward encouraged Ruth to reveal herself, he could be obtuse when she did and sometimes had to be, as he said in a letter, "clubbed with the obvious." Ruth sent him "She Speaks to the Sea," a poem that reveals her wish for death as a longing tinged with erotic desire. Edward found it "ambiguous." She must have told him then about the struggles with suicide that lay behind her poem, since he next apologized for his lack of understanding, making one of the few very personal remarks in his letters, "You must have suffered much to be able to write it" (SF, 28 May 1924). Later, he told Ruth that he thought it one of her best, coming "on the crest of an emotional wave" (SF, 26 Nov. 1925).

Edward's wife died that spring of 1924 at the age of thirty-four. Her death followed complications from yet another operation to drain lung abscesses. Edward's grief was acute and shot through with guilt and anger. He had no religious beliefs to sustain him, writing to Ruth: "Death for myself does not seem such an evil, then why should it for Florence? Well, I suppose it is partly because I had always hoped the future would soften and reinterpret some grievous stretches of the past. That was a selfish motive, like absolution held in reserve. But there was also the feeling that Florence knew so well what to make of life, if only given her due chance" (SF).

Perhaps psychoanalysis could have helped Florence, he thought, but the cost would have been prohibitive. Edward now financially supported his father, who was increasingly senile and living alone, as well as his mother, who continued to take care of the children. He had considered analyzing Florence himself, but fortunately heeded advice that he would have been insufficiently detached to do the job well. The tragedy of his wife's mental illness was a continuing puzzle. Her nature, he felt, "was infinitely richer than mine and . . . so ardently craved and required a deeper comprehension of the pure life of feeling than I could ever summon" (SF, 26 Nov. 1924). He put his most violent feelings into a poem called "Sing Bitter Song" (RFB, Box 101), writing accusingly,

> Sing bitter song, my soul, sing for the dead
> Who would not stay but panted into death,
> And you gazed wildly from a hated life
> And would have thrown your body for her bread.

When in 1926 Sapir met the psychoanalyst Harry Stack Sullivan, who was to become a close friend, the two talked for ten hours straight, Edward agonizing over his guilt that Florence had given up her studies to marry him when all he could provide was a home in a faraway city, where "isolation and loneliness had . . . shattered . . . her mind and body."[7] So if Edward was not always attuned to Ruth's inner world, at least he might now understand that, as a sensitive and clever woman, her life and sanity depended on her finding a place for herself in the outer world. Still, her ambiguity could make him uncomfortable: "You know how I feel about even toying with the idea of dissociation of personality," he once remarked to her on the occasion of one of his frequent attacks on her use of a pseudonym (SF, 23 March 1926).

During the summer following Florence Sapir's death, Edward Sapir and

Margaret Mead met at the convention of the British Association for the Advancement of Science in Toronto. Margaret, the youngest person to present a paper, was attending her first professional conference. Ruth, who had most likely introduced the two in New York, was not present, much to Edward's disappointment. Instead, she had decided to brave a field trip to the Southwest. The anthropologists at the convention formed a small clique among the large crowd of scientists. Sapir and Goldenweiser had lively arguments about Jung, whose work was becoming popular, and Margaret was interested to meet a woman anthropologist whose "contract" marriage, without benefit of church or state, had caused gossip in their circles, especially because she had a child.

There was endless talk in the group about fieldwork in the Arctic or among the Bella Bella or Nootka, and Margaret felt very much the novice. She recalled: "Everyone there had a field of his own, each had a 'people' to whom he referred in his discussion. I had entered anthropology with the expectation of working with immigrant groups in the United States and perhaps of doing some research on American Indian groups, among which I had not yet learned to distinguish very sharply. At Toronto I learned the delights of intellectual arguments among peers. I, too, wanted to have a 'people' on whom I could base my own intellectual life" (BW, 135).

Margaret, who eventually would become a mover and shaper in this "classical" period of anthropology, realized that finding one's own "people" was an act of self-definition for the new anthropologist.[8] Even Ruth was now venturing into the Pueblo cultures of the Southwest. Determined not to be left out, Margaret turned her mind to possibilities farther afield. If the men could be adventurous, why not she?

But for the moment, the chief delight in Toronto was Edward Sapir. There was an instant chemistry between Margaret and this man who was old enough to be her father. It was her first experience of an intense, adult heterosexual attraction. As she later recalled,

> He was 23 years older than I was. I was 23 and he was 46. But talking to him was just magnificent. He would say half a sentence and I'd say half a sentence and he'd say half a sentence and things just seemed to be in fireworks that were delightful. . . . He was the most brilliant person I ever met and the most satisfactory mind I ever met. . . . And he was terribly vulnerable and desperately unhappy . . . somebody you had to protect. (JH)

Margaret, of course, was quite at ease with the idea of protecting her elders, though in fact she gave the age difference incorrectly. She was twenty-two when they met. Edward, at forty, was her elder by eighteen years and closer to her father's age.

Sapir wrote to Ruth, now in Zuñi, informing her that a highlight of the convention had been "getting to know Margaret Mead. . . . She is an astonishingly acute thinker and seems to be able to assimilate and invent ideas at breakneck speed." Ironically, he was as concerned about her vulnerability as she was about his, probably having noticed the extent to which neuritis wore her down. "She must be told to think far more of her health . . . than she seems to," he wrote to Ruth (SF).

Margaret returned for the rest of the summer to her family in Pennsylvania and later went back to New York with Luther. All the while she corresponded with Ruth, whom naturally she missed a good deal. She felt intellectually isolated after all the excitement at Toronto: "I wish we could go on a field trip together," she wrote, "only in my present state I'd talk you insane. I don't seem to be able to stop talking any more than I can stop thinking" (AW, 285). Now she and Edward were correspondents, too: "I suppose it's a very bad sign that Sapir has time to write letters, but I do enjoy them. It's such a satisfactory friendship, defaced by no tiresome preliminaries (that's thanks to you) and founded on such sure ground of like-mindedness" (AW, 286).

What were Ruth's reactions to the news of this alliance between Margaret and Edward? Did she feel gratified that the two people she loved now liked each other; did she experience twinges of jealousy or foreboding? For Margaret, at any rate, life was becoming very interesting. She was already benefiting immeasurably from Ruth's loving her and now there was Edward, a fascinating older man and a leader in her chosen field. Emotional complications might be foreseen, but after all, if she became immersed she would only be catching up with her friends. No longer aloof from the fray, she was beginning to consider the benefits of being fascinating herself.

Through her letters she kept Ruth informed about her thoughts and plans, including her wish to find "a people." She had talked with Alexander Goldenweiser about her doctoral thesis, and he had persuaded her to analyze Polynesian boat building as well as tattoos. She was also writing an essay on deviance, in which she referred disparagingly to "a husky group of normal people bigoted beyond disturbance" (AW, 286). This is the first evidence of conversation between Ruth and Margaret about deviance and normality, a frame of reference Ruth was to develop into a theoretically important tool which helped her move beyond her personal (and generational) battle with Puritanism and into her own distinctive formulation of a modernist anthropology.

Ruth's two field trips to the Southwest in the summers of 1924 and 1925 laid the foundation for her great theoretical work.[9] Yet as a fieldworker she showed no exceptional talent and she never found "a people of her own" as

Margaret Mead hoped to do. Mead later commented that Ruth "never saw a whole primitive culture that was untroubled by boarding schools for the children, by missions and public health nurses, by Indian Service agents, traders, and sentimental or exiled white people" (AW, 206).

The cornerstone of Benedict's work was meticulous scholarship. She had pored over the writings of early travelers to the Southwest, feeling a particular affinity with the Jesuits who had left unparalleled records of their contacts with cultures which had not been previously exposed to European influence. Ruth's capacity to synthesize these diverse materials with the contemporary work of her colleagues reflected her humanistic, literary imagination at its best, and she built on her slight fieldwork experience to produce outstandingly original work.

The trips to the Southwest, though not especially challenging compared with anthropological standards of the day, gave Benedict a feel for Native American cultures not to be had from the library at Columbia or the displays at the Museum of Natural History. They allowed her to experience the spirit and geography of the region and familiarized her with the practicalities, as well as some of the hardships, of work in the field. On a more personal level, the journeys marked a further commitment to anthropology. They meant negotiating with Stanley about her absence from endless summers at the lake, and along with her weekday room on the Upper West Side, the trips demonstrated her serious career intentions. Clearly, by this time Ruth was increasingly committed to her own needs rather than to ministering to her husband's. She had finally moved beyond the role of underoccupied wife and out into the world.

Ruth's Manhattan friends probably envied her trip, for the Southwest was fast becoming a fashionable destination among the literary and artistic set. Mabel Dodge was now living in Taos, New Mexico, after her marriage to Tony Luhan, a Native American. She had found permanent fascination in the Pueblo cultures, whose virtue, she claimed "lay in wholeness instead of dismemberment."[10] She encouraged artists and writers to visit Taos, including D. H. Lawrence. The writer of *Lady Chatterley's Lover* disappointed Mabel as a "typical lower middle class, puritanical conventional Englishman," but Lawrence was suitably impressed: "Taos pueblo still retains its old nodality. Not like a great city. But, in its way, like one of the monasteries of Europe. . . . When you get there, you feel something final . . . the pueblo as it has been since heaven knows when, and the slow dark weaving of the Indian life going on still."[11]

Georgia O'Keeffe, whose original paintings stunningly captured the extraordinary colors of the local landscape, was another artist whose imagination was captured by the region. Capitalizing on the surge of interest around this time, the Santa Fe railroad company began an extensive advertising campaign, which brought more and more tourists to the Grand Canyon and "Indian detours."

Ironically, in their search for the untouched, the timeless, and the whole, escapees from the soulless life of modern America themselves contributed to the dismemberment of traditional native American cultures. Anthropologists were not above or beyond this process, even though they often saw themselves as advocating for Native Americans when they explained the subtleties of ancient cultures to progress-minded contemporaries. How anthropologists were seen by native Americans was sometimes another matter.

Many tribes placed a great value on secrecy. Aspects of ritual, ceremony, and esoteric knowledge were hidden from outsiders and often known only to those who had earned a certain status within their own community. The European respect for scientific knowledge was completely foreign, as was the romantic image of the fearless scientist who penetrates the secrets of nature, or, with the growth of human sciences, the secrets of culture. Native Americans strongly resisted anthropologists' attempts to pry into their secrets, though they often welcomed them into their villages and into their lives.

Anthropologists were often not content with what they were allowed to see. A common practice was the use of paid informants to teach the language, tell stories, and explain myths and customs, as was the purchase of artifacts. Trouble arose when informants were bribed to tell secrets, when photographs of esoteric ceremonies were taken without anyone's consent, or when sacred objects were removed for museum display. Before Ruth arrived in the Southwest, a photographer had been stoned in Taos, and Elsie Clews Parsons, who had made Ruth's visit possible, often found herself in hot water with her relentless quest for information.

Parsons might well have been unscrupulous in her work with Native Americans. She had first gone to Zuñi in 1915 and since then had visited the Southwest once or twice a year for intensive fieldwork. She was a highly principled woman, but her principles included the sincere belief that the cultures she studied were bordering on extinction and that it was imperative, both for science and for the sake of people's need for their own history, that all aspects of their culture be recorded. She believed, with justification, that native oral traditions and the wealth of knowledge contained in them were at risk of vanishing. But what she would not recognize was that stealing knowledge was also a violation and likely to contribute to the dismemberment of a culture just as surely as the more obvious forms of colonization. As well as studying Zuñi rituals, for example, she was an assiduous collector of interesting items for museums, and Alfred Kroeber once referred jokingly in a letter to their "robbing shrines at dusk."[12]

Parsons, whose relations with Native Americans were often close and affectionate, worked with paid informants, sometimes interviewing them in secret away from their homes. She would try to piece together information from a wide range of sources since individual informants, often resorting to subterfuge in order to earn their payments without putting themselves at risk, rarely provided all the material she wanted.

For those who revealed details of tribal life to outsiders, penalties could be severe. In earlier times informants had occasionally been executed. Commonly, they believed that they could sicken and even die as a result of their betrayals. Ostracism was another form of punishment; Tony Luhan had been put out of his own pueblo for marrying Mabel Dodge. Parsons took special precautions to prevent local people from learning about the contents of her scholarly works. In the 1930s she made it a condition of the publication of Taos Pueblo that Yale University Press not allow any copies to be sent to New Mexico, for if the work was known there "it might cause conflict in the pueblo and create difficulties for future ethnographic investigations there."[13]

In the event, her books inevitably did fall into the hands of the peoples they described. Parsons was told by a man from the Jemez Pueblo that his family had been singled out as informants and were publicly humiliated and denied their irrigation rights so that his crops failed. The Taos Pueblo also launched an investigation and, discovering that their identified informer had since died, they divested his son of an interest in communal lands.

As Ruth Benedict was setting out on her first trip to the Southwest in the summer of 1924, such matters were probably far from her mind compared to the practicalities of travel and housing, the heat, the bedbugs, and the unaccustomed diet. She had a companion in Ruth Bunzel, or Bunny as she was known, Boas's secretary now that Esther Schiff had decided to study anthropology. A Barnard graduate who had taken Boas's anthropology course, Bunny had heard about the job through her older sister, a friend of Esther's. With Boas in Europe during her first summer though, she was at loose ends. She had become friendly with Ruth and suggested accompanying her to the Southwest to help out with shorthand and typing. When told of her plans, Boas "heard me out, snorted in his inimitable fashion and said, 'Why do you want to waste your time typing? . . . Do a project of your own.' But I said, 'Professor Boas, I'm not an anthropologist. I can't do that.' He said, 'You're interested in art. They make pottery there. Go do a project on the relationship of the artist to her work.' "[14]

Boas immediately enrolled Bunzel in the Ph.D. program, giving her "about four or five weeks to become an anthropologist and plan a project. . . . I had to swim. I assumed that Zuñi artists were not going to be any more articulate about what they were trying to do than the poets and painters I had met in Greenwich Village."[15]

The two Ruths arrived in Zuñi after a journey of several days by train and a trip of thirty-six miles from Gallup. Parsons had arranged for them to stay with a local schoolteacher, but when they arrived to find their contact had left town and their letters were still at the post office, undelivered, "our hearts went down into our toes," Bunny recalled.[16] Fortunately, they were befriended by Flora Zuñi, a local teacher who spoke English and who arranged the rental of a house on the edge of the village. There Ruth Benedict spent her days collecting stories, which were eventually to be published as *Zuñi Mythology*, while Bunny watched the potters at work, beginning a study which was to result, after five trips to the region, in her classic, *The Pueblo Potter*.

Sharing life in the field meant the start of a long friendship between Ruth and Bunny, though Ruth now had to do all her own note taking and typing. She was handicapped by the fact that she spoke no Native American language, her Spanish was poor, and she was partially deaf. Nevertheless, using an interpreter she worked with informants in marathon sessions of note taking. She later described to Margaret how she would sit under a tree, and "with flying pencil and aching arm, [write] down verbatim hundreds of pages of translated tales to be redictated when she returned to New York" (AW, 202–3). She valued the regular correspondence with Margaret, who wrote telling her not to work too hard: "Your letter sounded about eight times too industrious. Aren't you really awfully tired out? Eleven hours of dictation makes me think of the day I gave thirteen Binets [to the Italian children], and the memory is a most unsavory one" (AW, 287–88).

Ruth also kept in touch with Edward, who envied her sojourn in the strange landscapes of the Southwest which he had not visited. He wrote "Zuñi" for her, a sonnet he considered one of his best, imagining Ruth in the "dry glitter of the desert" watching Native American priests in a "slow, dreaming ritual."[17] Warning Ruth of the mysteries and dangers of fieldwork that might not always be apparent to a novice, Sapir admonished her to "hear on the wing, see in a flash, retreat" and to "put wax into your ears and close your eyes." He joked to her about the poem: "You see I am warning you against the Desert Siren. It would be terrible to have you come back over-punctuated with Oh and Ah like any well-behaved acolyte of the Santa Fe school. Of course it is all pure envy" (SF, 26 Aug. 1924).

Locating informants who were willing to divulge what the anthropologists wanted to know was, as Ruth might have expected, a troubling issue. Before her second trip, during which she planned to study several pueblos besides Zuñi, Ruth was roundly warned about informants by a colleague,

Jaime de Angulo, a half-Indian linguist to whom she had written for advice. He replied angrily that Frank Hamilton Cushing, an earlier anthropologist, had killed the Zuñi, and that Elsie Clews Parsons "is doing her best to kill Santo Domingo."

> As for helping you to get an informant, and the way you describe it 'if I took him with me to a safely American place' . . . 'an informant who would be willing to give tales and ceremonials' . . . oh God! Ruth, you have no idea how much that has hurt me. . . . Do you realize that it is just that sort of thing that kills the Indians? . . . It kills them spiritually first, and as in their life the spiritual and the physical element are much more interdependent than in our own stage of culture, they soon die of it physically. They just lie down and die. That's what you anthropologists with your infernal curiosity and your thirst for scientific data bring about. (RFB, Box 35)

Ruth did not heed his warning, it seems, though the native emphasis on secrecy must have had some resonance with her own history as someone who had always resisted divulging her own secrets.

Ruth and Bunny found a willing and interesting informant in Nick Tumaka, a man whom Alfred Kroeber had called "the outstanding intellectual of the Zuñi."[18] In his youth he had been tried for witchcraft and "hung by the thumbs until he confessed."[19] Despite his high status, he appeared something of an outsider. As Ruth commented in a letter to Margaret, "There's something impressive in the man's fire. He might have been a really great man. And yet I think any society would have used its own terms to brand him as a witch. He's too solitary and too contemptuous" (AW, 292).

She was thrilled to listen to Nick telling the "sacred" stories which he narrated with "fire in his eye," in a singsong manner, endlessly going through the necessary repetitions of the same episodes (AW, 292). Ruth thought his information reliable, but Ruth Bunzel wrote to Boas that Nick was "an old rascal who wants to see which way the cat jumps."[20]

Bunny had an easier way with the Zuñi than Ruth, whose talent for friendship did not so readily extend across cultures as it did to the interesting and different among the New York set. Bunny was initiated into Flora's clan and given a Zuñi name, "Bluebird," representing the color of the artist's smock she habitually wore, and Nick once asked Bunny to marry him.

After Nick died his relatives accused Bunny of having caused the death by taking away his religion and leaving him defenseless. Nick himself, shortly before he died, had told Bunny of a dream in which a white girl had come to him with prayer sticks. He interpreted it to mean that he was going to die since he had told her Zuñi rituals and poems and had lost his protection. "It was a chilly experience," Bunzel recalled when she was herself an elderly woman; "I haven't quite recovered from that."[21]

But in the twenties such concerns must have seemed a little remote. Days in the Pueblo were crowded with events. "The Zuñi are a ceremonious people," Ruth wrote; "a people who value sobriety and inoffensiveness above all other virtues. Their interest is centered upon their rich and complex ceremonial life. Their cults of the masked gods, of healing, of the sun, of the sacred fetishes, of war, of the dead, are formal and established bodies of ritual with priestly officials and calendric observances. No field of activity competes with ritual for foremost place in their attention. Probably most grown men among the western Pueblos give to it the greater part of their waking life."[22]

By her second trip in 1925, Ruth was more familiar with the territory and she found that she was pleased to be back, writing to Margaret; "I've discovered in myself a great fondness for this place—it came over me with a rush—We drove in with the rain pouring down in great white separate drops and sunlit clouds, and soft veils of rain sifting and forming against the far off mesas. The red terraced hillock of Zuñi never looked better in any setting" (AW, 291).

After Zuñi, she went on to Santa Fe and then to live in Pena Blanca with a Mexican family. Next she moved on, probably by horse-drawn cart to Cochiti, a Keres-speaking village of around two hundred inhabitants on the far side of the Rio Grande, where the people were known for their hospitality to outsiders and where informants were more easily found. In Cochiti Ruth had a house to herself, "next door to an underground kiva with its ladder thrust up to the sky. An adobe staircase ascends from one side. . . . [The houses have] twisted acacias to sit under in the front, and porches covered with boughs whose leaves have turned just the color of the adobe" (AW, 299). American food was difficult to procure, with bread and milk unavailable, and the bugs were such a problem that she had to take her bedding onto the roof and sleep under the stars.

Boas, with the safety of his "children" always in mind, had warned Benedict that she "ought not to set foot . . . in Cochiti . . . with an informant." But Ruth had a different feeling about the situation, writing to Margaret that "I never do get this sense of the spiked dangerous fence that Elsie, and Dr. Boas in this case, make so much of" (AW, 299). After a couple of days, she wrote, "I have male callers, mother callers, innumerable children who've heard I have candy, and the family of the house wander in at least every day from the farm across the river" (AW, 300). In fact, the callers came to seem excessive: "The complete gregariousness of it staggers belief in a hermit New Yorker! . . . As soon as I go out for water the men begin to come in. One amorous male I think I have got rid of, dear soul! He's stunning, with melting eyes and the perfect confidence which I can't help believing has come from a successful amour with a white woman. He hopes I'll be another Mabel Dodge; . . . It was when I bribed a little girl to come over and sleep with me under my trees that he took to heart that if I let him kiss my hand six times with much heat, on departing, I meant nothing that interested him" (AW, 301–2).

Ruth paid her informants a dollar for three hours of storytelling, and she found that "the whole village vies to sit with me for a seance. Joe disperses appointments as he would a poor fund and I'm in luck that my old shaman is poor—otherwise he'd be frowned on. One of those who rob the poor working girl, you know!" (AW, 303). She sought esoteric stories, but to her disappointment she was given only the ones fit for public telling. Her favorite storyteller was an old man, Santiago Quintana, made famous through the work of Cochiti potter Helen Cordero. Southwest folklorist Barbara Babcock reports that many years later Benedict was remembered among the Zuñi and Cochiti as gentle and generous.

The purpose of Benedict's field trips, as well as the collection of tales that were eventually published as Zuñi Mythology and Tales of the Cochiti Indians, was to investigate whether folktales accurately represented tribal life. Some did seem to characterize present day events, while others had their origins in the more distant past. Particularly puzzling were tales containing themes that seemed to contradict current practices, such as the stories they told about infant abandonment which Ruth could never corroborate in real life. Ruth figured that this type of story was what psychoanalysis would call a compensatory daydream, a wish fulfillment. But whether or not these tales reflected accurately the events of their life or culture, she believed that "people's folktales . . . are their autobiography and the clearest mirror of their life." For the human imagination with its artistic imperative helps to fashion a culture just as strongly as material factors do: "The world man actually lives in . . . always bulks very small in relation to the world he makes for himself," she wrote with imaginative insight.[23]

In her analysis of folktales of the Southwest, Ruth was influenced by Edward Sapir's developing interest in the psychology of culture. Boas had always emphasized the importance of studying the mental life of peoples, but Sapir, with his interest in psychoanalysis, had encouraged Ruth to look for psychological patterns in the material. His publication of "The Unconscious Patterning of Behavior in Society" in 1927 is usually seen as the beginning of the "culture and personality" school in anthropology, a development which for some time would be virtually synonymous with the names Sapir, Benedict, and Mead.

Since Margaret's thesis was on Polynesia, that part of the world seemed a logical destination for fieldwork. She set about persuading a friend, Isabel Gordon, to plan an expedition with her. Ruth, on the other hand, faced uncertainties about her future, for Stanley had ideas of moving to Detroit; perhaps Ruth could commute to Ann Arbor. Sapir was not impressed: "Can't you persuade someone to make it worth your husband's while, financially speaking, to stay in New York? It seems a thousand pities to have you migrating to the provinces" (SF, 15 Nov. 1924). Sapir sympathized with Ruth's plight at Columbia, where she was being used as "the cheapest of cheap labor" but was amused to hear the latest gossip, that Alexander Goldenweiser and Elsie Clews Parsons would be publicly debating the question of monogamy: "I hope it's going to be as idiotic as it sounds" (SF, 19 Jan. 1925).

At New Year 1925, Sapir passed through New York en route to a conference in Washington, D.C., and accompanied Ruth on a visit to the Mead-Cressman household. The visit was uncomfortable for Luther, who could not match the urbanity of their conversation and felt condescended to, though "they tried to be polite and courteous to me."[24] Perhaps he also detected undercurrents of tension caused by Margaret's infatuation with Sapir and his seemingly returning her interest. Before leaving Ottawa, Edward had written a poem, "Star-Gazer," in which he described Margaret as "of hazardous and strange conceit," probably because he was concerned at the rashness of her plans for the South Seas (MM, Q15). After meeting her in New York he wrote "Ariel," dedicated upon its publication to "M.M." The poem likens Margaret to the sprite of Shakespeare's *Tempest*, a free spirit reaching for the sky, oblivious to the risks she took. "Reckless, be safe," he implored, hoping that "her little wise feet" would not lead her into danger (AW, 88–89).

Returning from his conference via New York, Edward showed Margaret "Ariel." Ruth, acting as an intermediary, in turn showed him a batch of Margaret's poems. After his return to Ottawa, he told Ruth, "A trip to New York used to stimulate me, of late it seems to induce a melancholy vacuity" (SF, 19 Jan. 1925). Perhaps he avoided referring to the immediate cause of his melancholy, which seems to have been an altercation with Margaret. Toward the end of Edward's New York visit she had written "Unmarked Grave," dedicated "To E.E.S." (MM, Q15). The title was a little thoughtless in view of Edward's recent bereavement, but tact was never Margaret's strong point. The gist of the verse was indignation at someone who murdered her feelings so that they were now buried in an "unmarked grave."

What lay behind all this? A most likely scenario is that Margaret had told Edward of her feelings for him and been rebuffed, not because Edward was not attracted to her, but because Margaret, as she says in the poem, "did not ask to see, in love's eyes fidelity." Edward would not have entered lightly into an affair with a very young woman, and a married woman at that. He did not believe in free love, and he was not used to New Women. If he were to love again, so soon after Florence's death, it would be a serious matter. Margaret's pride may have been wounded by his rejection, and she appears to have taken on board the idea, probably his, that her attitudes to fidelity were "shallow." In the poem she attributes them to her family patterns, rather than to the intellectual repudiation of Puritanism that she had announced to Ruth only that summer.

Though she did not name Edward in *Blackberry Winter*, Margaret referred to the confusions and misunderstandings that marked her relationship with him when she wrote, "We did not bargain with men. After college many of us fell in love with an older man, someone who was an outstanding figure in one of the fields in which we were working, but none of these affairs led to marriage. Schooled in an older ethic, the men were perplexed by us and vacillated between a willingness to take the love that was offered so generously and uncalculatingly and a feeling that to do so was to play the part of a wicked seducer. . . . It was a curious period in which girls who were too proud to ask for any hostage to fate confused the men they chose to love" (BW, 116–17).

Edward probably inflicted a further hurt when he told Margaret that her poetry was not particularly good: "I wrote Margaret yesterday," he told Ruth, "and decided to tell her gently but frankly how her verse affected me. She won't take offence, I am sure, especially as I make the positive point she should go in for simple narrative verse, and I don't think it would have been really frank or friendly for me to have passed over her verse in utter silence. That kind of charity would have seemed an insult to me if I had been she" (SF, 14 Feb. 1925). This rebuff had come on top of a similar one from Ruth, not very long before, to which Margaret had responded, "I knew the verse was poor. . . . I didn't quite understand your query about its being an expression of my mood—in your sense. I wrote them rather to be rid of moods that bored me or plagued me. And they were a very diverse picture because of some things I didn't finish which came in between. Most of them conformed to your description of saying 'ouch when your corns are stepped on' " (AW, 288).

Franz Boas was uneasy about Margaret's plans. He would have preferred that she go to the Southwest, his usual destination for women students, but she had suggested Tuamoto in the Marquesan Islands. To put her off,

Boas "recited a sort of litany of young men who had died or been killed while they were working outside the United States" (BW, 128). If young men were not safe, young women were even less capable of protecting themselves from physical danger, let alone withstanding the heat, the risk of tropical disease, and the unaccustomed diet; their vulnerability to sexual endangerment also needed to be considered.

Though Margaret had confidence in excess, she was small in stature and hardly tough, what with the undermining of her health from the constant pain of neuritis. Had she proposed that Luther accompany her, Boas might have relented, but Margaret had no intention of taking her husband. Instead, she set about exercising her not inconsiderable manipulative skills: "I did what I had learned to do when I had to work things out with my father. I knew that there was one thing that mattered more to Boas than the direction taken by anthropological work. This was that he should behave like a liberal, democratic, modern man, not like a Prussian autocrat. It was enough to accuse him obliquely of exercising inappropriate authority to have him draw back. . . . Unable to bear the implied accusation that he was bullying me, Boas gave in" (BW, 140).

At the same time, she told her father that Boas was trying to force her to work in the Southwest "instead of letting me go where things were interesting. My father, rivalrous as men often are in a situation in which someone else seems to be controlling a situation and where they believe they have a right—and may also have failed—to control, backed me to the point of saying he would give me the money for a trip around the world" (BW, 141).

The compromise was Samoa with its strong American naval presence and where on outlying islands there remained villages whose traditional life appeared relatively unaffected by westernization. Margaret wanted to research culture change, but Boas suggested studying adolescence. He was beginning to direct students toward studies of individuals in their cultural setting, partly a continuation of his challenging the biologically oriented psychologies of the day. Boas's choice of topic may have been inspired by a wish to take on his old enemy, G. Stanley Hall, president of Clark University, from which Boas had resigned on a matter of academic freedom. In an influential book on adolescence, Hall had argued that the storminess of this stage of life was an inevitable outcome of biological changes at puberty. Boas wanted to investigate whether the phenomenon of adolescence was culturally determined. As a young woman with some training in psychology, Mead seemed ideally suited for this task.

Edward's reaction to Margaret's triumph was studiously casual: "Good for Margaret," he wrote Ruth; "She'll enjoy Samoa, but the thought of a grind of field-work out there somehow makes me yawn. How perverse we can be!" (SF, 26 Jan. 1925). But he could not leave alone the issue of Margaret's health: "I am glad to hear that Margaret Mead is buoyant and industrious in spite of her physical suffering," he wrote in March 1925. "Work is a great thing, isn't it?" And again: "Poor Margaret! She'll have to stop being driven. Can't you take her in hand and lay down the law?" (SF, 6 March 1925). A fortnight later it was, "It's too bad she has such a frightful time with the neuritis. Can't something be done?" (SF, 18 March 1925). Ruth shared his concern. That spring she arranged for Margaret to be seen by specialists, but a neurologist found no physical disorder and diagnosed Margaret as suffering from nervous fatigue (AW, 290).

Ruth was anxious on her own account about the risks Margaret would be taking, and the prospect of parting was a source of great distress. In "Riders of the Wind" she hears the wind at her beloved's heart, a wind which "tears apart" her own "slight cocoon" and sets her drifting "forever lonely, beyond reach" (RFB, Box 45). Comparing Margaret to a bird soaring, she wrote;

> I see you lift in the passion
> Of my own heart;
> But we ride it in different fashion
> Worlds apart.

"Lift Up Your Heart"—a poem Edward called "difficult and splendid . . . [with] diction [that] sounds almost like a literal translation . . . of some difficult Greek poet" (SF, 27 Feb. 1925)—describes how Ruth felt now that the date had been set and time marched relentlessly toward the separation.

> When you shall lie abandoned to that hour
> Scrawled star-incised upon your horoscope,
> Do not be comforted. Admit no hope
> Warm-lipped upon your breasts, nor folded flower
> From any south-turned slope. (AW, 481)

There is no consolation for the lovers in this poem—"I who have loved you leave against this sorrow"—so they must experience life fully in the here and now ("Be desperate in that hour / Lift up your heart as any cup / and drink it desolate.") In the event, Margaret would take Ruth's advice to live life fully, though not in the manner Ruth would have wished.

"Fulfillment," another in a flood of poetry from around this time, expresses Ruth's feelings of powerlessness about Margaret's leaving for "coral oceans lovelier, than any still midnight."

> She put aside our offerings
> With slight unheeding hands,
> Impatient for more tenuous wings,
> More strange untraveled lands. (RFB, Box 43)

Another part of the poem ("Our wine was vapor to her thirst, Our air, stale element") alludes to the "wine" metaphor, with its rather incongruous religious overtones, which Margaret liked to use to express her capacity to love nonexclusively.

Margaret thought that emotions should be simple and straightforward, though experience should have taught her otherwise. As Luther recalled, Margaret often said, when bested in an argument, "If it isn't [the way things are], it ought to be" (GJ, 194). As usual, her intellect outstripped her feelings, and she remembered this period as a time of confusing personal relationships: "I alternated between complaining that life was too full . . . and drawing diagrams which compared people to different atoms with different valences, so that some people could manage more relationships that others, and some of those relationships would be to others who could themselves manage many fewer" (BW draft). To some extent her differences with Ruth and Edward were a generational problem; yet even those not so much older, like Luther and Marie, seemed capable of an emotional steadfastness which was out of Margaret's reach.

On the eve of May Day 1925, the old Ash Can Cats, Margaret, Léonie, Pelham, Louise Rosenblatt, and Bunny McColl gathered willow, moss, ferns, and flowers to make their May baskets. As they prepared to deliver them, Margaret received a telegram informing her she had won a National Research Council fellowship which would pay her a salary in the field; this, alongside her father's contribution, would finance the trip to Samoa. She was overjoyed, and hers was not the only triumph of the evening. Léonie told the group that her first book of poetry, *Those Not Elect*, had just gone to press, and Louise Rosenblatt announced she had won the Duror fellowship from Barnard which Margaret and Léonie had missed out on earlier. The young women were ecstatic as they roamed uptown and then down to Greenwich Village, distributing seven baskets in all, with one to Ruth Benedict, one to Louise Bogan, and one to the poet they admired from a respectful distance, Edna St. Vincent Millay. At midnight, they gathered outside Millay's house, calling out to her. She responded graciously to her enthusiastic fans, and in an "extravagance of delight" they basked in her "magical" presence.[25] Léonie was flattered that Millay had heard of her, and as they departed, tossed her glove over the wall as a memento (BW, 132).

Elated, Margaret now felt sure she would be successful in her new career, which she intended to pursue joyfully: "If I could skip as I went along, I would be able to work in a world that had not been constructed for a woman to work in. I was beginning to realize that the freedom to work as one wished was the important thing" (BW, 132).

Edward, on learning of the fellowship, congratulated his "highly gifted young lady" (MM, Q11) and wrote to Ruth that he was "very glad that Margaret has obtained her desire. She will enjoy the year in the South Seas hugely and will profit greatly by it, I feel certain. She lives intensely in the outer world and it will all mean a great deal to her" (SF, 2 May 1925). But his letter continued with a warning note, "I hope her neuritis is letting up. She can't go on indefinitely with it." He was pleased to announce that he had reconsidered Margaret's poetic talents and now found her verse "delightfully fresh . . . It is nothing short of marvelous how she has leaped from the ineptitude—really, you know—of the things you showed me in New York to the kind of thing she's doing now. She must have been practicing all the time but wisely refraining from showing anyone the transitional capers of her Muse."

Edward also congratulated Ruth on her plans for another trip to the Southwest that summer. His own "disoriented and bluish mood" continued. He had arranged to teach two ethnology courses at Columbia's summer school, but to his great disappointment neither Ruth nor Margaret would be there, for Ruth had to put time in with Stanley at Winnepesaukee Lake and Margaret would be in Pennsylvania making her final preparations.

Time was passing rapidly. One day in May Margaret, in a departure from convention, visited Ruth at her suburban home in Bedford Hills. Stanley may have been out of town, though perhaps this was the occasion when he sought refuge in the barn to avoid her. During the visit Margaret penned "Hollow Heart," a verse with a cynical edge featuring a "proud and secret" woman, in whom "sweet joy" was "sieved through dear agony"; whose "pallid smile could never be / Dim echo of their ecstasy," and who seemed to have lost everything she held dear in life (MM, Q15). Margaret by now may have experienced Ruth's jealous, passionate side, usually well hidden. A poem of farewell that Margaret wrote a few days later is suggestive of guilt as well as sadness at the emotions her leaving had aroused in Ruth. The original title was "Wanderer to Wanderer," but she changed it to "Traveller's Faith":

> Someday when I no longer lean
> In aching transport on your banks of green,
> And your clear fingers may not bless

An absent lover with a cool caress,
I shall not weep nor feel to blame;
Knowing the smooth brown pebbles are the same
But that the waters of your spirit flow
Past other banks in woods I do not know. (MM, Q15)

Margaret often used the color green in poems that seem to have been inspired by Ruth. In one of her later dream interpretations she noted that red, to her, signified love. Green, as opposed to red, would seem to suggest calmness rather than passion. Comparing her lover to a cool stream hints metaphorically at the relationship's being, for Margaret, more nurturing and enlivening than passionate, though "aching transport" introduces a different note.[26]

Margaret showed these poems to Edward, who congratulated her on their "charming simplicity" and complained that his Muse had deserted him for the company of "you and Ruth and the rest of you singing bluestockings" (MM, Q11).

On 8 May there was a further triumph for Margaret, when she emerged successfully from her doctoral examination. Her friends came to celebrate and Luther arrived home to find her in a state of "benign shock." Luther had also just completed his doctorate and had won a scholarship for a year in Europe. The arrangement was that husband and wife should meet in France in the spring of 1926, after a separation which would stretch to nearly a year.

Luther was conscious of tensions in their marriage at this time, although he did not really know their cause. He put the trouble down to sexual incompatibility, with the honeymoon having been a "storm flag of warning." For him, sex and love should be a joyous, creative unity at the center of a marriage, but Margaret cut him out of her life and put up barriers between them. The apparent calm in the marriage was more of a truce. They never quarreled, but Luther thought that this was because they did not dare, for fear of irrevocably souring the atmosphere. A quarrel would "settle nothing. . . . The tensions, indefinite as to cause—perhaps a feeling of not communicating, with not getting through to the other, that left a sense of uncertainty, ill-defined and meaning unclear, as in a state of being mistlike—increased during our second year as the time for our separation [drew near]" (GJ, 129).

Margaret's final days in New York were a flurry of activity. She enlisted Marie Eichelberger's help with provisioning and Marie gladly slipped into a role that would last a lifetime. She took care of Margaret's clothing, helping her buy cotton dresses needed in the tropics, and as a hopeful parting gift gave Margaret a writing case. Equipment for the novice anthropologist consisted of a portable typewriter, a strongbox, a Kodak camera, typing and carbon paper, and six large notebooks, a skimpy outfitting by later standards. On the final night in New York, Margaret and Luther went out to dinner at a French restaurant and speakeasy on Twenty-eighth Street and then to James Joyce's *Exiles*, playing on the Lower East Side. Luther was particularly struck by a line from the play, "We are all exiles, exiles from happiness." Their outing ended on a somber note; they returned in silence to their apartment with its twin beds, Luther overwhelmed by a sense of foreboding about the future.

Ruth drove up to West Alton with Stanley. They too had problems to sort out. Any pretense of a shared life was fading, and although Ruth loved Margaret, there seemed no possibility there for the permanence she so prized. She hoped that her sexual and emotional longings might still find an outlet in her marriage, but she had thoroughly alienated Stanley and he had developed a romantic interest in another woman. "Stanley finds me sexually undesirable," she wrote in her journal, "[which] has tended to fixate my interest in him as perhaps a more normal relation might not have" (RFB, Box 36).

Sexual rejection also meant the death of hope in terms of Ruth's desire for children. "Blossom-time shall flaw to arid seed-bearing," she says in "For Seedbearing," one of her poems from this time (AW, 71). Another poem, "The Worst is Not Our Anger," shows her despair at the failure of the marriage: "Love departs / Thus numbly always, nor leaves behind / One red-lipped fagot of the fire / Of her incredible and dear desire" (AW, 70).

In this unhappy time Margaret and Luther paid a last visit. They borrowed a car and went first to Louise Bogan and Raymond Holden, now living in Boston at "rather a nice horse-hair-and-black-walnut kind of address," as Louise put it in a letter to Ruth.[27] Margaret gave Louise some hand-hemmed dishtowels. "She would!" Louise wrote acidly, adding, "She said she omitted the aspidistra she intended decorating them with, merely out of lack of time." Leaving Boston, they spent two or three days at the lake, the only occasion that Margaret ever spent any time in Stanley Benedict's company. Luther recalled the stay as "pleasant," but then Luther was pleasant himself and not always sensitive to emotional undertow. He was not even aware that Ruth's marriage was unhappy (GJ, 91).

The next stop for Margaret and Luther was Narragansett Bay, where they spent a week in a holiday cottage, a week Luther remembered as "the most significantly happy of our married life. . . . All competing affairs had been laid aside . . . [and this was] a kind of second and true honeymoon" (GJ, 130).

Perhaps this was so for Luther, but the relationship between Margaret and Edward was becoming more complicated. Their correspondence continued, and Edward received his copy of *The Measure*, featuring Ruth's "Ariel," with its dedication to Margaret, who had lent him Kurt Koffka's *Growth of the Mind*, a contribution from the new Gestalt school of psychology and a book that she later credited with having stimulated Sapir's interest in psychological approaches to anthropology. In his personal life, he continued to be despondent. Like Ruth, he saw no future in his relation to this surprisingly appealing young woman, though he was flattered by her interest. He judged Ruth and Margaret to be in a far better state than he, for he could concentrate only on the technicalities of linguistics, not on poetry or anthropology. He wrote sadly to Ruth, "I have no desire to help or save humanity but merely to try to keep myself as systematically busy as my innate waywardness will allow up to the moment when the demonstrator in anatomy gets tired of his demonstration. You and Margaret have more to ask of the hosts of this party, and the entertainment is correspondingly keener (certainly in Margaret's case and I hope in yours too); my main job will have to be to school myself against absurd regrets" (SF, 14 June 1925).

The years at Ottawa were coming to an end for Edward, and it seemed likely that he would be offered the chair in anthropology at Chicago. He had dearly hoped to succeed Boas at Columbia; the old man was unwell but seemed unwilling or unable to arrange his successor. The year 1925 was an "annus horribilis" for Boas, with stress from his wife's illness compounded by the horror of having recently lost an adult son in a railroad accident and a daughter to polio. Edward expressed concern to Ruth about "our beloved hero," but nevertheless, he was resentful at Boas's dilatoriness (SF, 19 Jan. 1925). At least the Chicago post would mean a change of scene. His mother was now ill with nervous exhaustion, and he himself had succumbed to a fit of the blues around the anniversary of Florence's death.

Edward was deeply hurt when he learned that Boas had supported Goldenweiser for the Chicago position. Ruth explained that Boas still held onto the hope of Edward's replacing him at Columbia, but Edward replied, "I have the curious and somewhat amusing satisfaction of knowing that when Boas roots for me at Columbia, he can't have his way, but when he roots for others at Chicago I can slip in" (SF, 3 Oct. 1925). From Chicago he would have fewer opportunities to visit New York, but then he might have work to offer: "I shall miss you and Margaret very much. That would have been my chief reason for preferring New York, aside from the obvious advantages of New York as New York, but perhaps you girls can come to Chicago yet" (SF, 22 June 1925).

In early July, before removing the family to their new home, Edward accepted an invitation to spend a weekend with Margaret at the family farm in Pennsylvania where Sapir hoped the two would be able to "thrash out . . . all outstanding matters . . . between us" (MM, Q11). It proved to be a fateful encounter. Margaret recorded in her journal that they strolled to the ravine, the picturesque spot with a brook running through that had originally captivated Emily Mead. There Edward's feelings overcame his common sense and he began to make love to her. They were disturbed in their encounter by Margaret's mother, who arrived without warning to call them to dinner (MM, A21).

Edward's version of the stay for Ruth was that it had been "an extraordinarily pleasant weekend at Margaret Mead's farm. A charming spot and lovely people . . ." (SF, 17 July, 1925). Margaret's younger sister Elizabeth was wonderful, "a regular Saint of the Primitives," but "Margaret is still more wonderful. She is ever so much bigger than I had imagined her. In that beautiful rustic atmosphere she comes into her own." Somewhat insensitively, he added, "Won't you feel lost without her? Melville [Herskovits] will have to be your staff, I'm afraid" (SF, 18 July 1925).

Edward now realized that he had fallen in love with Margaret, and the intensity of his feelings perhaps surprised them both. Samoa was fast approaching, and the two wanted time to be alone together. Margaret had not planned to visit New York again, but luck was on her side. Only a few days after Edward's visit, Pliny Earle Goddard called her up to the natural history museum for an interview for the position of assistant curator. The job looked interesting, though curatorships were not as prestigious as academic jobs. Museums were the traditional homes of amateurs and collectors, rather than of those who defined the discipline, and curatorships were often seen as women's work. Still, the job would be a beginning, and the public education aspect of the brief appealed to Margaret, who had already developed a sense that anthropology was not something to be kept to a small group of insiders. Moreover, the interview proved the perfect excuse for a meeting with Edward.

They had dinner together and then went to the hotel room that he had arranged for them. The episode was something of a fiasco. Edward was out of practice and nervous, seeing himself as a "wicked seducer." Margaret was twenty-three and unused to romances with men. Edward was impotent that night, or at least that is the interpretation to be drawn from comments Margaret made about a dream she had much later on. The following morning Edward could not remember the assumed name he had chosen to register under at the hotel, and the pair were embarrassed in their dealings with reception.[28]

Margaret's dream was of Edward with the second wife he had recently married, whose image dissolved into that of a woman in a play she had just seen, a woman who was "homosexual, so not minding impotence." In her notes she compared Edward to her father as lacking in virility and "intensely masculine mentally only," suggesting that, despite her free-thinking nature, she still had, at this stage of her life, fairly conventional notions about sexual roles (MM, A21).

Margaret may have hoped that Edward would fall in love with her, but she also realized she had a problem on her hands. Edward's conservatism came to the fore as he took the affair seriously. According to his social assumptions, a mere dalliance was impossible; making love to a young woman implied an intention to marry, a logic which held even though the young woman in question was already married. Edward seems to have hoped that Margaret would make a suitable wife and companion to him and a mother to his three lively and argumentative children, even though it became clear that his opinion of her was that she was neurotic and unstable.

Margaret must have been flattered by Edward's plans for the future, but she almost immediately assessed the situation as impossible. She had no intention of stepping into Florence's shoes and being "mamma" to the brood. In fact, she was horrified by these expectations, partly, she recalled, because she did not approve of Edward's parenting style: "He treated the children so awfully and I immediately saw myself flinging myself in front of the children, protecting . . . them against their father" (JH). As a result of her upbringing, Margaret had progressive ideas about child rearing, and she assessed a potential husband in the light of his suitability for father-hood as well as for joint anthropological work.

If Margaret was in two minds about Edward, forthcoming events certainly made her more resolute, for Edward embarked on a campaign to prevent her from going to Samoa. First he told her that he thought she was being foolish; then, within a day or two of their night in New York, he took up the issue with Boas, arguing that the Samoan trip posed a great risk to Margaret in terms of her physical and mental health. Boas had just written Margaret a farewell letter, giving her advice about her research and remind-ing her of the importance of paying attention to her health, going so far as to tell her: "If you find you cannot stand the climate do not be ashamed to come back" (AW, 289).

Immediately after his entreaty to Boas, Edward wrote to Ruth in West Alton, expressing his concerns: "I am worried about her—distinctly so. What is she going to Samoa for? . . . Are you inclined to think one ought to do something to stop the whole infernal business at the eleventh hour? Answer at once. I communicated my uneasiness to Boas today but he thought it would be a distinct mistake to interfere. He is still a little nervous about her going, but seems inclined to minimize the danger. Apparently he considers the main thing to fear is her frail health but I fear the latent neurotic situation, which I feel to be rather grave. . . . Tell me what to do, Ruth" (SF, 17 July 1925).

Ruth received this letter at the same time as one from Boas, who had also written immediately to her for an opinion he could trust: "Sapir had a long talk with me about Margaret Mead. You know that I myself am not very much pleased with the idea of her going to the tropics for a long stay. It seems to my mind, however, . . . that it would be much worse to put obstacles in her way that prevented her from doing a piece of work on which she had set her heart, than to let her run a certain amount of risk. In my opinion Sapir has read too many books on psychiatry on account of his wife's illness to trust his judgment; he does not really know the subject and therefore always sees abnormal things in the most disastrous forms. Of course I know that Margaret is high strung and emotional, but I also believe that nothing would depress her more than inability on account of her physical makeup and her mental characteristics to do the work she wants to do. . . . Besides it is entirely against my point of view to interfere in such a radical way with the future of a person for her own sake. . . . Of course, Sapir takes that point of view, but if he were right, then who should not be restrained?" (RFB, Box 103).

Ruth's response to Boas was heroic, considering her own anxieties and her unhappiness at the prospect of being without Margaret. Showing a loyalty her culture saw as more characteristic of friendships between men, she took Margaret's part without hesitation. "The mental condition I think Sapir is unduly alarmed about," she wrote to Boas, and she reassured him about Margaret's physical condition as well. She told him about having taken Margaret to a neurologist, who had found nothing organically wrong, diagnosing only "nervous fatigue" and prescribing "rest." She suggested as well that "the natural relaxation of a tropical climate . . . , far away from the strenuous setting she is used to, may be the best possible change for her." And she also reassured Boas about Margaret's willingness to take precautions for the sake of her health (AW, 290–91).

Ruth's good judgment prevailed. For the rest of her life, Margaret strongly resented Edward's interference, seeing his motives as self-serving. His "advice that I would do better to stay at home and have a child than go off to Samoa to study adolescent girls seemed peculiar to me. After all, men were not told to give up field work to have children!" (BW, 266). Sapir, in fact, was given to making ironic comments about women intellectuals: "Alas!" he had joked to Margaret on hearing of her doctorate, and he had also made witticisms about the "darning of bluestockings" (MM, Q11). Margaret wrote "a bitter little verse of feminine protest" directed at Edward, imagining his ideal woman laboring at her domestic arts:

Measure your thread and cut it
to suit your little seam
Stitch the garment tightly, tightly,
And leave no room for dream . . .
Head down, be not caught looking
Where the restless wild geese fly. . . . (BW, 11)

Although Ruth had worked to control the effects of Sapir's intervention, Margaret's immediate problem was how to deal with Edward's urgent protestations of love and his arguments that she must divorce Luther and marry him. She felt that he was "terribly vulnerable and desperately unhappy" and might not be able to stand a rejection (GJ, 132). Time was running out, and what with the feverishness induced by inoculations against tropical diseases as well as by the emotional issues there was no way that the situation could be put on a better footing before the date of departure.

Ruth, still at the lake, prepared for her second visit to the Southwest. She and Margaret planned to begin their trip together on 28 July, 1925, meeting on board the train. They intended to travel together for the first part of the trip and disembark to make a short side trip to the Grand Canyon before going their separate ways. Ruth had only one day in New York and Edward expected to spend the day with her, inviting her to attend his summer school class if she had time. Praising her recent poem in *The Measure*, he told her she should bring poems to show him. He also told her that Fran Herskovits had picked out the "Anne Singleton" poems as the best in the magazine and had asked Margaret the identity of this promising new poet. Margaret, Edward wrote, had lied to her, claiming that Anne Singleton was "an unknown person who wrote in, apparently, from Texas." He went on to warn her, "Melville and she know you are writing verse. It seems absurd to make such an ado about concealment, don't you think? . . . [But] we look to you now for our standard-bearer. The chrysalis is broken" (SF, 7 July 1925).

Ruth found Edward bursting to tell her all about his feelings for Margaret. There is no record of what he said, and Ruth may have already known something of the situation from Margaret's letters, but according to what she later told Margaret, his words came as a shock. In fact, she said that day had been "the worst day of her life . . . when Sapir came in and told her that he and . . . [Margaret] were in love with each other" (BW draft).[29] Ruth was appalled, judging that a relationship with Edward would be a "disaster" for Margaret and feeling she needed to intervene. But it is hard to imagine the worst day of Ruth's life being occasioned entirely by anxieties about Margaret's welfare—clearly, she was devastated by Edward's and Margaret's feelings for each other. Her own love for Margaret must have seemed a poor thing if it was so easily displaced by a man's. And how humiliating that the two people closest to her, the two people she loved and whom she hoped loved her, had now fallen for each other.

Back in Pennsylvania, Margaret had a final, lively family dinner and was driven to the Baltimore and Ohio railroad station, where the atmosphere became subdued. Luther described the farewells: "Darkness was lowering when we arrived. How filthy that station housing the boarding platforms with the coal dust of years and the hissing steam of waiting locomotives! *Gloom* is the only word adequate to describe the atmosphere enveloping our small group, almost inarticulate in the face of imminent separation, a new experience. Feeling my intimacy with Margaret was of a different kind from her family's, I embraced her warmly, said a few endearing words, and kissed her au revoir. With a 'Good luck and see you in Marseilles next spring,' I stepped well back from the family group, a fitting distance for my swirling feelings.

"As I stood watching the family's lingering farewell, I think I appreciated perhaps more than anyone else could have this lovely, not beautiful, young woman, my wife, willful at times, stubborn, sometimes quixotic, never simple, brilliant, goal-oriented and her course laid out, not permitting any interference with her steady progress in that direction, with an absorption in her work to which everything else had to be secondary in the long run. She was hitching her wagon to a star, and I felt grateful I had never stood in her way. . . . At the last call she climbed aboard her pullman, turned, and waved to us from the platform. The porter closed the door, and she was gone. We waited on the concrete platform until the last car cleared, then suddenly the yawning emptiness of the station enveloped us, empty, empty. . . .

"I took Margaret's mother's arm to walk slowly, and thoughtfully toward the car—the men were already there, continuing their platform discussion on the desirability of buying new tires for the car—and she said in a voice asking for reassurance, 'You will meet her in Marseilles next spring, Luther?' " (GJ, 130–31).

Margaret's recollections were more matter-of-fact: "I kissed them all good-bye and walked through the gate. Afterward my father said, 'She never looked back!' This was the next step in life. I was going to the field and Luther had a fellowship to travel in Europe, the thing he wanted very much to do. No one was permanently bereft. I would be coming back to the farm when the hollyhocks were in bloom again" (BW, 14).

Margaret did not write to Luther until she reached San Francisco, just before she embarked for Honolulu. It was a brief note, beginning, "I'll not leave you unless I find someone I love more." To Luther, the note was: "cryptic and in context truly enigmatic, what did it mean? It was a strange letter, an au revoir letter to a husband after two years of apparently reasonably happy marriage, albeit with tensions and facing a year's separation. It was the first real suggestion, not teasing, that she might be even considering such a step" (GJ, 12).

Not until years later, in conversation with Ruth Benedict, did Luther understand, when Ruth told him about Edward Sapir's "insistent attentions" toward Margaret in the days leading up to her departure for Samoa. He then realized the extent to which the situation had colored her feelings toward him. Margaret's version of events was different, and less credible. She told an interviewer that "Luther knew about [her and Edward], and said, 'Poor dears, it's a pity they didn't have more time together' " (JH).

In her autobiography Mead implies that she began her momentous journey alone (BW, 14). Yet in the draft of *Blackberry Winter* she referred to Ruth's traveling with her, though with the white lie that Ruth would be getting off the train at Gallup to go to Zuñi. In truth, they were both to disembark at Gallup for the Grand Canyon, before Ruth returned and Margaret went on westward.[30] Even at the time there was some secrecy and deception about their traveling arrangements. Pliny Earle Goddard from the natural history museum was also traveling in their direction that summer, but "Ruth and I had to hide our plans to keep him from joining us" (BW draft).

When Ruth and Margaret met on the train, they had not seen each other for more than a month. There had been no chance to talk about the affair with Edward or about Ruth's having experienced "the worst day of her life" when Edward told her about it. The reunion must have been fraught with emotion and colored by Ruth's disappointment, distress, and, perhaps, jealousy. But after the inevitable stresses of the journey, they awoke on the final day to sunrise in the desert of New Mexico, described by Margaret to her grandmother as covering "the whole bowl of the sky, instead of just one edge of it" (MM, O40). They passed through pueblos with adobe houses and watched Indians bailing alfalfa, and for a day or two they were tourists, not anthropologists. The Grand Canyon lived up to its reputation. Margaret wrote to her grandmother: "Ruth and I got very different things out of the Grand Canyon, but we both loved it. She was most impressed by the effort of the river to hide, a torturing need for secrecy which had made it dig its way, century by century, deeper into the face of the earth. And the part I loved the best was the endless possibilities of those miles of pinnacled clay, red and white, and fantastic, ever changing their aspect under a new shadowing cloud. . . . There were many clouds, and in the afternoon a little rain, which did not stop the sun from shining, and later a dark blue cloud which threatened rain, in earnest. We had everything except the canyon by moonlight."

With both projecting their personalities onto the scenery, Ruth her secretiveness and Margaret her vivid sense of possibilities, the Grand Canyon was like a Rorschach test. Awed by its grandeur and magnificence, the two reached a resolution. Margaret had decided that the affair with Edward could not continue, but in light of his emotional vulnerability, she devised a strategy to make him reject her. In her letters, she would emphasize that she was in her outlook much more of a New Woman than Edward could possibly tolerate. She figured that "All I had to do was to present my theory of relationships between people, that they weren't exclusive, which to him meant absolute wickedness, promiscuity" (JH).

Such manipulativeness was foreign to Ruth's nature, but she agreed that Margaret's strategy was defensible, or, as Margaret put it, at least "she didn't say it was wrong." Ruth felt such deliberate provocation would not be easy for Margaret; she did not know anyone for whom this "would be harder to do than you" (JH), but she was hardly a neutral bystander. She was in love with Margaret and had been shocked by the pace at which things had developed between Margaret and Edward. Overt jealousy was against her principles, but she must have felt deeply disappointed and threatened.

But for now they were on their own, and in the splendor of the canyon, cloaked in the colors of late summer, Ruth prevailed. They reached a decision that their love for each other was most important and that "neither of them would choose further intimacy with Sapir." Margaret never described this pact in any of her published writings, of course. The sequence of events was relayed by Margaret to Marie Eichelberger, who years later told Margaret's daughter.[31]

Ruth, reassured that she had Margaret's heart, must have found her joy mixed with overwhelming sadness that this triumph was the occasion of their parting. They would not be reunited until they would meet in Europe, nearly a year away, and although Ruth had roundly defended Margaret's wish to journey to "strange untraveled lands," she still shared Boas's and Sapir's fears. Their friendship was not to replay the biblical story of Naomi and Ruth which Ruth had adored as a child. Margaret was not a follower, and "Whither thou goest, I shall go" was not her style at all.

The pact was sealed with gifts. Ruth gave Margaret an anthology of favorite verses that she had typed out and had specially bound. She may have also given her Phi Beta Kappa key to her young protégée.[32] That evening the two parted at Williams, Arizona. The triangle was now a twosome, or so it must have seemed. Husbands hardly entered the picture.

# 6

## In Coral Oceans Lovelier Than Any Still Midnight

MARGARET BEGAN HER FIRST FIELD TRIP as a complete novice. At twenty-three, she "had never been abroad or on a ship, had never spoken a foreign language or stayed in a hotel by myself. In fact, I had never spent a day in my life alone."[1] Shipboard life was tedious, but on arrival in Honolulu she was taken to the palatial house of an old college friend of her mother's. Every day for a week she was driven to the Bishop Museum and given a lesson in Marquesan which, if not Samoan, was at least an Oceanic language. Before leaving Honolulu she was presented with a little silk pillow, which was such a successful gift that a small pillow became one of Mead's traveling necessities, sometimes her only symbol of hearth and home.

She was seasick en route to Pago Pago, on the island of Tutuila, where she arrived on 31 August 1925. Margaret was surprised by her first view of the capital of American Samoa. The harbor was crammed with U.S. navy vessels blaring ragtime music, airplanes screamed overhead, and no one met her at the dock, though the "natives . . . , laden with kava bowls, tapa, grass skirts, models of outrigger canoes, bead necklaces and baskets," looked interesting (LF, 23). She made her own way to the hotel, where she was eventually found by a Miss Hodgson, from the native nurses' training school, who had missed her on the crowded dock. She was pleased to be offered a dry closet for storing her evening dresses, "which is the greatest help of all; otherwise they rot or get rust stains from cockroach bites" (LF, 24).

For the first six weeks Margaret concentrated on Hodgson's Samoan lessons. Her friendly "cook-boy" Fa'alavelave ("Misfortune") prepared "dreadful meals . . . which were supposed to accustom me to Samoan food" (BW, 159). She rearranged her room so that she felt "civilized," hanging prints from an art magazine sent by Louise Bogan, setting out books, and laying her green steamer rug on the bed (LF, 25). She traveled the "fiendish" roads around Tutuila in "rattletrap buses . . . packed with

Samoans, baskets of food, ice, pigs, and chickens in sacks and baskets . . ." and listened to "endless speeches" at village ceremonies (LF, 26). Staying at the hotel helped her adjust to the new environment, and besides, she was unable to leave because the bill could not be settled until her grant money arrived.

After considerable inquiry, Margaret identified the island of Ta'u in the Manu'an archipelago as an appropriate place for her fieldwork. It was relatively unspoiled yet had a naval outpost where she could stay with the one white family on the island, the Holts. Beforehand, she would be able to meet Ruth Holt, who was off the island awaiting the birth of her second child. Margaret wrote to ask Boas whether he thought living with westerners would detract from her study. She did not expect to hear back from him before she made the decision, but she knew that Boas himself was used to staying in European quarters when he worked in the field with his "dear Kwaikutl."[2]

Before leaving Tutuila, Margaret stayed briefly in one of the chief households of Vaitogi, a small village where she spent the most "peacefully happy and comfortable ten days in my life" (LF, 31). Her constant companion was Fa'amotu, the chief's daughter, who spoke a little English and taught Margaret to wear a sarong, to bathe Samoan-style, and to negotiate many of the intricacies of rank and custom. They slept together on mats in a curtained-off area at the end of the communal sleeping house and by the end of the visit had become such friends that they remained in contact for the rest of Margaret's stay in Samoa and kept up a correspondence afterward. Margaret was made thoroughly welcome and given, as a courtesy, the title of *taupou*, a ceremonial virgin or maiden of high rank; she kept her marriage a secret from the Samoans.

Despite the pleasure of her new Samoan family, Margaret was confirmed in her belief that Ta'u would provide the best conditions for working, writing to Boas that "such advantage as might be reaped [living with a Samoan family] would be more than offset by the loss in efficiency due to the food [she found the starchy native food difficult] and the nervewracking conditions of living with half a dozen people in the same room, in a house without walls, always sitting on the floor and sleeping in constant expectation of having a pig or a chicken thrust itself upon one's notice" (LF, 29). Further, a *taupou* status would impose on her a set of obligations and prohibitions which would have limited her ability to mingle freely.

In early November Margaret boarded a minesweeper bound for Ta'u, sixty miles from Pago Pago. There was no wharf on the island and the passengers were ferried by whaleboat in treacherous conditions across the narrow entrance through the coral reef. On its first trip, the whaleboat rolled on the bar and its school-aged inhabitants were dumped. Seasoned swimmers that they were, there was a flurry of excitement but no harm done. Margaret, however, could not swim, and must have been quite anxious until the passage was safely accomplished and she arrived at her new home, a small village occupying the foreshore of a mountainous island about fourteen square miles in size.

Margaret's quarters were a screened-off part of the back verandah of the dispensary in the only European-style house. A Samoan-style house near the dispensary served as a small interview room and in the Christmas vacation she would be able to use the nearby schoolhouse as well. Her new family comprised the Holts and "Sparks," the radio operator, and as before, she was "presented" with a Samoan girl as a companion because "it would have been unsuitable for me ever to be alone." Felofiaina, who spoke no English, was a "good Christian girl" according to the pastor, and would arrive at eight each morning to help until siesta time with one of the first tasks, a census of the village households and kin relationships (BW, 162).

Makelita, as she was called, proved a popular curiosity. As she walked around the village a gaggle of girls usually accompanied her and she often paid visits to nearby villages where she could "summon informants to teach me anything I wanted to know; as a return courtesy, I danced every night" (BW, 165). She entered into village life with flair, and soon boys as well as girls crowded into her room day and night, chattering ceaselessly, singing, dancing, and strumming on ukuleles and guitars. Little ones gathered outside "to peek through the holes and display their few English words or chatter endlessly in Samoan about her various belongings." They were particularly fascinated by her picture of Franz Boas hanging on the wall (LF, 37). The children turned up as early as 5:00 A.M. and stayed as late as midnight; at first Margaret did not "dare chase them for fear they won't come back" (MM, 1206).

After her first month on Ta'u Margaret described a typical scene:

> Four of my promising pre-adolescents and two babies are peering at me through the Dispensary window now. My pre-ads. are much the most ubiquitous and attentive group. You should see them seated in semi-solemnity on the floor of my porch; Filialosa, with soft brown curls and the gentlest expression in the world, who nevertheless comes and wakes me up when I may have the rare good fortune to have gotten to sleep; Va, a little shaven haired gamin who I can never remember is a girl; Sio and Potasi, the sisters who have a most flaming crush [on] one another that what ever one gives the other is bound to appear wearing the next day; (Sio kills flies with second best effi-

ciency and does not have a *loto leaga* (jealous heart) so she's a long way towards being the favorite); Siualoas, whom a[n] ex-teacher christened "monkey," a lean, triangular face, agile young animal, for whom the children have made up a song about being a monkey to which she dances a fascinating and loathesome monkey dance; Anovale, the only really cross, cranky little creature who likes to hit the other children over the head with my fan if they open their mouths. I have to tell her a dozen times a day "Le pule 'oe", which is really "you aren't the boss." Lastly there is Ailafo who was prettiest of all and the queen of fly-killers, but she has shaved off her hair and presents a naked and heart-rending baldness to the world, and Leialofa, who was white blood, is the prettiest child in the three villages but pays for her beautifully shaped little face and small hands and feet with a terrific shyness. (MM, I206)

Entering into Samoan life was relatively easy, but Margaret felt thrown in at the deep end, ill-equipped to begin a systematic study of adolescence. Her training had alerted her to esoteric comparisons between exotic languages but had not taught her how to learn a language in the field; she had learned the intricacies of kinship systems but not how to prize the information out of villagers. An exasperated novice anthropologist once exclaimed, "How anyone knows who is anybody's mother's brother, only God and Malinowski know" (BW, 151).

Boas had advised Margaret not to use her precious time on ethnological research, the core fieldwork method of anthropology. He set her a new task: to examine whether adolescence in Samoa was a time of conflict for girls. It would be, as he described it, a study of the "psychological attitude of the individual under the pressure of the general pattern of culture," a new approach which Ruth Bunzel, in her study of individual artists of the Pueblo, had also been told to pursue. Dishearteningly, Boas had said "it is, of course, impossible to tell from here what the most promising lines of attack may be." But he promised that "Great, of course, will be the satisfaction if you succeed in getting even part of what you would like to find and I believe that your success would mark a beginning of a new era of methodological investigation of native tribes"—an extraordinary statement of faith in the resourcefulness of a twenty-three-year-old novice (MM, N1).

Boas did suggest that Margaret take note of any rebelliousness or sullen behavior, that she investigate whether Samoan girls were as bashful as girls in the Indian tribes he had observed, and that she should look at the "interesting question of crushes among girls." She might also ask whether older girls experienced romantic (heterosexual) love, a phenomenon he thought most likely under a system of arranged marriage (MM, N1).

Mead later deplored the lack of advice and practical training for field-workers: "if young fieldworkers do not give up in despair, go mad, ruin their health, or die, they do, after a fashion, become anthropologists" (BW, 142). Now she was forced to innovate and improvise. Against Boas's advice she did begin an ethnological study and for the adolescence research fell back on psychological techniques with which she was familiar. Her young Samoan friends were subjected to intelligence tests which she had translated, to color naming tests she had devised with little painted squares, and to a picture naming test made up of images cut from a magazine story about the South Seas. She remembered reading social work case records collected by her Aunt Fanny from Hull House, the Chicago settlement house, and these inspired her to document the personal histories of the sixty-eight local girls aged between nine and twenty. She interviewed each one, mostly in Samoan, asking a multitude of questions about their families, schooling, menarche, experience of menstrual pain, and life experiences, such as witnessing births and deaths or having traveled off the island.

Extensive socializing with the girls gave Margaret information on their relationships with other girls, falling in love, experiences of jealousy, vocational and marriage plans, what happened if they didn't get along with their parents, and what they did with boys under the palm trees. She also made a study of younger girls, so that she could put her adolescents into developmental perspective, and her detailed plan of the village households enabled her to understand each girl in her family context.

In her last letter home before Christmas, Margaret told her friends, "If you wake up in the wee small hours of the morning, picture me lying on my face, perhaps with a pillow for my elbows, playing 'sweepy' Casino, with a group of blandly cheating young people, or inquiring into the intricacies of a new selipusi (fishing stick) or the methods by which jealous wives amputate their rival's ears, or explaining that unless I write a good book about Samoa, I'll never get any more money to make any more malagas [journeys]" (MM, 1206).

In Samoa Margaret began a lifelong practice of recording her impressions of the field in group letters written for friends and family. With her grandmother in mind as the ideal reader, she developed in these letters a writing style that later made her work popular. She also wrote and received many individual letters which came every few weeks in a deluge of seventy or eighty at a time. No doubt speaking of herself, Margaret once commented on the tendency of women alone in the field "to be preoccupied with present or possible future relationships," more so than men.[3] The letters were surely a lifeline back to the United States, although they did have the disconcerting power to "wrench one's thoughts and feelings inappropriately away" from the matter at hand, the immersing of oneself in a strange culture (LF, 7).

Correspondence with Ruth Benedict was especially important. Although only extracts from the Samoan letters have been published, and the letters from this period have not been made available to scholars, one of the few people who had the privilege of reading the originals described them as love letters.[4] Certainly Ruth's letters were not, as Margaret later suggested, solely expressive of teacherly concerns for a "student to be followed with solicitude" (AW, 284). Ruth poured out her heart in them. After their parting in Arizona, she had begun her second trip to the Southwest with Margaret very much on her mind. Missing her constantly, she wrote obsessively and often: "I try to bring you close by the nearest, most routine facts—be thankful I spare you menus and Indian callers. . . . I'm getting a taste of what these three week gaps between letters will be. . . . I shall count off the year with the steamers' coming as the Indians do with their prayer-stick plantings . . ." (AW, 292).

Ruth's letters displayed anxiety about Margaret's health and well-being. One problem had improved, though; by the time Margaret got to Honolulu her neuritis had subsided considerably. Ultimately, Ruth felt sure Margaret possessed depths of resilience: "you are you and indomitable in the long run. After all this is the only safety in life . . . and we always fight through to it in agony of soul. . . . There is only one comfort that comes out of it—unbelievably—the sense that there is that sure something within us, no matter how often it is laid in ruins, that cannot be taken away from us." She went on, "Be very good to yourself. Eat all that is stupid and wholesome, sleep when it seems impossible, experiment with the light touch when it seems treachery . . ." (AW, 291–92). A month later she wrote, "Develop all the expedients you can against weeping—companionship is only one of them. I've had excellent ones: they range from brushing your teeth and gargling your throat with every onset, to playing you're your own daughter for a year. . . . But I know there is no clear-sightedness nor course of reasoning that will help—you have that already. God bless you . . . and make life easier for you" (AW, 299).

Away from Zuñi for a couple of days' rest at Santa Fe, Ruth walked in the mountains and day-dreamed about Margaret, who had written that she was appreciating the poems Ruth had given her at the start of her trip. Ruth replied, "I am glad you know how much of me is shut into your book of verses—I shall delight in having you feel me speaking them to you. Will you do one thing?—jot down the verses you wish you had or the ones that haunt you brokenly, and I'll send them to you" (AW, 294).

They continued to exchange comments on each other's verse. Ruth sent

Margaret two poems she was reworking, dealing with the disintegration of her relations with Stanley. She also sent them to Edward, though she told Margaret she thought he would misinterpret "For Seedbearing," with its reference to "the ecstasy she knew on summer mornings." Edward would no doubt find "an echo of his playgirl" in the poem; evidently he had wondered whether Ruth was just as much a New Woman as Margaret was. What she really had in mind, Ruth explained to Margaret, was "that time after heart-break when one is thrown back upon oneself," and the poem is full of imagery mourning Ruth's infertility (AW, 303).

But Ruth was more preoccupied with Margaret and the inevitable delay in their communications than with Edward's possible misunderstandings: "It will be one of this year's crosses not to be able to have your comments on my verses while they are fresh in my mind (AW, 303).

"Parlor Car—Santa Fe" most likely dates from this time. Ruth is on the train, chatting casually with a friend, perhaps Bunny, and hiding her emotional turmoil about Margaret beneath a veneer of conversation about art, theater, and philosophy:

> We are so wise! And out across these sands
> Men plant their feathered prayer-sticks in the moon
> Tonight, praying the gods of ancient pueblo sires.
> And we would dash our pride with naked hands
> To bury once a prayer-plume in the moon
> And pour in hearing ears our hot desires. (RFB, Box 108)

Margaret considered printing "Parlor Car" in An Anthropologist at Work, but evidently thought better of it. Perhaps it was too revealing.

Ruth, of course, had her own fieldwork to manage. She confided in Margaret that she was pleased to be handling the life of isolation: "Three years ago it would have been enough to fill me with terror. I was always afraid of depressions getting too much for me. . . . But that's ancient history now" (AW, 294). Her language skills remained poor. "I shouldn't learn Zuñi in three years," she wrote, expressing the hope that Margaret would pick up Samoan more quickly; "but then I compare our memory and our ears and [I] am quite prepared to have you speaking it in three months. It's lucky you never have been on a field trip with me, you'd be outraged at my slowness in language" (AW, 292).

Margaret kept her cheerful side for the field bulletins. In her letters to Ruth she poured out her troubles and woes. As she said later, "Matters of this kind are best kept for letters to the one person who may be expected to understand and sympathize with some particular heartache" (LF, 12). The effect was that Ruth worried about her more, forming a different impression than other friends.

A theme running through their correspondence was, of course, Edward Sapir. Ruth kept Margaret up with all the news. Louise Bogan, who had taken the plunge and married Raymond Holden, had told Ruth of Edward's visiting her in Boston before he made the move to Chicago. His timing had been unfortunate; it was the day "when Raymond's mother had elected to come and give her sanction to our wedded state." But Edward was "very swell," although he was also worried: "[He] thought Margaret looked very worn and tired when he last saw her. Do you think she'll bear up under that journey's long grind? Perhaps Samoa hasn't the aching, tearing kind of tropical oppression that Central America [where Louise had once lived] has. Perhaps it's higher and wilder." And she concluded, perhaps unfortunately given the later controversy about Mead's work in Samoa: "I trust Margaret to make something of nothing in almost any circumstances."[5]

Ruth found Edward increasingly disgruntled. She ventured a comment about the loveliness of individuality; his reply implied that she was perverse: "There is something cruel, Ruth, in your mad love of psychic irregularities. Do you not feel that you extract your loveliness from a mutely resisting Nature who will have her terrible revenge?" (SF, 18 Aug. 1925). Edward's emotional rivalry over Margaret was beginning to manifest itself in a clash of values, with Edward defending an increasingly conservative position. Behind his dismissive remarks lay a sense of aversion to those aspects of life that Ruth would come to term deviance and would be central to her anthropology and her sense of herself.

Margaret once recorded a dream about Ruth Benedict and Florence Sapir which emphasized Ruth's "mad love of psychic irregularities," the aspect of her character that Edward abhorred since it reminded him all too much of his wife's madness. In Margaret's dream the figure representing Florence had a face that was "dead white, the eyes were frozen pits of hell, the face was like a mask which reveals more than any mere face. . . . She was mad, and yet much more real and vivid and convincing than any of the other people." As horrible as the face was, Ruth appeared to be "exulted," taking Margaret by the hand and saying, " 'Here is a face where we can really look at stripped reality!' " Margaret remembered that in reality Florence Sapir had given the opposite impression, "of someone wasted to nothing, not heightened to everything, by madness." But she understood that the point of the dream was really to "comment on R's use of terror and horror as documentation" (MM, A21).

Ruth arranged to visit Edward on her way home from Zuñi. In Chicago she had dinner with him, his mother, and the children. Afterward, Edward took her back to her hotel where she patiently listened to his outpourings until after midnight. He had received his first batch of letters from Margaret and was willing to show her the first group letter and the suggestions that Margaret had made about his poetry manuscript. The personal letters he kept to himself.

According to a letter Edward later wrote to Ruth apologizing for his behavior that night, they also quarreled, with Edward accusing Ruth of being a go-between who always took Margaret's side and "of being a self-appointed confirmatory gloss." But now he wondered, "How could I fail to know that you say nothing that is not sincerely yours and that you are not a diplomat?" and begged her to "forbear for the present, please, and put me on indefinite parole" (SF, 3 Oct. 1925). Although the rift was healed, the accusations that Edward had made that evening in Chicago were the beginning of the end for their friendship.

Back in New York, Ruth's life resumed its outer form much as usual, though without Margaret. She returned to Stanley at Bedford Hills and, as usual, rented a weekday apartment near Columbia for the academic year, when she would continue in her honorary lecturer's position. She earned a little extra money from teaching in Columbia's extension program and allowed herself to be nominated for the council of the American Anthropological Association.

In continuing on her independent path, Ruth relied on Stanley's forbearance, but on her return from the Southwest she found him "brooding over a chance remark overheard about her poems," which had been published that year in the prestigious *Poetry* magazine, as well as in *The Measure*. Stanley jealously guarded his privacy and was serious about keeping up conventional appearances. As Margaret told it, Stanley "had her take a copy of a poetry magazine which contained a group of her poems and paste new postage stamps over the name of every author; then he set himself the task of identifying the poems that were hers. She wrote me triumphantly: 'He got every one right' " (AW, 93).

Ruth wrote in her diary that she was more pleased that Stanley showed some insight into her inner life than alarmed that the poems might be traced to her (she had not even told Boas about "Anne Singleton") (RFB, Box 37). According to Margaret, the episode "inaugurated the best years of their marriage," though this must have been something of an exaggeration. Mead also acknowledged that "This was a temporary state, however, for the things she said in her verse were uncongenial to him. But it made it possible for her to work toward the publication of a book which would have appeared as the work of Ruth Benedict" (AW, 93).

It is hardly surprising that Ruth's verse was uncongenial to Stanley. Perhaps what Margaret meant was that when Stanley took an interest, Ruth in turn was courageous enough to expose something of herself and realized she could survive his disapproval. Sometimes he might even understand and sympathize; whatever the outcome, she could continue without brooking active opposition.

Cracks continued to appear in Ruth's friendship with Edward. There was the usual give-and-take about poetry, but with a change in Edward's attitude. Now he insisted on the importance of Ruth's poetry to the disparagement of her career in anthropology, making remarks such as, "It is no secret between us that I look upon your poems as infinitely more important than anything, no matter how brilliant, you are fated to contribute to anthropology" (SF, 11 March 1926). He did applaud Ruth's professional successes, though, and tried, unsuccessfully, to help her win a research fellowship. But it was to Margaret, not Ruth, that he now spoke of offering a position at Chicago. He continued to share news of Margaret, writing to Ruth in October: "Margaret's batch of letters from Samoa were in variable mood but towards the end she was very happy. It was a joy to read her last letters and know her so joyous and confident. . . . She evidently talks Samoan by now. It was a foregone conclusion she would master the language very quickly" (SF, 15 Oct. 1925). A short while later, he asked Ruth for news of Margaret and commented plaintively: "Now she will be at Tau, in the thick of the real work. I do wish, Ruth, somebody could explain to me once and for all why one studies primitive customs" (SF, 9 Nov. 1925).

Christmas brought the usual deluge of letters for Margaret. There were Ruth's, of course, and Edward was writing voluminously. The plan to drop Edward, which Margaret had devised with Ruth's cautious approval, was now in action, but in response he sent a torrent of letters arguing his case, accompanied by such overheated poetry that Margaret came to feel that romantic love had clouded his perceptions. She had become a figment of his imagination, "just an idea in his head," some idealized representation of womanhood (JH). In Edward's poems, her eyes and her hair changed color as his fantasies ran riot evoking this oddly sophisticated and pigheaded young woman with whom he was in love. "Nostalgic Ditty," "one of my favorites," as he told Ruth, whom he had the nerve to show it to, suggests the unrestrained and undignified nature of his emotions.

> My sweet by the fleet billows of the southern sea,
> Under otherworldly willows, wistful, she
> Dreams back, a little weeping, to ecstacy
> That lovers, we, did come on casually.
>
> The little yellow-haired girl dreams back from the south
> To where true Heaven blossomed between a mouth and a mouth. . . .

Oh sweet, write me the name of the exotic tree
Whereunder, the fingers locked in a revery,
You chose once to have a dream of beloved me
And all the faint secrets of our ecstacy.
(SF, 6 Sept. 1925; MM, Q15)

Edward was surprised at Margaret's reluctance to pursue her proper destiny which, he was convinced, must surely be linked with his. She responded angrily, yet even this failed to convince him that he had made the wrong choice. In a verse ("He Implores His Beloved Not to Answer Contumely with Silence") that was remarkable, or perhaps unremarkable, for its egotism, he declared,

when you twist wild words of pain for me
I know that rage may but a loving be.
Howe'er you point the tongue and shoot the arrow,
Your voice is love in my most inward marrow. (MM, Q15)

Margaret had few skills for dealing with the tumultuous feelings that she seemed to have provoked. In "Grave Clothes," insensitive to his bereavement, she wrote:

When love was dying
Pain torn and bowed
In resolute frenzy
I stitched it a shroud. . . . (MM, Q15)

As Christmas drew near, Margaret found that her supply of materials suitable for gifts had become severely strained. Samoans brought her presents "with much flourishing," she wrote in a group letter, "then they fold their hands and say complacently: 'Now I am ready.' And I explain that it is our outlandish custom to give Christmas presents on Christmas" (MM, I206). She grew annoyed at the constant demands, and more than sixty years later Fa'apua'a, a now elderly Samoan woman who had been one of Mead's closest friends on Ta'u remembered, "We were like real sisters but sometimes when we were out together and gifts had to be given, she would cry, saying all her things were being given away, even though she knew that presents had to be given."[6]

Christmas passed, with Makelita bedecked in garlands from her Samoan friends. She decorated her room with a wreath from the Ash Can Cats bearing the motto "Home is Where Your Halo Is." At New Year on the island the wind began to rise and the "otherworldly willows" and "exotic trees" of Edward's imagination began to sway in a decidedly unromantic fashion. The whole population of the three villages of Ta'u had been planning to assemble in front of the dispensary after their church service and dance until they were given food, but this round of New Year festivities was canceled because of the weather. Instead, the Holts, Margaret, and two naval men then on the island made their own festive dinner and ate it themselves.

After dinner, with the winds still rising, the *papalagi* (Europeans) stood on the porch and watched the Samoan buildings topple one after another. The eye of the storm came, all was menacingly still, then the wind ripped furiously across the island from the other direction. The house was abandoned and they all crouched in the cement water tank which had been emptied as a precaution. There they remained, ankle deep in water and holding the babies until the storm abated. The hurricane left only five houses standing in the village, theirs one of them.

News of the destruction of Ta'u soon made its way to the United States. Ruth had spent New Year's Eve in New York with Edward, who seemed surprisingly free of his agonizing over Margaret. Ruth confided in her diary, "I've never seen him more alive; all his turmoil has gone like a last week's thunderclap, nor even bitterness for a residue. It's evaporated. He couldn't summon the nerve to tell me about 'something else,' but 'he'll write.' Obviously another love affair. O gods and little fishes!" (RFB, Box 37).

Edward put Ruth on the 1:55 A.M. train for Norwich and as it sped northward, she spent two hours writing to Margaret, no doubt telling her this news. New Year at Norwich was a family occasion, with her sister Margery and her family visiting from California. Ruth spent a morning in the attic rummaging through antiques and reading a family diary that had survived from the eighteenth century, with its "good 1776 pessimist pages" (RFB, Box 37). Two days later, back in New York, she went with some anthropology friends to a disappointing party, populated by "soulful females and maiden aunts and uncles" (RFB, Box 37). Next day she had tea with a fellow anthropologist, Paul Radin, who was bursting with gossip about Edward, telling Ruth all about Jean, the new woman in Edward's life: "It's a full grown affair" (RFB, Box 37).

Edward, apparently, was entirely serious. "It's to be as noble as ever the virtues in their day," Ruth wrote in her diary. "I stormed. I don't know why it was so much worse to know than to guess it. Fortunately Ruth B[unzel] took me home to dinner . . ." (RFB, Box 307). Ruth had been hurt by Edward's affair with Margaret but had struggled to keep her feelings at bay while she counseled them both from the unenviable position of someone whose heart was torn in both directions. Now all the effort seemed to have been a matter of little consequence.

The same day Ruth had letters from Margaret, who had been ill. "I could hardly bear it," Ruth exclaimed in the diary. She would have been able to bear it even less had she made time to look at the newspapers that day, as they contained news of the hurricane. She replied the following day, so as to catch the outgoing mail. The next day brought a devastating letter from Margaret's mother "referring to the tornado in Samoa. Telephoned everywhere and could find no news. Then Mrs. Bunzel found it in Monday's paper—Manua especially razed. Wrote Mrs. Mead and sent last letter to M.M. for this boat. Sent cable for Dr. Boas to M—asking for reply" (RFB, Box 37).

Ruth waited anxiously each day that followed. To distract herself she worked intently proofreading her Cochiti tales. Marie Eichelberger matched this state of high anxiety, telegraphing her four times in nearly as many days. Finally, on 12 January, nearly a week after news of the hurricane, Boas phoned Ruth late in the evening. She noted in her diary: "Margaret cables, 'Well.' I sent telegrams to the Meads and to Marie, and took a hot bath like a ritual" (RFB, Box 37).

It was Ruth who told Luther about the hurricane and that Margaret was known to be safe. Margaret seldom communicated with her husband; he usually had to read her group bulletins to find out what she was doing. Several days after the good news, Ruth herself received a cable from Margaret. Succinctly, it said, "Love." Then Ralph Tynkham, an engineer who had known Margaret in Samoa, contacted Ruth and they lunched together. The next batch of letters from Margaret contained a description of the hurricane. Coincidentally, the same post brought Edward's confession of his new affair: "One from Edward telling me the 'something else.'" He apologetically told Ruth that "it needed distance from what had gone before." "Just so," noted Ruth acerbically (RFB, Box 37).

But if she felt worse about Edward, she was beginning to feel better about Margaret. "I'm more at ease about Margaret than before," she wrote in her diary. "Heaven knows whether I have any reason—but her letters seemed to me to have a better ring" (RFB, Box 37). Perhaps this was because Margaret had come through danger unscathed and was now halfway through her sojourn in Samoa.

By 1926 Ruth was suffering far less from the nervous strain she had been subject to in the early twenties; in fact she was blossoming, despite Margaret's absence. She was fond of Léonie Adams, who was still in the midst of her great preoccupation with Louise Bogan and told Ruth that she could not stop thinking about her. Léonie was thrilled that Margaret had sent her the ideal birthday present, a fare to Boston so that she could visit the object of her affection. Louise also visited New York from time to time; on one occasion they all went to *Hedda Gabler* together. Louise, Ruth remarked, "isn't happy but that would be a miracle. She's one of the most loveable of beings" (RFB, Box 37).

Stanley barely featured in Ruth's social life. Many of her friends, including Edward, never met him at all ("the shadowy Stanley," Edward once called him) (SF, 29 Sept. 1927). Margaret herself met him only three times. He was Ruth's companion during quiet weekends and summer vacations, and of course she was still financially dependent on him. But now Ruth had her own significant others, for all that they might cause her anxiety, grief, or disappointment. Her work preparing the Zuñi and Cochiti tales for publication was absorbing; it had supplanted the increasingly tedious work on the Southwest concordance, which she managed to pass on to someone more junior (and which, as a result, was never finished, despite the huge amount of money Elsie Clews Parsons had put into it).

Ruth had now gained a measure of professional recognition. Her teaching was popular despite her obvious handicaps and she had a gratifyingly large enrollment in her mythology class. Taking the risk of exposing herself as a poet, she gave a reading ("to those doubly elect," joked Edward in a play on the title of Léonie's first book) (SF, 11 May, 1926). Altogether, the entries in the diary she kept over January and February 1926 showed a much happier and more confident person than the woman of the 1923 diary, who had been close to a breakdown.

Around this time Ruth began to form a friendship with Natalie Raymond. Several 1926 diary entries refer to Nat, though they were excised when Mead published extracts. Nat was twenty-one years old, a couple of years younger than Margaret. Her stepfather was a wealthy businessman and her mother a well-known hostess in Pasadena, where Ruth's sister, Margery, lived and where Ruth had spent two unhappy years teaching high school. Probably she met Nat through a family connection. On Monday, 11 January 1926, after the outrage about Edward and in the midst of her anxiety about Margaret, Ruth noted, "Also called on Nat in passing. Home at 1.30 A.M." On the following Monday she wrote verse, had lunch with Bunny, endured a session in the afternoon with Elsie Clews Parsons, and then went "down to Nat's at 6. She opened the door in the dark in her pajamas—Kate was in bed sick and they'd been asleep. She's out of a job but about to look for one with more pay. Left Kate and and took Nat to Waverly Inn. A gay soul" (RFB, Box 37).

A couple of weeks later Ruth invited Nat, her roommate Kate, and a couple of others to a reading by Louise Bogan. But first they had to endure a tortuous performance from a less accomplished poet: "We just saved ourselves from the disgrace of hysterics. . . . It was a riot but I hope she didn't guess—we were behind her. . . . Louise was a lovely figure—read with an accent of disdain, very becoming" (RFB, Box 37). Nat does not crop up again in records of Ruth's life until the early 1930s, but the motif of an attractive, fun-loving young woman who could not hold down a job was to be recurrent.

Ruth's battle against Puritanism was certainly encouraged by her circle of friends. Now she could note with amusement the naiveté of an acquaintance who said of a friend's escapades, " 'Her husband is living, did you know? And she has men friends. That's so broad. I think it's just fine, don't you?' " Ruth wrote in exasperation, "What shall we do with the creature?" She also thought it amusing when someone she lunched with announced that she was "Miss by choice and not by necessity" and kissed Ruth "coming and going" (RFB, Box 37).

The attractions, affairs, and heartbreaks, both heterosexual and homosexual, that the supposedly New Women confided to Ruth provided her with a continuing source of entertainment. Margaret's college friend Marie Eichelberger was by now a confidante and she always had an ear for the latest gossip. Marie had recently told Margaret that a mutual friend had "once accused me of having a silly crush on you . . . [and] censured me for that extra-ordinary admiration and emotion." That friend, she went on, had not believed that Margaret was "capable of being fond of anyone properly, as she could not understand your marriage." Marie thought her friend was hypocritical, since "at the same time she was having an affair with Madge, which she must have recognized as being out of the ordinary" (MM, TR1). So it went on with the "oh-God-the-pain-girls," to use Léonie's phrase.

Margaret was fond of Edward, and though she was sincere in her plan to make him reject her, she was enraged when Edward wrote "that he didn't want to hurt me terribly but he had fallen in love with another young woman, despite his '10,000' letters of protestation." In an uncharacteristically impulsive action she made a bonfire of all his letters on the beach at Ta'u. She later told an interviewer, with some regret, that they were the record of one of the most "scintillating" minds of the day (JH). Edward, too, smarted. On one of the several occasions that he urged Ruth to drop her pseudonym, he added bitterly, "Lie outright if you have to, but for God's sake don't stylize the lie into a pretty institution. Leave those dodges to Margaret" (SF, 23 March, 1926).

Margaret's fieldwork had been substantially affected by the hurricane. As the villagers set to work rebuilding, the regular interviews with girls had to be suspended: "Informants were not to be had by love or money" (LF, 45). But untoward events are grist to the anthropologist's mill and Margaret turned to ethnological observation, recording the way this small society got itself back into shape. She watched the men building frameworks for new houses, the women weaving the walls and floor mats. She helped them sweep floors, learned to weave fine mats herself, went to church, and took part in moonlit fishing expeditions. She bathed with the children, enjoying the fresh water pool "with half a dozen handmaids to pour cool fresh water over you from coconut shells and wash your clothes, fetch your shoes and dry your hair" (LF, 47). She watched a pig being sacrificed for a birthday feast, and stood close enough for her white dress to be spotted with blood.

She also witnessed birth and death, and along with curious children, she stood at the side of a grave to look at a foetus being cut with a machete out of its mother's dead body for fear that it might come back as a ghost and take its revenge. This event haunted her in later dreams in which she imagined finding her own baby dead and decayed, accompanied by the vividly remembered smell of rotting flesh (MM, A21).

As time passed she felt more and more at home with the Samoans: "I find I am happiest here when I am alone with the natives, either bathing or lying on the floor of a Samoan house, watching the sea or making long flowery speeches to some old chief" (LF, 47).

As always, there were endless field notes to type up. Young, inexperienced, and with no colleagues to guide her, Margaret continued to worry about whether she was taking the right approach. She had written to Boas telling him how she was tackling the problem ("Margaret Mead sends encouraging reports," he wrote to Elsie Clews Parsons. "I believe she is getting a good deal that will clinch the point that fundamental individual natures depend upon cultural setting more than upon hereditary or innate characteristics.")[7] But Margaret could expect no reassuring reply until near the end of her stay. She was not sure whether she should present her material statistically or as case studies, so she gathered material for both, realizing that the full writing up would have to wait until the fieldwork was over. The immediate recording of events and inquiries needed all her attention, and it would have been "flagrant wastefulness" to be diverted because she was worried that her funders would want to see a detailed report (MM, N1).

In a letter to Boas written within three weeks of her arrival on Ta'u, Margaret outlined her impressions of the life of the adolescent girl, commenting that "discussion of sex and religious matters will have to wait upon my obtaining greater linguistic practice" and bemoaning "the fact that no one has ever learned this language in less than 18 months" (MM, N1). Months later she received his reply, reassuring her and advising that often the very best information came across in the last few days in the field, as "by the time of your departure the people will become more and more attached to you and more and more willing to tell you what you want to know" (MM, N1).

Later on Margaret reported that "my work is going nicely. I have finished, with the exception of a few gaps." For her intensive study of sixty-six girls, she now knew around thirty percent "intimately" and was "acquiring new intimacies every day," giving her the information she needed for the case studies and the tabular chart of details on each. She went on, "There will remain for special investigation, her sexual life and any philosophical conflicts. These are of course the most difficult to get at, requiring the greatest facility in the language and the longest intimacy. And of course I have a good deal of material on both subjects already . . . [which] indicates a minimum of sexual activity before puberty and great promiscuity between puberty and marriage, coupled with a normal amount of laxity in the married state" (MM, N1).

Toward the end of her stay Margaret became friendly with Fa'apua'a, a young woman of her own age and the only taupou (ceremonial virgin) on the island until the title was graciously conferred on Margaret as well, as it had been in Tutuila earlier. Here she was given the name Fua-i-lelagi ("Flower of Heaven"). Accompanied by Fa'apua'a and visitors from the Bishop Museum in Honolulu, Margaret made the arduous journey by foot to the village at the other end of the island, Fa'apua'a's birthplace, where they stayed several days. Shortly afterward the opportunity came to take a voyage by rowboat to the outlying islands of Ofu and Olosega. With her "merry companions," Fa'apua'a and her best friend, Fofoa, Margaret made a ten-day journey. The girls acted as Margaret's "talking chiefs," cooking for her, washing her clothes, and seeing that she handled formal occasions with proper etiquette. For their efforts they were handsomely rewarded with three new dresses each.

In mid-April, Margaret made her farewells to the villagers of Ta'u before returning to Tutuila for a warm visit to Fa'amotu and her family. From Pago Pago she sailed for Sydney, Australia, where she would begin the ocean voyage to Europe underwritten by her father in his fit of generosity. Secure in the knowledge that she had the job at the Museum of Natural History, she looked forward to picking up the threads of her life again. In Europe she expected to be reunited with both Luther and Ruth.

Any account of Mead's work on Samoa must consider the controversy surrounding its accuracy. In 1983, several years after her death, Derek Freeman published his detailed refutation of her work. More recently, Freeman has continued his attack with attempts to prove that Mead built her description of adolescent sexuality on scanty information gleaned from a hoax perpetrated by her informants.[8] He has also argued that she was young and credulous, that she had a poor grasp of the language, that she did not carry out her investigations properly, that *Coming of Age in Samoa* is littered with errors, that she twisted the facts to suit her (and Boas's and Benedict's) preconceptions, and that she was entirely wrong in her portrayal of Samoa.

Freeman's work caused an instant furor. Its publishers, Harvard University Press, organized unprecedented publicity for an academic book and the media enjoyed the opportunity to dent the reputation of a celebrity. Many anthropologists leaped to Mead's defense and Freeman was censured at an American Anthropological Association meeting, but her public image had by then been thoroughly tarnished.[9]

In the wake of Freeman's claims, there have been endless debates and reexaminations of Mead's Samoan work, both in the United States and in the Pacific, some of them favorable toward Mead, most including points of criticism, and most also taking issue with Freeman's perspective. The discipline reeled, aghast, as one anthropologist put it, that the field had become "a shooting gallery, not a scholarly discussion."[10]

Freeman himself kept stirring the pot, and in 1996 his views again received a thorough airing in the Southern Hemisphere when David Williamson, a well-known Australian playwright, made Freeman the hero of *The Heretic*.[11] The play showed the now elderly, New Zealand-born academic pitted against the contemporary forces of cultural determinism, sexual radicalism, and political correctness. The mother of these forces was, of course, Margaret Mead, whom it was heresy to challenge.

Freeman's *Margaret Mead and Samoa* is a scholarly book researched with painstaking attention to detail. No one would dispute that Freeman, with his lifelong interest in Samoa, is more knowledgeable about his subject than Mead was at the tender age of twenty-three. However, many have argued that his picture of Samoan life as crime-ridden and marked by competition, aggression, jealousy, and strict controls on sexual expression is just as far off the mark as Mead's.

Freeman's work is imbued with a hostility that goes beyond the usual bounds of academic rivalry. Though he has often insisted that he admires Mead, he appears to have taken excessive delight in his role as the instrument of her downfall. "She's doing a 22," he told an interviewer, "22 feet per second being the rate of speed at which bodies fall. . . . The opposite of doing a 22 is rising like a phoenix. But I don't think Margaret is going to rise from the ashes. If she does, she'll be a bedraggled old bird. . . . Her reputation is going to collapse inwards. She is going to be a black hole. . . ."[12] In a grandiose manner, Freeman seemed to believe that his critique felled the whole of cultural anthropology; he told an interviewer proudly that his students called him "the death-watch beetle of cultural anthropology."[13] He has also tried, with undeniable malice, to demonstrate that Mead's private life colored her view of Samoa. He asserted to colleagues that Mead had sex with a young Samoan man: "that's what really distresses Samoans . . . these implications of Margaret Mead that Samoan women are promiscuous . . . [when] She had an affair with a profligate Samoan."[14] He accused her of being prejudiced against men: "Mead was known as a castrator: she went for men and put them down."[15] And after Mary Catherine Bateson's disclosures about her mother's relationship with Ruth Benedict, he claimed that it had been a *folie à deux* that had distorted Mead's work (Howard). "Her own daughter has destroyed her in a way I never could have," he is said to have asserted after the publication of Mary Catherine Bateson's book.[16]

Freeman's accusations have raised two issues of concern about Mead's work in Samoa. One has to do with the book that resulted from the fieldwork, *Coming of Age in Samoa*, and Freeman's claim that it is a deeply flawed piece of work. In many ways his argument rests on a purist strain of scientific realism and a belief that Mead's work, when measured against those standards, is wanting. In light of today's understanding of the social construction of science, the suggestion that anthropology says as much about anthropologists as it does about the cultures they study would not be a startling claim; it would be more of a truism than a slur. We need to ask, then, whether *Coming of Age* is, as Freeman claims, a false book or merely an inevitably imperfect one. Indeed, Mead herself knew well that observers bring their own preoccupations to the field, speaking often about "disciplined subjectivity" and the necessity of working without undue interference from one's personal reactions to the material (LF, 5). These issues, however, will be discussed in chapter 8, "The Deviant and the Normal."

The other question has to do with Mead's experience in Samoa, rather than the ways she interpreted and transformed those experiences once she put pen to paper. Freeman's claim that she had had an affair with a Samoan man may well be true. She observed that Polynesians, being "sophisticated" and "sexually attractive" to Europeans "will not hesitate to approach a European woman, and women fieldworkers may be tempted into inappropriate friendships."[17] She apparently told Luther that she had received advances from one young man and had rebuffed him, though there is a different story in Samoa, passed around by the man himself. Though it seems unlikely that the truth of the story will ever be sorted out entirely, her comment about "inappropriate friendships" suggests that she may indeed have developed some sort of entanglement which, not surprisingly, she later glossed over.[18] But any dissimulation engaged in by Mead about her own personal life (and there are several instances in this biography) hardly reflects her character as a scientist. Western culture expects sexual life to be private and not subject to the high standards of evidence, truth telling, and replicability required by scientific investigation.

The suggestion of Freeman that Mead was the victim of a hoax in Samoa is a much more troublesome charge, however, and one that bears examination.

It is not possible to establish exactly how Margaret broached the issues of masturbation, homosexual and heterosexual experiences, and related topics, for she left no records of what questions she asked or of whether she ran into difficulties with her informants. Other commentators on Samoa make it clear that talking about the intimate details of sexual experience is not common practice, though certainly joking and teasing about sexual matters abound in young people's conversations. They point out that the Samoan language does not contain many of the words to describe sexual experience that westerners use in research or medical contexts, a difference that has become problematic in recent efforts to prepare educational materials about AIDS.[19] Mead, however, conducted several long and detailed interviews with informants other than the young girls, including a male Samoan schoolteacher, almost certainly English-speaking, who provided her with considerable details about sexual practices. Her notes include explicit terms referring to the details of sexual anatomy and sexual positions (MM, N4).[20] She also relied for her information on "the Samoan love for pedantic controversy," often finding that she could simply propound a question to a group and listen to the ensuing argument.[21]

The extent to which she conversed with her young women in English has also been a matter of controversy, and it must be said that Mead misled readers of Coming of Age about the matter, just as she provided inconsistent information about the length of time she spent on her investigation.[22] It is also true that while Mead had copied from a Samoan dictionary a list of words pertaining to childbirth, the list did not cover all the areas of experience that she investigated. On the other hand, it did include terms for hermaphrodite (fa'afafine, not a strictly correct translation), abortion (tampapa), menses ('ele'ele), and pregnancy (ma'ito) (MM, N2). Furthermore, Mead, who was certainly resourceful, most probably asked amidst the usual joshing, teasing, and gesturing that characterized conversations among girls, such unspecific questions as "do you do it with so-and-so?"[23]

There are no specific words or concepts in Samoan language referring to lesbian activities, though the fa'afine, the womanly man, is a well-known feature of Samoan life. However, we know from the history of love between western women that a lack of words does not rule out experience or communication about sexual matters, and Mead did have English-speaking informants.[24] Moreover, women talk to each other in ways that exclude men. Still, it would have been helpful if Mead had more thoroughly documented this aspect of her investigation.

Mead's data on the young women was recorded in the form of pen portraits describing each girl's appearance, personality, family relationships, and life situation; additionally, there are charts which appear as appendixes in *Coming of Age in Samoa* which denote by means of a tick or cross whether each girl, identified by means of a pseudonym, had had particular experiences, including homosexual and heterosexual ones. These would have been of no more than technical interest had Freeman not challenged the validity of Mead's entire study with the specter of a hoaxing.

Freeman argues that hoaxing occurred when Margaret made journeys with Fa'apua'a toward the end of her stay. His trump card, displayed after the publication of *Margaret Mead and Samoa*, was the tracing of Mead's "merry companion," now in her eighties, with the help of Samoan friends in high places. Fa'apua'a told him that she and her friend had misled Margaret, swearing on the Bible that Margaret had embarrassed the two of them so much by interrogating them about sexual practices that they had resorted to a time-honored Samoan custom of teasing and making up stories about their exploits. "We said that we were out at nights with boys," Fa'apua'a said; "she failed to realize that we were just joking and must have been taken in by our pretences. Yes, she asked: 'Where do you go?' And we replied 'We go out at nights!' 'With whom?' she asked. Then, . . . Fofoa and I would pinch one another and say, 'We spend the nights with boys, yes, with boys!' She must have taken it seriously but I was only joking. As you know Samoan girls are terrific liars when it comes to joking. But Margaret accepted our trumped up stories as though they were true."[25]

In a video excerpt from this same interview, Fa'apua'a, with Samoan elders standing over her, can be observed rubbing her nose as she makes her "confession," a gesture that may raise some doubts about the veracity of her testimony.[26] She may also have been involved in a face-saving strategy among the Samoans, some of whom were not happy with the image of their culture associated with *Coming of Age*. Mead probably was teased by her "merry companions," as Fa'apua'a claims. Whether she believed what they told her is another matter. She was not one to be easily duped; "She was never duped by anyone," was the categorical assertion of one anthropologist who had worked with her in the field.[27] And when the occasion called for it, she could be a reasonably accomplished liar herself—for example, in Samoa Mead passed herself off as unmarried so that she could easily mingle with the girls.

Our examination of the "Samoan hoax accusation" shows that it does not stand up against the evidence on other grounds as well. A recent detailed investigation by Martin Orans, an anthropology professor at the University of California, Riverside, has carefully examined the extensive collection of Mead's Samoan field materials in the Library of Congress.[28] Nowhere among them are any records of the supposed hoax, though Mead assiduously kept records of extended conversations with informants. There are frequent references in her notes to cultural practices concerning sexuality, which make it clear that Mead understood these reasonably well, given her brief study. Although Orans is harshly critical of some aspects of Mead's work, claiming that she made many mistakes of detail and interpretation and that she went beyond the evidence, he is utterly convincing on the point that Freeman's claim about a hoax is unjustified.

# 7

*Never Break a Date With a Girl for a Man?*

P REPARING TO LEAVE S AMOA FOR E UROPE, Margaret wrote to her father that she loathed traveling alone (MM, N1). The first leg of the voyage from Pago Pago was miserable enough, the ship and its passengers surviving one of the worst storms for decades. At Sydney Margaret boarded the *Chitral*, which was unexpectedly confined to port because of a strike. Among the few passengers with nowhere to go, she remained on board; here she met Reo Fortune, a New Zealander on his way to graduate study in England. Missing her friends after months in the field, deprived of regular letters because she was in transit, lonely and starved of intellectual stimulation, Margaret was primed for an emotional adventure. She was immediately drawn to Reo, a tall, good looking, intensely serious, and rather awkward young intellectual.

Neither had money, so while the ship was in port they occupied themselves with incessant conversation. They were assigned their own dining table and when they did set sail fellow passengers seemed to assume they were having an affair: "We were not," said Margaret, "but we were falling in love, with all the possibility of a relationship that I felt was so profoundly unsuitable. Reo was so young, so inexperienced, so fiercely ambitious, and so possessively jealous of any fleeting glance I gave another person" (BW, 161).

A year younger than Margaret, Reo had an unusual background. His father was an Anglican priest who in late middle age turned away from the church to become a dairy farmer at Raumati, near Wellington in the North Island of New Zealand. Reo's mother resented the social comedown and disliked milking and other chores which fell to her. Since Peter Fortune had long decided that his true love was his wife's younger sister, sourness pervaded the family atmosphere. Arguments between husband and wife were common, and Reo's father may have occasionally used physical violence against his wife. Certainly, Margaret listened in surprised disbelief when Reo told her about his Irish grandfather, "who was said to have locked his wife in the kitchen with a stallion, telling her 'I hope he damn well stamps you to death!' " (BW, 161).[1]

The Fortunes placed a high value on education and were united with pride over Reo's academic achievements. His name, the Maori word for "language," meant, in the biblical sense, "The Word." As a student Reo had worked his way through university, missing classes as he could not afford lodgings in Wellington all year round. He showed a strong aptitude for languages and might have become a classics scholar had his interests not turned to psychology, a newly developing discipline at Victoria University College. While still an undergraduate he began research on dreams and on graduating won a scholarship to Cambridge University. This was the pinnacle of achievement for a young scholar; many Pakeha New Zealanders (those of European descent), in one of the most farflung British dominions, then looked to Britain as their intellectual, cultural, and economic home.

Reo had embarked on the journey troubled by romantic problems. Despite his wooing her with screeds of poetry, a girl had rejected him; he was sexually inexperienced and told Margaret that his romance with Eileen had been unrequited. She believed him at the time, but later scribbled, with a stab of doubt, "Or was it?" on a draft page of her autobiography. Reo may have seemed a little unsophisticated and rough around the edges to Margaret, a full-fledged New Yorker, but they delighted in finding much in common beyond a consuming interest in anthropology and psychology and their love of poetry. Both were eldest children whose parents had experienced marital difficulties; their fathers, with whom they had ambivalent relationships, were atheists and stood out as unusual, even eccentric, in the small rural communities where they lived. The tradition of strong-willed, career-oriented, and opinionated women in Margaret's family was not, however, a pattern familiar to Reo.

Before long Reo had prevailed on Margaret to record her dreams as a contribution to his research. The newly available collection of dreams in Mead's papers dates from this time and, supplemented by Margaret's interpretive comments, the dreams illustrate her misgivings about the developing romance and her anxieties about meeting Luther in Marseilles. Other themes include conflicts about sexuality, fear of being a bad influence on others, and anxieties about her own work and health. Margaret was not well during the voyage, suffering from seasickness as well as accumulated exhaustion from her intensive fieldwork. She wrote to Boas and also recorded in her dream notebook that she was worried about making little progress in writing up her materials (MM, N1, A21).

The first dream she recorded most likely drew its impetus from a real life event, Reo's convincing her they should drop their inhibitions and tell their dreams. In another dream, Reo contracts scarlet fever from nursing (scarlet fever symbolizing to Margaret both falling in love—the color red—and Margaret's being a "contaminating influence") (MM, A21). In another dream she rushes to catch a train, fearing that if she missed it she would be too late to meet Luther. This reflected, according to Margaret's analysis, "a general sense of guilt" about meeting Luther in Europe and the fear that it might be "too late" to save the marriage (MM, A21).

The "contamination" theme took a lesbian turn in another dream, where she and a woman friend are working in Margaret's bedroom. The woman "suggested we go to bed to keep warm. I consented. She insisted in wrapping herself all up in a piece of mosquito netting, for 'hygienic reasons,' so that she wouldn't get my breath. I reflected that the listerine was all gone so perhaps that was just as well." The character in the dream, Margaret noted, stood for a friend "whose work and capacity for thought were definitely ruined by marriage and a sinking into domesticity" and who had scolded Margaret for "behaving in an unnatural fashion and leaving my husband for a year" (MM, A21). Margaret comes across in the dream as "unnatural" in her devotion to work, her neglect of men and, symbolically, in her relations to women.

Anxieties about her field trip surfaced more pointedly in a dream she called "The Mockery of My Work," in which Margaret realizes with "wounded pride and annoyance" that her book on Samoa had been published with a silly and inaccurate cover reminiscent of another book that she considered "a decorative and unscientific piece of work, showy and unsound" (MM, A21). Mead's own book, embarrassingly, is titled "Seekings for Sin." A related dream drew on her apprehensions about her relationship with Reo harming his career.

However one might judge the outcome of Reo's and Margaret's collaboration in anthropology—it was Margaret who persuaded him to switch from psychology—at the beginning it was Reo whose interference was detrimental, contributing, she believed, to a problem that occasionally surfaced throughout Margaret's career and erupted into scandal after her death. This, of course, was the question of the validity of Mead's work on Samoa. The first wrong step was taking Reo's advice not to attend the conference of the British Association for the Advancement of Science in England that summer. Bronislaw Malinowski, the Polish anthropologist whose recently published *Argonauts of the Western Pacific* had set a new benchmark for ethnographic fieldwork, was to be there, and Margaret told Reo how much she looked forward to meeting him. Reo obviously knew the story of Margaret's romance with Edward Sapir, which had begun two years earlier at the same conference in Toronto. He developed the fixed idea that this would be a repeat performance: "Reo was already fascinated by Malinowski, but he was also jealously determined that I should not go to the meeting in England, where, he was convinced, Malinowski would certainly seduce me" (BW, 159).

Malinowski did have something of a reputation as a womanizer, as Margaret knew from Ruth's letters. But Ruth's initial impression was favorable: "I had such a good time yesterday with Malinowski. . . . You'd like him a lot. He has the quick imagination and the by-play of a mind that makes him a seven-days' joy. . . . It's intriguing to find an intelligent person discovering with such force the things we've been brought up on with our mother's—or Papa Franz's!—milk" (AW, 305). Edward Sapir met him as well, finding him brilliant, but also "damned conceited" and a "belligerent romanticist" (SF, 11 May 1926). Malinowski, who enjoyed shocking his contemporaries, had arrived in Chicago exclaiming, "My God, will somebody find me a woman!" and in New York he had offended Zora Neale Hurston, who was then a Columbia anthropology student, by slipping money into her stocking (BW, 159). Malinowski's reputation, according to Margaret, was "very likely [mostly] a pose, but in Reo's New Zealand eyes, [his] behavior appeared to be that of a shocking roué" (BW, 159).

Reo's jealousy was so unremitting that Margaret gave way, but she would always regret missing the opportunity of meeting Malinowski, who became one of her principal detractors. On his American visit he had told people that Margaret's Samoan trip "would come to nothing, that nine months was too short a time to accomplish any serious research, and that I probably would not even learn the language" (BW, 160). She came to harbor the suspicion that Edward Sapir, who had grown hostile toward her in the aftermath of their affair, might have influenced Malinowski, and she may have been right; Derek Freeman says that a decade later Sapir told another anthropologist that Mead was "a prostitute and a pathological liar" (Howard).

To have such an eminent detractor always troubled Margaret considerably, even though Malinowski, with his competitive nature, was well known for insulting remarks. Had Margaret met him at the conference, his attitude might have been hardly different. Malinowski was trying to create a new British school of social anthropology so named to distinguish it from Boasian cultural anthropology.[2] A charismatic leader, he surrounded himself with loyal disciples, liking to emphasize that his approach was entirely new and different, though Boasians believed it was not. However, they did acknowledge the outstanding quality of Malinowski's work, and the competitiveness seemed mostly his.

With his flair for self-publicity, Malinowski played a major role in creating that cultural icon of the twentieth century, the anthropological fieldworker, who, "by pitching his tent in the middle of the village, learning the language in its colloquial form, and observing native life directly," did what no European had ever done quite like this before. Malinowski laid the foundations for the myth of the anthropologist-as-hero, "the lone Ethnographer [who] encountered the precontact Primitive, distilled the essence of a particular cultural 'otherness,' and brought back to civilization an exotic, esoteric knowledge of universal human import."[3]

Margaret, with her work in Samoa, was also engaged in the heroic quest. But as a woman on her first fieldwork expedition, limited to some extent by her sex and youth and subject to her own frailties, she was clearly outclassed by Malinowski. And generosity toward potential rivals was not his strong suit. Though he was a wonderful mentor to his own students—including a number of women who went on to make their mark, such as Hortense Powdermaker and Camilla Wedgwood—it was well known that "belligerence characterized many arguments with his peers."[4]

Malinowski's reputation suffered after his death, just as Mead's has. The publication of his fieldwork diaries in the 1960s caused a scandal nearly as significant as Freeman's attack on Mead. The diaries revealed a tarnished hero who had more contact with the colonizers he so reviled than he had given his early readers to understand, who made frequent derogatory references to "niggers," and who was prone to fits of murderous rage.[5]

Luther Cressman waited anxiously for Margaret in Marseilles. He had heard from her infrequently during his year abroad and in England he had met Dorothy Loch, an older woman more sympathetic than Margaret had ever been. Observing the proprieties, they had "respected" Luther's marriage, the only lapse being when Luther sent Dorothy a "fervent love letter" shortly before setting off for France (GJ, 175). As the Chitral drew into port, Luther paced the wharf. The passengers disembarked with no sign of Margaret. She was still arguing with Reo who wanted her to continue with him to England. "Finally," as she later wrote, "sensing that the ship was not moving, we walked around the deck and saw Luther standing on the dock, wondering what had happened to me. That is one of the moments I would take back and live differently, if I could. There are not many such moments, but that is one of them" (BW, 162).

Luther recalled that he was "almost ill with disappointment and the fear that something had happened to Margaret. Just then she appeared at the head of the gangplank with a tall, rather handsome young man, who zipped back out of sight when he saw me. Margaret, very crestfallen and completely without enthusiasm, met me as I hurried to her. . . . The luckless nature of our meeting and Margaret's sense of depression and lack of enthusiasm enveloped us both in a smothering cloud of dejection." He had booked a hotel room; they made love, though the rapprochement was brief. Margaret reminded him of their pact that neither would stand in the way of the other's loving someone else and let it be known that she wanted to marry Reo. Luther, though upset, was proud of responding sympathetically toward Margaret rather than "as a husband whose honor has been challenged" (GJ, 176).

It seems likely that Luther conveniently avoided telling Margaret about his feelings for Dorothy Loch, allowing himself the role of the wronged one. When Margaret shouted at a cabdriver, he decided that she "was obviously in a state of extreme emotional tension to the extent of being capable of irrational behavior" (GJ, 177).

Louise Rosenblatt, who had spent the year at Grenoble, joined the unhappy couple, who "pretended things were all right between them," for a tour of the South of France.[6] It was a torturous time, Luther recalled. Less forthrightly, Margaret noted that "those days remain etched in my mind" (BW, 162). The time she had spent in Samoa put her at a distance, a feeling of estrangement which is commonly experienced by returning fieldworkers. A figure representing Katharine Rothenberger appeared to her in a dream that resonates with conflicts about sexuality and loss, while in her conscious mind she battled with the dilemma of whether to divorce Luther and marry Reo. At Carcassone she decided in favor of Luther. It was a decision that would not last for long.

When Margaret, Luther, and Louise arrived in Paris, friends from New York were congregating. "Everyone in the world is here and I have difficulty in dodging people long enough to see Europe," Margaret wrote to her grandmother (MM, O40). Although exhausted, anxious, and unwell, there was café life, sightseeing, theatergoing, and shopping. One commission was to buy a wedding dress for her Samoan friend, Fa'amotu, who wanted to be seen in haute couture. Margaret bought the dress at the Galerie Lafayette, while Parisian dresses with outrageous prices appeared in her dreams. She mailed it off, but instead of the expected thanks, she had this reply: "Makelita, make your heart smooth, do not be angry, but something awkward has happened, my fiancé has married someone else" (BW, 156).

Tensions between Margaret and Luther became so obvious that Margaret felt Louise needed an explanation and confided in her. She had received a letter from Reo giving no return address and telling her he was coming to Paris. Dreams from this time show Margaret's apprehensions about his unscheduled and potentially disruptive visit. One features an argument between the men in her life about whether she "should be allowed to do as she liked about men," with Luther defending Margaret's right to choose. In another, Margaret sets off to meet Reo, "terribly uncertain" as to whether he will come or not, and Luther helps her pick blackberries (a fruit with a markedly different color to the red strawberries of her earlier dream about Reo) (MM, A21).

Reo's visit to France did not begin well for him, as he recorded in an account of a disturbing dream, replete with phallic images, of being beaten on the buttocks at customs because he had undeclared cigarettes (RF, Box 18). When Reo was due to arrive at the hotel, Luther, trying to remain calm in the face of competition, decided to go out, but as he was explaining to the concierge that Margaret was expecting a young man, "a tall, good-looking young lad stepped up beside me and interrupted my conversation with the concierge without apology. 'Tell Miss Mead that Mr. Fortune is here.'" Luther introduced himself: "I am Luther Cressman, Reo, and Margaret is expecting you." "Reo was speechless," he recalled (GJ, 178–79).

Margaret was thrown into confusion by these events, as dreams following Reo's arrival indicate. In one she dreamed that Marie Eichelberger was sure that Margaret was keeping a secret from her. In another, Reo, Edward, Ruth, and Marie all turn up at Margaret's family home and there is confusion about the sleeping arrangements.

One dream from this time was used, in a disguised fashion, by Reo in his subsequent monograph on dreams, The Mind in Sleep. The original dream is available in manuscript form, and Reo's published interpretation throws light on some of the conflicts at the time. In the dream, Margaret fails to perform certain religious duties (lighting a candle and swinging a censer). Reo suggests that the underlying issue is that the dreamer is embroiled in a conflict over whether to let down her defenses and embark on an extramarital affair. The "censer," according to Reo, also alludes to the dreamer's censoring a "deeply repressed sex tendency."[7]

Reo's interpretation implies that Margaret had worked through, at an unconscious level, her conflicts concerning fidelity to Luther and was ready to begin a sexual relationship with him. It is interesting that the dream interpretation also focuses on religious conflict, for Margaret's own accounts of this time emphasize practical and emotional dilemmas and her advocacy of open marriage, rather than religious issues. In contrast, Luther tells us that he and Margaret viewed adultery as unacceptable, even though they believed that marriage should be based on love and should end if either partner fell in love with another. At that time, of course, Luther was unaware of Margaret's attempted adultery with Edward Sapir and he seems not to have understood the nature of her relationship with Ruth Benedict.

Reo, too, seems to have been insensitive to Margaret's same-sex relationships. The "censer" dream contains a Ruth Benedict figure, a "rather heterodox female" who comes to Margaret's aid, lighting the candle and swinging the censer for her. Reo's interpretation does not refer to this other woman in the dream, whereas much could have been made of her role, especially since Benedict's arrival in Paris was also imminent. Whether Margaret herself felt that homosexuality counted as adultery is unclear; perhaps she did not, since it could be seen in its culturally acceptable guise as romantic friendship. But whatever Margaret's views on fidelity, her most pressing problem was the threat Reo posed to her marriage. That she did not love Luther made the situation no less threatening.

Luther decided to return to New York early, offering the excuse that he had just accepted a job teaching sociology at City College. In the days before leaving he tried to make himself scarce, although one evening, when he returned earlier than expected, he could not avoid the sight of Margaret and Reo embracing at the hotel entrance. Luther made a gesture of friendship toward Reo, inviting him to a dinner he gave for Margaret and her friends. Reo seemed to find this mystifying, expecting outright hostility from someone whose wife he was forcefully wooing.

Although Luther was distressed, his tolerance went as far as his helping Margaret with contraception after she had asked for advice "in case she and Reo went together." Luther had studied the birth control movement and in England had met Marie Stopes, the woman who set up the first birth control clinic there. He gave Margaret the address of a place where she could purchase the necessaries, a gesture that surprised her slightly, since in their marriage he had always taken the responsibility for contraception. Margaret later told him that she had made use of the address, but that her sexual relationship with Reo over the summer had been "frustrating and disappointing." No "intimacy" had taken place, she said, and Luther understood Margaret to mean that Reo had been impotent. Margaret's dreams from this time include reference to "spermatozoa," Barnard faculty members demanding an explanation of her behavior in church, Reo's things scattered over the floor, and racing around Paris with Reo in an automobile, trying to keep out of sight of the automobile's owner.

When the time came for Luther's departure, Margaret and Louise saw him off at the station, where Margaret cried and pleaded with him to tell her what to do about Reo. He told her that she needed to make up her own mind, "for through three years of marriage I had learned that Margaret did not welcome advice on behavior from men, and a husband in particular" (GJ, 180).

Ruth Benedict was not aware of the chaotic situation that would greet her in Paris. Communication between the two women had been slow while

Margaret was in Samoa, but at least it was regular. Once Margaret boarded ship it was difficult to exchange letters since Ruth was also leaving for Europe, along with Stanley, who would be presenting a paper in Sweden. Louise Bogan had initially hoped to travel with Ruth but changed her plans when she was offered a residency at the Yaddo art colony. After visiting Louise in Boston, Ruth spent her twelfth wedding anniversary alone before traveling to the lake to join Stanley. In England, she saw Stonehenge and Salisbury Cathedral, colleagues at Oxford, revisited Mary Wollstonecraft at the National Portrait Gallery, and noticed enough poverty and unemployment to be quite depressed about the state of the country. The couple then toured the Scottish Highlands, Norway, and Sweden, after which Stanley returned home, leaving Ruth free to meet Margaret in Paris.

Shortly before her arrival, Ruth had a letter from Margaret. The contents were a great shock to her because she had had no idea of Margaret's situation and she found it hard to forgive her. This was a sore point with Margaret even years later when she leaped to her own defense: "Letters could not catch up with me. . . . This was something Ruth never fully grasped; periodically, through the years, she would reproach me for that long six weeks without letters, when she had no idea what I was thinking, and when I was falling in love with Reo" (BW draft).

Margaret may have been protesting a little too much. Knowing how upset Ruth would be, she was most likely reluctant to break the news. She may have tried to soften the blow by having Louise Rosenblatt write to Ruth, for in the one available letter from this period, a hastily scrawled note, she asks Ruth anxiously if she has received Louise's letter and then makes a plea for sympathy, launching into an apology for the mess Ruth will find her in:

> Are you prepared to play nurse to a cranky invalid? I'm all of that. My sinuses are ghastly. I'm so tired I can't stay up for more than two or three hours at a stretch and just at present I'm cutting a wisdom tooth in a very wholesale fashion. It makes me sick. I did so want to enjoy Europe. I might just as well be in Kansas City. I've almost given up and gone home but I couldn't rest with my family and it's cheaper to live here. I haven't much money either. Only I'm not willing to spoil your summer with all my aches and pains and miseries. . . . I meant to bring you something better back. (MM, B14).

As she had done with Reo, Margaret dreamed anxiously about Ruth before her arrival. In the dream in which Reo, Edward, Ruth, and Marie all turn up at her father's house, she pictures Ruth as wearing her old feather hat and looking "shabby and tired":

She kisses me most affectionately & only then do I realize that this is the first time I have seen her for a year. She tells me how much she has liked some gift I've given her & gives me a picture she's written me about. It's the picture of a Zuñi ceremony . . . and is in a frame like my little Easter Madonna. She says might that be a valuable addition to a collection & I say "Yes" rather doubtfully. Then I notice that Sapir hasn't come and I ask why. (RFF, Box 18).

The image of a shabby, tired, and badly dressed Ruth bearing gifts of doubtful value shows Margaret in a frame of mind that did not augur well for a reunion. Her comments on the dream reveal her concern about paying sufficient attention to Ruth since she was so preoccupied with Reo.

Another dream has Margaret dwelling on the inevitable meeting between Ruth and Reo. She is in a railroad station waiting for Ruth when she sees a huge placard announcing "Mrs R. Benedict." Then Margaret sees Ruth "approaching very eagerly." Margaret takes a while to get to her, having to go around several obstacles. She kisses her and takes her back to a railroad carriage or taxi where Reo is waiting and introduces Reo to Ruth. He fails to stand up and his "lower lip sticks out very curiously." Later in the dream, she asks Reo why he behaved like that and he tells her that he was struck dumb by the difference in age between Margaret and Ruth and felt "awfully tender" (MM, A21).

Margaret's dream life at this time took her on a guided tour of her emotional connections to women. She dreamed of Ruth, she dreamed of Katharine Rothenberger, and she also had a dream about Marie Eichelberger being obsessively in love with someone who has been away in France. Marie consults a doctor who tells Margaret that when the love object returns, "it will start all over again. It would be better for them if one of them were dead." Margaret asks, "But can't you do anything for her?" and the doctor replies, "Not when she knows what's wrong and doesn't mind" (MM, A21). Marie did seem to know what was wrong with her emotional life, and she may have minded, but she also seemed resolved about the situation.

The real life reunion between Margaret and Ruth is not on record. It was surely an occasion of mixed emotions, probably including guilt and apprehension on Margaret's part and distress and jealousy on Ruth's. Margaret gave Ruth a tapa cloth as a souvenir of Samoa, and Ruth's gift, if she brought one, is recorded only in Margaret's anticipatory dream. Margaret managed to find time to spend with Ruth—it is not clear if Reo was still in Paris and Luther had already returned to the United States—and together they visited the tourist spots. Ruth was depressed, in the grip of her "blue devils." As they sat in a little churchyard looking at the splendid view of Notre Dame cathedral across the Seine, she said to Margaret, "Isn't it unbearable that that is all about nothing?" Margaret wrote later, "I can still recall the passionate repudiation in her voice" (AW, 85).

Paris in the 1920s was home to a sophisticated lesbian community, some of whose members were American expatriates Natalie Barney, Gertrude Stein, and Alice B. Toklas. Margaret and Ruth could hardly have been unaware of Parisian lesbian chic, as they would have been familiar with a similar phenomenon in Greenwich Village. It is not known whether they encountered this culture in their Parisian explorations, though in the 1970s, when Mead wrote about bisexuality in one of her popular *Redbook* columns, she mentioned the Parisian lesbian community.[8] Certainly while Margaret was in Paris, possibly in Ruth's company, she saw the Edouard Bourdet play, *The Captive*, about a young woman whose marriage is jeopardized by her obsession with another woman. That same year the play opened on Broadway and became a cause célèbre when it was closed down by the police because of its lesbian content. It is interesting that in *Blackberry Winter* Margaret mentions seeing the play but does not say whom she was with or that it was a play with a lesbian theme; her mention of the play functions as another oblique reference to homosexuality.

At some point Ruth and Reo did meet, but there is no way of knowing whether Reo curled his lower lip, refused to stand up, or was struck by the difference in ages. No doubt it was not a pleasant occasion for Ruth, though she would come to like Reo very much. For now, the young woman whose motto was "Never break a date with a girl for a man" had let her down most bitterly.

Ruth and Margaret parted after some days, planning to meet again in Rome for the Congress of Americanists. Margaret made a short trip to England with Reo, though in accord with his wishes she stayed away from the British Association conference. She wrote to her grandmother from England, making no mention of her new lover (MM, A1). Their time together was hardly idyllic, given her poor health, their sexual awkwardness, and Reo's continued insistence that Margaret get a divorce.

Ruth, meantime, went to the South of France on her own. Her depression deepened. She and Margaret, watching the sun set over the Grand Canyon, had made a pledge to each other and Margaret had failed to honor it. In a journal entry from St. Paul sur Nice, she insists that

> This mood that haunts me with such persistency has nothing to do with any nihilism. It passes for such, but it's really a refuge from it. I know to the bottom of my subconsciousness that no combination of circumstances will ever give me what I want. But death will. Passion is

a turn-coat, but death will endure always; life is a bundle of fetters or it isn't worth living, and for all our dreaming of freedom, only death can give it to us. Life must be always demeaning itself, but death comes with dignity we don't even have to deserve. We all know these things, but in me it's bred a passionate conviction that death is better than life. Why do people fear and resent it? Shouldn't they hanker for it? Isn't it good to know that we'll be the plowed earth of this planet through hot human generations that will disport themselves as we did, millions of ants upon their ant hill? And my mood has nothing to do with suicide. It's a cheap way of attaining death, and death at least need not come cheap. I shall come by it honestly, and I wish I could think that people would feel that same honor for me that I feel first at any news of death—the honor for anyone who has held out to the end. (AW, 153–54)

In this period Ruth's hair changed color dramatically. Though she was only thirty-nine, after cutting short the long strands that used to fall over her face, she emerged with "a silver helmet of white hair" that would make a strong impression on Margaret when they met in Rome. From the start, Margaret had been conscious of Ruth's beauty, hidden though it was; she would now think Ruth "extraordinarily beautiful," as she must have looked when she was a girl (BW, 163).

Ruth's outward change in appearance was matched by a process of inward transformation. She did not return her to her previous state, a shy, unconfident woman overshadowed by the unhappiness of her marriage. Instead, she began to develop a characteristic air of remoteness, not one that cut her off from intimacy, but that removed her from the turbulence of feeling marking the early period of her relationship with Margaret. There would be times when this cultivated detachment wore thin, but she would never again fling herself so wholeheartedly into a great passion.

These changes were reflected in her poetry. From 1926 onward themes of eroticism and desire no longer feature so strongly. "Earth-born," for example, is a poem of repudiation: "I have put spirit from me as a cheat," it begins. No longer is there any "food of comforting," no longer is she blessed, as she once was, by "your wandering hands" (AW, 487). She is severed from "rooted earthy things" and no longer beset by desire: "I have such need of you as petals shed, / Before the wind one burning hour ago." She dedicated this poem to Margaret and sent it to her with the comment that it represented only "*one* mood" (MM, TR2).

"But the Son of Man," (which Louise Bogan described as "succinctly, a knockout"), was also from this period and was later published in an influential anthology of American poetry.[9] It takes its title from Matthew, "Foxes have holes, but the Son of man has nowhere to lay his head," and it describes foxes wintering: "they sleep, not knowing bereavement, content, worthy / The ecstacy withdrawn." The poet experiences "the winter of the blood" as she seeks, like the foxes, to quiet crying flesh, to find oblivion (AW, 475).

In her usual anticipatory mode, Margaret had dreamed of Italy before arriving: "I was eating in a French restaurant in Italy. There is ice in the wine and I have put a small piece against my clitoris with stimulating result. Eleanor Phillips is very contemptuous of eating in a French restaurant in Italy but I say that this [is the] only place where they understand what I want" (MM, A21). No interpretation is recorded, but Italy must have been associated with Ruth in Margaret's mind, and wine functioned metaphorically for Margaret to describe the selective attention that allowed her a multiplicity of relationships. The reference to her clitoris would most likely have summoned up the popular association between clitoral sexuality and lesbianism. "The only place where they understand what I want" could refer to a feeling that only a woman, Ruth, provided Margaret with the understanding that she needed. Luther was determined to leave her to her own devices and was not simpatico, and Reo, argumentative and passionate, was more intent on pursuing and winning her than on understanding her needs. A dream is susceptible to many interpretations and only when Margaret interprets her dreams are the workings of her emotional life exposed; nevertheless, this interpretation squares with the facts.

Margaret and Ruth met in Rome as planned and spent a week together. They had time for sightseeing, visiting Keats's grave in the Protestant cemetery where, absorbed in talking, they were locked in and had to ring a bell to be released. At the Sistine Chapel they had "one of the most violent disagreements" ever, with Margaret repelled and Ruth delighted by the "outsized demigods . . . She smiled mischievously, saying, 'I knew you wouldn't like it.' "[10] Ruth's penchant for the unnatural and perverse, disliked by Edward, was again at the fore.

Pliny Earle Goddard, Margaret's new colleague at the museum, whom Ruth and Margaret had avoided on the trip to the Grand Canyon, was also in Rome for the congress. He was traveling with Gladys Reichard, who had taken the job at Barnard Ruth had hoped for, and the two were widely rumoured to be having an affair.

Goddard and Reichard figure in a nightmare Margaret experienced while she was in Rome:

> Ruth and I were in a room and I was lying down. Ruth was standing near a window. Gladys came in and said "Now I've got 12 of the 15

letters which Goddard wrote you during the year." And I said "Hump! People who really care about me wrote me more letters than that by every boat." . . . Then she said "And you had a fellowship and you lay down on the job. . . . You were sick for a whole week." . . . Ruth exclaimed against the cruelty of this, and Gladys began to beat me with a tapa beater. The impact of every blow was intensely painful. Ruth rushed over to stop Gladys, but her dress was glass (not transparent but brittle) and when she and Gladys grappled with each other the glass broke and cut Ruth. Then Gladys pushed her out of the window onto a roof—and she fell to the ground. I could hear the glass smash when she fell.

Then I dreamt that I awoke with all the sensations of awakening from a nightmare and told the dream to Ruth, Gladys and Goddard.

Then I really awoke, feeling sore all over with all the nightmare feeling. (MM, A21)

With her dress of glass, the figure of Ruth appears as a fragile recasting of the mythic knight in shining armor, saving Margaret from enemies who would detract from her work. Gladys Reichard was hardly an enemy; nevertheless, Margaret and Ruth were not fond of her and disappointment about the Barnard job was very real. The dream does not have a happy ending, for Ruth does not win her prize but falls out of the window and shatters. Margaret believed that her dream pointed to Ruth as more vulnerable than she had realized (MM, A21). Having already experienced the suicide of a friend, Margaret had reason to be alarmed about Ruth's state of mind. The dream also told her what she knew from experience, that Ruth, as her mentor, would defend her should anyone care to criticize her fieldwork. Illicit sexuality also features in the dream; the interchange between Margaret and Gladys about letters can be understood by recalling that Margaret believed Goddard and Gladys were lovers and that Margaret had received a constant stream of letters from Ruth and Edward Sapir.

Margaret was aware of changes in Ruth, revealed by the almost overnight graying of her hair, but perhaps she tried to avoid understanding her own role. Her dream spoke more truthfully, and she noted to Reo that it gave her a "new appreciation of Ruth's vulnerability as a person." That Margaret forwarded this dream to Reo is interesting, but suggests a reason for reticence in her interpretive remarks.

The congress was dull, Ruth wrote to Sapir (SF, 21 Oct. 1926). Margaret was fascinated by the fanfares that greeted Mussolini's appearance. The pageantry, designed to impress the international participants, seemed more like a comic opera.

After the congress, Margaret rushed to France to meet Reo, but with real life playing a Freudian trick, her train was stopped by a blocked railroad tunnel and she had to stay in Italy. After some delay Reo managed to join her and the two continued to argue about what Margaret should do. In Florence, Reo, plagued by mosquitoes, dreamed he and Margaret were gazing at a statue of St. Citronetta (reminiscent of the mosquito repellent, citronella), who wore the face of an ass. He thought this meant there could be no solution to his conflict (RFF, Box 18).

At the end of September Ruth and Margaret boarded their ship for the ten-day journey to New York. Reo was there to make his farewells before beginning the journey back across Europe, his sleepless nights punctuated by a dream in which he addressed a crowd, asking them "What is the good of the greatest number, anyway?" In another dream he worried that Margaret was unwell and went through a long tunnel (which he interpreted as a vagina) to some cloisters, where he met a cadaverous monk begging for alms, a Luther figure whom Reo fought, to Margaret's fury. A couple of nights later he dreamed that Margaret and his father were in love and went away together past the cow shed on the farm at home, leaving Reo bareheaded, with no possessions, and afraid that his father might kill him. At one point he copied down the injunction from Ecclesiastes, perhaps to stop taking himself too seriously: "Who so regardeth dreams is like him that catcheth at a shadow and followeth the wind. For dreams have deceived many" (RFF, Box 18).

Now Margaret and Ruth, for the first time since their reunion, had time to talk without distraction. Ruth began to recover from the intense feelings of disappointment that had plagued her. Their mutual work put the relationship back on a more even keel. On shipboard, she and Margaret "began a discussion that continued for many years," focusing on psychological problems and anthropology.[11] Margaret's and Reo's long discussions of dreams and psychoanalysis rekindled their mutual interest in psychology. Ruth read Reo's monograph on dreams and they debated it, Ruth going as far as to write to Reo arguing against his interpretation of one of his own dreams. The dream reflected his temperament, she said, wherein he cast his lot with a despised group and welcomed unpleasantness in a good cause. This was, as Ruth wrote, "an essential endowment for all knights of the holy grail, as it were." She went on to comment: "If only we could get everybody to record his own recurring types of dream, with his own interpretations, I wonder how much light they'd throw on personality. That correlation—of the dream and the dreamer—is the most interesting of all to me. . . . It might be found that dreaming is a little laboratory where each person turns over his perplexities and convictions, with all the differences in psychological approach that mark him off from his neighbour in the daytime" (RFF).

The ocean journey marked the beginning of a significant and close period of collaboration between Benedict and Mead in which they developed together the ideas about deviance and culture and the relationship between personality and culture, first included in Margaret's account of coming of age in Samoa and later central to Ruth's work on cultural patterns. Their friendship could have foundered, but they were able to move on, finding together the permanence that Ruth so valued in a close friendship and collaboration. They may have continued as lovers on occasion, but it was now clear that Margaret, whether she ultimately chose Luther or Reo, would continue to be intimate with men.

# 8

## The Deviant and the Normal

CREATIVE WORK, WHETHER ARTISTIC or scholarly, is often shaped in collaborative relationship with others, yet little is known about collaborations between women. The emphasis on true friendship as a masculine quality means that the work of women in productive partnerships has been neglected. Moreover, the very fact of women engaging in intellectual and artistic work of significance has been regarded as anomalous: it breaks the rules of gender. The prevalent view that individual genius and solitude are needed for eminence also contributes to the neglect of women's cocreativeness; "women's ways of knowing" were scarcely explored before the boom in feminist scholarship of the 1970s.[1]

Feminist scholarship has excavated stories of women who worked in partnership, mostly with men in which their contributions were thoroughly submerged, and these lives have served as cautionary tales. There was Auguste Rodin, who reaped fame and fortune from his relationship with Camille Claudel, whose lot was madness and ignominy. The marriage of Ted Hughes and Sylvia Plath is sometimes portrayed in like manner. In contrast, some heterosexual relationships are viewed as liberating and generative, such as Simone de Beauvoir's and Jean-Paul Sartre's.[2] There are few accounts of women whose collaborative relationships were successful, Vita Sackville-West and Virginia Woolf being a notable exception.

The nature of collaboration itself is not well understood.[3] It is often viewed as a process of joint production which excludes the possibility of other collaborative relationships. This need not be true, as is demonstrated by the intellectual careers of Ruth Benedict and Margaret Mead. Their anthropological work was collaborative from 1926, when they returned from Europe together, until Benedict's death in 1948. They did not produce jointly written publications, but their close relationship was crucial to their work. They conversed often, usually on a daily basis when Margaret was in New York, and they corresponded at length during her field trips. Their interactions laid the basis for their individual contributions to anthropology. Each gave the other the gift of close attention. They elaborated on each other's material and engaged in lively challenges and disagreements, usually—though not always—in a supportive, encouraging atmosphere. Ruth—her best critic—invariably read Margaret's work in draft, and in turn Ruth showed Margaret hers, or at least discussed key ideas, the structure of her argument, and the anthropological examples she needed to illustrate her points. Margaret provided vivid accounts of her own fieldwork, giving Ruth a much wider range of experience, at close second hand so to speak, than her trips to the Southwest could afford. When Ruth died, Margaret said, "I had read everything she had ever written, and she had read everything I had ever written" (BW, 113).

The process of developing a collaborative partnership worked to resolve the tensions of the early years. During the period 1926 to 1928, time together was plentiful. The two even shared an apartment for a summer. Though the sexual dimension still partly defined the relationship, Margaret was no longer the student and protégée but rather the colleague and equal. Yet she was always tempted to keep Ruth on a pedestal as a "Mary" figure. Ruth's achievement was to accept with sadness that her love for Margaret would never be exclusive or take the form of domestic partnership, but that as an emotional and intellectual alliance it could have staying power. In a variation on the permanence she so valued, she found a sense of continuity that would subdue "her most obsessive quarrel . . . with life as endless episodes" (AW, 292).

Both Mead and Benedict initially saw their work as Boasian. They soon moved beyond their mentor, with Boas encouraging them. Though he never fully incorporated into his own work the new psychological directions pioneered by his two protégées, he was "the ground under my feet," as Margaret put it, and Ruth continued as his "left hand" (AW, 341).

Edward Sapir remained an influence, although his and Margaret's falling-out soured his friendship with Ruth. Sapir had provided a framework for a psychological approach to anthropology in his "brilliant" summer session courses at Columbia in 1925, but hostilities between the three disturbed the collegiality of those who pioneered the "culture and personality" school in anthropology.[4]

Mead and Benedict were joined by other collaborators, notably Mead's second and third husbands. Reo Fortune was part of the school for a time, though he would later repudiate it. Gregory Bateson contributed his particular genius. Ruth's graduate students brought in new blood, and her association with Columbia linked Margaret to the academic world, especially during her years in the field.

The Benedict-Mead intellectual collaboration was energized by issues from their personal lives. As they struggled with problems and possibilities inherent in their love, their scholarly work examined cultural meanings of sexuality, femininity, the body, and personal identity. Ruth concentrated on the way conceptions of normality and deviance lay at the heart of cultures, shaping the lives of individuals whose temperaments led to tension or harmony with their social worlds. Margaret examined cultural formations of gender, the body, and sexuality and was perpetually fascinated by the links between biology and culture, especially in the lives of the women and children she described so vividly. Both women used their work on "primitive" societies as a tool for critical reflection on reformist endeavours within their own society. They were part of a generation of anthropologists who, in engaging with "the primitive," laid the foundations of a cultural relativism that has profoundly influenced western twentieth-century thought and practice.[5]

Margaret and Ruth arrived back in New York in September 1926 to an exuberant reception. Luther was on the pier, outnumbered by a crowd of Ash Can Cats who had not seen Margaret since she left for Samoa. Léonie Adams and Pelham Kortheuer were so eager for her return that one of the "girls" at Columbia later asked Ruth if Margaret was homosexual (MM, A21). Léonie urgently wanted to talk to Margaret about how unhappy Louise Bogan was making her. Pelham's news was that she had fallen in love with a man.

Luther had found a high-rise apartment at 610 West 116th Street between Broadway and Riverside Drive. Convenient to his work at City College, it was also close to Ruth's weekday apartment, as Margaret had requested; it was close to Columbia and not too distant from the American Museum of Natural History, where Margaret was due to take up her new position.

Starting as assistant curator, Margaret Mead began a working relationship with the museum that outlasted any of her domestic arrangements. Perhaps this was surprising, since museum jobs were not of high status; they were seen as especially suited to women who were unlikely to win scarce academic jobs. Margaret's new boss, Clark Wissler, had been known to remark that museum tasks resembled housekeeping. Bright young women were often given low-paid jobs cataloguing collections that had expanded rapidly in the acquisitive years of the later nineteenth century, though by the time Mead began her association with the museum the work was becoming more professional.[6]

Watching aging curators "puttering among their books and specimens" gave Margaret a sense of security (BW, 15). The endless warren of corridors in the upper floors, lined by locked cupboards, stored treasures. One summer Wissler brought in the family silver and it ended up being misplaced; it was found eleven years later, as safe as the stashes of Peruvian gold hidden nearby.

Margaret's own office was an attic under the eaves of the west tower. Margaret felt it was: "just like the . . . kind of room I had always chosen in each rented house we lived in" when she was a child (BW, 14). She inherited an old roll-top desk, shabby filing cabinets, and bookshelves and supplemented the spartan furnishings with Samoan mats, tapa-patterned curtains, and kava cups. The kava cups soon came to serve as ashtrays; Margaret, like most of her circle of New Women, including Ruth, was now a dedicated smoker.

Everyday duties at the museum were not taxing. Margaret's special responsibility was Pacific materials, a task for which she was now undoubtedly competent. Settling into her new life was not easy, however. A 1926 sample of her handwriting—analyzed by the graphologist whom Margaret consulted in the 1940s and whose interpretations she set great store by—showed her as having low vitality, unstable ego development, and a lack of direction. Although she had a "drive to maintain performance and handle duties adequately," she was beset by "a waning clarity of her direction and goals. A very strong impression prevails that despite all her excellent abilities, she is psychologically jobless, for she cannot bring the best of her abilities to bear on what she is doing" (MM, Q35).

Despite the dubious validity of handwriting analysis, many of the interpretations were uncannily accurate. It took time for Margaret to learn to take advantage of the flexibility inherent in her new position. She was still experiencing, as returning anthropologists often do, a sense of foreignness and alienation. A faltering marriage added uncertainties. Her briefly revived commitment to Luther weakened when a medical examination showed a tipped uterus and she was advised that pregnancies would always result in miscarriage. Margaret kept this news from Luther, who only learned it when Ruth Benedict mentioned it casually years later (GJ,267).

Margaret's graphological analysis also suggested that although at that time "she might be moved by sudden impulse to pregnancy, . . . an actual desire for motherhood appears lacking" because of "her attitude towards the sexes" which contained "an unresolved adolescent or homosexual component," along with insecurity, fright, and unconscious inhibition in relationship to men (MM, Q35). As Margaret recounted it, the prognosis that she would not be able to have children tipped the marriage scales toward Reo. Whereas Luther would have made a good father, Reo, jealous and demanding, would not. But marriage to Reo offered a professional partnership that would enhance Margaret's fieldwork opportunities. Her dilemma remained.

Ruth's reaction to Margaret's medical news, colored by her own disappointments about infertility, was that Margaret had accepted medical opinion too blandly. Margaret later wrote in her memoir that "even though neither [Ruth] nor anyone else questioned the doctor's verdict, she felt that I was somehow making an ascetic choice, a choice against the fullness of life" (BW, 245).

During the academic year 1926–27, Ruth replaced Gladys Reichard at Barnard while Gladys stayed in Europe on a fellowship. Margaret was appointed her assistant. Now Mead assisted Benedict instead of Benedict's assisting Boas, which was how it was when the two first met. Ruth was earning, at last, a respectable salary of two thousand dollars. During that year, conscious that deafness impaired her teaching, she experimented with an earphone but "didn't have the nerve" to take it out in class and returned it to the manufacturer (AW, 74). Margaret was a great aide in Ruth's communications with others, and of course, she did not confine herself to mere translation. Around Columbia she came to be referred to jokingly as Ruth's "talking chief."[7]

Edward Sapir continued to prey on Margaret's mind. His new romance had progressed rapidly and by the time she returned from Europe he was married to Jean McClenaghan, a twenty-six-year-old social work intern. Jean became stepmother to the three Sapir children, the role Margaret had dreaded, and within a year had given up her career. Edward wrote to Ruth that "Jean, poor girl, has resigned so she may contemplate at closer range the different types of complex-formation of her husband and his three children" (SF, 29 Sept. 1927). Jean had found it "rather fatiguing" to combine the demands of the job with household duties; soon she became pregnant and gave birth to a son.

Margaret, who remained hurt about the misunderstandings with Sapir, was not to meet Jean until years later. Long after Edward's death, when she was gathering material for her biography of Ruth, she was dismayed to find that Edward had told Jean that Margaret was "a wicked, promiscuous, terrible creature." In Mead's eyes this portrait was especially ironic. Jean had behaved no differently from her, but had been perceived by Edward as an "innocent young girl who was seduced before she married him, but she married him, so that made it all right." Mead took great satisfaction in telling Jean that no man but Luther had kissed her before Edward. Of course, she said nothing about women. A further blow was that Jean, apparently following Edward's instructions, had burned all Margaret's letters (JH).

During the winter of 1926, Edward figured in one of Margaret's dreams. The evening before she and Luther had been talking about whether to divorce. Margaret went out to visit Ruth, who told her about a Columbia colleague's wondering if Margaret was homosexual. The two of them gossiped about Edward and reflected on Ruth having been in love with him. Did Ruth think Margaret had fallen in love with Edward because he was "unavailable," too? Ruth "wasn't sure, it was a possibility." Margaret ended the conversation feeling strongly that she could never divorce Luther (MM, A21).

That night she had the long and complex dream that clearly referred back to the failed assignation with Edward before the trip to Samoa. The dream involved meeting Edward, Luther, her father, and Jean and being told that Jean had insisted that the Sapirs live in a hotel because keeping house had been too much of a strain. In her interpretation Margaret dwelt on themes of virility, impotence, marriage failure, and homosexuality. She wondered whether her father represented virility, in contrast to Edward, but decided this was unlikely. The Jean figure looked like the younger sister in a play she had seen recently, someone who was homosexual and therefore did not mind impotence in a man. In the dream Margaret said to herself that if Edward's marriage to Jean "proved a success, I should have all my theories upset" (MM, A21). Margaret had recently remarked to Léonie that she had "daydreamed that marriage into failure because I *had* to believe success was impossible" (MM, A21).

Ruth was Margaret's principal confidante. It must have sometimes been hard to lend a sympathetic ear to Margaret's heartbreaks about men when she herself had been let down so badly. Ruth did show signs of impatience, even jealousy, as Margaret's poetry indicates. "Star Bread" begins with a comment that someone, almost certainly Ruth, has flung at Margaret, "Oh, you have love enough."

> "Oh, you have love enough," you said.
> How could you think I'd make
> Your star-meal into common bread,
> Or let you bend that lovely head
> Above a need another heart could fill.
> I hold you far too high to count
> Such usufruct of love;
> Yours the gold apple swung above,
> Mine but the worshipping hands
> Which only will
> To brush it with the dreams of you
> Grown poignant in my finger tips,
> And with your name upon my folded lips
> Be softly still. (MM, Q15)

Margaret contrasts Ruth's "star-meal" with "common bread," the ordinariness she wished to avoid in her love relationships, and she suggests to Ruth that their relationship had a specialness beyond the everyday quality.

"Your Gift," dedicated to "R.F.B.," expresses Margaret's gratitude and love for Ruth as a mentor, as does "Green Sanctuary": "Your branches curve beneath my head / Lending from earth a sweet release / With sweet tongued leaves above my bed / You hold me in a singing peace" (MM, Q15). "Misericordia," one of the few poems Margaret publicly acknowledged as written for Ruth, recalls "a certain September evening" when a woman prone to depression is tricked and betrayed by the return of warm weather, which thaws her out, unlocking her lips with "empty promises." When she published this poem in *An Anthropologist at Work*, Mead omitted, perhaps as too revealing of her attachment to Ruth, the last two lines: "Hearts that are human were born with no defense / Against this beauty unconfused by sense" (AW, 89).[8]

"Our Lady of Egypt" also may have been inspired by Ruth, who was prone to wondering whether she might have been more at home in ancient Egypt. Passion has died, it seems: "Only the bones of passion lie / a fragile heap upon the floor / of a once fertile valley." The Ruth figure is ascribed "a fervent forced abstemiousness" whose "touch can bring no semblance of the old fire back" (MM, Q15). Margaret did not keep these sentiments to herself; it was Ruth who submitted "Our Lady" to a magazine on Margaret's behalf, so she most likely acknowledged the truth of the portrait.

Having settled in at the natural history museum, Mead took up work on the manuscript *Coming of Age in Samoa*. Her discussions with Ruth about the field materials, begun by letter and continued on the voyage home from Europe, led her to ask what she, Ruth, and her friends would be like had they been born Samoan, beginning an endless conversation on the theme of temperament and cultural patterning. In *Coming of Age*, Margaret, as well as exploring themes that would remain of interest for a lifetime, made a start on investigating the issue that held a particular fascination for Ruth, the role of the deviant in a culture.

Nervously, Margaret submitted her completed manuscript to Boas. Would the old man decide that his protégées had strayed too far, especially in their fascination with psychological questions? Would Margaret's breezy style offend his austere scholarly standards? Boas asked both Margaret and Ruth to a conference about the book. Margaret was terrified. " 'What is he going to do?' I asked Ruth. 'Make you bowdlerize it' was her response." Before the meeting she paced anxiously up and down her office, but at lunch "after a lot of aimless talk he turned to me, brows beetling ferociously, and remarked, 'You haven't made clear the difference between passionate and romantic love.' That was the only criticism he ever made of it" (BW, 121).

Harper Brothers rejected the manuscript, but it was taken by a new publisher, William Morrow. He advised Mead to add extra material comparing young Samoan women to young Americans, though he warned Mead that its popular style might rebound unfavorably on her professional career. Certainly Coming of Age showcased Mead's talents as a writer with an engaging style who could lead her readers into unknown worlds and invite comparisons with their own culture.

The book's central thesis was, of course, a confirmation of Boas's hypothesis that adolescent Sturm und Drang was not a cultural universal. Mead presented Samoan adolescence as untroubled, arguing that western socialization causes sexual, vocational, religious, and family conflict and that educators and parents should do more to ease the pathway for girls into womanhood.[9]

In a disarmingly forthright manner, Mead wrote of the sexual life of Polynesians, displaying what Ann Douglas, using the words of Raymond Chandler, called the "terrible honesty" of New Yorkers of her time.[10] Perhaps her disturbing dream of publishing a book with a lurid jacket and a title Seekings for Sin was not entirely off the mark, for the sexual content of Coming of Age was to make it a best seller. From the first sentence Mead lured her readers with an evocative, sensual description of Samoan life reverberating with the centuries-old western romanticizing of the South Pacific: "As the dawn begins to fall among the soft brown roofs and the slender palm trees stand out against a colorless, gleaming sea, lovers slip home from trysts beneath the palm trees or in the shadow of beached canoes . . ." (14). This style led British social anthropologist Evans-Pritchard to refer to Mead as from the "rustling-of-the-wind-in-the-palm-trees school," while another Britisher, Haddon, dismissed her as a "lady novelist."[11]

Mead's account of growing up in Samoa emphasized the burgeoning of sexuality. Her little girls were free of inhibition. Nude bathing, scanty clothing, outdoor toileting, and communal sleeping arrangements meant that the body held no mysteries for them. Though adults sought privacy for sexual expression—even affectionate interchanges like kisses or holding hands were unseemly in public—the children spied on their elders and soon found out all there was to know. Masturbation was "an all but universal habit (136)" from the age of six or seven. Preadolescent girls and boys avoided each other's company and there was "no heterosexual experimentation and very little homosexual activity" in that age group, though young boys often masturbated in groups (138).

During adolescence masturbation was largely discontinued. Young people engaged in "horseplay" and "romping," which "is particularly prevalent in groups of women, often taking the form of playfully snatching at the sex organs" (135). Premarital heterosexual activity began and "casual" homosexual practices were commonplace (147). Mead says that "these casual homosexual relationships between girls never assumed any long-time importance. On the part of growing girls or women who were working together they were regarded as a pleasant and natural diversion, just tinged with the salacious. Where heterosexual relationships were so casual, so shallowly channeled, there was no pattern into which homosexual relationships could fall" (147–48). She went on to explain the Samoan attitude to homosexuality: "The general preoccupation with sex, the attitude that minor sex activities, suggestive dancing, stimulating salacious conversation, salacious songs and definitely motivated tussling are all acceptable and attractive diversions, is mainly responsible for the native attitude towards homosexual practice. They are simply *play*, neither frowned upon nor given much consideration" (149).

Mead argued that there was a difference between perfectly acceptable, yet socially unimportant, homosexual practices and "the real pervert" who was "incapable of normal heterosexual response," a rare figure but one recognized in the culture (147–48). The one "real pervert" Mead described was a male, regarded by the girls as "an amusing freak" and by men he approached "with mingled annoyance and contempt" (148).[12]

Some of the girls Mead knew were involved in homosexual relationships that were less than casual. However, they were not "real perverts" but "mixed types" (148) like Lita, a "clever and executive" girl with a "crush" on her older girl cousin which "was accompanied by the casual homosexual practices which are the usual manifestation of most associations between young people of the same sex" (165). Lita's crush was driven not merely by passion, but also by ambition. She lived in the pastor's house and wished to become a nurse or teacher; her well-educated older cousin was a role model. Using the term that she and Ruth Benedict were coming to rely on, Margaret named Lita a "deviant" but an "upward deviant" (169), one of those girls who "demanded a different or improved environment, who rejected the traditional choices" and who, "in making their choices, come to unconventional and bizarre solutions" (171).

Comparing Samoans with Americans, Mead saw Lita as similar to college girls who plan careers that might prevent marriage and children and are frowned on and seen as deviant in American culture. Throughout their work Mead and Benedict used "deviant" as a nonjudgmental term. It derived from statistical measurement, whereby divergences from the norm are expressed in terms of standard deviations, and it was more neutral than the common expression, "misfit," also used by Mead.

Mead's question concerning deviance, which "Ruth Benedict had taught me to ask" (AW, 208–9), was: "Were there no conflicts, no temperaments which deviated so markedly from the normal that clash was inevitable?

Was the diffused affection and the diffused authority of the large families, the ease of moving from one family to another, the knowledge of sex and the freedom to experiment a sufficient guarantee to all Samoan girls of a perfect adjustment?" (158).

In her chapter, "The Girl in Conflict," which Mead once mistakenly referred to as "The Deviant Girl" (BW, 195–96), she explored deviance Samoan-style, using the example of homosexuality to exemplify upward deviance, whereas downward deviance, or delinquency, was shown by girls who thieved, who were insubordinate, quarrelsome, and generally troublesome.

Romantic love, which Boas had asked Mead to examine, was not, she concluded, a feature of Samoan life.[13] It was not evident in either heterosexual or homosexual pairings and indeed, Samoans had a recognition of "the essential impersonality of sex attraction which we may well envy them" (222). Marriages were arranged, by which time both partners were skilled at lovemaking, so that sexual adjustment was seldom a problem, although women were slower to reach maturity in their sexual feelings and men were held responsible for satisfying them. Mead went as far as to claim that in Samoa "there are no neurotic pictures, no frigidity, no impotence, except as the temporary result of severe illness and the capacity for intercourse only once in a night is counted as senility" (151). Marriages often lasted, but if they were unhappy they were easily dissolved at the behest of either partner. "Old maids" and "frustrated wives" were not part of the picture. Adultery did not necessarily end a marriage, and while jealousy sometimes occurred, it was seen as curious if prolonged.

Long-term homosexual partnerships were not a feature of adult life in Samoa, Mead explained, because sexual feelings in that culture were not specialized: "As heterosexual relations are given significance not by love and a tremendous fixation upon one individual, the only forces which can make a homosexual relationship lasting and important, but by children and the place of marriage in the economic and social structure of the village, it is easy to understand why very prevalent homosexual practices have no more important or striking results" (149). Referring to the arts of love, she went on to say that "the recognition and use in heterosexual relations of all the secondary variations of sex activity which loom as primary in homosexual relations are instrumental also in minimizing their importance" (149).

Mead understood women's sexuality as culturally shaped and inclusive of lesbian sexuality, although "lesbian" is a word that she does not use in *Coming of Age*. Repressive cultural standards such as Americans were used to might distort the natural range of sexual expression in men or women, causing frigidity or fixations. Mead makes an important distinction between homosexual practices that are within the normal range of behavior and may or may not be frowned on in a culture, and "psychic perversion" or an incapacity to respond heterosexually. She also argues that sexuality is linked with practical choices, as with the link between same-sex relations and careers for women.

Mead and Benedict surely tried to understand their own sexuality and relationships using this framework. Most likely neither saw herself as "psychically perverted" because they each had a history of heterosexuality, although Mead's experiences with male impotence in her affairs with Edward and Reo seem to have raised anxieties about whether she might really be the "castrating woman" a college friend said she was. In general, homosexuality as a "perversion," in Mead's circle, was defined less by sexual interactions with women and more by a failure to achieve satisfactory sexual relationships with men.

Mead and Benedict, in considering Samoan culture, would have been well aware of their singularities as Americans who believed in romantic love, the virtues of individuality, and the existence of neurosis, capacities that made the casual attitudes of Samoans unavailable to them, despite Margaret's envy of Samoan "impersonality of sex attraction." For Benedict, from an older generation, such casualness was an even more remote possibility, regardless of the sexual frustrations she often experienced.

Mead's Samoa is a sensual utopia, a romantic island culture where pleasure and choice are a feature of women's sexuality and where lovemaking is skilled and separated from emotional entanglements.[14] However, it is also portrayed as flawed, for it is not an intellectual, cultural, or even emotional utopia, since individuality and the possibility of deep intimacy and self-exploration are practically nonexistent. In dwelling on the nature of her relationship with Benedict, Mead must have wondered at the possibilities of being partnered by a woman, but this choice she associated with earlier feminist attempts to make the best of the separate sphere allotted to women. As always, her "have your cake and eat it too" attitude prevailed; she would find herself able to exercise freedom in her career, to enjoy the socially sanctioned partnership of marriage, eventually to have a child, and to love whomever she wished, male or female.

At the age of twenty-five Margaret still found life confusing. She was "uncertain of the kind of deviancy I was experiencing" (JH). She knew that though she was attracted to women, she was quite feminine. She liked being a woman, she felt satisfied with her own body, and she did want children someday. "What's this about Margaret thinking life is strange?" Louise Bogan wrote Ruth. "Léonie said she had a dreadful blue fit a while back."[15]

Christmas 1926 found Margaret in Pennsylvania, writing Reo love letters which included gripes about her family, accounts of her dreams, and plans for their future. They might live in New York and plan fieldwork together, perhaps returning to Samoa, though she told W. F. Ogburn, her former Barnard professor, that if she wanted to return there, publication of *Coming of Age* would have to be delayed, since "it would allienate [sic] too many people down there and complicate my fieldwork" (MM, N1). Family life was driving her to distraction, a mixture of "gravel in the honey. Twenty-four hours of it left me worn out and Priscilla says she has just steeled herself never to sympathize with Mother or she'll cry all the time" (MM, A21).

Margaret insisted that she liked the members of her family as individuals but did not care about them just because they were family. "I fail to see that blood relationship entitles anyone to special affection," she wrote frankly to her mother, striking an odd note for an anthropologist whose discipline specialized in understanding kinship.[16] She appreciated what Emily and "Dadda" had done for her *as herself*; what they had done only because she was their daughter she valued less.

Vacation time was also spent with the "good, genuine" Cressman family, where Margaret was treated like one of the boys, an easier environment after her "great failure" at home, though it did induce a "dream-like feeling of complete unreality." She went to midnight mass on Christmas Eve and took communion for the first time in many months. No longer a believer, she told Reo that Christianity "is still the most beautiful thing I know." It was something she could improve on, her amendments being an anthropological golden rule, "Do unto others as they would be done by" and a new commandment, "Love thy neighbor for himself." Perhaps to reward herself for this theological revisionism she dreamed she was sent a set of yellow satin kneeling cushions from the Archbishop of Canterbury (MM, A21).

Back in New York, Margaret continued to miss Reo: "I vacillate between putting your picture away and taking it out, for the waves of longing that come over me leave me weak with wanting you" (MM, A21). Mrs. Holt from Ta'u visited with her baby, and Ruth was disappointed to miss seeing Margaret subdued by her former landlady. Margaret wrote to Reo telling him that Ruth Holt's brother was a hermaphrodite, and "on the strength of that" she dreamed that Reo was, too. In the dream she consulted someone about this alarming problem, a figure who was both a sociologist of sex and a homosexual poet whose hand "was soft and fine like a woman's and as small as mine" and who embraced her, a scene immediately followed by thoughts of Léonie (MM, A21). She told Reo, disingenuously perhaps, that there was no value to the dream.

A week later Margaret had one of her the "murdered baby" dreams, following the party where her Barnard friend Deborah Kaplan, "as biological as a roan stallion," had criticized homosexuality and Margaret had defended it. This was the dream about having left a baby unattended in a box, which she interpreted as an "expression of a suppressed fear that I after all am primarily a homosexual person and only really fall in love with unavailable men; my work mitigating [sic] against my full acceptance of a women's [sic] role in a heterosexual relationship." Her confusion was apparent in her recording of the dream; where she wrote *heterosexual* she had originally written *homosexual* and crossed it out (MM, A21).

Life was "chock full of events and people" and the feeling of unreality persisted. "Really, it's not my life at all," she told Reo, "not one half so real as the weeks we spent together" (MM, A21). She continued her dream records: more neglected babies, an odd baby with gold hair and "four extra high blue eyes in the top of its head," and one in which a man made love to her in a woodshed, resulting in "enormous sensation on my part but no organism [sic]—I thought, 'He'd never know enough to give me one'" (MM, A21).

Unsurprisingly, Luther was feeling left out. After a dinner party where Margaret was feted as the traveler from exotic places and told entertaining stories all evening, he wondered if he would always be referred to as Dr. Mead's husband. However, he had still not told Margaret the extent of his feelings for Dorothy Loch. Margaret suggested she might move out and live with Marie Eichelberger; if they divorced, he should consider marrying their friend Edna Lou Walton (MM, A21). Luther, of course, had no intention of complying with Margaret's schemes to alleviate her guilt. It was a stressful period for Luther, since as well as experiencing marital uncertainties, he was considering leaving the priesthood.

Margaret arranged to meet Reo in Germany in the summer of 1927. By then he would have completed his degree in anthropology from Cambridge and Europe would serve as the first leg of his journey back to Australia where he had won a fellowship to study with Radcliffe-Brown. The ostensible purpose of Margaret's trip was to tour museums examining Oceanic materials. She also wanted to visit the well-known Homosexual Museum, begun by Magnus Hirschfeld and later destroyed by the Nazis. Professor Ogburn had suggested that Margaret should follow up on the Samoan work by making a career of sex research, though Margaret later said she thought it would have been boring (BW draft). Interestingly, despite the sophisticated airs of *Coming of Age* not everyone thought Margaret was able to discuss sexual matters with maturity. Margaret Sanger once crossed her name off a convention list because she had found Mead unhelpful in the early days of the birth control movement when Mead had "scoffed and giggled like an adolescent over the subject."[17]

Luther said farewell to his wife from the pier. Though they were at sixes and sevens, he believed she still wanted the marriage to work; she wrote telling him so just before her boat docked, though this turned out to be another fluctuation. Her dreams, as usual, were troubled and emphasized the theme of contamination: she had abscesses on her breast, the doctor diagnosing syphilis so she had to be segregated; her mother was trying to wash Margaret's stockings which had an unremoveable stain.

In Hamburg, Reo was not on the wharf to greet her; Pelham Kortheuer, who had been traveling with Margaret, recalled how much this irritated her: "She bared her teeth and stamped her feet."[18] But Reo soon arrived and the romance blossomed as before. After three days in Berlin, Margaret wrote to Luther that she wanted a divorce; she would marry Reo. Luther claimed he was shocked at this sudden change of heart, but before the summer was out he had crossed the Atlantic and begun to woo Dorothy Loch in earnest.

While Margaret was in Germany her grandmother died suddenly. It saddened her that she could not attend the funeral of the woman she had loved wholeheartedly and whom she saw as the most decisive influence in her life. Margaret was now devising her own future as links with the past were breaking.

Margaret and Ruth corresponded over the summer of 1927, but letters from this time are unavailable and it is not clear how Ruth reacted to Margaret's decision to divorce and remarry. Early in the summer Ruth seemed particularly under a strain. Her old friend Marguerite Israel Arnold wrote to her, "The trouble is, both you and Stanley have too much brain power, and you tend to work too hard. Don't be old before your time. I hope you will move to the village and have a good time, and several love affairs, next year." Marguerite argued that Ruth would benefit from psychoanalysis, and knowing she would resist the suggestion went on to give her own view: "You are in many ways a very suppressed person. You have built up two personalities, more or less consciously, a public and a private, and the strain is rather heavy. It isn't that you can't do it, but that it will wear you out to do it. And scholarship may become . . . just a retreat, much as it may benefit the world!" (RFB, Box 1).

That summer Ruth went to the Southwest for a third time, traveling as usual with Ruth Bunzel. In Santa Fe she gathered more Cochiti tales and may have been able to visit Louise Bogan and Raymond Holden. Then it was on to a new fieldwork site at Sacaton, Arizona, where she lived comfortably in the Indian school guest room while studying the Pima and their ceremonies. They involved drinking a beer brewed from cactus until states of exultation ensued. She wrote to Boas that the Pimas' emphasis on passion as the path to esoteric truths formed an "unbelievable" contrast to the peaceful lives of the more familiar neighbouring Pueblo tribes (AW, 206).

This contrast, familiar to Ruth from the two worlds she experienced in her own life, gave her the crucial insight she later expressed in *Patterns of Culture*. As a Boasian, Benedict paid close attention to the ways in which cultures influenced each other through contact. Yet there were enormous differences among tribes that were geographically close. Her insight was the understanding that cultures have characteristic temperaments just as individuals do. This temperament or, more accurately, pattern, provided a key to understanding how a culture developed out of a rich array of influences. A long-time devotee of Nietzsche—she had sent *Thus Spake Zarathustra* for Margaret to read on the boat from Samoa—Benedict chose his description of Greek tragedy, with its Apollonian and Dionysian themes, to characterize the contrast between Pima and Zuñi. Apollonian cultures, like Zuñi, emphasized moderation, while Dionysian cultures, like Pima, valued ecstasy.

Ruth's description of cultures in terms of varying cultural temperaments also derived from Sapir's notion that different cultures emphasized different styles of behavior. Sapir, Mead, and Benedict had all read Freud and also were interested in Jung's psychology of personality types and of temperament. They were further influenced by the German school of Gestalt psychology, with its emphasis on patterns and holistic thinking. From these influences, Benedict developed the idea of typologies of culture, but not in the simplistic, categorizing manner of which she has sometimes been accused. For Benedict the pattern of a culture is the organizing, dynamic principle at its heart. As with temperamental influences on the individual, patterns do not work in a simple cause-and-effect manner, nor do they set limits on development. They configure events, absorbing and shaping them in their own distinctive ways.

Over the following years, Ruth developed these ideas into her own theoretical approach. For now, the insight crystallized thoughts she had so often shared with Mead and Sapir and formed the perfect means of expression for understanding deviance. As Margaret joked, Sapir thought what was important was "the mystic breaking of the pattern," whereas Ruth was driven "to absolve all individuals by proclaiming how strong the pattern is" (MM, B14). Ruth's temperament, with its gentleness, tolerance, and fundamental sense of estrangement, had found a congenial vision.

Poised on the verge of her most important contribution to anthropology, Ruth, ironically, had nearly given up on her career. The Barnard position was only temporary; and it had been humiliating to ask Stanley for money for the Pima field trip. Offered a job at Smith College, she declined it, perhaps reluctant to leave Columbia, distance herself from Margaret, or take a definite step toward divorce. Boas, realizing that Ruth might not continue her work without financial assistance, tried to find her a paid position. He continued to make efforts on her behalf over the next three years, but to no avail, despite her increasing professional recognition. In 1927 she became president of the American Ethnological Association and the same year joined the three-person executive group running the American Anthropological Association. Edward Sapir encouraged Ruth to apply for research grants. He told her "for God's sake" not to be "so remote and technical" and jokingly suggested she try a fashionable topic, such as a study of the "declining, or increasing, mentality of Mayflower stock" (SF, 4 Dec. 1926). The postwar censure of Boas and his removal from the National Research Council meant that projects on racial superiority still attracted funding.

Around this time Ruth recorded for Margaret a dream that seemed to highlight her predicament. In the dream, Boas has a grandson, a baby boy named Robert—the name Ruth's parents had chosen should she have been a boy—who falls from a tower and is killed. The boy, according to Ruth's interpretation, represented "a stake I supremely valued, a stake life dashed to nothing" (MM, A21). Early in the 1927–28 academic year, she wrote to Sapir that she was considering throwing it all in. He replied with irony, yet in a manner that was undermining: "Your plans for the role of a lady of leisure sound most attractive. I hope to sample your cooking some day. Maybe I can even meet the shadowy Stanley" (SF, 29 Sept. 1927). Jean Sapir, of course, had only recently abandoned her career to look after her husband and this, no doubt, accounted for Sapir's newly complacent attitude toward Ruth's career, which he had previously encouraged.

Sapir now showed more interest in fostering Ruth's identity as a poet. Both were seeing their work in print, Ruth more regularly than Edward. Both now had manuscripts prepared for publication. Edward's manuscript, "Chronicle" (a title Ruth did not care for), was dedicated to the memory of Florence. "Winter of the Blood," a title Edward regarded as "too self-revealing" (SF, 4 Feb. 1928), Ruth changed to "November Burning," dedicated "To M.M.—with these verses."[19] Both manuscripts were submitted to Harcourt Brace, and after an awkward moment when Louis Untermeyer told Ruth he was recommending hers but not Edward's, they were both rejected. Edward received the rejection first, and with hurt feelings he told Ruth he intended to take his manuscript somewhere and bury it. Ruth's manuscript was rejected a week later, and following these events the commitment of both to writing poetry waned.

By 1928 Ruth's poetry had become more detached than despairing, carrying few echoes of the earlier immediacy, sensuality, and urgent desire, though in "Countermand" she recalled "a singing, lost now, forgotten, and its dream betrayed" (AW, 426). Perhaps she had begun to transcend the life-changing emotions Margaret had inspired, though the poem of dedication in "November Burning" alludes to secrecy ("Haws when they blossom . . . flaunt their bodies / secret and quick, to eyes incurious") and can be read as an allusion to love between women. The poem also includes an example of Margaret's favorite wine metaphor:

> Still through their roots runs the most secret liquor
> No wind shall tamper, no hurrying bee shall sip;
> Let the haws blossom, let their petals scatter,
> In covert earth wine gathers to their lip. (AW, 473)

On Margaret's return from Germany in the autumn of 1927, she and Luther spent their last week together "unmarred by reproaches or feelings of guilt" (BW, 15). They made arrangements for a Mexican divorce. Luther left for a short visit to England and Dorothy Loch, telling Margaret mischievously that Dorothy was "sort of a cross between Léonie Adams and Ruth Benedict."[20]

Everyone knew that Margaret planned to divorce Luther, but he continued to keep his own romance quiet. Over the following year, while seeing Luther frequently, Margaret was annoyed that her friends saw her as heartless and "trifling with his affections" (BW, 166). Luther had always been popular with her crowd; at least one of her friends, possibly Louise Rosenblatt, fell in love with him. Continuing to see Luther after their separation also shocked Margaret's father, "who held to the opinion so common in earlier generations that it was revolting—somehow like incest—for a couple who were getting a divorce to spend time together" (BW, 166).

Margaret moved into a Greenwich Village apartment at 507 West Twenty-fourth Street with her "group of neurotic friends"—Léonie Adams, Louise Rosenblatt, Pelham Kortheuer, and Hannah Kahn (whom they all called "David") (MM, TR2). She had not taken up the idea of living with Marie Eichelberger, who seems to have been jealous of Margaret's attention to Léonie. Bohemian life in the Village was flourishing. The culture, though not predominantly gay and lesbian, provided an atmosphere of tolerance. The young were expected to be sexually confused, and drag balls with "punks," "fairies," "wolves," and "queers" were popular, as were jaunts to the nightclubs of Harlem where blues singers of all persuasions could be heard. The years 1927 and 1928 were a time of visibility for lesbians in New York. The Captive, which Margaret had seen in Paris, was raided, and Radclyffe Hall's classic novel of the tortured lesbian, The Well of Loneliness, was published, attracting immense publicity and also running into censorship difficulties. Wanda Fraiken Neff, whom Margaret may have known at Barnard, published *We Sing Diana*, a novel of college life which showed that by the twenties the flaming crushes that had once been acceptable had been cast into suspicion by Freudian ideas, and "intimacies between two girls were watched with keen, distrustful eyes."[21]

*Dusty Answer*, a novel about the confusions of a young bisexual woman by English author Rosamund Lehmann, had just appeared. Margaret must certainly have read it, since many years later she gave it to her daughter when she was confused about the nature of her feelings for another young woman.[22] Lesbian chic, though, had a short life, as Lillian Faderman has shown in *Odd Girls and Twilight Lovers*, her history of twentieth-century lesbianism. It was not long before "lesbian-smashing" became a popular pastime among young men in Greenwich Village, with Edna St. Vincent Millay one of the first to succumb to these attempts at conversion.

Léonie Adams, struggling with a sexual identity she found more torturing than "chic," traveled in the summer of 1927 to Santa Fe in pursuit of Louise Bogan. It proved an unhappy time, Louise telling her to "be good" and accusing her of arrested development. Léonie, under Margaret's influence, recorded her own dreams, finding that the process helped her poetry. Those of Léonie's dreams that are in the Mead collection contain many references to homosexuality and to her fear of sexual disapproval, just as Margaret's do (MM, A21). An indication of Léonie's unhappiness is evident in her early poem, "Those Not Elect," which includes these lines: "Never taste that fruit with the soul / Whereof the body may not eat / Lest flesh at length lay waste the soul / In its sick heat. . . . Never, being damned, see paradise."[23]

Margaret continued to collect dreams, especially from her friends in the apartment, and homosexual themes loomed large in them. Hannah Kahn ("David") dreamed she visited Ruth Benedict in a country house and when Ruth greeted her with "considerable affection" she was surprised and did not respond. Another roommate dreamed about being in bed with David, and Louise Rosenblatt dreamed about Ruth's kneeling before a shrine marked *Margaret* (MM, A21).

Ruth, exercising characteristic reticence, selected a few of her own dreams for Margaret's collection and completed a questionnaire on daydreams, which Margaret wanted to use in a project inspired by her interest in Ruth, a study of "the relationship between day dreams and the development of a double personality" (MM, N4). In a reverie before sleeping, Ruth visualized the hen house from the farm at Norwich, into which a procession of "idiots" marched, taking up their position on perches covered with droppings and leering at Ruth with their "deformed and hideous bodies"; this was symbolic to Ruth of "a repulsive world" (MM, A21).

In a dream, the farmhouse had been left to Ruth and she had remodeled it in a tasteless fashion. This followed a lecture she had delivered at Mt. Holyoke College in South Hadley, Massachusetts, in which she felt she had not performed well; in the dream she wears an old ripped nightgown and Stanley tells her she ought to be ashamed. Humiliated by her performance at the lecture, she felt that she had been given "an especially ludicrous and uncongenial role." The badly remodeled farmhouse, Ruth thought, symbolized having "rebuilt my life according to a most uncongenial pattern" (MM, A21).

Ruth's daydreams were motivated by the desire for escape that had been part of her mental life since childhood. Death fantasies were common—"If I could stop *now*" is the way she described them—and to stop them from becoming too appealing she would keep props to remind her of unfinished tasks, such as "certain disorderly Zuñi notebooks." She schooled herself against daydreaming: more productive was the regular time she spent exercising "the concentration and 'stillness' of the mystics" (MM, A21).

Even Franz Boas was not too aloof to contribute a dream to Margaret's collection. It converted a "perfectly futile" committee meeting characterized by backbiting into a dream image of a bagful of mice biting each other's backs.

Ruth's 1928 appointment diary records lunch dates and evenings with Margaret, who sometimes stayed overnight. At Easter, Stanley went to the lake on his own and Margaret stayed in town with Ruth. Margaret was ill on occasion during this difficult year and would turn to Ruth, presumably allowing herself to be cared for. One day in May, when the diary entry said, "MM at apartment *upset*," Ruth had dinner with Luther, perhaps so she could soothe some frayed nerves.

Ruth was occupied with other friends besides Margaret and her circle. There were lunches with Papa Franz, Ruth Bunzel (Bunny) was now a frequent companion, and Louise Bogan had returned from Santa Fe. Marguerite Israel Arnold was still around and there was someone new, Lydia Simpson, who had fallen in love with Ruth. They met for lunches, dinners, and trips to the theater; at one point Lydia and her children stayed for some weeks in Ruth's apartment. Margaret was irritated by the interference with her own intimacy with Ruth. An entry in Ruth's datebook suggests the complexity of keeping all these friendships going: "All day at home. Léonie cried at review [of her poetry]. Lydia at me. . . . Eve[ning] M[argaret] M[ead] but Léonie there" (RFB, Box 42). Years later Margaret, bristling with resentment, likened Lydia to a "hellhound of a psychopathic female" who relentlessly pursues her quarry. Ruth seems to have terminated the friendship firmly. Several years later she received a letter from Lydia, "lonely and ill" in the hospital. "I offer no excuse for writing," she said. "I loved you for many

Margaret Mead around
ten years of age with
brother, Richard, 1911.
*Courtesy of the Institute for
Intercultural Studies, Inc.,
New York*

Ruth Fulton around ten
years of age with her
sister, Margery, c. 1896.
*Special Collections, Vassar
College Libraries*

Margaret Mead and
Katharine Rothenberger
as king and queen of a
pageant, 1920. *Courtesy of
the Institute for Intercultural
Studies, Inc., New York*

Luther Cressman, c.
1922. *Courtesy of the
Institute for Intercultural
Studies, Inc., New York*

Marie Eichelberger.
*Courtesy of the Institute for
Intercultural Studies, Inc.,
New York*

Margaret Mead
graduating from
Barnard, 1923. *Barnard
College Yearbook*

Ruth Benedict at home
in the suburbs, c. 1924.
*Special Collections, Vassar
College Libraries*

Franz Boas. *Special Collections, Vassar College Libraries*

Edward Sapir. *Special Collections, Vassar College Libraries*

Margaret Mead
in Samoa with
Fa'amotu. *Courtesy
of the Institute for
Intercultural Studies,
Inc., New York*

Margaret Mead and
Reo Fortune in Ma-
nus, 1928. *Courtesy
of the Institute for
Intercultural Studies,
Inc., New York*

Ruth Benedict in 1931.
*Special Collections, Vassar College Libraries*

An Ash Can Cats reunion, 1935. *Left to right:* Léonie Adams, Louise Rosenblatt, not identified, Pelham Kortheuer, Margaret Mead, two others not identified. *Courtesy of the Institute for Intercultural Studies, Inc., New York*

Margaret Mead and
Gregory Bateson in
mosquito room,
Tambunam, 1938.
*Courtesy of the Institute for
Intercultural Studies, Inc.,
New York*

Ruth Benedict with two
men from the Blackfoot,
field trip, 1939. *Special
Collections, Vassar College
Libraries*

Ruth Benedict in later
life. *Special Collections,
Vassar College Libraries*

Margaret Mead at the
American Museum of
Natural History. *Courtesy
of the Institute for Intercultural Studies, Inc., New York*

years. I long for a friendly gesture—despite knowledge of how inconsiderate you may [undecipherable handwriting]" (RFB, Box 35).

In the summer, Margaret's co-op broke up and she arranged for Ruth to move in with her. She told her mother she was going to Mexico rather than to Nevada for the divorce so that she would have money to spare "to be here with Ruth this summer."[24] Margaret had been finding the co-op tense: "most of my friends, when they had time to spare from their own complicated lives, were accusing me of heartlessness" in relation to Luther (BW, 167). There were other tensions. Much later, when Margaret in her autobiography referred to Léonie's heartbreak, Léonie was annoyed to have been singled out for her suffering and wrote to Margaret's assistant, "Margaret will know in her own heart a more fundamental reason for not alluding to the tangled emotional situation, which was a source of pain for a part of that year." She referred darkly to Margaret's "principal critics" outside of the apartment, though who these critics were and exactly what situation Léonie had in mind is not clear (MM, Box I204). But she seems to have been making a veiled reference to a homosexual attachment, since according to Marie Eichelberger it was Margaret's very slight reference to the subject in her book that had aroused Léonie's ire (MM, Box B14). In 1928, at any rate, Margaret was "relieved" when everyone went their separate ways and the Mexican divorce was straightforward. Margaret testified untruthfully that "Mr. Cressman, without justifiable cause, abandoned the conjugal domicile" and she did not ask for alimony, though she and Luther argued when he refused to pay half the legal costs.[25]

That summer was the first and only time Margaret and Ruth shared a domicile. In early July, Ruth came back from the lake and began teaching at summer school. That summer they were shocked by Pliny Earle Goddard's death, which occurred while he was with Gladys Reichard. Rumors flew about Reichard's liaison with Goddard; it seems that her promotion had been blocked and she was at least once threatened with dismissal from Barnard because of it. Extramarital heterosexual liaisons were more dangerous at Barnard than relationships between women. Dean Gildersleeve, "generally assumed to be homosexual," was responsible for these punitive attitudes.[26] In this climate Ruth and Margaret's living together presented no problems at all.

The two women kept busy. Ruth laid her unfinished book on religion to rest, reworking her material into a chapter for a book Boas was editing and turning her insights about the Pima into a paper she would present in the fall. Margaret prepared for her first field trip with Reo, with the Admiralty Islands the destination they had decided on. She would have to leave before Coming of Age hit the bookstores, and she needed to complete her ethnography of Manu'a.

The Manu'a monograph presented the first exposition of Ruth's insights about cultural patterns in a section for which Margaret and Ruth "thrashed out . . . every detail of the phrasing" (AW, 205): "We spent hours discussing how a given temperamental approach to living could come so to dominate a culture that all who were born in it would become the willing or unwilling heirs to that view of the world. From the first Ruth Benedict resisted any idea of schematization in terms of a given number of temperaments—Jung's fourfold scheme, for instance. She saw the relationship between a culture, which was 'personality writ large' and 'time binding,' and any individual who might or might not fit in, as a way of so phrasing all deviation that the unfortunate could be pitied and the world seen as the loser because of gifts which could not be used" (AW, 206).

The view of culture as "personality writ large" enabled Margaret and Ruth, particularly Ruth, to incorporate into anthropology an understanding of deviance, represented by people who, through no fault of their own, found their temperament and inclinations had no satisfactory outlet in their "deeply uncongenial" culture, but who may have been quite at home in another.

Regarding homosexuality, the approach they developed was both shaped by, and functioned as, a form of resistance to new professional discourses in which lesbian relationships no longer could be considered innocuous. Ruth always had a sense of herself as a deviant, an outsider, but Margaret never found the label fitting. She tussled with the issue and worried about her homosexual leanings but was not, by temperament, what Margaret Caffrey in her book about Ruth Benedict called a "stranger in this land."

Indeed, Mead's references to herself as deviant are disingenuous. In *Blackberry Winter* she insisted that she was deviant in comparison with other career women because her interests were so traditionally feminine, an analysis perhaps partly genuine and partly functioning to throw her readers off the scent. As she says, "I puzzled about the contrasts between Ruth and myself, especially when she made what seemed to me contradictory remarks, such as that it was quite impossible to imagine me as a man and that 'you'd make a better father than a mother' " (BW, 196).

Amidst these efforts, the two managed a rare holiday together in West-port, Connecticut, a seaside community favoured by writers and artists. Ruth would later tell Margaret that for the rest of her life she retained fond memories of this special time (MM, B14). Clearly, they had managed to find happiness in their personal relationship; the parting at summer's end was less fraught than the previous one. Margaret was now twenty-six, Ruth in her early forties, and the terms of their relationship had been negotiated. They were committed to a loving friendship and an intellectual partnership and any passion was the secret wine they savored, not their daily bread. Margaret's preference had won out.

Ruth was, of course, sad at the parting, but probably not distraught. "I Shall Not Call," from this time, is a poem of farewell and renunciation. A final reference to "witch fires" that "feed my years with star dust" resignedly echoes Margaret's imagery from "Star Bread" (MM, Q15). As Margaret had asked, "How could you think I'd make / Your star-meal into common bread?" Ruth's reply was:

> We shall go straitened upon sundered ways;
> Be lonelier than ghosts who may not lay
> Cheek against rose-flushed cheek, nor ever say
> The word the living weep for all their days.
>
> Ghosts have doubtless compensate ecstacies
> Of bodiless satisfactions; and I, being human,
> Shall I have nothing but the cup a woman
> Dips any day from unexhausted seas,
>
> Or bend me to the comfort that is all
> Our appetites shall get them for their need?
> There are witch fires at morning that shall feed
> My years with star dust. Go. I shall not call. (RFB, Box 45)

The two would spend a year apart; Margaret expected to return from the field married to Reo.

# 9

## Strange Untraveled Lands

THE ANTHROPOLOGIST LOLA ROMANUCCI-ROSS, who once worked with Margaret Mead, observed that anthropological field trips echo the heroic voyages of classical literature. Not just scientific expeditions, they are "voyages of self-discovery" and "metaphors for finding oneself. . . . In magical flight, far from creatures of their own kind, [anthropologists] . . . go to other worlds and return with their versions of them."[1] Margaret Mead's trip to the Admiralty Islands in 1928 initiated a voyaging decade, while closer to home Ruth Benedict continued to explore what she called in "Fulfillment" the "strange, untraveled lands" of her imagination (RFB, Box 43). Securing her position at Columbia meant that her commitment to anthropology, once more tenuous than Margaret's, was now solid. The women's private lives were also characterized by self-discovery. Margaret struggled to interweave fieldwork and marital partnership; Ruth was estranged from Edward Sapir, ended her marriage, and discovered the possibility of new intimacies.

Margaret, according to plan, met Reo Fortune in Auckland, New Zealand, on 8 October 1928. Since A. R. Radcliffe-Brown, Professor of Anthropology at Sydney, had suggested that Margaret might be fickle enough to change her mind, Reo insisted that they marry there and then. After rushing to a jeweller to adjust the size of Margaret's ring, the couple had just time to get to the registry office. They were married, and their boat sailed that evening.

In Sydney, they prepared for the Melanesian expedition and Margaret got to know Radcliffe-Brown. Tall, handsome and suave, he gave "the impression of enjoying being an Englishman in voluntary exile, but he also seemed lonely. His long cape and high hat, which he wore on social evenings, his level of sophistication, as well as his brilliance, set him off from his Sydney colleagues. . . . [His] relations with men seemed easier than those with women . . . [and he] gathered about him a group of worshipping disciples [who later seemed] to belong to an ancestor cult."[2] Radcliffe-Brown, along with Malinowski, was pioneering functionalist approaches to anthropology, though the Americans found it hard to discern differences between the British school and their own Boasian style. Reluctantly they tolerated, nevertheless, its vigorous promotion as the new direction for anthropology.

Margaret showed Radcliffe-Brown a draft of *Social Organization of Manu'a*, her formal monograph on Samoa. One of her points, she told Ruth, made him "so mad that he was barely civil to me. . . . He really is rather insufferable because he is so sulky and rude whenever he is crossed. . . . Any disagreement, tacit or uttered, with his ideas he takes as a slap in the face" (AW, 309–10). Yet though he could be difficult, Margaret was impressed with his approach and was always respectful of his scholarship.

From Sydney, it was twelve days to Rabaul, the capital of the Australian-governed Territory of New Guinea. Margaret and Reo traveled in an "evil-smelling little tub" with a menu that "boasted eighteen curries, different in name only." From there they sailed to the government station at Lorengau, the largest town in Manus, one of the Admiralty Islands. This, Margaret wrote "will be our metropolis for a year. There are some two dozen white people. Everyone speaks to everyone else and hate is rampant. It was really better at Pago Pago where they didn't speak to each other" (LF, 62).

The district officer was a "solitary and disgruntled" man; another local, Charlie Munster, had been a "famous blackbirder" (a Pacific form of indentured labor that at times was virtual slavery). He now traded pearl shells and owned the only refrigerator on the island: "The government is now out looking for prisoners to build a good road to Munster's place so that all the staff can have a pleasant little walk over in the afternoon, after tennis, for some good beer." There was a storekeeper "who makes 100% on every sale," a few planters, some not very successful missionaries, and that was it (LF, 62).

Margaret often spoke disparagingly of colonial society: "Such flimsy structures of a hundred or so white men govern and exploit this vast country—find gold, plant great plantations, trade for shell, hide their failures in other lands, drink inordinately, run into debt, steal each other's wives, go broke and commit suicide or get rich—if they know how" (LF, 63). Yet anthropologists relied on colonials for local knowledge and practical assistance, and they tended to overlook their own role in the colonizing process. They, too, contributed to westernization through transactions with money and tobacco and the introduction of western medical practices. Although not bent on economic exploitation or evangelism, they returned from the "colonies" with intellectual capital, which they used in the service of progressive, reformist ideals by demonstrating that their own cultures' sexual practices, family systems, childrearing, economic, social, and leadership arrangements were open to challenge and change. They also gave voice to the romantic preoccupations of the alienated westerner and fed the popular imagination with dreams of alternative societies.

Melanesia was a more formidable region for the anthropologist than Polynesia had been, with its hundreds of languages and "thousands of tiny communities" relating to each other through trade and sometimes warfare. Manus was only forty miles in length, yet had a population of 14,800 and eight distinct languages. "Blackbirding" had been modified into a system of "forcible persuasion" whereby young men were recruited into contracts requiring them to work for the colonists for three to five years, a practice that meant that anthropologists, too, had a ready labor supply. Pidgin, which enabled communication between indigenous peoples and colonists and across language groups, was becoming the preferred language in the region, though in villages it was usually only spoken by men who had labored away from home.

Nevertheless, field prospects looked good. Margaret's research topic, a study of the "mental development of young children among primitive people," could be investigated almost anywhere, so she allowed Reo to choose their site, the village of Pere, a day's trip up the coast by canoe.[3] From Lorengau she sent Ruth a cable which read simply "Auspicious. Devotedly" (MM, B14). Their local interpreter, Banyalo, whom they had met up with in Rabaul, was reluctant to return to Pere, and when they insisted he teach them Pidgin as well as the fiendishly complex local language, they found him "five foot six of sulky uselessness most of the time" (LF, 73).

Their new home was "a primitive Venice," a small fishing village of more than forty houses a quarter of a mile out from the mainland where "all life is conducted by means of canoes" (LF, 67). The houses, built on stilts over waterways, had thatched roofs and verandahs and were constructed with an airiness suited to the hot climate. Margaret and Reo settled into the house for government visitors, which all villages were expected to provide, while the men built them their own house.

The opportunity to move back and forth between two houses proved useful. In one, Margaret studied the playing children, who had few responsibilities beyond learning not to drown from inevitable tumbles into the water. The children were happy to draw pictures—thirty-five thousand in all—for Piyap, "Woman of the West," as they called Margaret. Reo learned the men's secrets in the other house. A horde of adolescent "cook boys," paid mostly in tobacco and eager to learn the ways of their prospective employers, made a lively background to the daily routine. Margaret reluctantly deferred the pleasures of smoking so that she would not have children constantly wheedling for cigarettes.

The food was better than expected, which pleased Margaret, since in Samoa she had been concerned that the local diet might affect her health and had chosen to eat mostly as the Europeans did. Fish was a staple, supplemented by taro, the indigenous starchy vegetable, a variety of tropical fruits, and occasionally a duck shot by Reo. Pigs were killed for festivities, and Margaret sometimes baked bread in a camp oven. The medical bag prepared by Marie Eichelberger helped the outsiders make a good impression when Margaret revived an unconscious child by breaking a phial of ammonia under his nose.

Soon after her arrival, Margaret sent an "at home" announcement to her friends. Louise Bogan, writing to Ruth, found this amusing: "Margaret is one to be quite At Home in any Mandatory Territory."[4] She was pleased to be there and happy with Reo on the "best field trip we ever had," though there were "few pleasures" and Reo's competitiveness was already in evidence (BW, 169). Her first impression of the Manus was that they were "gay and open-hearted," though she soon decided that they were not nearly as relaxed as the Samoans (LF, 71). Reo, whose first field trip had been among the more hostile Dobuans, found the contrast a great relief.

As time passed, Margaret observed that Manus adults were unlike their carefree children. Warfare and pillaging were not far in the past. She judged the people "anal" in personality formation, because they were "puritanical, materialistic [and] driving" (BW, 200). Their lives were dominated by the ever-present spirit world, with offenses against the spirits causing all sorts of illnesses and disasters.

Margaret and Reo worked with persistence during their months at Pere, learning the language, observing festivities, ceremonies, rituals, and ordinary interactions. They both had bouts of malaria, and Margaret fractured her foot and hobbled around on crutches for some time. Still, they managed to keep their notes in good shape and Reo also worked on his Dobu manuscript. He sent it to Ruth, who responded warmly that she loved what he had written, wondering how he could have survived in such an inhospitable culture. Toward the end of their time in Pere, thanking Ruth for a book of poetry she had sent him, he told her that they were "looking forward to getting out of primitive society with overpowering pressure" (AW, 313). He hoped Ruth would help him procure a fellowship at Columbia, since the couple planned to return to the United States and he would need a base there.

Ruth still missed Margaret. Around the time of Margaret's marriage to Reo she woke early one morning "with a back and forth rocking restlessness" and consoled herself by reading a booklet of "ruminations" given to her by Margaret before leaving for the field. Ruth later wrote, "I save the little

manuscript book like a too scant water supply on a voyage in an open boat"
(AW, 94).

She was also worried about the other person she loved most, Franz Boas.
He was unwell from time to time and suffered family misfortune. After
losing an adult son in a railway accident and a daughter to polio, there was
a further tragedy when his wife Marie, on whom he was utterly dependent,
was run over in the street and died shortly afterward. Boas was in Chicago,
and Edward Sapir accompanied him on the long, sad journey home, arriving in time for Boas to sit for a night with his wife before the burial.

Boas could not be discouraged from coming to the office even when he
was ill, and, as Ruth once remarked to Margaret, he insisted on "putting
his iron will to its worst possible use. He pushes his poor body as if it was
his . . . galley slave" (MM, B14). Ruth implored him to stay home on various
occasions and let her teach his classes, even though "there's no one in the
world I miss as I miss you when you're not in your room. I can't think how
poor I'd count myself if I hadn't known you. It should be enough just
to know you exist, but I'm terribly dependent on seeing you too" (FB,
28 March 1929). But she decided that in pushing himself to the limit he
was, after all, following his lifelong pattern, and she wrote to Margaret that
"he means to hold off death to get the Kwaikutl texts translated" (FB,
30 Dec. 1931). Edward once referred to Boas sarcastically as Ruth's "divinity" (AW, 95). Ruth herself joked to Margaret about having been brought up
in anthropology "with our mother's—or Papa Franz's!—milk" (AW, 305).

In September 1928, Ruth helped to organize an International Congress
of Americanists in New York, roping in Margaret's friend Hannah Kahn to
entertain international visitors; Stanley Benedict would not have been a
willing helper. The congress was a high point for Ruth; here she presented
her groundbreaking theory of psychological types in the Southwest. She
had a twenty minute time slot, sufficient to make an impression on her
audience. Edward said that the lecture was good and that he agreed with
her ideas; Alfred Kroeber wondered about Boas's reaction, asking, "How
does the old man take a paper like that?" (AW, 308); one of the overseas
visitors flattered her, thinking it the most important paper of the congress.
Margaret's boss, Clark Wissler, "scowled through a great deal of it and I
haven't seen him since," and Elsie Clews Parsons "was speechless and rose
to make all sorts of pointless addenda when she'd recovered her breath"
(AW, 308). Later, though, she helped Ruth edit the paper for publication
and even praised it. "Pretty good to fetch conviction from Elsie on so
alien a point," Ruth wrote Margaret (AW, 311). Most important, Boas, to
whom Ruth had been nervous about showing her work, "said nice things"
(AW, 311).

But Ruth's relationship with Edward was marked by increasing acidity.

Now safely married again, with Margaret half the world away and married to Reo, she hoped that at the congress the two of them would restore their friendship. But she told Margaret, "We spent one evening on a bench in the park. It took an hour or two to get him over a discussion of—how would you guess—jealousy. He nearly repudiated me and our conversation because I didn't agree that jealousy was necessarily the reverse of any important love and that you measured the size of the love by the size of the jealousy. . . . Finally, to avoid having to give chapter and verse out of my life, I had to pacify him by saying that after all I'd never been tested; but he bore away the resentment at my lack of understanding of his holy point . . ." (AW, 307). The "chapter and verse" from her own life must have referred to her feelings for Margaret and her experience of jealousy, an emotion she did not admire and had been able to master.

After the congress, Sapir wrote to Ruth, grumbling about his inconsequential talks with his male colleagues and insisting that what stood out was the time spent with her. Surprisingly, he did not even refer to the triumph of her paper. Ruth's poetry and friendship were what he valued, not the new psychological ideas she was bringing to anthropology, even though some of her inspiration derived from his work.[5]

Ruth found Edward's increasing conservatism thoroughly irksome. A few months later, she wrote to Margaret about her conversations with him at the American Anthropological Association's 1928 Christmas meeting: "Out of the evening I spent with Edward there was one hour of free reciprocity and a couple of excellent moments" but for the rest of the evening Sapir annoyed her by preaching about the exigencies of modern life, holding up the businessman as the ideal and dismissing poetry as irrelevant (AW, 95). Ironically, Edward privately published his rejected manuscript of verse, whereas Ruth put hers to rest until Margaret resuscitated it after her death, publishing many of the poems in *An Anthropologist at Work*.

Tensions came to a head when Edward wrote an opinion piece about the "sex problem" in America, published in the *American Journal of Psychiatry* late in 1928 and later on in the magazine, *American Mercury*.[6] It was some time before Ruth read it, because Edward avoided sending her a copy. When she eventually stumbled across it, she was outraged.

Edward's argument was that Americans were in a transitional stage in their attitudes to sex. They were "painfully near" to the "old Puritan morality which looked upon the sex act as inherently sinful." But the fashionable new radicals had gone overboard in rejecting the past: the "present excited and puzzled attitude, shifting back and forth in a single individual's mind all the way from orthodox acceptance of the restraints of Puritanism to a reasoned religion of promiscuity" was equally unhealthy. The radical, suggested Sapir, fails to recognize "the naturalness and the universality of love. . . . One hears it said that among the truly enlightened love, in so far as it exists at all, is merely the casual association of the sex impulse with certain warm feelings of companionship or friendship." The result of sexual experimentation is that "life is being measurably cheapened by an emotional uncertainty in matters of sex." The supposed "enrichment of personality" by way of multiple sexual experiences is really just "a weary accumulation of poverties."[7]

Edward next took what had to be a direct swipe at Margaret, as well as Malinowski: "The present sex unrest has been nibbling at more or less reliable information presented by anthropologists from primitive communities. Any primitive community that indulges, or is said to indulge, in unrestricted sex behavior is considered an interesting community to hear from. . . . It does not seem to occur to readers of excited books about pleasure-loving Samoans and Trobriand Islanders that perhaps these communities are not as primitive as they seem." Sex, he argued, is not unregulated in primitive societies, and "if we cannot sympathetically understand their sex taboos, why do we pretend to understand their freedom from our sex taboos?" He made pointed jabs at the "smart and trivial analysis of sex by intellectuals who have more curiosity than intuition" and attacked feminism, dismissing the idea that ownership of women is at the root of sex restrictions: it was "one of those theories that are too plausible to be true."[8]

The modern woman confused sex radicalism with her own ambitions: "The aftermath of the feminist revolt is still with us. Every psychiatrist must have met essentially frigid women of today who have used sex freedom as a mere weapon with which to feed the ego. And this all too common sacrifice of love and the possibility of love on the altar of ambition that is essentially insatiable, because it is so much of a compulsion, is met by the complementary need of 'fair minded men' to accept the free woman at her word. . . . Is it a wonder that the sexes unconsciously hate each other today with an altogether new and baffling virulence?"[9]

Arguing that sexual freedom made it difficult for men and women to develop "true psychological intimacy," Edward went on to lambast homosexuality: "In extreme cases—one dreads to acknowledge how appallingly frequent these extreme cases are becoming—the constantly dampened, because never really encouraged, passion between the sexes leads to compensation in the form of homosexuality, which, if we are reliably informed, is definitely on the increase in America. . . . Love having been squeezed out of sex, it revenges itself by assuming unnatural forms. The cult of the 'naturalness' of homosexuality fools no one but those who need a rationalization of their own problems."[10]

A discussion of jealousy—his "holy point," as Ruth had put it—gave Edward an opportunity to take another dig at Margaret: "As one young emancipated woman once expressed it to me, it would be an insult to either her or to her husband to expect fidelity of them." What was worse, these emancipated young women were not even sexy: "Our intellectual mistresses of sin play a sadly pedantic part—their ardors are in the head rather than in the heart or even in the 'erogenous' zone. To put it bluntly, the 'free' woman of sophisticated America, whether poetess or saleslady, has a hard job escaping from the uncomfortable feeling that she is really a safe, and therefore a dishonest, prostitute. . . . The battle glows in the hard, slightly unfocused, glitter of the eye, and in the hollow laugh, and one can watch the gradual deterioration of personality that seems to set in in many of our young women with premature adoption of sophisticated standards."[11]

Ruth wrote angrily to Edward. Why had he not shown the paper to her? He had not sent her a copy, he replied, because he took it for granted that she would not care for it. Ruth may not have been surprised by Edward's virulence, but it was outrageous that he had gone into print obliquely calling Margaret frigid, dishonest, trivial, and essentially a prostitute. If this were not bad enough, Edward's remarks about homosexuality seemed to target Ruth. She evidently accused him, as he replied, "I do not wish to have our relations unnecessarily muddied by irreconcilable differences, but that you were outraged by a supposed quotation shocked as few things have shocked me. . . . You will probably not believe me—and yet it is the sober truth—when I say that you were never once in my thoughts when I wrote the paper on sex, which I did, by the way, rather reluctantly at the request of Harry Stack Sullivan. No, it was Margaret and a lot of drivel in her letters which I was quoting. . . . She is hardly a person to me at all, . . . but a symbol of everything I detest most in American culture. But I have always loved you too much to drag in everything I know or sense of your life and its tragic problems" (SF, 29 April 1929).[12]

Ruth had once loved Edward romantically; now he dismissed her life, her sexuality, and, if he but realized it, her passion for Margaret as "tragic problems." He was one of the few people she had been able to confide in and the first in anthropological circles. She had taken risks in her intimacy with him; now, given his complete misunderstanding, she must have felt their friendship had always been suspect. No doubt Margaret had defended homosexuality to Edward; perhaps his comment was directed at Margaret. It was nevertheless insulting and his reply made matters worse.

Ruth seems not to have replied to Edward's letter, as their regular correspondence now ceased. In later times she was cordial toward him, but the earlier intimacy was never reinstated.

In the summer of 1929, after a year's absence, Margaret and Reo returned. In San Francisco, Margaret had an operation on her sinuses aimed at correcting her "Samoan eye trouble" and the pains in her arm. The operation was nearly fatal, and she later remarked that the doctor, a friend of her mother's, was "somewhat monomaniac in his diagnoses" (BW, 180). Certainly this encounter with western medicine put her in more danger than any tropical situation Ruth had worried about.

In spite of Margaret's worries about the reception of Coming of Age, she returned home to find it wildly successful. She had dreamed in Sydney that the book had "failed completely" and been withdrawn by the publisher, and she thought that another dream, in which the dedication to Ruth was left off the monograph on Manu'a, meant that "I'm dissatisfied with [it]" (AW, 311). But the anxiety proved unfounded. William Morrow had already written excitedly that Havelock Ellis had been generous with his praise of the book, and comments from the high priest of sexology were placed on a bright red band around the cover.

Malinowski had also come up trumps despite the gossip and Margaret's fears. He wrote that Samoa was "an absolutely first-rate piece of descriptive anthropology . . . an outstanding achievement."[13] Sales far exceeded expectations and reviews from fellow anthropologists were good, though Morrow's warning that in popularizing her work she should pay some regard to "the possible attitudes of your fellow-scholars" led Margaret to write articles about Samoa for American Mercury and The Nation rather than Smart Set or Cosmopolitan, as she had initially planned.[14]

Louise Bogan liked Coming of Age, though she could not resist a little jibe, writing to Ruth: "I read Margaret's book with much pleasure. The argument goes as cleanly as a piston; the cause falls, the effect rises, but not mechanically—brightly and humanly set going."[15]

Waiting for Margaret were royalties of five thousand dollars, a small fortune representing twice her annual salary. The financial atmosphere in New York was heady; friends were gambling on the soaring stock market and Ruth suggested that she speculate, but her father predicted a crash and her grandmother had always advised, "Lucky at cards, unlucky in love" (BW, 183). She kept her money safely in her hometown bank; Reo, though not a gambler, was caught when his New York bank failed. Her investment shielded Margaret when the Depression started to bite and the museum lowered salaries.

Stanley Benedict, like many others, lost money in stocks. Among their mutual friends, Louise Bogan was most affected when her husband Raymond Holden's inheritance was wiped out. The two had returned from Santa Fe, buying a farmhouse in the countryside outside of New York. It was later destroyed by fire, forcing them back into the city. The stress contributed to Louise's mental breakdown and hospitalization in the winter of 1929–30. She later described this time as a "sojourn in hell."[16] Ruth's friendship with Louise, perhaps never intimate, did not survive the trouble.

Marie Eichelberger, overjoyed to have Margaret home, remembered as one of the best days in her life the Saturday Margaret took her to lunch in Greenwich Village and presented her with a copy of *Coming of Age* (MM, B14). It was probably Marie who found an apartment for Margaret and Reo, a brownstone on 102nd Street with a study for Reo, now enrolled, thanks to Ruth's efforts, in the doctoral program at Columbia.

Margaret's premonition that "life would be uncomfortable for Reo in a country in which I was at home and already well-known, but he was a stranger" was accurate (BN, 185). Visitors found their household "stable though rather tempestuous" (BW, 177). Margaret, with admirable good sense, had vetoed Reo's plan after leaving the Admiralty Islands to go to New Zealand, where he would work as a laborer while she wrote up her field notes. A conventional New Zealand man of his time when it came to sex roles, Reo found it difficult not to be the breadwinner. They lived carefully, Margaret saving her royalties for future fieldwork. Reo did not like to see her doing housework—nor did he do any. She learned to tidy up stealthily, though they also employed a cleaner.

Reo revised *Sorcerers of Dobu* and worked on *Manus Religion*, while Margaret, content to keep a relatively low profile in her work place, wrote *Growing Up in New Guinea* in the museum tower. Though not a great collector, Margaret was always committed to the educational role of museums; one of her achievements in this period was a display of the village of Pere. Her book on New Guinea is a model of psychological observation and contributed to debates about progressive education by showing that the youngsters of Pere, despite growing up carefree, developed a rigid personality in adulthood. Her argument showed that the dictates of society could overcome the lessons of childhood and she urged educators to examine the imperatives of American culture.

Margaret often found it difficult to share her friends with Reo because he was awkward or jealous. As a couple, they did get on well with Eleanor Steele and Howard Scott, the founder of "Technocracy," an idiosyncratic, anti-Marxist political ideology which Margaret found compelling. Toward Ruth, whom he would have seen frequently at Columbia, Reo seems to have mixed feelings. He respected her intellect and experience. Ruth seems to have been friendly to him, encouraging his work, lending him money, and finding common ground through their mutual interest in poetry. One indication of Reo's attitude toward Ruth comes from a dream he recorded during his early days in the United States. He was struggling to cook popovers and make coffee while Ruth watched mockingly; "Finally she said something about using the hot water & I made believe I didn't know there was anything wrong about that & she said, 'Well I just think that using cold water is a more adult way of making coffee' " (MM, A21). Reo thought the dream reflected Ruth's judgments on his work, though people often mistook Ruth's reserve as mockery and Reo typically dreamed of put-downs, arguments, and other aggressive themes.[17] He may well have resented Ruth's influence on Margaret, who continued to see Ruth for lunches and in the evening.[18] He was younger than both women; Margaret, if not bossy, was certainly self-assured; and Reo's sense of male prerogative was hard put to find a satisfactory outlet in his situation. As a couple, they accommodated each other uneasily.

One of the few books Mead cites in *Growing Up in New Guinea* indicates her growing conservatism regarding homosexuality, a change from the carefree attitudes she had endorsed in *Samoa*. *Love in the Machine Age* was the work of Greenwich Village writer Floyd Dell, Edna St. Vincent Millay's first male lover.[19] Dell believed that homosexuality was unnecessary in the age of free love; it was only in patriarchal societies where marriages were arranged that unfulfilled desires took the form of homosexuality, prostitution, or adultery. With the intellectual woman becoming more independent, the typical man of Greenwich Village, as one observer noted, "felt like a victim deprived of his property."[20] Reo may well have shared this attitude, though Margaret was loyal and tried to make the marriage work.

In December Léonie Adams arrived home from Europe, staying for a time with Ruth and then with Margaret and Reo. She was full of stories about France, where she had met Gertrude Stein, and of England, where she had become acquainted with H. D. and Bryher, the lesbian literary couple. Before her trip to Europe she had succumbed to Edmund Wilson's persistent attentions, and on her return they broke off. As was his habit, Wilson memorialized his encounters with Léonie in characteristically obscene passages in his diaries, while in print he listed her as one of the most distinguished among emerging American writers.[21]

Margaret and Reo were planning another field trip. Boas had vetoed a study of the Navajo, who supposedly belonged to Goddard and Reichard— territoriality was still the norm among anthropologists. Eventually they arranged a trip to Nebraska in the summer of 1930 to study the Omaha, Ruth's having helped Reo find his share of the funding. They bought a Ford and drove across country into the heat, Margaret frightened by Reo's erratic driving which on occasion took them off the road. Three months among the Omaha, living in the midst of a "broken" culture marked by dependency on welfare, drunkenness, family breakdown, and child neglect were dispiriting. Margaret wrote complainingly to Ruth, hoping that she would not be thought "a thankless wretch" (LF, 96), and concluding that if she were an Americanist, she would remain in a library most of the time. She doubted the authenticity of research by her fellows if all their fieldwork were carried out in such unpromising locales.

The Omaha trip brought out a streak of paranoia in Reo. He thought he had been set an impossible task so that he would fail and disgrace himself. Ruth had set the task, so his suspicion must have turned in her direction. *Omaha Secret Societies*, his book from that trip, bore out his presentiments in that it received little appreciation. Margaret's monograph, *The Changing Culture of an Indian Tribe* (whose working title was *Reservation Women* until she realized that was the term the army gave to prostitutes), dealt with the mistakes in the government's Indian policies which had brought this community to a state of aimlessness and despair.

In the summer of 1930 Ruth was forty-three. At the lake she brooded. Her friendship with Edward had ended on a bitter note, poetry was less absorbing, her relationship with Margaret had become more settled and less preoccupying. She was still married and financially dependent, yet she and Stanley no longer shared any sexual intimacy, to Ruth's disappointment. One Saturday the previous spring, after Thursday lunch with Margaret, she "lost a good day reviling myself for the wave of self pity I'm inundated by," describing herself as "a lonely woman whose sex demands could get out of hand at a moment's provocation—*are* out of hand on a day like this." Suffering from menstrual pains and "spring fever," she recalled that it was five years since Stanley had shown any sexual interest, except for one night the previous summer (RFB, Box 37).

A heat wave made even the lake unpleasant. Ruth had a bad dream that seemed to reveal the lack of intimacy between herself and Stanley: "I was being served with a mess of new ground meat, and I was picking it over in an agony to find some limit of the beauty of the living body that had been brought to this—some bit of the soft skin of the cheek or the rounded arm. I woke sobbing, shook myself out of the dream, but I could not choke myself out of the agony" (RFB, Box 37).

Ruth knew her nature could allow her to be sensual, carefree, and happy, but the great artists and spiritual thinkers she admired either lacked sensuality, like Jesus, or managed to subdue it, like Buddha, or wrestled with a divided self, like Dostoevsky. Did civilization really mean breeding out the "pull of the senses and of simple healthy animal indulgences"? Ruth was sometimes repelled by mysticism and its overcoming of the body: "When touch seems such a sweet and natural human delight, I resent rooting it out even in favor of my dearest dream of achieving some sort of dignity in living." She went on: "Temperamentally my stakes are on the side of the spirit—I am given over to these unhealthy growths, pity and fidelity. But that doesn't settle the matter. I'm too healthy, and when I pass up the animal joys of human nearness, it's my pity that tears me. The pleasures appear to me like lovely children and if I were an animal they would be. The fact that some human turn of the screw committed me to the pursuit of permanence in relations, to a yearning for the kind of human intercourse that can only come out of much more complicated arrangements than spending a night together—that hasn't yet become enough to keep me from yearning over the murdered pleasures of the senses" (RFB, Box 36).

Ruth and Stanley returned from the lake in mid-September before the new academic year. Although she still had no permanent job, Ruth was expecting heavy responsibilities, since Boas had arranged to take a sabbatical amongst his "dear Kwaikutl" in British Columbia and she would run the anthropology department, doubling her teaching load.

One rainy Tuesday in early November 1930, a public holiday, Ruth spent the morning with Margaret. Recording "misery" afterward, she went home to bed, then back to Bedford Hills in the evening. There she and Stanley must have had a painful quarrel with perhaps an attempt at reconciliation since Stanley, most uncharacteristically, spent the next night in Ruth's apartment. The following day Ruth recorded in her datebook that after sixteen years of marriage she and Stanley had separated (RFB, Box 42).[22]

Judging from later remarks she made to Margaret, Ruth was the one who initiated the separation (MM, B14). The next week a letter from Stanley arrived, laying out his terms for the separation, which evidently were unacceptable. The following day, Saturday, she wrote "All day laid out campaign! Night slept 7 P.M.–9 A.M." On Sunday, with no Bedford Hills to draw her away from Manhattan, she "worked *alone* all day in the apartment" (RFB, Box 42).

At the time of her separation, Ruth was seeing a younger man, Thomas Mount. According to Margaret, who wrote to him when she was working on Ruth's biography (MM, TR2), Ruth was fond of Tom, though the nature of their relationship is unclear. It did involve friendship and support. Tom was an aspiring writer who worked in advertising. How he and Ruth met is not known; perhaps they had been introduced by Marguerite Israel Arnold, who had also worked in advertising and had urged Ruth to have an affair. It seems that Tom helped Ruth lay out her "campaign" in reply to Stanley's letter, and a month after the separation, just before Christmas, she noted cryptically, "Tom—overture" (RFB, Box 42).[23]

Was this a sexual advance, or was it a request for financial assistance or a place to stay? A few days later Ruth rented a new apartment, went to a party of Margaret's, and noted that Tom got home at 2:00 A.M., so by then he was staying with her. The new apartment on West Seventy-fifth Street was more spacious than her usual small rooms, with room for the truckload of furniture she brought from Bedford Hills. Her datebooks note several engagements with Tom over January 1931. Later that month he sailed for Europe. If Tom had made an advance to her, whether or not accepted, Ruth would have been flattered at a time when affirmation was especially welcome.

Despite the separation, Ruth helped Stanley buy and furnish a new house in Scarsdale and worried about whether he was looking after himself. He did not seem to want much contact. When she heard he was in bed with the flu, she restrained her impulse to help, knowing he was "exceptionally comfortable" on his own. In the first few months after the separation he was angry with her, but became more amicable, telephoning from time to time "with great cordiality and pleasantness." In mid–1932 Ruth reported to Margaret that he had managed to keep up "excellent behavior" all year, and perhaps he felt there were some compensations to be had from their separation. Ruth wrote to Margaret that "as long as he hasn't been irreparably hurt I'm content" (MM, B14).

Tom settled in Spain to work on a book which never seemed to eventuate despite his reassurances that it was forthcoming. Ruth helped him financially from time to time; after a while he married a young European woman. It was not long before she was pregnant and her dowry nearly used up. Tom approached Ruth for a contribution toward his fare to the United States so that he could work for the summer before returning to Europe, a scheme Ruth thought was unrealistic and would spoil her own summer. She "vigorously" advised him to stay put, as she was "weary of his vagabondage" and, as she told Margaret, she was "giving thanks to God that there was no man living whose whims and egotisms I had to take seriously" (MM, B14). Ruth continued to contribute financially to Tom's "ménage," according to Margaret, though it was an arrangement that Ruth had "very little time for" (MM, B14).

For a while Ruth was in an emotional limbo. Having lived for years in the shadow of Stanley's apparent dislike or disapproval, and having been hurt and disappointed in her intimacy with Margaret, she wondered if she would ever experience another partnership. In a note fragment from around this time she wrote, "It would be different with another person, of course, and I know that with my *self*. I don't daydream about another deep personal relation. It would be bad for me really to believe in it" (RFB, Box 37).

She was not inclined to be public about the separation but did eventually mention it in a letter to Edward that was largely about professional matters, since their correspondence was now seldom personal. Edward replied that he was quite shocked at the news but was "sure you would not allow such a thing to happen if it were not inevitable, as you say" (SF, 4 Feb. 1931). Her friends knew, of course, and she saw Margaret frequently, rarely accompanied by Reo. She began adjusting to her new freedom.

Supporting herself was now an even more pressing matter. But the separation galvanized Boas into action. Two days before her forty-fourth birthday, on 3 June 1931, Ruth was thrilled to accept an assistant professorship at Columbia. Her salary would be $3,600 per year and she could earn a further $1,000 with extension courses. Initially, the dean had offered a one-year lectureship at $3,000, but Boas negotiated a better deal. It was nearly a decade since Benedict had commenced her academic career and she was roundly congratulated by her friends and colleagues. Gladys Reichard called her appointment "a grand scoop for feminism,"[24] and even Edward wrote kindly that it was "a modest and criminally belated acknowledgment of your services, and I hope it won't be long before they raise your rank" (RFB, Box 62).

The appointment came days before Ruth was due to leave for the Southwest, with Margaret bidding her farewell rather than the other way around. By the time she returned, Margaret and Reo would again be en route to New Guinea, expecting to be away for at least two years. So there was a final round of visits, a dinner alone with Reo, a Samoan party, most likely organized by Margaret and—during Ruth's final evening in New York—a farewell visit just with Margaret. Ruth's diary is silent about the occasion.

# 10

*Witch Fires at Morning*

RUTH'S 1931 TRIP TO THE SOUTHWEST came about because Edward Sapir had asked her to lead a field expedition that summer. Perhaps offering the leadership to Ruth was an astute move, since Boas had accused the organizers of these summer laboratories of prejudice against women. The venture had originally been planned at the Yale Club, and because women were not admitted to those august premises Elsie Clews Parsons, despite her wealth and expertise, was left off the invitation list, an omission that had become something of an embarrassment.

By 1931 women were more generally accepted as part of the landscape of anthropology, but they still ran into difficulties when they wanted to do fieldwork. Mead had gone to Samoa on her own, with opposition from Sapir and trepidation on the part of Boas, but now her work took place in a husband-wife partnership, a widely accepted fieldwork model. The idea of women and men who were not married to each other working together as colleagues or students in the field had always provoked disapproval from most of the men in anthropology. Parsons, whose whole life was a campaign to overturn the conventions of polite behavior which kept women in their separate sphere, helped to lay down new standards for behavior in this area by traveling with male anthropologists such as Kroeber and Boas and refusing to tolerate gossip—although romantic attachments to Parsons flourished among her male colleagues, and someone like Pliny Earle Goddard, who delighted in a good story, could not be controlled altogether. But Parsons's seriousness of purpose could never be faulted, and her social position and financial generosity toward anthropology put her beyond criticism.

Evidence from the time suggests that while the issue of women's safety in the field was often legitimate, male concerns about working with women were often the primary cause of anxiety. As Desley Deacon, Parsons's biographer, points out, "Despite the inroads of feminism in advanced circles of

American society, most men considered women a different, and somewhat dangerous, species." Alfred Kroeber told Parsons that the Harvard men were afraid of her because "you are a lady, so must be treated as one; but ladies don't talk of sex, and they would be ever so much more comfortable if you were a bit off-color and they could cut you."[1]

Edward Sapir, still smarting from his entanglement with Mead, often played the liberal, but he showed his true colors in correspondence with Parsons about women students being excluded from the first Santa Fe summer school. He thought she must have heard "a prejudiced or heated version" of the selection process, arguing that the men had not discriminated and that if there had been "a really strong woman candidate" she would have been chosen. He went on to say, though, that "there are of course difficulties about a mixed party in the field. . . . The type of woman who really means business scientifically, like Gladys Reichard or Eva Horner or Ruth Bunzel, is welcomed by all, but I am afraid there are some—and they may be among the ablest intellectually—who create highly disturbing and embarrassing problems. . . ." Alfred Kidder, from Harvard, who was involved in the selection, defended himself to Parsons by saying that if women were to work alongside men in the party, there would have to be at least two, and there had been only one candidate who was qualified. Even her friend Kroeber let her down. He was to lead the party and wrote to her, "does anyone see me wanting to lead a little harem around an Arizona railroad town for two months . . . ? If ever Anthropology gets to be prevailingly a feminine science I expect to switch to something else. So, I think, will you!"[2]

Deacon documents several instances of career-wrecking discrimination against women at this time, behavior that displayed both men's fear of sexual distractions in the work place and also the ways in which they used sexual innuendo to discredit women's work and obtain positions for themselves and their male protégés. Sapir's slurs on Mead were not an isolated example. Ruth Bunzel's work in Guatemala came to a swift end in the early 1930s following malicious gossip that she was "Padre Rossbach's mistress; that we had indulged in wild orgies at the Convent . . . ," and so on.[3] One of the Harvard anthropologists told Bunny directly that it was Boas's responsibility to provide positions for the women he had trained—even though his male students found all doors open to them, filling the most prominent positions available to the next generation of American anthropologists. Moreover, as Bunzel was told, she had a family that could take care of her.

Ruth's plan was to take students to an Apache reservation at Mescalero, New Mexico. Phenomenal organization was required, and she found herself ordering huge stores of canned sausages and cornmeal, budgeting for tennis equipment and magazines, and purchasing an Ediphone recording machine with one hundred cylinders, all at the end of an exhausting academic year.[4]

Before taking on this project, Ruth vacationed at her sister's home in Pasadena. Here she met Natalie Raymond again, the "gay young soul" she had befriended in New York in 1926. Previous biographers of Benedict have had little or nothing to say about Natalie, who was now in her mid-twenties and spending time with her wealthy stepfather, Albert Bradley, and her mother, Undine, known for vibrant, entertaining parties. Nat had been scientifically educated, at some point working with laboratory animals. Her circle of older friends included Richard Tolman, a physicist at the California Institute of Technology, his psychologist wife, Ruth Tolman, and their next-door neighbour, Ruth Valentine ("Val"), also a psychologist. Val had taken her doctorate with Edward Chace Tolman, Richard Tolman's brother and Professor of Psychology at Berkeley. Since Val's thesis was an experimental study of learning in rats and Natalie also worked with laboratory animals, it seems possible that Natalie also may have studied with or worked for Edward Chace Tolman.[5]

Richard Tolman was also the probable connection between Natalie and Robert Oppenheimer. A brilliant young physicist from a wealthy New York family, Oppenheimer had recently taken up teaching positions at Berkeley and in Pasadena. Later he would become known to the world as "father of the bomb" for his leadership of the American atomic weapons program during World War II, and, after the war, a cause célèbre in the highly publicized McCarthy hearings where he was accused of being a Soviet agent.[6]

Oppenheimer's biographers never mention a romance with Natalie, though published correspondence makes it clear that the two enjoyed each other's company, and a friend of Natalie's remembers that at one time Natalie said she and Oppenheimer planned to marry. It is unclear whether politics was a common interest, since Oppenheimer's involvement with left-wing causes did not begin until the mid-thirties, but certainly they shared scientific and cultural interests. They both loved the outdoors, too, and Natalie spent several vacations with "Oppie" and other friends at his small cabin in the Pecos Valley, New Mexico, where they rode horseback and hiked along mountain trails.

Oppenheimer was known for his reckless driving, and Natalie herself was not averse to taking risks. In the early thirties, before Ruth's visit to Pasadena, the two were in a serious auto accident. Oppenheimer had boasted that his prized Chrysler, a gift from his father, would do seventy five easily. Racing against the coast train near Los Angeles, he crashed it.

Natalie was knocked unconscious and Oppenheimer thought at first that he had killed her. By way of recompense for his son's foolishness, Oppenheimer's father gave Natalie a Cézanne drawing and a Vlaminck painting.

By the time Ruth and Natalie met in Pasadena, any romantic elements in Natalie's relationship with Robert Oppenheimer may have been in the past, though the two remained friends. Natalie never married, and there is no suggestion of any later involvements with men; perhaps by then she considered herself a lesbian. Between Ruth and Natalie the attraction seems to have been immediate. Two and a half years younger than Margaret Mead, Natalie has been described as slim, vivacious, and of medium height (there are no available photographs). She was witty and intelligent—a friend from the New York publishing world recalled that "Nat" was one of the brightest people she had ever met—although unlike Margaret, she was not particularly determined or serious and was unsure of her life plans.[7]

Before Ruth's brief stay was over, the two had arranged that Nat, who had probably intended to visit the Oppenheimer ranch that summer, would also stay with Ruth at Mescalero. So Ruth left for the Southwest and in the scorching heat of New Mexico began the field trip.

Lodgings were the dormitory of a native school, Ruth sharing a room with Regina Flannery, the only woman student, while the four "boys" were in one large room. Anthropological work was interspersed with swimming in the mornings, trips to the mountains, and sitting outdoors in the evening. Jules Blumensohn (later Jules Henry) soon became a personal favorite of Ruth's; she had a ready sympathy for anyone different, and the other young men, "hearty extrovert boys . . . snubbed him pretty badly," possibly on account of his Jewishness (AW, 317).

Nat spent three weeks with the group, making occasional forays elsewhere on her own. She was a hit with the students, leaving an impression of a young, physically exuberant woman with a strong personality. Morris Opler, one of the students who later kept in touch with Ruth, referred to Nat as a "very vigorous young lady" who "stormed about . . . menacing the lives of all gentle and well-behaved young men, dogs and cats." He joked that Harry Hoijer, the linguist in residence, "still trembled at her name" and had nightmares about driving around with her (RFB, Box 62). The auto accident apparently had done nothing to repress Nat's love of speed.

Ruth was unwell part of the time. Occasionally she spent an entire day in bed, and toward the end of Nat's stay, when they traveled to El Paso and then on to Juarez on the same day, she fainted and had to stay in bed while Nat went off to a ceremony with Harry Hoijer. On their final day together, Nat left for Albuquerque to catch an eastbound train, while Ruth's party returned to Mescalero hoping to observe a rain dance. The nature of Ruth's illness is unclear, but she was already tired when the trip began, her responsibilities were taxing, and the emotional whirlwind arising from her feelings about Nat may have exacerbated any physical complaint.

Nat's presence did not deter Ruth from her customary correspondence with Margaret, and she still became agitated when mail was delayed. Just what she told Margaret about Nat is not known, but she did mention the visit (FB, 18 Aug. 1931).

It seems likely that Ruth and Nat became lovers early on. By the end of Ruth's time at Pasadena, Nat had decided to return to New York, where she would live with Ruth and take up studies at Cornell medical school. Whether these professional plans were formulated before or after meeting Ruth is not clear, but Nat was capable of rapid decisions. "Nat has gone east, having worn out the Pacific Coast," Robert Oppenheimer wrote to his brother.[8]

Sudden action on the personal front was not Ruth's forte. She had endured years of an unhappy marriage; her disappointment in Margaret's marriages had been submerged so as not to poison their friendship, and despite her hunger for sensuality, short affairs were not to her taste since she valued permanence in relationships. On the other hand, years of deprivation must have made a love affair all the sweeter. And if Ruth was one to measure her decisions carefully, Nat was impulsive enough for both of them.

Ruth's personal happiness was clouded by a tragedy which occurred during the Mescalero expedition, one that was horrifying in itself and also threatened women's future chances at fieldwork.[9] A week after Nat arrived, on a day when Ruth was ill, there came horrifying news that her graduate student, Henrietta Schmerler, had been murdered. After she had been turned down for the field laboratory Schmerler had persuaded a hesitant Benedict and Boas to allow her to make a field trip on her own to an Apache reservation in the White Mountains on the other side of Arizona. Ruth thought her student naive and idealistic, but how could she not support a woman with an independent streak? Margaret had been her first great success, against the opposition of Sapir and with the reluctant consent of Boas.

Since Ruth was ill when she heard about the murder, Gladys Reichard rushed to the Apache reservation from her nearby location with the Navajo. As the circumstances surrounding the murder became known, the only possible conclusion was that Schmerler had taken risks that Benedict and others had warned her against. They had told her to work with the Apache women, and she had duly reported to Ruth that she was learning needlework at the feet of an old woman. It seems, however, that her actions were not so judicious. She had camped in the woods on her own rather than lodge with a family, causing offense to her hosts. She had also endangered herself greatly in her attempt, as an admirer of Margaret Mead's Samoan work, to investigate the sex life of the Apache. It was suggested that the men mistook her research questions as a sign of "looseness," and further, that she became romantically involved with one of them. Then she rode out on horseback with another young man, a sign to the Apache of willingness to be courted. He made advances to her, she apparently rebuffed them, and he sexually assaulted and murdered her.

Ruth was shocked and upset, but moved quickly to control the damage, for important matters were at stake. Had she made a mistake in authorizing Schmerler to go into the field alone? Schmerler's father clearly thought so and initiated a suit against Columbia University. Would the murder set back the progress of women in anthropology and fieldworkers in the Southwest generally? Would it stir up hostile racism in the press? How would Boas, now in Europe, take the news?

Ruth wrote to Margaret, sending her to Columbia to try to stop Gladys Reichard from telling Boas the full details. In fact, Ruth and Margaret hatched a plot so that Boas would not know Schmerler "had made the mistakes we both feared" (FB, 10 Aug. 1931). They wanted him to think of her as a martyr to the cause of anthropology rather than as a naive and wayward young woman. But their plot failed—Gladys could not be made to understand the "martyr" script and her letters "did not soften the blow." Indeed, Boas was extremely upset. Schmerler's death preyed on his mind all summer and he wrote to Ruth, "How shall we now dare to send a young girl out after this? And still. Is it not necessary and right?" (AW, 409).

The newspapers made as much of the murder as Ruth and Margaret had feared. Months later, as the trial approached, Boas was determined to testify on behalf of Columbia. He booked his train tickets to New Orleans, though Ruth was relieved when ill health meant he could not travel. She wrote to Margaret: "His idea was that he could see that it was kept sweet and pure, I suppose. Can't you see what a target the lawyer for the defense would have made of him? . . . At least that's one thing he's mercifully spared. Papa Franz as the butt of an Arizona murder trial that has carte blanche to play up the motifs of sex and race!" (FB, 27 Dec. 1931).

Ruth was put forward as a witness in place of Boas but was most reluctant to go. "Ach! can you think of any worse way of spending the month of March?" she wrote Margaret (FB, 24 Feb. 1932). In cahoots with the departmental secretary, Ruth Bryan, Benedict maneuvered Boas into coming up with the idea of sending Ruth Underhill, a mature, responsible graduate student with a background in social work. Underhill was excited about the responsibility and Ruth discharged her duties by writing to the Indian Bureau that Schmerler had disobeyed instructions. "I've not tried to shield her except with her family," she told Margaret (FB, 24 Feb. 1932) and was relieved when Schmerler's father, whose suit against Columbia was settled out of court, sailed to Palestine to join the Zionist movement: "Thank God he's out of the picture" (FB, 25 July, 1932).[10]

Ruth was so relieved to have avoided testifying that after Underhill's departure she held an "excellent and convivial" party for Columbia people at her apartment, breaking open a bottle of Cointreau that had been part of a bet as to who would have to go (MM, B14). In Ruth's and Margaret's view, it seems, anyone who violated the mores of a culture was fully to blame for the consequences. Yet their lack of outrage at women's vulnerability to male violence seems a little surprising, viewed from the present. Schmerler was not alive to tell her story, there were no witnesses except the accused, and the supposition that, among the Apache, it was perfectly natural to murder following sexual rejection seems not to have been contested in their circles. Moreover, their private attitudes suggest a callousness about the victim that was uncharacteristic, perhaps demonstrating just how threatened women anthropologists felt about their legitimacy as fieldworkers.

With Marie Eichelberger now living in Detroit, the full burden of looking after Margaret's affairs fell on Ruth. On the whole she was willing, but she did once complain to Esther Schiff Goldfrank that "whenever Margaret goes out into the field she throws a batch of manuscripts on my desk and says, 'Please get these ready for publication.' "[11] When Margaret and Reo left for New Guinea, Ruth took charge of their finances, filing income taxes, investing the royalties from Margaret's two books, and arranging to send money to New Zealand for the education of Reo's younger brother. She acted as quartermaster, arranging for their provisions to be sent and arguing with stores over shipping procedures to such a faraway place. Overseeing Margaret's increasingly complex program of publishing (and Reo's, as well) involved keeping track of manuscripts, proofreading, arranging for copies of publications to be sent to fellow scholars, and providing critical readings they always offered each other. During the Depression it was more difficult to find publishers for scholarly manuscripts, and Reo's monograph on Manus religion was delayed for several years, much to his distress.

Margaret's biographer, Jane Howard, has argued that Ruth's "busy-work" on behalf of Margaret was a sign of a role reversal in their relationship: "As Mead's stature grew, the difference between her and Benedict's ages mattered less. Increasingly it was Mead who told Benedict what to do."[12] But Margaret Mead had always told people what to do and Ruth was no exception: "Will you, will you, will you," she exclaimed at the end of one letter containing a whole list of requests, "It's frightful the number of things I bother you with. And I never pay it all back in doing things for you" (MM,B14). But role reversal there was not; Ruth had never been accustomed to telling Margaret what to do. More accurately, their professional status had become more equal, which Ruth had always wished for. Margaret was her "companion in harness" and she would become irritated if Margaret insisted on respecting her as an elder, or continued to behave as a protégée to a mentor. Ruth had no interest in maintaining inequalities in the relationship.

Margaret's and Reo's route to New Guinea was by way of New Zealand; this time Margaret would meet her in-laws. She must have anticipated the visit with some trepidation, for Reo's parents had been embroiled in conflict. A year previously, Mrs. Fortune had fled the farm at Raumati, not telling anyone where she was going. A few days later she wrote a short note and then vanished again. Reo's father tracked her down and somehow patched things up. He told Reo that he loved his wife, though he recognized that their living arrangements had "tried her too severely." His "coarseness and abuse, however indefensible and regrettable in themselves, were not of the essence of things," he believed (RFF, 14 Feb. 1930). Mrs. Fortune's version, of course, may well have been different as abused wives in those times had even more difficulty than they do today, with respect to financial resources and lack of understanding and support.

When Margaret arrived with Reo it was springtime, a forgiving season though a time for hard labor on the farm. This part of New Zealand was beautiful in the spring, with its native bush rising into the hills beyond roughly fenced paddocks, creeks running down to the wild and lonely beach, and the native cabbage trees, a New Zealand variety of the palms Margaret would have remembered from Samoa. Margaret made a favorable impression on the Fortunes. She was well used to adapting to new environments, even if life at Raumati must have seemed a somewhat bizarre, down-under twist on *Cold Comfort Farm*, the British comic novel of country life popular at that time.[13] Reo's mother wrote to Margaret later that she wished their home had been more "comfy" and that she was sorry she needed to go out to "the nasty cows" while her daughter-in-law was visiting. She said, sentimentally, "I will always see you both sitting on the sofa, Reo reading to you and you doing his nails, in front of the old black stove." Margaret was "a frail little soul," yet "it has been a comfort to know Reo is so happy and loves his Margaret dearly" (RFF, 9 Sept. 1932). After the visit the couple corresponded regularly with Reo's family. Barter Fortune, who admired his elder brother, wrote too, signing his letters with such endearments as "yours till hell freezes over" (RFF).

In Sydney a "lady reporter" coined the term "gender consciousness" for the forthcoming research that would produce some of Margaret's best known work (LF, 108). She and Reo were in the field from December 1931 until late 1933; initially her task was not clearly formulated, but she wanted to examine how primitive cultures patterned the behavior of the sexes. They decided to work among a people known for the richness of their ceremonies who were living inland from the northern coast of New Guinea, and they looked forward to more success than they had experienced with their disappointing work in Nebraska.

Carriers to take the couple over the mountains were hard to find. The local people were used to European traders and could not be tempted by the usual bartering. While Margaret remained in comfort on a plantation, Reo went off scouting. He went "from one village to another, unearthed their darkest secrets which they wished kept from the government, and then ordered them to come and carry" (LF, 103). With 250 porters thus coerced, the expedition was on its way and Margaret, who had insufficient stamina to make the journey on her own, was carried by six reliable boys lent her by the plantation owner. As she described the experience, "They strung [the hammock] on a pole and laced me, with banana leaves over me to keep out the sun and rain, for all the world like a pig. It was a little sea-sickish being handed up and down some of the mountains, but it was a great improvement on walking," even though half the time she was upside down (LF, 103).

The pair did not travel lightly and Reo seems to have resented the amount of luggage that Margaret took.[14] One of her packing lists includes silver slippers, silk underwear, jewelry, a black velvet jacket, and a camel hair coat, though no doubt some of these were left at European outposts (RFF, Box 5). They carried extensive food supplies, guns, cameras, lanterns, typewriters, notebooks, a medicine chest, a mosquito room, pots and pans, furnishings, and gifts for exchange. Two days inland from the plantation, at the village of Alitoa among the Mountain Arapesh, their porters abandoned them. Alitoa was where they would remain, a place Reo reported as not having "any culture worth speaking of—sisters-in-law are friends!" (BW, 194), and which Margaret described as "an exceedingly simple culture, one in which the personality and roles of men and women alike were stylized as parental, cherishing and mildly sexed" (LF, 101).

Reo set out to study the language—at least that was complicated, with eleven genders, twenty-two third person pronouns, and irregular plurals. He made a speech to the villagers assuring them that as long as the Fortunes were in residence there would be no lack of matches or salt, and he immediately commissioned a house to be built. Here they would stay for eight months, during most of which Margaret, disabled by a weak ankle, remained "virtually a prisoner" in the confines of the village. With its thirty or so houses it was the length of a New York avenue block and often deserted while people were off in the bush cultivating their plots. Reo was not unhappy at her confinement, Margaret recalled with some bitterness; "[Men have a] sense that their very life depends on women staying still, on the woman at home waiting, who makes the venture abroad safe and certain" (BW draft). He often left her for days while he made expeditions in the neighborhood. Once the villagers prepared her for the shock of his death, having misinterpreted a message which merely asked Margaret to send more tea.

This was the only time in her life Margaret ever experienced depression that was other than momentary, or so she said later on (BW draft). Life in the field was narrow, spent as it was "with only one person, every thought and almost every breath shared, no possible privacy and no place to cough in the night without waking the other, no place to recover from a burst of tears and fix a proper smile on one's face" (BW draft). But at least she was able to write uninterruptedly, making use of the ambidextrous skills she had learned when first suffering from neuritis. This enabled her to work using two typewriters, a feat of digitation which contributed to her prodigious output.

Ruth returned to New York in September 1931, and two days later Natalie Raymond joined her. Shortly afterward Ruth took out a lease on a new apartment on Central Park West, at 247 West Seventy-second Street, which would become a permanent home. Natalie enrolled for doctoral studies in histology at Cornell medical school, where she must have met Stanley Benedict, since he was in the biochemistry department there.

Ruth wrote to Margaret about her new household: "I'm not a bit oppressed. I'm feeling quite gay, even. Nat and I are getting used to our basis of familial affection, and are very happy together" (MM, B14). She may have spared Margaret the details of her romance; Margaret once said that Ruth kept people in separate rooms, and Ruth may have felt uneasy lest her new commitment intrude on their relationship. With Margaret on the other side of the world, Ruth wrote in a reassuring tone that she was cheered by picturing the two of them "heads down on the scent of the culture" and habitually closed her letters on very affectionate terms: "I'd be glad to have you in New York for a little while. It is too far to the Sepik, sweet. I love you"; or, "I love you dear. Be good to yourself, and then be good to yourself again. My dear one, I send you kisses" (MM, B14).

Ruth's daily routines with Nat involved dining together and spending a leisurely evening, punctuated occasionally by work. "I wouldn't make any change in my life except I'd have you within reach," she wrote to Margaret (MM, B14). Nat, who loved animals, was taking a "messy" physiology course where she had to cut up "live cats and dogs on experiments that none of the little boys can make work" (MM, B14). A friend wrote to Reo in late 1932: "I called on Ruth Benedict last night. Her friend Natalie has been bringing home a succession of small beasts from her medical school laboratory. First there was an insane kitten, too young to see, too young to walk, but old enough to attend to her various processes of elimination in the most conspicuous portions of the living room rug, and to suck your ear or finger like the vampire. . . . Last night I walked in to find a touching domestic scene with Ruth seated in front of her fireplace, watching tenderly as Natalie, with yearning motherliness, fed with a medicine dropper three youthful rats whose mother is dying" (RFF, 9 Dec. 1932).

Ruth, eighteen years older than Natalie, took an almost maternal interest in her young lover. Interestingly, a small survey of lesbians in New York around this time showed them disagreeing with any suggestion that they took on male and female roles; they felt there were more mother-daughter resonances in their relationships. So it seems to have been with Ruth and Natalie.[15]

Ruth told Margaret that she was working well, in good health and no longer plagued by her "devils," adding: "But you belong especially to seasons when there are no devils—you belong to both, but I've a special hunger for you when my blood pressure goes up! And I'm terribly impatient for letters" (MM, B14). Margaret probably genuinely applauded Ruth's newfound contentment, though perhaps she felt a little envious. Life among the Arapesh with Reo was not enthralling. A tinge of regret showed when she pointed out to Ruth "the difference it would have made" if she had known Ruth "without Sundays—and all they meant—counted out." Their relationship had always been a weekday one, even when they had been lovers, except for the rare holidays together, such as the one they took at Westport and the several weeks of summer together in New York in 1928. Ruth evidently told Nat of Margaret's remark and passed on Nat's reply that she did appreciate having Ruth around the house on Sundays (MM, B14). Ruth gave Nat a key to her strongbox containing Margaret's valuables, a precaution in case anything happened to her (MM, B14).

In 1931 Edward Sapir left Chicago for a more prestigious position at Yale. He evidently felt he had reinstated himself with Ruth and urged her to come to New Haven, "partly to help you get over shop [the field trip] before you shake down to work at Columbia, partly to help us get our curtains hung. . . . We did see a very nice apartment, and if we take it, as seems possible, I hope you will assist us to make it as liveable as you can" (RFB, Box 62). It seems unlikely that Edward took notice of her new domestic arrangements, but Ruth did visit eventually, writing to Margaret "it was more trouble jollying him along than it could possibly be worth. I know enough to keep off conversation about you, but I praised Reo's book and talked of Papa Franz some. And he glowered. Oh darling, I'm glad neither you nor I am bound to care what his pleasures and displeasures are. I kept thinking of Jean and being sorry" (MM, B14).

Margaret's long absences meant that the friends she and Ruth shared grew fewer. Marie remained a constant link. Ruth saw "David" frequently and kept in occasional contact with Margaret's sisters, passing on family news of Margaret. No longer an active poet and overworked at Columbia, Ruth moved less in literary circles. She seldom saw Léonie Adams, who finally buried her feelings about Louise, married a college teacher, William Troy, in 1933 and moved out of New York. As with many of her circle, Léonie flirted briefly with Communism in the 1930s; she later turned full circle and became a Catholic.[16] She remained a heavy drinker and Edmund Wilson commented sourly that she had become "brutalized by living with that low-grade Irishman."[17] Louise, though she might have been relieved at Léonie's marriage, thought the turnaround had gone too far: "wifehood is too damned full of hero-husband worship."[18]

Natalie, of course, had her own group of friends, who accounted for some of Ruth's social time, though "I've cut off all kinds of social obligations and not made any new ones, and I wonder why I ever bothered," she wrote Margaret. "Nat is a good playmate, and when she's home we read or work or listen to a concert over the radio, or go to a theater or a movie. Thoroughly phlegmatic, but we both like it" (MM, B14).

Ruth had so improved in health that "I'm looking like an after-taking advertisement," she wrote Margaret in 1932, describing herself as "a quite cheerful and easily pleased matron" who no longer writes verses because "in my present mood I can well do without them." After 1928 Ruth had stopped using her pen name Anne Singleton but had continued to write poetry occasionally, using "an older name, 'Sally,' for the self who came and went and who would 'dictate' lines only when it suited her" (AW, 94). Ruth's tendency toward dissociation, expressed in poetry and daydreams and at times when great stress threatened to break through into everyday life was no longer so apparent.

In early summer 1932, Ruth and Natalie celebrated the younger woman's twenty-eighth birthday and caught a train for Detroit, where Ruth, no doubt encouraged by Nat, purchased her first car, a new Ford. The opportunity to make Marie Eichelberger "tremendously happy" was another reason for the trip (MM, B14). Marie was curious about Natalie and wrote to Margaret, somewhat disingenuously, "Does my comment on her [Ruth] and Nat interest you?" (MM, B14). They went swimming in Lake Erie and drank champagne on the beach (RFB, Box 42). Nat bought Ruth flowers, and after a few days the couple turned east to make a leisurely trip through the spectacular scenery of upper New York State, Vermont, and the Berkshires.

Nat then left for the West Coast for the rest of the summer, and Ruth went to Norwich, where she was joined by her mother and Marie. Marie was recuperating from a stressful period in her job, where the atmosphere was strained by repressed homosexual feelings between a colleague and a supervisor (Marie's "madhouse boss," as Ruth called her [MM, B14]). "The dummies out in the Center are so conflicted on the subject of homosexuality," Marie wrote to Margaret, "that they speak of it with bated breath when it is apparent in a patient, and so among P.S.W.'s [psychiatric social workers] it is simply inconceivable" (MM, B14).

While Marie deplored the hypocritical attitudes of her colleagues, Ruth prepared a paper championing homosexuals for a mental hygiene conference in Syracuse. "Anthropology and the Abnormal"—the first of Ruth's writings to tackle the issue of homosexuality as a form of deviance—was praised by Margaret as one of Benedict's "two most outstanding theoretical contributions" to interdisciplinary thinking.[19] Its argument was a precursor to *Patterns of Culture*, which Ruth was also working on.

Taking up the point that they had established in discussions of Margaret's Samoan work, Ruth argued that normality is culturally defined and that we make the mistake of identifying "our local normalities with universal sanities." Western culture, with its emphasis on ego gratification, finds nothing socially unacceptable about men who are "unbridled and arrogant egotists" and who are "probably mentally warped to a greater degree than many inmates of our institutions," Benedict wrote.[20] On the other hand, types we regard as abnormal, such as sadists, people with delusions of grandeur or persecution, or those who have trances or periodically run amok "function at ease and with honor" in many cultures.

In this context she considered the place of homosexuality in our culture, in which being a homosexual "exposes an individual to all the conflicts to which all aberrants are always exposed. . . . We tend to identify the consequences of this conflict with homosexuality," she said. "But these consequences are obviously local and cultural. Homosexuals in many societies are not incompetent, but they may be such if the culture asks adjustments of them that would strain any man's vitality. Wherever homosexuality has been given an honorable place in any society, those to whom it is congenial have filled adequately the honorable roles society assigns to them. Plato's *Republic* is, of course, the most convincing statement of such a reading of homosexuality" (268).

Benedict gave other examples of acceptable homosexuality, such as

Siberian "men-women" and Native American berdaches. Moreover, she thought that "so-called normal" individuals are malleable and "in a society that institutionalizes homosexuality, they will be homosexual" without difficulty (278). Mental health professionals should show tolerance for the "less usual types." With respect to the homosexual patient, "If he can be brought to realize that what has thrust him into his misery is despair at his lack of social backing he may be able to achieve a more independent and less tortured attitude" (278–79).

It is notable that in Ruth's paper, homosexuality is always male. Though her own experiences undoubtedly inspired the work, she was careful to avoid any reference to lesbianism. However, she was true to her principles, and when the book in which this paper was to appear had its title altered to "something like 'Our Neurotic Generation,'" she withdrew it (MM, B14). She was years ahead of her time in her stance, since it was not until the early 1970s that homosexuality was removed from psychiatric diagnostic categories.

*Patterns of Culture*, Benedict's classic exposition of cultural relativity and one of the most popular works of anthropology of all time, was begun the previous spring. It progressed slowly since Ruth, unlike Margaret, was not a quick writer and considered writing "drudgery." "Darling," she wrote to Margaret, "What wouldn't I give for your ease!" (MM, B14), and later, "I'm getting on creditably—for me—with the book, though I can always imagine how much faster you'd have turned it out" (AW, 319). She missed Margaret's critical contribution, as her colleagues were either "riding some patented horse" of their own or "too silly to pay attention to" (AW, 319). "I'm sick to have an intelligent person to talk anthropology to!" (MM, B14).

Ruth had just read Virginia Woolf's *The Waves*, and the novel influenced her ideas for *Patterns* and her thinking about temperament in general. She thought she would "set down everyone she knew in a similar fashion. . . . I'm disappointed that she [Woolf] didn't include any violent temperaments, and I want my group of persons more varied. I want them to include, not just persons who have a shrug of the shoulders like mine, but persons who haven't, like you and Stanley." She understood the theme of *The Waves* to be "about life's being a wrapping and wrapping oneself in one's own cocoon. What you can spin is all you have to work with, and the result is altogether dependent on that" (MM, B14).

Ruth kept the plan for a book a secret: "If I get the book done I can say I put some articles together and made a book. . . . [No one] need . . . know that I had to slave to get it together, and that I deliberately did not ask their criticism" (AW, 319). By early August she had managed forty thousand words and was vastly encouraged. She worked on field materials others had collected, the kind of scholarly work she preferred to her own ventures into the field; at least, she told Margaret, "I don't have to go around to feasts or lay myself out to stupid old women" (AW, 324).

Ruth was also encouraged by Ruth Bunzel's writing a book. An anthropologist who was critical of Benedict once expressed surprise that although Ruth could be a wonderful mentor, she appeared to give little encouragement to Bunny, despite their personal friendship.[21] Certainly, Benedict and Mead were inclined to pass judgments on their colleagues, and although Ruth was fond of Bunny, she did not regard her as a first-rate thinker. In fact, Bunzel's *Pueblo Potter* is a remarkable study which has become a classic.

Edward Sapir may have been one of the colleagues Ruth did not want to consult about her work. He appeared unenthusiastic to her. At an "awful" dinner, he did not even acknowledge Ruth's latest article, "Configurations of Culture in North America," and when she inquired he claimed that Ruth's ideas were largely unoriginal. She had "said a great many things . . . that he'd used in his classes for years," Ruth reported to Margaret, and where she was original she was wrong headed. "Apollonian and Dionysian were too literary terms for him" and her description of the Northwest culture ("the megalomaniac personality type") was "too lurid" (MM, B14).

Whereas Ruth would characterize the personality of a culture and then examine the fit, or lack of fit, between individual temperaments and the particular cultures they inhabited, Edward disliked this sociological way of thinking: "There are as many cultures as there are individuals," was his view.[22] One commentator, Richard Handler, argues that for Benedict the greatest of cultural evils was intolerance, whereas for Sapir it was "spuriousness," or facile imitating of intellectual or social currents, as in Margaret's apparent advocacy of free love.[23] Perhaps that is why Benedict referred to Edward's conception of culture as his "quarrel with the universe" (AW, 325).

While she was working on *Patterns*, Ruth also corresponded with Reo. She needed more examples and wanted to use "his" Dobu. She already had her Apollonian and Dionysian contrasts and Papa Franz's Kwaikutl and, as she wrote to Margaret, "I hadn't really thought I'd need to take one of yours or Reo's cultures—because you do them so well I can only parrot your points" (AW, 321). Reo agreed to her request. She told him of the favorable reviews of *Sorcerers of Dobu*, which had just come out. Everyone liked it "enormously," Ruth reassured Reo, apart from the occasional detractor (AW, 320). In letters to Margaret, Ruth was less circumspect. She suspected Malinowski of jealousy when he called the Dobu the "most attractive" people he had met in Melanesia, forming an uncomfortable contrast to

Reo's picture of them. Ralph Linton, whom Margaret and Reo had met in Nebraska, was also offensive, saying that the Dobu were "just the sort of culture that Reo *would* find" (MM, B14).

Ruth missed Margaret's editorial eye: "I wish you were here to red pencil and suggest" (AW, 319). But she may well have regretted sending a section of the manuscript to Margaret, for Margaret's red pencil was so extensive that Ruth was taken aback. Margaret did not just question some details; she told Ruth that the work should be completely rewritten and rearranged and that much of the material, including the first chapter, should be omitted. Understandably, Margaret was afraid that Ruth would be annoyed: "I'd give anything to have you here so that I could watch your face as I talked, and then perhaps I wouldn't say anything wrong. . . . And I keep thinking, that it's so very important that you should write the book and that I've been wanting you to write it for the last five years and that if I should discourage you about it, I'd be miserable. And on the other hand, we're really all you have to depend on to save you from the wolves, and therefore we ought to say everything that we can think of. So here goes, and try to see me saying it, wrinkling my brows and making awful faces to get it clear, and ready to fly if I should say the wrong thing" (AW, 335).

Margaret argued that Ruth did not write with a clear audience in mind. Some sections were "cryptic," as if Ruth were talking to Margaret alone, and that "has had a bad effect on your style, the texture is all uneven and choppy, sometimes intimate, sometimes heavily formal, sometimes colloquial or journalese, sometimes in the jargon of anthropology and sometimes in the phrases of good literature" (AW, 336). She should avoid trying to write for Boas or Lowie or Malinowski; instead, she should show it to an intelligent lay reader like David. Ruth was aghast, replying that she was "distressed that you don't like it, the part that you've seen," and that she had shown it to others who were not nearly as critical. In the end, she did rearrange some material and left out some at Margaret's suggestion, but overall the effect of Margaret's response was discouraging. She wrote, "I wish you'd sent the book MS with your marginal notes, and perhaps I'd have been able to do something about it. The blanket disapproval I can't do much with, but I've tried to bring the first chapter closer to my own standards" (AW, 337–38).

Margaret Caffrey, Benedict's biographer, argues that Ruth's wish to "strike a general blow against homophobia" drove her in the writing of *Patterns*, which she characterizes as "the final thread weaving together the themes of her work and her life."[24] Margaret did not see the final chapter of the book, which Ruth had adapted from her paper on the abnormal with an expanded section on homosexuality. Sadly enough, it was mislaid in the mail; it would have been interesting to know Margaret's reaction, which was often very cautious on this issue. Ruth told her that the chapter provided a chance to "introduce a little sophistication into the discussion of the deviant in a culture" (AW, 324).

Caffrey suggests that Benedict may also have exercised caution in this chapter, diluting the issue of homosexuality by adding a discussion of trance as another example of deviance and taking care to distance herself personally. The text renders lesbianism invisible; as with the paper on the abnormal, it refers only to male homosexuality. Further, Ruth insisted that her name on the title page be "Mrs. Ruth Benedict," even though by the time the book appeared she had lived with Natalie for three years and had been separated from Stanley for four.

While Ruth was leading a life of unaccustomed contentment, things were going steadily downhill for Margaret. Marooned among the Arapesh for eight months, she and Reo had explored its "very transparent social processes" thoroughly. They scrutinized incest prohibitions, always of interest to anthropologists, confirming that they did not arise from some "obscure psychological prohibition" as the Freudians thought, but were practical rules enhancing social cooperation in a small society. On the other hand, monogamy was a selfish waste of resources: "Keeping your women to yourself is strictly parallel to keeping your surplus yams to yourself," wrote Margaret, who must have found the Arapesh eminently sensible in this respect (LF, 129).

By September 1932 the two were more than ready to move on. Their next location was also chosen in a relatively haphazard manner. The Sepik River, New Guinea's central waterway, was a possibility, but that was the stamping ground of Gregory Bateson, a Cambridge man known to Reo and whom Margaret had yet to meet. Eventually, they decided to travel to a tributary of the Sepik, the Yuat River, where they found themselves among the unappealing Mundugumor. Margaret wrote home in a mood of cynicism: "The natives are superficially agreeable, but . . . they go in for cannibalism, headhunting, infanticide, incest, avoidance and joking relationships, and biting lice in half with their teeth" (LF, 133). They were the antithesis of the more gentle Arapesh, for the predominant personality combined ferocity with jealousy and rivalry. Adults treated each other ungenerously—their lovemaking "took the form of a violent scratching and biting match, calculated to produce the maximum amount of excitement in the minimum amount of time"—and the children fared even worse.[25] Unwanted babies were simply tossed in the river to drown or to be preyed upon by the ever present crocodiles.

The one point of similarity between the Arapesh and the Mundugumor that Margaret could discern was that neither seemed to expect differences in personality between men and women. As with most societies, certain behaviors and prohibitions were sex linked, but their rules highlighted cultural contrasts rather than sex differences: "In Arapesh the women were kept away from the gardens for their own protection, because yams disliked anything to do with women. In Mundugumor people copulated in gardens belonging to someone else, just to spoil their yams" (BW, 205).

Margaret was the first white woman that the Mundugumor women had ever laid eyes on. She must have been a sight, wearing a huge straw hat and Reo's old pajama bottoms underneath her dresses as a protection against the voracious river mosquitoes. She learned to bathe holding a whisk in her hand and worked in the cagelike mosquito room on the house verandah. As always, she made the best of things. Crocodile eggs could be used to make corn fritters, bread could be baked, and since supplies were more easily brought in by river than across the mountains, there was the luxury of tinned asparagus from time to time. Reo carried a revolver, which gave them a feeling of security.

It was Reo, again, who allotted the work. He told Margaret to study the simple Mundugumor language, the children, and the technology, while he would investigate the larger culture, including kinship. Margaret was finding him more and more impossible. He made a virtue of stoicism and took pride in physical endurance; as she later recalled, Reo was the sort of man who would fight an attack of malaria by climbing the nearest mountain to knock it out of his system. In their early days together he had nursed Margaret with kindness through her first bout of malaria, but those times were past and now he treated her as "a wife—and so a part of him—he turned on me the same fierceness with which he treated his own fevers" (BW, 206).

The Mundugumor seemed to bring out the worst in Reo, who "was both repelled and fascinated. . . . They struck some note in him that was thoroughly alien to me, and working with them emphasized aspects of his personality with which I could not empathize" (BW, 206). Reo wrote to Ruth that the culture was "more incest ridden" than any place he knew and was "very much more pathological than the Dobu. . . . The limits of outrage are not nearly plumbed yet" (AW, 330). Ruth replied in the tone of the amused voyeur safely ensconced in New York, "I'm already imagining more details of your scandalous Sepik culture. . . . You know I like them scandalous" (AW, 331).

Reo's obsessions and paranoia, his anxieties about his work, his fits of fury and harshness were hard to bear, but the worst crime in Margaret's book was that his high-handedness was counterproductive. "I did not mind a division of labor based on what Reo wanted to do," she later said, and "in which I was left to do whatever he thought was least interesting, as long as the work got done" (JH). In more harmonious times they had always read each other's work every day, but now Reo refused to cooperate. Margaret was annoyed that his behavior meant they almost missed a very interesting point about the kinship system—Mead's "rope" theory, describing a unique kinship pattern found only among the Mundugumor, which anthropologists later, after much dispute, decided she actually had got wrong.[26] Margaret's forbearance was being tested, and although she wrote to her mother that "this wild duck is comfortably married for good," trouble was definitely brewing (MM, O40).

# 11

## Points of the Compass

IN DECEMBER 1932, Margaret despondently celebrated her thirty-first birthday among the Mundugumor. Then she and Reo began their journey up the Sepik in search of a third and final field site, desperate for the company of congenial people and looking forward to stopping overnight in a Iatmul village to meet anthropologist-in-residence, Gregory Bateson.[1]

Bateson, six-foot-five and thin as a beanpole, was twenty-eight, two-and-a-half years younger than Margaret. Gentlemanly, charming, and starved for company too, he completely fulfilled their desire for a congenial friend. Margaret always remembered their first encounter; Gregory took one look, exclaimed "You're tired," and sat her down in a chair. "These were the first cherishing words I had heard from anyone in all the Mundugumor months," she wrote later (BW, 208). Gregory then pleased her even more by pulling out his copy of *Growing Up in New Guinea* to challenge something she had written. The three-way conversation between Mead, Fortune, and Bateson had begun—and would not let up for weeks.

They spent Christmas together at a government station along with "Sepik Robbie," the likeable and alcoholic district officer, a dozen hard-drinking white men, and "a most ambiguous female with a rattrap mouth, mascara eyes, and a wholly suspicious and deadly restraint of manner" (LF, 140). Apparently, she had just finished serving a prison sentence for killing her baby. The drinking grew wilder, and when the beer ran out the Australians smashed open a case of someone else's champagne, which they saw as an inferior substitute. Dishes were broken, furniture was tossed around, and Reo, who usually found it hard to stay out of trouble, was threatened with fisticuffs.

Reo enjoyed Gregory's company as much as Margaret did, but Margaret and Gregory were attracted to each other, an attraction that inevitably excluded Reo. Gregory, described by one male acquaintance as "the most physically unattractive man I've ever known,"[2] charmed women. In Sydney, according to the gossip, he had had affairs and had been the cause of women's leaving their husbands. Reo found himself increasingly on the outside as Margaret and Gregory "established a kind of communication" he did not share, and Gregory once offended him with his easy assumption that they would all swim together in the nude (BW, 211).

The vacation over, they all explored the Sepik in Gregory's native canoe, complete with outboard motor, and Margaret and Reo settled on their third culture, a group living on the edges of Tchambuli (sometimes called Chambri), a beautiful lake where herons and osprey fed among lotuses and water lilies. Margaret felt she had been "let out of jail" (LF, 140). She wrote to her mother that she was "healthier than I have ever been in my life and very happy" (MM, O40), and cabled Ruth in early January to tell her that they would be extending their time in New Guinea. A change in the gold standard meant their funds would stretch further, though Margaret worried about the effects of the Depression on her museum job. Still, she wrote to Ruth that "I think my job is safer with me out here. . . . It would seem like cruelty to children to fire me alone among the cannibals" (AW, 334). Ruth was worried about Margaret's safety: "I shall be happier yet when you're out of that Sepik. I don't like it. Be careful down to the last detail." But she was also heartened by Margaret's evident good spirits (MM, B14).

Extending the trip was shrewd, Ruth wrote to Margaret, for at the December conference of the American Anthropological Association, Radcliffe-Brown had been "stern with people who stayed short whiles and wrote books. . . . You'd better dig yourself in [in] the manner of B[ronislaw] M[alinowski] in the Trobriands and make yourselves comfortable. It will be counted to you as a virtue" (MM, B14). The specter of Malinowski as a potential critic lurked; he told Reo he had critical remarks to make about Margaret's work (RFF, 18 Feb. 1931). Attitudes toward fieldwork were changing. Not many years earlier W. H. Rivers, whom both Mead and Fortune admired, had argued that scientifically trained observers with no knowledge of the local language could produce far more worthwhile information than that casually acquired by European residents; Mead, in *Coming of Age*, had asserted that "a trained student can master the fundamental structure of a primitive society in a few months."[3]

But Malinowski had set new standards. Since anthropological fieldwork is, in the words of one anthropologist, "as the blood of martyrs . . . to the Roman Catholic Church,"[4] Mead and Fortune needed to guard their reputation, although, as Ruth remarked to a friend, most unkind jibes about them were based on envy, nothing more (MM, O38). In later years Mead grew less sensitive to criticism, explaining that since anthropologists of her generation thought of each other as kin, their relationships were tinged with incestuous overtones which accounted for "the violence of some of the internecine fighting."[5]

Tchambuli, their new culture, was only a short distance from Iatmul, so Gregory Bateson was a frequent visitor. When he was not around he kept in touch via messengers who sometimes brought notes written on palm leaves for Margaret's eyes only.[6] He would usually sit with Margaret while she worked, leaving Reo at the other end of the village. At first Bateson was startled by his colleagues' methods: "They bully and chivvy their informants and interpreters and hurry them till they don't know whether they are on head or heels. But in the end I was converted and I am going to do some bullying too. . . . I spend hours feeling my way and getting into rapport with natives and it is all quite unnecessary."[7] Reo maintained that at least they were kinder than the imperialistic Malinowski, who "grabbed natives by the collar so they couldn't get away."[8]

Tchambuli culture proved likeable and satisfying, though the language was complex and it was the third one Margaret had learned in a year. She floundered in her research until struck with an insight. Unlike the Arapesh and the Mundugumor, the Tchambuli did seem to expect that the sexes would differ in personality. In this they were like westerners; however, the characteristics they expected of men and women were exactly opposite to the assumptions of western culture. The women, while not exactly in charge, were the breadwinners, capable and hearty, whereas the men, no longer able to follow their customary pursuit of warfare, were vain and catty, spending most of their time sitting around in groups gossiping and adorning themselves. Perhaps, Mead theorized, the key to the organization of a culture lay in the ways it molded the biological foundations of sex and temperament into cultural expectations of behavior, thus providing a way of allocating the tasks of living.

This theory, which Margaret elaborated in *Sex and Temperament in Three Primitive Societies*, was hammered out in daylong discussions with Reo and Gregory, intensified by the trio's explorations of their own personalities and relationships. It was a time of great excitement and, increasingly, great stress. Ruth was not uninvolved in these dynamics, as her *Patterns* manuscript had arrived and the three of them pored over it. Their intense explorations of temperament relied heavily on Ruth's formulation, which argued that out of the whole range of human potential, cultures select certain traits to emphasize. Many people are flexible enough to fit perfectly into their cultural pattern, but some are not, whether through inherited disposition or early learning. Such misfits find themselves marked as deviant.

Bateson was working on a similar concept; he used the term *ethos* to describe the emotional tone of the cultures he was studying, presenting his analysis of Iatmul to Margaret and Reo. He was also interested in the sexual organization of cultures, analyzing the sex role reversal of the *naven* ceremony, after which he titled his notable book, *Naven*. For this ritual the men assumed a "grotesque femininity" and the women strode around in "male finery." Reversals also cropped up in typical fights among Iatmul woman, who would yell insults to each other, such as "I'll copulate with you!" (not unlike a more modern expletive).[9] The exaggerated mimicry, Bateson would argue, had the effect of emphasizing sexual difference among the Iatmul.

As the trio continued to talk, analyzing themselves, their friends and relatives, their own cultures, and the cultures they were studying, they devised a scheme to describe human temperament based on the points of the compass. The gentle Arapesh, both men and women, were southerners, whereas the hostile Mundugumor men and women were northerners. Tchambuli women were located in the Northeast, Tchambuli men at the opposite point, in the Southwest.[10] Reo, absorbed in his own feelings and jealous, possessive, and suspicious toward others, was, like Margaret's father, a northerner and fitted the masculine expectations of his New Zealand culture. Margaret and Gregory were southerners, concerned and responsive to others but lacking possessiveness. Gregory, an unaggressive man with a tinge of the easterner's withdrawal, was a deviant in his own culture, and Margaret felt herself deviant, too, because "my own interest in children did not fit the stereotype of the American career woman or, for that matter, the stereotype of the possessive, managing American wife and mother" (BW, 219).

Margaret characterized the other important people in her life by their scheme. Ruth Benedict was a northeasterner. The eastern aspect, with its remoteness, fitted her well, but Margaret's characterization of Ruth as having the northern dimension of possessiveness and self-concern was perhaps surprising. But as Mead's daughter, Mary Catherine Bateson, argues, Margaret was taking into account Ruth's "capacity for intensity, for jealous passion," a characteristic she knew well though it was hidden from others.[11]

The trio's interest in the "squares," as they described their temperament theory, spun into obsession as tensions increased. They argued about temperament and its effect on personal relationships. Reo decided that Margaret and Gregory, in describing themselves as southerners, were cementing their alliance and rejecting him; he "periodically announced he was going to go and find a woman who was a Northerner." Margaret can hardly have been flattered by his description of a typical southern woman as "the kind of girl whose shoulders are so rounded that her shoulder straps fall off [and who] will dance with you all evening just because you want her to."[12]

In this situation, Margaret wrote, "cooped up together in the tiny eight-foot-by-eight-foot mosquito room, we moved back and forth between analyzing ourselves and each other, as individuals, and the cultures that we knew. . . . The intensity of our discussions was heightened by the triangular situation. Gregory and I were falling in love, but this was kept firmly under control while all three of us tried to translate the intensity of our feelings into better and more perceptive field work" (BW, 217).

Margaret's marriage was failing as a professional collaboration, and another issue was bothering her too. Her desire to have children had been fuelled by disgust at the callousness of the Mundugumor in throwing unwanted babies to the crocodiles. Though Reo did not want children and in her opinion would not be a good father, Margaret made "a somewhat unilateral decision" that "one child wouldn't wreck his career" and allowed herself to become pregnant. Liable to miscarriage, as she had once been told, she lost the baby after an episode in Tchambuli when Reo assaulted her, almost certainly not the only time he had used physical violence against her, since she wrote later that he "came from a culture where boys were physically disciplined, and men struck women." Margaret found such behavior completely unacceptable, as she "came from a family tradition within which probably no man had lifted a hand to a wife or child for several generations" (BW draft).

The miscarriage remained a source of bitterness. Reo rationalized the failure of the marriage, imagining that his relationship with Margaret foundered because he had burned himself out while still young and was unable to give her a child. Margaret remained indignant forty years later: "Well, he was able to make me pregnant, which he will not remember. And he will not remember that I had a miscarriage because he knocked me down. . . . So then he said later, 'Gregory ate our baby' " (JH).

If the Arapesh environment had fostered depression, Margaret later identified the time among the Tchambuli as the period she had been closest to madness. Locked in a "rigid, boxed drama," where everyone was overly sensitive to each other, her mood became elevated until it was almost manic (JH). Reo later claimed that among the Tchambuli Margaret no longer knew quite who she was; to Malinowski he once wrote that he had a "psychopathological case" on his hands in New Guinea and that he had to get her out to "save her from a permanently deranged condition."[13] His intent may have been malicious, but Bateson confirmed his report, saying, "all three of us together were pretty well psychotic."[14]

The personal stresses did affect Margaret's intellectual judgment, for although she thought at the time that they had made a world-shattering discovery, she never published the temperament theory and the others never did either. By the time they reached Sydney in mid–1933 she was still enthusiastic about it, sending Boas an excited cable from herself and Reo and writing to Ruth, "We've made what we think is a most important discovery—and we hope you and Papa Franz will think so." She apologized for not writing much, but "all my letters become completely invalid before I send them. Life has begun to move at an extraordinary pace. . . . Civilization seems unbelievably dear and friendly and Sydney a beautiful place. . . . As soon as life becomes a little clearer I'll send you a fuller account—As it is I can only say—we are frightfully excited, personally, scientifically and in every way—and so will you be when you hear about it" (MM, TR1).

The new theory, with its emphasis on innate temperament, went against the Boasian grain—Gregory, after all, was trained as a biologist. Margaret later justified the lack of publication by arguing that the three were "very clear about the possible dangers of emphasizing any inborn differences between human beings, and this held us back from publishing our hypotheses at the time" (BW, 220). However, it is likely, as Mary Catherine Bateson suggests, that Margaret realized their discovery owed as much to the heated state of their personal relationships and malarial fevers as it did to careful observation and deduction. Reo repudiated the "squares" soon after leaving New Guinea, and Ruth was never enthusiastic about a scheme that seemed too Jungian and too rigid (AW, 206). Nevertheless, as Mary Catherine Bateson points out, the model did extend Ruth's approach by suggesting that cultures may not be best characterized by a uniform ideal, or pattern, but can "incorporate sharply contradictory or contrasting themes, often but not always organized on gender lines."[15]

Before their arrival in Sydney Margaret and Reo had talked of parting. Margaret dreaded returning to New York, subject to his "frantic fits of jealousy or fury" and had already begun to discuss the possibility of a future with Gregory (JH). The time in Sydney was confusing, and Margaret confided in Caroline Tennant Kelly, a friend there who would last a lifetime and always provided hospitality, support, and the latest gossip, despite friction in her marriage when she and her husband took different sides over Margaret's domestic problems (MM, B9).

Reo was offered a job at the University of Sydney and ill-advisedly turned it down. He also sought consolation with another woman, one Muriel. Whether she was the northerner he longed for we do not know, but Timothy Kelly described her as a "blowsy barmaid type" (MM, B9). Margaret claims not to have been jealous; she later confided to Caroline that in the eyes of the world he had given her the perfect "conventional" excuse for leaving him, but she was concerned that her reputation would suffer should she divorce again (MM, B9). In the end, the trio left Sydney at different times and bound for different destinations. Margaret, though she had more or less decided to separate from Reo, agreed to stop off in New

Zealand on the way home to pay a reassuring visit to his parents. From there she wrote to Caroline that she would like help in encouraging Reo to agree to a divorce ("that made G[regory] very pleased and happy," replied Caroline). However, only a little later, perhaps on the journey home, Margaret became indecisive; perhaps she would remain with Reo "on some basis or other." Caroline, who seems to have passed on all the news without fear or favor, replied, "I had until then thought G rather unresponsive but my hat did that poor soul blow up?" (MM, B9). The upset happened the day before Gregory sailed to England, with a farewell from Reo, who was still unsure of his plans, marital and otherwise; when Gregory's boat was delayed the two men played a last amicable game of chess.

Increasingly, Ruth was finding friendship among the Columbia crowd. As Boas's health grew worse, she also played a more significant mentoring role among graduate students. Her favorites were usually the "deviants" like Jules Henry, Ruth Landes, Regina Flannery, and Cora Du Bois, the women, homosexuals, and Jewish students whom she mentored as she had mentored Margaret. She struggled to find them jobs in the unfavorable economic climate, lent them money, books, even her car on occasions; she listened to their woes, engaged them to take risks, wrote them letters in the field, drank with them, and made them coffee. The most favored were invited to her apartment where they met Natalie.

A direct consequence of Benedict's and Boas's combined influence was that Columbia achieved an equal sex ratio in graduates from 1921 through 1940, an astonishing result when compared with any other university department of anthropology. If some had the feeling that Ruth indulged in favoritism and neglected the white middle-class "boys," one of her male students recalled her "complete evenhandedness" with men and women.[16]

Margaret learned of up-and-coming anthropologists through Ruth's letters. The time was approaching when Boas should retire, but as the Depression bit deeper it seemed unlikely that Columbia would appoint a successor. Margaret tried to exert her influence from afar, and it seems that she never took Ruth's potential candidacy seriously, perhaps believing it thoroughly unlikely that a woman might be chosen. She wrote to Radcliffe-Brown suggesting he try for the position. Ruth was not pleased, telling Margaret that although she had tried to like the man, it was no use hoping that she could "trump up any fellow feeling" because she found him condescending, "impenetrably wrapped in his own conceit," and possessing a "fatal" tendency to promote divisiveness and factionalism (AW, 327). Margaret was forced to agree that though he was charming, liked by his students, and had done excellent fieldwork, he had "no tact and no political sense . . . and needs a nurse" (AW, 334). One has to wonder whether Margaret, well aware of Edward's hostility toward Radcliffe-Brown, backed him for Columbia in a hostile move of her own.

Malinowski dropped by to check out his prospects, annoying Ruth: "He is affectionate to the point of imbecility," she told Margaret. He managed to say a few unkind words about his rival, Radcliffe-Brown, sniping at his "peculiar personality" and spoiled students: "months of work has [sic] to be put in to get them over the poisoning effects of his teaching. After an hour of this I loved R-B with all my heart, and felt like using a whip on M—" (MM, B14). To a former student, Ruth wrote with even more asperity that Malinowski was "one of the most annoying individuals I can well imagine, vain to the point where any respectable culture would have to lock him up in a madhouse" (RFB, Box 34). Ruth's dislike of Malinowski made Margaret uneasy; she later wondered if some "deeply competitive feminist note" had colored Ruth's attitude and perhaps triggered some of the scorn Malinowski showed toward Margaret's work (BW draft).

For the summer of 1933 Ruth declined Edward's suggestion that she direct a further field program. She and Natalie spent early summer in New York, happily making short excursions into the countryside while Ruth worked hard on *Patterns*. She was pleased that Nat would not head west until August, "so there won't be a very long break" (MM, B14). Although Ruth looked forward with excitement to the end of Margaret's longest absence, no one was as eager as Marie, who implored Margaret to break up her journey across the continent with a stop in Pittsburgh "even for two hours" (MM, B14).

Marie, though handicapped by her distance from New York, was more reliable than Ruth in attending to Margaret's numerous requests from New Guinea. "Aren't I a good shopper for you anymore?" Marie once complained, while hoping that Margaret would continue to commission her; "When others *fail*, you do fall back on me" (MM, B14). As the Depression grew inexorably worse and banks continued to fail, Marie worried about Margaret's money. She hoped Margaret would not play the stock market, as Nat was doing: "If for any unthinkable reason you should decide to gamble on the market, I *beg* you that you will not tell me. I could not stand it. . . . I follow Nat's plunges with bated breath: one week she's cleared up $1550; the next week she's lost all her original capital. I think it's all right for her to do it; of course I'm fond of her. I wonder what you will think of her. It's not, either, that I'd just be fond of anyone who made Ruth so happy. That's true, of course. But I value her for herself" (MM, B14).[17]

Marie had an encouraging development to report. She thought she might be falling in love with an older woman. If Margaret did stop over, she did not want Margaret to meet Clara, as it would be "one of those queer mixed situations." But, "Oh, my dear, it will be so good to see you and say things, and hear things" (MM, B14).

On her return in August 1933, Margaret did find a day for Marie, leaving her admirer in raptures: "It was a beautiful day together, wasn't it, a day to be laid away and always kept along with all the other precious things we've had. It was nice because you knew I was happy and I knew you were, and you looked so charming and pretty and the day wasn't hard on you." Marie was overwhelmed when Margaret gave her one hundred dollars in gold and felt bound to reassure her friend that while the old obsession was not getting out of hand, she still kept "all the feeling for you that we both know I have, and yet I'm not writing to you even once a week. My sweet, my sweet, I love you and I'm so touched. The universe seems sure with you alive in it" (MM, B14).

Nothing comparable is known about Margaret's and Ruth's reunion. Did they meet alone, or was Margaret immediately introduced to Natalie in "one of those queer mixed situations"? How did Margaret and Natalie react to each other? Later there was no love lost between them. Margaret found Nat irritating, she admitted decades later (MM, Q23), and neither did Nat like Margaret, once telling a friend that she regarded her as "an opportunist."[18] A pattern was quickly established for Ruth's seeing Margaret alone. They lunched and dined together as they had always done; whether Nat was jealous on these occasions is unknown. But she must soon have realized that a central place in Ruth's affections was forever set aside for Margaret.

Ruth was not particularly pleased over Margaret's feelings for Gregory; apparently she protested.[19] But the situation was hardly comparable to the 1926 disaster when Margaret had come back from the field in love with Reo. Ruth's relationship with Margaret had stabilized into a loving friendship, perhaps marked by occasional intimacies, and she had transferred her impulses toward domestic partnership to Natalie.

Margaret had more need of Ruth's friendship on her return, as the world had changed in her two-year absence. Though she was buoyant about the new relationship, Gregory was in England, linked only by letters and the prospect of her seeing him in a year. This was the same situation she had been in with Reo seven years earlier. Margaret set about reopening the apartment she had shared with Reo, put his name on the door and in the telephone book, and generally made a pretense to the outside world that he would arrive in due course. She reinstated herself with her old friends and began making new ones. Once again she was a celebrity, newspapers relishing the outlandish details of the "woman explorer's" sojourn among the "sweetest" of people who practiced cannibalism and infanticide.[20] In demand on the lecture circuit, Margaret settled down to a busy working life with public appearances, museum duties, and writing up the New Guinea material. Released from the confines of the relationship with Reo, she inaugurated a time "between field trips, and between marriages, [when] life would open up again" (BW draft).

The grim economic conditions of the Great Depression deeply affected the lives of most Americans in the thirties, but for Ruth and Margaret it was a period marked by financial security and independence, satisfying and innovative work, and the establishment of personal relationships that led to much happiness. Though Margaret spent long periods in the field throughout this decade, letters kept the friendship with Ruth alive and responsive, and their frequent contact when she was in New York nourished them and their shared circle. For both women the thirties was a time of peak achievement; now they would write the books most fully expressing their originality and their mutual inspiration.

Around Christmas 1933, Natalie attended a "wild, confusing and very amusing" drunken party with Robert Oppenheimer to usher in the New Year, and Oppenheimer was surprised at the great change in her appearance: "She has learned to dress," he wrote to his brother. "She wears long graceful things in gold and blue and black, and delicate long earrings, and likes orchids, and even has a hat." Knowing well Nat's taste for the dramatic, he also remarked jokingly, "To the vicissitudes and anguishes of fortune which have brought this change to her I need say nothing."[21]

That summer Margaret traveled to Ireland to meet Gregory for a secret holiday with another unmarried couple, the geneticist C. H. Waddington and his future wife. It was a happy time; Margaret left certain that she wished to marry Gregory and that the romance was not just the product of tropical heat. They continued their discussion of the "compass points theory," as Margaret was now writing *Sex and Temperament*, which in its emphasis on temperament as an innate quality would show the influence of Gregory and his biologist friends.

As usual, Nat went west this summer, probably on her own. With her Pasadena friends, Ruth Tolman and Ruth Valentine, she vacationed at the Oppenheimer ranch. Ruth Benedict went to Norwich, taking along Ruth Landes, a graduate student. *Patterns* was at the publisher, and the manuscript of *Zuñi Mythology* was at last nearly complete. Ruth had time for reflection. Though having largely overcome the despair that had dogged her for years, she still sometimes felt not fully engaged in life. Her work, "even when I'm satisfied with it is never my child I love nor my servant I've brought to heel," but "is always busy work I do with my left hand, and part of me watches grudging the waste of lifetime."

In close relationships Ruth saw herself working toward a state of detachment, an aloofness not present in, or valued by, those around her and which she saw as an indication that her temperament was really best suited to the spiritual life, where, as she wrote in her journal, "incidents of faith-lessness, of failure, of death, would not touch its being" (AW, 154). Around the same time she also wrote,

> I ought to have enough self-knowledge to know what would make life meaningful to me. Not my work in anthropology, much as I owe it, and committed as I am to it. Like eating and drinking it has a neces-sary place in my life and adds to it, but the role it plays in Margaret's life or in Boas' is impossible to me. Companionship comes closer to the core of the matter, and loving Nat and taking such delight in her I have the happiest conditions for living that I've ever known. If I have to cultivate a background role and school myself to the precariousness of my happiness—since she has so much of life before her and so many choices still to make—after all, that is something I can very well do in terms of my own temperament. I'm not possessive, and the happiness I have in her is nothing that can be taken away from me, though the outward circumstances of it may well be. This very differ-ence, though, touches the heart of the matter. To take it so implies a strength and collectedness in myself that is the strongest need I have. (RFB, Box 36)

Ruth understood that she must allow Natalie to make her own choices, which might one day exclude her; here was an echo of her difficulties with Margaret, but now Ruth happily, if perhaps temporarily, had an intimate companion. Possessiveness was not to her taste, though she could be roused to it, as Margaret had sometimes discovered. It would require some strength of mind to stand back; restiveness on Nat's part must have been at the back of Ruth's mind, for the younger woman was increasingly demon-strating an inability to follow through with plans.

*Patterns of Culture* was published in the fall of 1934. In the months be-forehand Ruth scrutinized every detail of the book's production. She passed on a request for biographical material to Margaret, asking her to "be a darling" and provide it, because Ruth found self-promotion so diffi-cult.[22] She had thought long and hard about the title, wanting to avoid anything too psychological; she argued with the publisher that the price should be affordable, the spelling English style, and the jacket an exact shade of southwestern turquoise. The book contained no dedication; in-stead, Ruth repeated the proverb she had quoted in that first anthropology class Margaret had attended so long ago: "In the beginning God gave to every people a cup of clay, and from this cup they drank their life."

*Patterns*, the culmination of Ruth's insights into the American Indian cultures she had observed, included an original theoretical approach which, in its psychological emphasis, moved beyond the work of Boas, her mentor. Yet despite Benedict's apprehensions, he seemed to approve of the book and wrote a generous introduction. Ruth had now moved beyond the task set by Boas, the historical study of cultural diffusion, to an emphasis on understanding cultures as wholes. She had been unable to finish her religion manuscript, which seemed too firmly wedded to the tradition she had been schooled in, rather than being something she had made her own.

Benedict's approach bore similarities to the functionalism of the British school of social anthropology, pioneered by Malinowski and Radcliffe-Brown. They, too, focused on the relationship between cultural traits within particular societies, but their approach was mechanistic, whereas Benedict favored holistic explanations. Though the scientific method was the foundation of her anthropology, Benedict insisted on the importance of the interpretive traditions of the humanities. Her central tenet was that "a culture, like an individual, is a more or less consistent pattern of thought and action. . . . The whole . . . is not merely the sum of all its parts, but the result of a unique arrangement and interrelation of parts that has brought about a new entity. . . . Cultures, likewise, are more than the sum of their traits. We may know all about the distribution of a tribe's form of marriage, ritual dances, and puberty initiations, and yet understand nothing of the culture as a whole which has used these elements to its own purpose. . . . The process, of course, need never be conscious during its whole course, but to overlook it in the study of the patternings of human behavior is to renounce the possibility of intelligent interpretation."[23]

The Boasian approach had laid a foundation of skepticism toward grand theories and insisted on the careful and disciplined collection of facts to establish the history of a culture. The new shapers of anthropology would attempt to understand how cultures actually worked, the relationship of parts to the whole and of structure to function. Radcliffe-Brown's innovation was to distinguish between Boasian ethnology, which reconstructed the history of cultures, and social anthropology, which aimed to discover the natural laws of society. Benedict, Radcliffe-Brown, and Malinowski were the key theorists ushering in a classical age of anthropology, and Margaret Mead was one of its pioneering fieldworkers. Anthropology as they conceived of it would become less drily historical. It would take on the form of a modern social science, its core being cultural relativism, arduous fieldwork, and scientific interpretation, and its popular face being the relativizing of familiar social arrangements and values.[24]

Benedict's key idea of culture as personality writ large provided a rubric under which cultural patterns could be examined, and it was an approach ideally suited for her theory of deviance, with its sense of a pattern laid down, easy adaptation by the majority, and the lifelong struggle of misfits who found their own culture uncongenial. However, in so sharply etching the configurations of different cultures, her work raised questions about whether she had done justice to the complexity of each one. And ultimately, the functionalism of her British peers, with its emphasis on the scientific method and distrust for the humanities, proved more attractive to her discipline. But Benedict's emphasis on cultural patterns and individual deviance had an underlying moral purpose that proved to be of lasting value. As Margaret put it when delivering her eulogy at Ruth's memorial service in 1948, the study of cultural difference would "breed gentleness in those fortunate ones whose culture fitted them like a glove; it could breed a forlorn selfless hope in those who found themselves strangers among their own people, that others of their kind might somewhere, sometime, be at home. . . . [In her work] the deviant ceased to be either a tragic or merely pathetic figure and became more and more a measuring device against which the pattern itself could be understood."[25]

The initial response to Ruth's book was favorable. It was widely reviewed and received a good press despite Margaret's forebodings; it went on to become one of the most popular works of anthropology of its era, selling over a million copies in its paperback edition. Ruth received accolades from friends and colleagues. Marie was thrilled to be personally presented with a copy. Reo Fortune told Ruth he was impressed with her use of the Dobu material, especially with "everyone else just doubting whether one didn't make it all up." Ruth's evocation of Dobu "looks grand," he told her, "and I'm pleased all round" (AW, 338). The only disappointment, by now expected, was in Edward's reaction. In a stiff, formal note, contrasting hugely with his former enthusiasm for her work, he wrote, "Dear Ruth, A few days ago I received a copy of your 'Patterns of Culture' from the publishers. I presume the book was sent at your request. I want to thank you cordially for thinking of me and letting me have a copy. I've only barely glanced through it so far but it is easy to see that it is an important and interesting work and I am looking forward to reading it. Yours as ever, Edward" (SF, 19 Nov. 1934).

Ruth was confirmed as a leading light among anthropologists, even if, at the age of forty-seven, she was still a lowly assistant professor. Honors came her way regularly. In 1932, even before the publication of *Patterns*, she had been named by the editor of *Science* as one of the five leading anthropologists in the United States; in 1933 she was one of only three women designated a notable scientist in *American Men of Science*. This honor led to interviews in *Time* and other newspapers and magazines in which she emphasized the employment difficulties of the new generation of women anthropologists. In 1935 she became a member of the National Research Council Division of Anthropology, the organization that had turned down her research proposals not long before.

Ruth reacted to such worldly achievements with a characteristic shrug of the shoulders. To Margaret she wrote about being singled out: "The list is pretty silly, but there were only two women: two zoologists and me. So we were figured like dancing bears. . . . The Tribune interviewer was a moron; she asked me about women anthropologists, and . . . if I liked domesticity, and what my hobbies were. . . . The Daily Mirror put in a write up under a column called Caviar, and I'm followed by 'Delicatessen in Grand St.' or something like that" (MM, B14).

Ruth had put Margaret's and Bunny's names forward for *American Men of Science* and tried to console Margaret by saying that "of course it's an age-group classification." In fact, Mead was slow to receive the distinctions that had come Ruth's way, not being starred for excellence in that directory until 1943. Boas had recommended Gladys Reichard, but she was not chosen either, Ruth told Margaret, and was "as sore as a corn on your toe" (MM, B14).

At home in the mid–thirties, between husbands and field trips, Margaret refreshed her ideas and made new friends, mainly psychologists and psychoanalysts, whom she also introduced to Ruth. In the summer of 1934, Lawrence Frank, a social scientist who had a genius for bringing out the best in people through the medium of the small group, organized a month-long interdisciplinary seminar on human development in the pleasant surroundings of the Hanover Inn near Dartmouth College in New Hampshire. Here Margaret found a delightful cooperative model of working, for this group, free from institutional hierarchies, was intellectually thrilling.

Larry, with his green eyeshade, oversaw the proceedings. Group members included John Dollard, the Yale psychologist known for his work on frustration and aggression, who inspired the others with his interest in life histories; Carolyn Zachry, a psychoanalyst who worked with adolescents and lived with a woman partner; Robert and Helen Lynd, who had written the sociological classic, *Middletown*, describing the life of small town America as if it were as foreign as Margaret's Samoa or New Guinea; and Erik Erikson, the émigré psychoanalyst, who convinced Margaret of the importance of body zones in child development.

The Hanover Conference was an extraordinarily productive collaboration. It was here, for instance, that Erik Erikson formulated his notion of developmental tasks in the human life history, proceeding from the infant's need to develop trust versus mistrust through later stages of childhood and adulthood to the final stage of hope or despair in old age.

Erikson's ideas were to prove more acceptable to Americans than Freud's harsher psychology, with its emphasis on unconscious conflict and sexual motivation. By the end of the conference a grand outline of human development to which all the participants had contributed—and nicknamed "the cauliflower"—had been designed; though it was never published.[26]

After the Hanover seminar Margaret met other psychologists, psychoanalysts, and child development specialists, including Gardner and Lois Murphy, Arnold Gesell, Gordon Allport, and Kurt Lewin. In spring 1935 she invited Ruth to a party at Erich Fromm's where she introduced her to Fromm's current lover, Karen Horney. Ruth and Horney became good friends, often lunching together. A recent immigrant and a medically trained analyst, Karen Horney, a couple of years older than Ruth, was known for her heretical quarrel with Freud's view of penis envy as the cornerstone of feminine psychology. Her friendship with anthropologists like Ruth and Margaret led her to a new emphasis on culture. Her classic work, The Neurotic Personality of Our Time, which examined the forms neuroses took in competitive, anxiety-ridden American society, was a groundbreaking work for what came to be known as the cultural school of psychoanalysis.

Ruth met the analyst Harry Stack Sullivan around this time, perhaps through Sapir, as he and Edward had been friends since their first meeting in 1926 when Edward had spent hours discussing his concerns about his wife Florence's illness and death. Sullivan hailed from Ruth's part of the world, Chenango county, New York State, though the Sullivans were impoverished Irish Catholic immigrants who had escaped the potato famine, while the Shattucks, Ruth's maternal grandparents, were well established in the county. Though the early death of Ruth's father caused financial strain in Ruth's immediate family, it has been suggested that Sullivan always envied her superior social status.

Sullivan's homosexuality, unlike Ruth's, does not seem to have interfered with his and Edward's friendship. Sullivan was in a domestic partnership with James Inscoe, whom he had met in 1927 when James, or Jimmie, was a young hustler of fifteen or sixteen. Inscoe had changed his name to Sullivan and was known to Sullivan's friends as his foster son, though clearly their relationship was of a homosexual nature. It lasted until Sullivan's death in 1949.

As a psychiatrist Sullivan pioneered the treatment of schizophrenia in young men using psychoanalytical methods. At a New York psychoanalytical meeting chaired by Ruth during the thirties, he created a sensation by standing up and announcing that he himself was schizophrenic, a self-revelation that apparently was greeted with applause. Exactly what Sullivan meant is unclear, though one biographer has suggested that many of his patients were actually gay men experiencing terror about their sexuality and that Sullivan may have had a schizophrenic breakdown in his youth. Sullivan also deliberately hired gay men as psychiatric attendants, creating a familylike atmosphere which was therapeutically successful for the patients.[27]

It is not known whether Sullivan and Benedict ever discussed homosexuality—or their personal lives—but Sullivan's work may have been the source of some ideas Ruth put forward in "Anthropology and the Abnormal." Like Benedict, Sullivan deplored the waste of talent resulting from the difficulties put in the path of homosexuals. However, his views about homosexuality as a flawed outcome of family processes were firmly rooted in a psychiatric paradigm. In 1927, around the same time he entered into his two-decade long partnership with Jimmie Inscoe, Sullivan wrote, "there is nothing more striking nor more pitiful than the invert's attempt to find peace and satisfaction in the achievement of a permanent union with some similarly conditioned man."[28]

Margaret and Edward Sapir were still unreconciled. They would never willingly be in the same room together, and it is clear that their falling out, and Edward's coolness with Ruth, were divisive for the "culture and personality" school that was now becoming an established part of anthropology. Margaret's friendship with John Dollard, Edward's younger colleague at Yale, must have functioned as an irritant, as Dollard and Sapir, despite similar interests, were famous for not getting on. Dollard most likely harbored rivalry toward his older colleague, and what better fly in the ointment than a friendship with Margaret?

John Dollard was particularly interested in the subject of individual and social cooperation and competition, a topic of particular interest in the radical thirties. Discussions with Dollard led Margaret and Ruth to undertake a joint research project, the first formal, rather than informal, collaboration between them. Money was found for a major study in which both worked with Ruth's graduate students to explore models of cooperation and competition in "primitive" societies. Ruth's students wrote up the Zuñi and Kwakiutl material, while Margaret worked on Samoa, Arapesh, and Manus. The project gave Margaret the pleasure of working in a small group on a sustained task and reinstating herself at Columbia, where she got to know Ruth's latest batch of students, including Jeannette Mirsky, Buell Quain, Ruth Landes, and Bernard Mishkin.

This path-breaking study of culture and personality, Margaret's first experience leading a team of anthropologists, resulted in an excellent, if inexplicably neglected book, *Cooperation and Competition Among Primitive Peoples.* Out of the group discussions about ways to organize the materials came the notion of shame and guilt as separate categories of experience and as differential social forces, ideas Ruth would develop in her classic work on Japan, *The Chrysanthemum. and the Sword.* The investigation of deviance, Ruth and Margaret's theme of the twenties, was now advanced by studies of shame and guilt as forms of social control. Both now developed a more psychological focus, examining the characteristic ways in which societies induce individuals to fit the pattern.

Mead's *Sex and Temperament in Three Primitive Societies,* was published in 1935. Along with *Coming of Age in Samoa,* it is her most widely known work and has achieved the status of a feminist classic. Fostering the belief that human behavior is determined by culture, it has been praised for having "kept the light of feminist scholarship burning" in the 1930s.[29]

As with *Coming of Age in Samoa,* the book has attracted its share of skeptics. One of the most challenging criticisms has to do with the unlikelihood of Mead's having stumbled across cultures that so exactly fitted her argument. In choosing Samoa somewhat haphazardly, or more accurately, in having it chosen for her, Mead, so the argument goes, would have needed extraordinary luck to have found a society that so neatly demonstrated an easy transition to adulthood. Similarly, when Mead argued in *Sex and Temperament* that Arapesh women and men were similar to western women, that Mundugumor women and men were similar to western men, and that Tchambuli men and women were differentiated by sex in a manner exactly opposite to the West, her good fortune in finding cultures that demonstrated such a neat pattern seems close to unbelievable. The fact that she emphasized that her fieldwork sites were, once again, chosen arbitrarily, raises the question of how preconceived notions might have entered her work.[30]

Mead's work on New Guinea has also been subjected to critical reappraisal, though not to the same extent as her Samoan work. But the conclusions to be drawn from examining the controversy are similar. It cannot be doubted that Mead was an excellent fieldworker. She worked with extraordinary speed and her notes are insightful, systematic, and impressive. In contrast, Reo Fortune's field notes are all but indecipherable.[31] Yet as Martin Orans has argued in relation to the work on Samoa, questions persist about Mead's possible oversimplification in the book of the complex material in her fieldwork notes. Her reputation has not been helped by the public, including textbook authors, who are guilty of further oversimplifying the conclusions of the published work. There is a strong argument to be made that rather than Mead's having produced "bad science," it is the critics who have misunderstood the nature of Mead's fieldwork and the processes by which she turned her material into a critique of American society.

In her analysis of male and female in cultures, Mead was advancing Benedict's project of understanding patterns of culture. Oversimplification is the almost inevitable hazard of a search for unifying themes of a culture; one might argue that oversimplification is the hazard of all theorizing, especially about human beings and their societies. Benedict had characterized cultures in terms of a single theme, using the figure of the deviant for contrast, a figure who for the outside observer illuminates the cultural pattern and who, within his or her own culture, acts as a safety mechanism, preventing cultures from imploding under the weight of their own rigidities. Mead extended Benedict's approach, contributing an analysis in *Sex and Temperament* that is more original and sophisticated than is generally recognized. She argued that whereas relatively simple societies are organized along a single theme or pattern—with men and women, though usually allotted different tasks, not expected to show marked differences in personality—more complex social arrangements are arrived at through the introduction of difference. Emphasizing difference allows for the development of a wider range of talents in a society. And though class and race are often used to distinguish among people, Mead's key point is that societies tend to choose sex, an obvious marker, as the carrier of difference. In her view, the Tchambuli, who emphasize sex differences, albeit in a contrary manner to westerners, were a more complex society than the Arapesh or the Mundugumor, whose cultures she and Fortune had found disappointing.

Mead argued that the characteristics assigned to male and female are arbitrary. This was the radical potential of her work—the idea that men and women can be other than they are. Her argument does not rest on the assumption that men and women have exactly the same talents and capacities; rather, she regards them as strait-jacketed in arbitrary fashion by the dictates of their culture. Where Mead did make an error of judgment was in contrasting cultures in terms of opposites, having in the back of her mind, no doubt, the inadequate "points of the compass" schema. Seeing Tchambuli men and women as the *opposite* of western men and women, rather than as merely differentiated along dissimilar lines, and seeing Arapesh and Mundugumor characteristics as somehow *the same as* western female and male characteristics took the theory to a point of oversimplification, leading inevitably to questions of credibility.[32] If Mead had paid more attention to Benedict, who did not think of different cultural patterns as systematically related and who disliked schema of both the Jungian and "points of the compass" type, she would not have fallen into this error of judgment.

Nevertheless, *Sex and Temperament* is a classic, and elements other than Mead's theoretical contributions made it so. In what has been called the "middle matter" of her books, Mead shows her exceptional observational skills.[33] More empirically oriented and psychologically minded than Benedict, Mead brought her cultures to life with finely drawn observations of real life individuals and their developmental processes. Though characterizing both Arapesh men and women as gentle and peaceful, Mead noted that Arapesh men did fight men of other tribes, albeit reluctantly, and also engaged in incidents of wife beating. When Reo Fortune later published his article, "Arapesh Warfare," whose title seemed chosen in deliberate contradiction to Mead, she wrote to him to applaud the work and appeared not to take it as criticism of her own (MM, TR1).

Mead's idea that cultures fostered two personality ideals arbitrarily assigned to males and females led her to theorize deviance differently from Ruth. She later remarked that while Ruth had discussed the deviant person in *Patterns*, "she had no theory of how they become deviant" (BW draft). Mead's deviants are large-as-life individuals, quarreling, miserable, and made unstable by demands they cannot meet, whereas Benedict's are hypothetical and abstract.

However, her discussions of social deviance, like Ruth's, are usually framed around the issue of homosexuality. By the time she wrote *Growing Up in New Guinea*, she had moved away from the carefree twenties of her *Samoa*, where homosexuality was merely one form of sexual behaviour, indulged in openly and with enjoyment in societies that did not forbid it and in some situations becoming a way of life for women seeking horizons other than marriage. For only the few was it a "true" inversion. *Growing Up in New Guinea* introduced the psychoanalytically fashionable idea of "inversion" arising from a mistaken identification with the opposite sex parent, a theme that Margaret saw played out in Ruth's life.

*Sex and Temperament* develops these ideas a step further, incorporating homosexuality into a new theory of sexual difference. Homosexuality, Mead now argues, occurs only in societies that markedly distinguish between male and female. Among the undifferentiated Arapesh and Mundugumor there was no homosexuality, unlike the Tchambuli culture in which women engaged in "rough homosexual play" or sexually aggressive behavior on festive occasions. The strangest form of sexual play Mead saw among the Tchambuli was a dance ceremony in which young men wearing female masks dance around in a group of women, who "bump against them in definitely provocative positions, tickling and teasing them. . . . They display aggressive sexual desire and flaunt their right to initiative."[34] This ceremony, Mead believed, expressed the complexities of Tchambuli society, where men nominally owned wealth and headed households, yet women had the actual power and initiative.

Turning to American society in her chapter on "The Deviant," Mead argues here that sexual deviance might result from a mismatch between innate temperament and the type of temperament expected for one's sex.

For example, if a culture assigns bravery to boys, then a shrinking boy has his gender identity challenged, as does a brave girl. In a culture in which bravery is expected, but not sex-linked, the coward does not have trouble with his or her gender identity. The coward may be a deviant, but he or she does not become a sexual deviant. Thus, where individuals are consistently made to feel unlike members of their own sex, they come to identify with the opposite sex. Some societies have institutions like *berdache* to successfully accommodate people who feel they belong to the opposite sex, but American society offers no solutions.

There are definite hints of Ruth in Margaret's writing. Margaret imagines a girl with a temperament closer to her father's than her mother's, someone who finds abhorrent the feminine expectation that emotion and pain will be freely expressed and who therefore identifies with the male parent. This means to everyone, including herself, that she is "mannish," with the inevitable corollary that she is attracted to women. Mead, like virtually all theorists of homosexuality, focused on explaining lesbians who display "mannish" characteristics, while women with more feminine characteristics who are attracted to the "mannish" woman were, by implication, not genuinely lesbian, but were drawn by happenstance into a homosexual partnership.

Mead by now rejected the cultural insensitivity of psychoanalysis, which focused on (western) family dynamics as the basis for mistaken identification with the opposite sex parent. Rather, she emphasizes this identification as a cultural accident, implying that there would be no such condition in a world that did not emphasize sexual difference in temperament, although there might still be homosexual behavior and, in a minority, "congenital inversion" (305).

Mead's approach in *Sex and Temperament* allows homosexual behavior to be considered normal and homosexual identity to be a suitable adaptation if successfully integrated into the prevailing culture. However, her theory also echoes the changing mores in American life, which were becoming hostile to sexual freedom and to the career woman who chooses homosexuality as a congenial way of life. Moreover, Mead's theory still confuses sexual orientation and gender identity.[35] Yet hers is a more complex theory than Benedict's, which tends to emphasize homosexual identity as an inherent and stable aspect of personality, a condition of deviance, whether innate or established in early childhood, which nevertheless is deserving of tolerance in the culture at large.

The theory put forward in *Sex and Temperament* must have allowed Margaret to feel that it was hardly surprising that a feminine woman, as she always considered herself to be, might be attracted to a masculine woman like Ruth, never forgetting the proviso that "feminine" and "masculine" refer merely to temperaments deemed culturally appropriate in American society. In assessing herself as feminine, she no doubt thought of her interest in clothes and housekeeping, her pleasure in babies and children, her lack of interest in outdoor pursuits and physical exercise, her lack of facility with tools despite early training in carpentry, and the fact that she never learned to drive a car. She later noted that on a personality test she came out at the extreme end of the feminine scale, except in the scope of her ideas, interests, and activities, where she did not share the feminine tendency toward self-limitation.

Now satisfyingly in love with Gregory, longing for children, and with many of her college friends, even Léonie, marrying, it was only Ruth and Marie from Margaret's inner circle who appeared to have settled into a homosexual identity. Mead's theories show her uncanny facility for sensing, indeed influencing, the direction of the times, for they almost exactly parallel historical changes in attitudes toward homosexuality in the United States.[36]

Gregory might have been in the forefront of her mind, but Margaret was having problems with Reo. Issues concerning ownership of field notes and intellectual property needed to be resolved. Margaret had written fully on the Arapesh, first in *Sex and Temperament* and later in detailed monographs, and she considered the Mundugumor and the Tchambuli more briefly in *Sex and Temperament*, expecting that Reo would provide a fully detailed account of these two groups. It was a source of frustration to her that he never did.[37] In fact, Reo published very little after Margaret was no longer cracking the whip, and he often displayed a note of bitterness toward his ex-wife and what he perceived to be her controlling nature. In 1934, en route to New Guinea and the Purari, he wrote a peculiarly rambling, disturbed or drunken letter to Malinowski saying that he was "not going to be any stage comedy edition of a Patriarch. . . . Better be beggar than owner of luv or wenshes. . . . I've told Margaret so. Whether she's in or out of a beggar's Party I don't know. She's a bit intense for good party manners, and apt to go off being intense and vicious Matriarch of a Small One and Only Family."[38]

Among the Purari Reo spent a difficult and dangerous time. He wrote to Ruth that he was trying his best not to get killed, and to Margaret, who passed the information on to Radcliffe-Brown, that he had "to keep an armed force, is separated by guerrilla warfare from his nearest neighbour, and [in relation to his problems learning the language] the verb has 39 parts. But he says the noun is alright 'if you let it alone.' "[39] Reo was apparently lucky to escape alive after a frightening confrontation when, weakened by malaria and deserted by his porters, he was left to defend himself from hostile tribesmen. He returned home to New Zealand unwell and mentally below par, and Margaret worried, both for his own sake and for the possibility that he might endanger her reputation.

Margaret's not inconsiderable manipulative skills were evident in correspondence to Reo's sister-in-law, Shirley Fortune, and to Caroline Tennant Kelly, her friend from Sydney. She focused on advice about managing Reo: his temper, money, job opportunities, and involvements with unsuitable women (MM, B9, TR1). Caroline was never to use the word "square" in his presence, lest it encourage Reo in his view that "the whole theory of the squares was just a new way of saying that one liked one's lover better than one's husband. . . ." Margaret continued, "I have got to get this Sex and Temperament book published under the status quo and while Reo is off the scene of action or he might attack it disastrously. If it gets a six months start of his attack, then the attack wouldn't matter. But there can't be any scandal about that" (MM, B9).

After two years of separation, Margaret pushed through a Mexican divorce on the grounds of incompatible character and Reo's alleged desertion. She asked for no alimony, being in a much stronger financial position than Reo, who was jobless. With Ruth sending him fifty dollars a month, mostly cobbled together by Margaret, he was somewhat like the remittance men of early colonial history whose relatives sent them to the other side of the world and paid them to stay away. Divorce was much more scandalous in New Zealand than in the United States. Reo said that his family was "too extraordinary altogether" about the matter (RFF,1936). Barter Fortune claimed that after his brother returned from the Purari he was a changed man, the once energetic and intellectually brilliant brother now heavy with "incomprehensible lethargy." Derek Freeman, no friend of Mead, claimed that for the rest of his life, Reo was permanently disabled by a suppressed "primal scream" directed toward Margaret.[40]

Any such primal screams were hardly suppressed. It was not long before Reo was to claim that Ruth had misinterpreted his materials on the Dobu and Margaret had made misleading statements about the New Guineans. As he wrote to Boas, when he escaped from the Purari and found a copy of Sex and Temperament, he was so annoyed with the description of the Arapesh that he returned for three months to gather further evidence that her account was incorrect (FB, 9 March 1937). He later complained to Margaret that when it was known what he had done, Ruth, asserting her influence as the manager of his funding, cabled orders that he leave the area immediately (MM, TR1). In 1937, he wrote angrily to Radcliffe-Brown: "I am not favourably impressed by Mead's Sex and Temperament hash! It's wrong—

or by that pseudo-psychological huddle of Benedict-Bateson-Mead, and it's wrong, apart from all personalities, and even if I were six feet below a bomb coming down" (RFF, 4 Dec. 1937).

Reo's lecture notes and his copies of Mead's and Benedict's books are studded with points of disagreement. Ruth's ill-considered advice had thwarted his career, the Dobu were not paranoid, and Ruth merely evaluated cultures in terms of her likes and dislikes. Where Ruth says in *Patterns* that she verified facts by consulting the authorities, he makes a bitter note in the margin, "what are such when misinterpreted."[41] It may have been little consolation to Ruth and Margaret to know that attacks on them did not mitigate his rivalry with Malinowski, whom he was to accuse of fabricating data. In a letter to Radcliffe-Brown he called Malinowski a "shady individual" (RFF, 4 Dec. 1937) and he later expressed his belief in the British anthropology journal, *Man*, that Malinowski's fraud was comparable to the Piltdown man affair.[42]

Reo's correspondence with Boas during the late 1930s is full of spiteful comments about Margaret's work. He described how deranged Mead had been in Tchambuli: "When her husband [Gregory Bateson] bid hard for her there against me, the nervous strain she submitted herself to was excessive. . . . Her mental condition rapidly became only fit for an alienist to deal with—and in the absence of any psychiatric possibilities, something had to be done. I did not get out until I was in great fear of her mind permanently unhinged—of that condition I keep some of her typescripts of that time, as my charter for having acted correctly" (FB, 10 Nov. 1936). In another letter he said, "I was sorry about Margaret Mead because she laughed at the 'fashion' of loyalty, as I did not; also such disagreement extended to the work, where she made up all manner of personalities as 'science,' a big pseudo-science on a large dramatic scale, and as false as she personally . . ." (FB, 9 May 1937).

During this time, Reo came to some theoretical conclusions which were stranger than anything he accused Mead or Benedict of devising. Ruth jokingly referred to them as Reo's "great discovery," in which he translated the "abortive discoveries on the Sepik into science" (MM, B14). The manuscripts he sent Boas on "The Social Psychology of Family Life" and "Matrilineal and Patrilineal Cultures in the New Guinea Region" resonate with personal resentment against the two women who seemed to Reo to be increasingly powerful.[43] Reo's work draws out a contrast between matrilineal and patrilineal codes. In matrilineal societies, lines of descent and inheritance are female. There is no seclusion of women or taboos on women's cooking for men during the time of the menstrual flow. Women practice black magic and are active in feuds; where cannibalism occurs, the vulva is eaten and the penis discarded. Sexual mores include sexual experimentation and prenuptial sexual freedom, while jealousy in marriage is frowned on and divorce common. Women expect satisfaction in the sexual act, which involves stimulation of the clitoris until orgasm occurs.

In patrilineal societies, on the other hand, descent and inheritance are organized through the male line, menstrual seclusion is common, and cannibalistic practices involve eating the penis and discarding the vulva. There is no prenuptial sexual freedom, jealousy is not acceptable, divorce is rare, men look to their own sexual pleasure rather than their partner's, and stimulation of the clitoris to the point of orgasm is taboo. Reo goes on to argue that in modern America, while no one would like to introduce outdated elements of the matrilineal complex (black magic and vulva eating?), there is pressure to change sexual codes in a matrilineal direction. These changes affect women in more ways than one might expect, Reo argues. For example, since the clitoris is a rudimentary male organ, its manual stimulation alters the endocrinal balance, making women more masculine. Thus, in matrilineal societies, culture leads to the narrowing of biological difference between the sexes. Clitoral orgasms are not an innate physiological necessity, although "a woman with matrilineal conditioning believes in good faith that most of the nervous ailments of women are caused by men who do not follow her code."[44]

Margaret and Reo fought their matrimonial battles on anthropological terrain, and one can only surmise what sexual misunderstandings and grievances lay behind Reo's seizure on clitoral orgasm as a key feature of the matrilineal society. Certainly sexual mores in New Zealand during Reo's youth were strict, emphasizing men's potency rather than sensuality and confining women's sexuality to the reproductive sphere.[45] Reo had broken away from some of the strictures of his culture, but he seems to have found Margaret's New York bisexual sophistication, such as it was, psychically threatening. Interestingly, no overt references to Margaret's sexual relationship with Ruth or other women have been found among Reo's papers. Perhaps she never told him, sensing his inability to cope with the knowledge. There are, however, plenty of references to homosexuality in the dream materials she shared with him. Perhaps with Reo she managed to think of herself as not really sexual with women. Or perhaps Reo did have such knowledge about Margaret but preferred not to leave any such comments lying around. His distressed letters to colleagues contained no accusations of lesbianism, and he was more disturbed, as far as we know, by Margaret's attraction to Gregory than to other women. Someone close to Reo, a family member, apparently used to refer drunkenly at parties to Margaret and Ruth as lesbians, insisting that it was their relationship that wrecked Reo's marriage; this may be a clue as to what Reo himself thought.[46] It is interesting, though, that he did not include lesbianism among his list of the features of matrilineal societies.

As part of the culture-and-personality explorations, John Dollard encouraged those involved in the Hanover seminar to write a life history. So it was that Margaret made her first attempt at autobiography, which years later would result in *Blackberry Winter*. Ruth also wrote a life history, for Margaret's eyes only. The manuscript consists of a school writing tablet with the words, "M Mead. Please forward unopened," written on the cover.[47] Margaret later remarked that the self-disclosure she and Ruth had shared in the early days, with "long intricate discussions . . . marked the beginning of the self-awareness that made it possible for Ruth to write 'The Story of My Life' " (AW, 90). This autobiographical piece, and other writings from the period, explore Ruth's childhood, organized around the distinction she made between her two worlds, the duality of her "primal scene" with her father, peaceful in his coffin, and her mother weeping hysterically. "The story of my life begins when I was twenty-one months old," she writes, "at the time my father died" (AW, 97). The "Dionysian" bouts of fury of Ruth's childhood gave way, she says, through the mechanism of repression, to her "truly Apollonian course of life," where the only guilt she experienced related to an inability to sustain in herself "what the saints call . . . a state of grace" (RFB, Box 36). Ruth's account of herself clearly was influenced by psychoanalytical thinking, especially the concepts of trauma and repression. However, she did not place sexual motives and repressions at the fore, and she did not anywhere use Margaret's compass points to describe herself. By the time Margaret wrote her own autobiography, "the squares" did not play a central role in her thinking, either. However, Margaret's lifelong fascination with temperament and its impact on relationships showed through in her fine-grained descriptions of personality, which she executed with a novelist's flair. As Ruth once said, the value of a life history is its ability to show the influence of an individual's experience in the context of a particular culture, whose imperatives are, in turn, apparent in those life stories.[48]

# 12

*Is Our Cup Broken?*

IN THE LATE 1930S, Margaret and Ruth's friendship was tested by Margaret's long absence for fieldwork in Bali and New Guinea. The trip lasted more than three years, and toward the end the closeness Margaret and Ruth had always maintained appeared to weaken. In midlife, Ruth had become somehow remote and detached, though perhaps more at peace with herself than ever before. This newfound calm persisted through the breakup of her relationship with Natalie Raymond and the hostility of Boas's successor at Columbia, Ralph Linton, and her correspondence with Margaret became less frequent. Margaret, happy with her new husband, Gregory Bateson, yet longing for home, was forced to realize how much she depended on Ruth's continuing attentiveness. She would protest vigorously in her letters that she was being neglected, and she suffered over whether she had lost her special place in Ruth's affections. A complete and newly available collection of their correspondence from this time documents the changes in their relationship and the tension that strained the friendship.

Margaret's sailing date was 14 January 1936, Ruth noted in her appointment book. Just before her departure, Margaret, saying nothing of her forthcoming marriage, told her parents she had divorced Reo and that she did not want to discuss the matter any further. Ruth had met Gregory Bateson in the spring of 1935 on his brief American visit; apparently Ruth took Margaret to a fortuneteller in Harlem, who said that Gregory was a good man and that his new wife should feed him well.[1]

A new friend, Geoffrey Gorer, an English travel writer and a lover of dance, inspired Margaret and Gregory with an interest in Bali. Jane Belo, a Barnard alumna from a wealthy New York family, also spoke of Bali with enthusiasm. Teeming with history and ritual, the island seemed to offer a pleasant way of life and a cultured community of freethinking expatriates who would be a contrast to the boorish and mercenary colonials of New

Guinea. In her applications for funding to study Balinese culture, Margaret used Gregory's term, *ethos*, rather than Ruth's word, *pattern*. Fortified by her renewed interest in psychoanalysis, Margaret intended to specialize in Balinese child-rearing practices; both Margaret and Gregory would look at the connection between schizophrenia and trance, the latter a phenomenon Ruth had used to illustrate her theories of deviance.

Gregory met Margaret in Batavia, where their plans to marry were thwarted by authorities who had turned down Charlie Chaplin three weeks earlier, not wanting to acquire a reputation for encouraging American immorality (MM, B14).[2] So the two flew to Singapore, and on 13 March 1936, Margaret, at thirty-four, embarked on her third marriage and Gregory, thirty-one, married for the first time. Gregory wrote rather apologetically to his mother, who came from a long line of Victorian intellectuals and atheists including Charles Darwin, that Margaret was a lady, "if you will ever allow that term to be applied to an American." He remarked, with some dissimulation, since Margaret retained her links to the Episcopal Church, that his mother should be relieved to know that Margaret came from a long line of religious dissenters and that she had "a good sound plain intelligent—almost female Darwin face."[3]

Margaret lied to her parents, saying that Gregory had followed her to Java and there persuaded her to marry him. The marriage plans had been a secret from Reo, too, and it fell upon Gregory to break the news to him. Margaret's cable to Ruth read simply, "Married." Ruth immediately replied, "I'm so happy about it. I shan't say anything about the wedding till letters come—except of course to the people who are on tiptoes waiting to know. I've told Marie, and I'll call Elizabeth [Margaret's sister] and Leah [Josephson Hanna]" (RFB, Box 37).

Jane Belo had provided the newlyweds with introductions to the bohemian community in Bali, including the artist and writer Beryl de Zoete, whom Margaret privately called "the witch," and the dancer Katharane Mershon (BW, 231). The men appeared to be mainly homosexual, delighting in the Balinese youth who were attractive and compliant; Mead wrote to Marie about the "inverts": "almost everyone in Bali is one, or, if female, is married to one." Walter Spies, a European artist and intellectual, quickly became a friend. Mead analyzed his fondness for the place as based on its "very dissociated impersonality [which] gave him the kind of freedom that he sought."[4] Jane Belo's husband, Colin McPhee, who was also homosexual, "doesn't exercise a single conjugal duty of bed, board or companionship," she wrote to Ruth.

Walter Spies, instructed by Jane Belo, had organized a house, complete with domestic staff, for Mead and Bateson until they could survey the territory and find a village to suit their purposes. The contrasts in Bali immediately fascinated Margaret, "the most extraordinary combination of a relatively untouched native life going along smoothly and quietly in its old way with a kind of extraneous, external civilization superimposed like an extra nervous system put on the outside of a body. . . . From shady corners where a dozen men in sarongs may be comparing the virtues of fighting cocks in wicker cages, police in smart green uniforms and broad-brimmed straw hats may step out to ask your chauffeur for his driver's license. . . . An anthropologist is presented with an unprecedented situation—quick, easy transport between dozens of versions of the culture" (LF, 160–61). And, just as they had been told, rituals were to be viewed for the asking. Within only a few weeks they observed as many ceremonies marking a variety of events, as they might have seen during a period of many patient months in New Guinea.

They chose for their fieldwork site the mountain village of Bajoeng Gedé, in twenty minutes' walking distance from the nearest road and off the beaten tourist track. Walter found a carpenter, and with surprisingly little trouble a small complex of buildings arose to house their ménage. The village had some five hundred ragged peasants and numerous pigs, chickens, and cows, which gave it "a pleasant barnyard murmur." Despite innumerable dogs barking constantly, Margaret told Ruth she found the life "extraordinarily pleasant, cool and placid, and full of work, and human."

They paid two dollars a month in rent, from which they deducted the cost of anything stolen from the house or any money begged from them. They paid separately for rituals, which they ordered like meals. As usual, Margaret put her medical kit to good effect, although with surprising equanimity she avoided interfering with native medicine when she wished to study its customary aspects. As she wrote Ruth, she had "just come back from burying a baby I saw born three nights ago—a foot presentation and as they won't touch a child till after the cord is cut, they can't handle foot presentation and so all such children die. In the higher culture, it's an insult to say 'Were you dragged into the world?' "

Margaret characterized the early years of her marriage to Gregory as "the perfect intellectual and emotional working partnership in which there was no pulling and hauling resulting from competing temperamental views of the world." There were differences in maturity, though, and these exaggerated the age difference, for "I had what amounted to a lifetime of completed work behind me; Gregory had a lifetime of work he wanted to do. . . . I had grown up at eleven and so had been grown up for over twenty years; Gregory kept his slight asthenic figure and adolescent silhouette until the war ended, almost ten years later" (BW, 224). For the moment these contrasts were a source of delight, not discouragement, and the couple managed to develop a collaborative way of working, Gregory seeming free of the jealousies that had spoiled work with Reo. He took rapid-fire photographs with his Leica or filmed "moving pictures" of the stylized rituals as well as of everyday events such as a mother's suckling a baby or groups gathering around a cockfight. Madé, their interpreter, who "turns out texts like a well fed threshing machine," recorded the spoken word, and Margaret made field notes to match up with words and photographs. As thyroid problems were endemic in the village, life "went on in a kind of simplified slow motion," making the anthropologists' task more manageable than usual. The final outcome of the Balinese work were some twenty-five thousand photographs, twenty-two thousand feet of film footage, exhaustive field notes, and the acquisition of hundreds of paintings and over one thousand carvings, an unusual effort for Margaret, who was not a collector by nature, despite her museum affiliation.

The emphasis on systematic collection of data did not mean Margaret suspended her interpretative activities. When faced with a new culture, she quickly identified "points" of theoretical importance, a process Gregory wrily called "culture cracking."[5] The two worked at "fever pitch" (BW, 235), and Margaret was proud to report to Ruth that they were getting "a nice point practically every day." Margaret was to characterize Balinese society as gentle and graceful, its people perpetually and effortlessly active. They "sleep in bunches like nests of kittens" and "stand in crowds all tangled up with each other," she wrote to Ruth, but despite the appearance of intimacy, she felt that relationships were "light, without enduring warmth." The Balinese, as Margaret and Gregory had anticipated back in New Guinea, filled in the final square in their temperament schema, with men and women qualifying as easterners in their remoteness.[6] Strong emotions were seldom expressed; using the forms of psychoanalytical reasoning that she now favored, Margaret argued that Balinese ritual, trance states, art, and dance were the sphere in which "disallowed feelings will be given graceful stylized expression."

Margaret rejoiced in her "extraordinary degree of communication" with Gregory. She maintained, perhaps against the odds, that they were similar in temperament; certainly, their styles of thinking were complementary. Gregory, slow and thoughtful, would often "throw out something wonderful" which Margaret would take up and develop (JH). He was fascinated by minute detail, she wrote to Ruth, like "the contractions of a muscle in the calf while the individual is in a trance," or by the most abstract ideas, such as those that foreshadowed modern systems theory. These he derived from Margaret's and Ruth's work on deviance and the question of why societies did not actually explode under the stimulus of disharmony.[7] Unlike Gregory, who was interested in the influence of scientists on their data, Margaret was seldom troubled by the possibility of alternative interpretations.

She was happy in the middle ground, observing behavior, on the lookout for cultural patterns and contrasts among the increasing number of cultures she knew.

The couple did experience some disharmony. Margaret's pace was frenetic and she hated to waste time or miss anything. Gregory would refuse to be interrupted in his reading or writing and could patiently endure long ceremonies or the long intervals between them, which drove Margaret to distraction when she thought about everything else she could be doing. She confided to Ruth: "The result is a pretty heavy situational [sic] on both of us, even though there is no strain between us. If there were any between us we couldn't stand it of course." As an observer once mocked, perhaps crudely, "Margaret is always shooting thousands of ideas out in all directions, like sperm, while Gregory, when he has an idea, sits on it, and develops it like a big ovum."[8]

Keeping in touch with Marie Eichelberger had sometimes been a chore for Margaret, but in the Balinese years she felt grateful for Marie, who could be relied upon for news about Ruth, especially domestic matters which Ruth neglected to mention. Biographers, equally, have reason to feel grateful to Eichelberger, since the newly released Mead-Eichelberger correspondence provides details of Ruth's life that were previously unknown, especially about the period of her relationship with Natalie Raymond. Marie, now living in financial uncertainty at Christadora House, a settlement house for women on the Lower East Side, congratulated Margaret on her latest marriage and joked, "Every time you love someone I have to take on a new responsibility, isn't it absurd, dear?"

Marie had fallen in love, but in the role of the "other woman." Initially unsure if a woman named Eugenia and her companion, Mary, were lesbian, Marie wrote to Margaret, "because of my own adjustment, I am sensitized to emotional relationships between women; one can tell from the physical ease with each other and tiny bits of thoughtfulness, which would pass unnoticed by the average person. I feel fairly sure now that they are articulate in their relationship." Marie wanted to tell Eugenia the history of her feelings for Margaret and was pleased when Margaret gave permission. Marie's affair was secretive; Eugenia would not leave her partner despite her declarations of love. The relationship lasted several years, Marie often fearful and guilty. As it dwindled, her symptoms of anxiety returned; she was lonely, suffered a permanent headache, and at times experienced depression of near suicidal intensity.

Marie loved to confide in Ruth but worried about "crabbing and moaning," in case she bored Ruth who could become "aloof and distant." She sought friendship with women at her work place, but they were moving into middle age and all seemed partnered. The only options seemed to be to "get your man or your woman and settle down," or "love and ask nothing in return," which was Marie's perpetual lot. Ruth suggested she write a life history, but Marie felt that "like Léonie [Adams], I can't because of the form of my attachments." She told Margaret that she thought about keeping a journal as an outlet for her feelings, "with the pretense that you were going to read it after I died."

From Marie's letters we learn that Ruth's relationship with Natalie was becoming increasingly strained. Nat had not pursued her studies with any enthusiasm and earned a small income from casual typing. Marie found her difficult: "One wonders what Nat thinks and feels. Not like me, with this urge to say it all." Nat's enthusiasm for animals was undeniable, but Marie thought Margaret would be scandalized to know that Nat's dog, Mary, now had six puppies in the "lovely" Central Park West apartment— and that there was another dog as well. They were "very hard on the place, . . . ; those upholstered chairs are torn and ragged, quite literally, with holes gnawed in them and the stuffing coming out. Pillows all finally had to be put away, after the dogs chewed them open and covered the apartment with feathers. Rugs could no longer be on the floor, because of constant staining. And everything was dingy from the dogs lying on them. They have decided to get rid of every last puppy and keep only Mary. I never minded Mary (tho you found conversation difficult with her). . . . On the other hand, the dogs are lovable and pretty, and Ruth as well as Nat does love them devotedly. Each night when they came in, they had to clean up after them, and there was never a murmur."

By the end of the 1935–36 academic year, with Boas unwell and close to retirement, Ruth had shouldered many administrative duties before formally becoming acting head of the anthropology department. Marie reported that Ruth looked withdrawn, tired, and thin. Nat was not going to California for the summer but refused to go to Norwich with Ruth; Marie hinted to Margaret that Nat was pursuing her own active social life and that she "plays around" with her brother's "crowd"; one of his friends was "paying attention, but she isn't interested." Nat did seem interested in Patty Brisbane, who worked at Brentano's bookstore. With Ruth in Norwich, Nat hung out at the bookstore "most of the time . . . helping Patty, or chatting with the people who come in." Patty, a self-sufficient young woman in her twenties, lived with Mary Murphy, an older "lusty, robust, whole-hearted Irish woman." Patty and Mary were "not in love," reported Marie; "Mary has a very good salary; Patty not so much. They keep open house and drink and go off on week-end parties with men and girls—often to their friends who lend them their homes in the country. Ruth likes Patty quite a lot. . . ." Indeed, Ruth had Patty choose some books to send to

Margaret in Bali, including *Gone with the Wind* and Huxley's *Eyeless in Gaza*. Marie confided, "Nat said that Patty was the kind of person who had joy in just being alive. . . . She is attractive to men and has many of them around, but in the spring when Nat talked about her, was not in love. I asked Ruth whether Nat was in love with her [Patty], and she said she couldn't be sure, but didn't think so."

In August, after Ruth had been three weeks at the farm, Nat had sudden and severe discomfort from gallstones. She made an emergency call to Patty and was hospitalized and operated on immediately. Ruth drove down by night to be at her bedside and found her in critical condition.[9] The younger woman was dangerously ill for some time after the operation. Marie reported that Ruth spent most of her days at the hospital, reading aloud for hours at a time and staying through all the medical procedures. Nat was at first a good patient, but as time wore on "she grew most impatient. Once when I asked Ruth how she felt herself, she said, 'I am alright, I am taking good care of myself, because I will need all my strength later when Nat comes home.' " Ruth feared that Nat would not obey doctors' orders and Nat refused to have a nurse. Marie asked Ruth how she would keep Nat in hand, since "you have never with anyone used authority," but Ruth believed that "she could and would."

Nat discharged herself from the hospital to Patty's apartment—the stairs at Ruth's were too difficult, and Patty "was devoting her vacation to Nat anyway." Ruth immediately began looking for a new apartment with an elevator and found a likeable one, but Nat vetoed a move. A friend offered Ruth and Nat a place in the country for the convalescence, but when Nat was well enough she went off for a few days with Patty to a house in Westchester. Marie reported to Margaret that "Ruth didn't know when Nat would be home with her again." She was looking "badly" and "very worried; puffy under the eyes and thin." Boas wrote a note of sympathy about Nat's illness and Margaret wrote that she was glad to hear Marie's version of events, since she could balance her overstatements with Ruth's understatements.

Ruth Benedict's friendship with Ruth Bunzel was a source of comfort. Over this difficult few weeks, Benedict took most of her meals with Bunny and her mother in their Greenwich Village home. The two had known each other for more than a decade, but the newfound companionship led Bunny to the realization that she was in love; it was, as Ruth told Margaret, "the first time she has been in love with a woman." Ruth did not return Bunny's feelings. Nevertheless, she invited Bunny up to the farm the next summer, reporting to Margaret that with "no other claimants for my attention" Bunny was "at her best . . . [and] like a pussy cat—liked any place to curl up under the stove." The peace did not last on their return to the city, Ruth remarking that "the best answer to prayer would be some man's proposal of marriage; but will anybody? She should have somebody to vegetate with, and till she's preoccupied with some man she'll think I'm the choice of her heart." Margaret replied, also condescendingly, that "with Bunny having so little idea what human intimacy is about, I imagine you can make her blissfully happy, happier than she ever has been in her life, and at the same time keep any reserve you set."

It is surprising that Ruth felt the attentions of a man might cure a crush on a woman, since she had clearly accepted a homosexual relationship for herself. But even Marie, who often remarked on her own homosexual "adjustment" indicated that others still saw her as potentially marriageable. She told Margaret that a party-going friend had been to visit and "brought around a man she thought I ought to know. . . . I don't like getting drunk, and don't; neither do I like petting going home in the taxis, which seems to be the accepted pattern. One man told me I was missing a lot, being so formal."

Eventually, Nat came home to Ruth, but she was unhappy. Six months after her illness, Marie described Nat as depressed, miserable, and troubled by prolonged and severe headaches, "going along as usual, with no interest in anything, or anybody . . . the world dust and ashes." "Ruth couldn't be sure it was neurotic," wondering if there might be a physical cause. Ruth herself was feeling "rottenly," as she wrote Margaret; the doctor had told her it was a "clear case of postmenopause glandular disturbance," her "circulation . . . all gaga," so she was having "enormous injections of glandular liquid" which had made a big difference.

Nat's disturbance had been in evidence for some time. Two years previously Robert Oppenheimer had told his brother that when he and Nat spent an evening drinking champagne cocktails at the top of Radio City, he had listened to her "always new & always moving miseries."[10] Around the same time, Ruth Benedict wrote to Nat's California friend, Ruth Tolman, "I'm distressed about Nat and her work at Cornell. She's so dependent on having good people around, either to respect or compete with, and there's not a soul over there. She just drives herself to go on, and there's no pleasure in it. Just the same, it would be folly to let it slip, so near the goal of the Ph.D." Tolman, with Ruth Valentine, sent "Natsie, their 'dear lamb,'" a present of a new typewriter, since hers had been stolen (RFB, Box 35). But it seems that Nat drifted in and out of work, with various part-time jobs including working for psychologists in an animal laboratory. She was offered a teaching position at Queens College but turned it down in order not to give up her freedom. She earned some money from stock exchange speculations, she had an income from her family, and Ruth no doubt contributed more than her share of the household expenses. Nat had ambitious plans, but they usually came to nothing. She tried various writing jobs, including a short stint at *Time* Magazine; once she proposed writing a physiology textbook.

Perhaps the knowledge of the special place Margaret occupied in Ruth's heart was not easy for Natalie to accept. She would not even consider the idea of psychoanalysis when Ruth suggested it and Ruth grew increasingly disillusioned, remarking to Marie that Nat was "getting older all the time." Marie thought that "Ruth's attitude of discouragement is more a reflection of fatigue than change in her point of view as to anything she ought to do about Nat." Nat grew her hair long, tied it back with a knot, lost weight, paid more attention to her clothes, and continued to spend time with Patty, though as Marie reassured Margaret, "neither one are in love with the other" and there were "no men in the picture." Marie did imply, though, that Nat had other relationships when she told Margaret that Nat's relationship with Patty had lasted longer than others and "seems to be more casual." Ruth's reaction is unknown; perhaps she was hurt and jealous, though she disliked jealousy; almost certainly she was downcast. One change is certain: she no longer delighted in Nat as once she had done. In her letters to Margaret from 1937 onward, she seldom mentions the woman who had given her "the happiest conditions for living that I've ever known."

In December 1936, Stanley Benedict died of a heart attack at the age of 52. He had been ill for several weeks, had hired a nurse and kept his problems to himself. His sisters, whom Ruth had known since Vassar days, arrived at his bedside shortly after he died. They did not inform Ruth, who was shocked to learn of his death from the newspaper, too late to attend the funeral. Marie also saw the notice and called Ruth, who seemed "calm and serious . . . but . . . not . . . upset." When Ruth was ill shortly afterward she attributed the problem to her glandular disturbance. Much later, after attending a conference, she made an overnight trip to Boston to visit Stanley's grave and was back in New York by the afternoon to lecture to Gestalt psychologists.

Stanley's estate involved Ruth in a dispute with his sisters over the will. His legal, signed will left Ruth a trust fund of $25,000 with an income of $125 monthly, the principal to come to her at the age of sixty. Despite mutterings from the sisters about Ruth's having forged the will—and the existence of an unsigned will made after the separation that left them a larger proportion of the estate—a court found in Ruth's favor. She wrote to Margaret, "for so many years I though that what I had to put up with from the Benedicts was probably much what everyone had to put up with from in-laws. . . . But now I feel much freer to look back and judge them as they are. . . . If I'd been as clear about it then as I am now I'd have pulled up stakes long before.—I used to think I was getting paranoid; but now I think it's a wonder they didn't *make* me paranoid."

Clearing out Stanley's household effects was difficult: "I thought I'd got over my nightmare of the impermanence of what one cares about most, but going through Stanley's possessions is an over-great test. All my letters were there since before we were engaged. It was only a matter of transferring all such things into the trash-heaps, but nothing had been sorted out so there was no shortcut."[11] A beneficiary of the cleanup, Marie was thrilled to have Stanley's old car.

Ruth was now financially secure, with tenure and now a small trust income. Since she could live comfortably, she engaged a maid for shopping and cooking; "Ruth does not even know what is to come on the table," Marie noted with envy. To the outside world Ruth was Mrs. Stanley Benedict, widow, and she described herself thus on resumés until the end of her life.[12]

After their first year in Bali, Margaret and Gregory moved from their small village to rent a palace at Bangli for nine dollars a month. No longer subject to "the native rhythm and accident rate," they also had "no natives" in sight "except cheerful servants and Madé," their interpreter, though in the distance young Balinese were "singing sacred chants in low sweet voices." Despite the pleasing environment and excellent social life, Margaret was increasingly frustrated by her isolation from the world of anthropology. She often used Ruth as an intermediary in attempts to influence field trips and job placements. It was becoming a source of special concern that she had no way of passing on her fieldwork expertise; without a university position there was no ready source of potential protégés. It was not that she wanted "satellites," she told Ruth. Rather, "it really is too tiresome to spend all these years learning how to do things and then have the results no use." Ruth, of course, kept Margaret's work alive with her own students, but Margaret's lack of protégés and her fractured relationship with Sapir and Fortune left her vulnerable.

Margaret's most successful mentoring was of gifted amateurs, travelers or expatriates like Geoffrey Gorer, whom she and Ruth had turned into an anthropologist, and Jane Belo, whom she had involved in the trance research. She tried to give advice to Columbia students she knew from the project on cooperation and competition, but, she wrote, "I feel thoroughly blue about my choice of people who were to carry on the various lines which I started—each and every one of them have flopped. . . . Do you think my judgment is rotten, or do I pick the wrong points of identification?" She worried that Ruth would now have new students and she, Margaret, having been away so long, would not know any of them and she worked herself up to a fit of temper: "Why is it that people don't ask my advice . . . ? Do they think I will bully them, or is it all just Edward and Malinowski [telling stories about her] . . . Why why is it? . . . Who is responsible for making me out some kind of ogre? Heaven knows if I stay away for three years the myth will have grown to enormous proportions."

Ruth replied soothingly that the myth was fueled mainly by people's inefficiency and thoughtlessness: "You put first things first and take planning seriously," unlike most anthropologists she knew. Also, "most people can't stand much comparison of themselves with people they know are better. When you feel you are pouring out your wisdom and sharing it with them, they are feeling sunk because you're so good (your brain, not your good-nature). Don't ask me why people are so stupid as that, but remember the whole 'kill the father' movement in anthropology against Boas. He often asks me the same questions you have: 'Why don't people consult me?' "

Margaret, of course, was not always easy to work for, since she set an almost impossible pace, could be impatient, and lost her temper from time to time, though her "appearance of belligerency," she believed, was sometimes misinterpreted. If she was under par, "in order to keep going I get up steam, speak with more force, pound the chair arm, etc., and give an impression of affect which is really just my attempt to deal with the question . . . as my thinking depends on speed."[13]

Margaret also worried about whether she was in Papa Franz's good books. He had not acknowledged Gregory's *Naven*, and Margaret was not sure whether she should write to him: "I don't think I have ever mattered seriously except as a Student with a capitol [sic] S." Ruth replied that Boas had "got past living in the world at all, and hardly knows that other human beings aren't just shadows."

Reo was also a concern for Margaret, although he was "settling down and behaving better." He planned to marry his former sweetheart, Eileen Pope, and had managed to find a position in China, at Lingnan University, after having competed with Gregory for a Cambridge position. Margaret tried to make sure that he lost out on another Cambridge job, since she could not contemplate living in the same town as he did, and Cambridge might be her next destination. En route to China, Reo wrote to Ruth that leaving New Zealand was like getting out of prison. His trip was not uneventful; he was involved in a fist fight over a woman and transferred to first class to keep the peace. "He must be a genius," Margaret wrote Ruth; apparently, he arrived at his new job "all bashed up around the face." So that he could do some useful work from his underfunded university, Ruth and Margaret arranged a loan from Margaret's sister Elizabeth, disguised as a grant from Columbia.

Margaret was vastly relieved that Reo planned to marry: "the fates do seem most terrifically bidable [sic]." This would put paid to any suggestions that she had ruined his life, about which she was enormously sensitive: "Anyone who seems inclined to paint me as an ogre who wrecks people's lives might be told about it. I feel quite pleased to consider that all the men who have ever cared about me have speedily embraced the married state, as if I, in some obscure way, typified it, perhaps by not being more consistently faithful to it. But anyway, it is a great relief to know that that has all worked out as it should." She continued to worry lest the marriage not take place, asking Ruth to cable "Married China" as soon as she heard of it.

Reo was the cause of a rare disagreement between the two women when he insisted that Ruth not tell Margaret about his marriage plans. Margaret could not understand why Ruth should have kept to the bargain when "there have been hundreds of instances when we have told each other things which would have infuriated the one told of . . . When it has been the affairs of someone close to you, you haven't hesitated to tell me, but when it is someone close to me, you do. If I couldn't be trusted, if I were likely to write Reo, or do something which would show I knew, it seems to me it would be different. But if my communication with you is to be held up or distorted because of Reo's fits of guilt over marrying Eileen and being pleased about it, until someone sends me a clipping the size of a house announcing his marriage, that seems a bit heavy tribute to pay to the Goddess of Fidelity." At first Ruth did not reply to this criticism, and Margaret reminded her: "I don't mean to fuss, if you think it is really better just to ignore an issue rather than meet it, but you have never answered my question about the whole matter of not betraying Reo to me. . . . I feel as if you were making the kind of point you made to Edward in refusing to have mine or Papa Franz's name mentioned. Unless I know what you do think it's bound to cramp my writing a little." Ruth brushed aside Margaret's concerns in a reply that came nearly a year after the original complaint, such were the vagaries of the mails: not telling Margaret would have only held up the news of Reo by about a week, she argued, and since "I had given Reo a sworn promise" and since "the wait was so trivial," she was of the opinion that it "didn't involve fundamentals in any way."

Franz Boas finally retired in 1936 at the age of seventy-eight and Ruth Benedict became acting head of the anthropology department, though she was still paid substantially less than the other associate professor, archaeologist Duncan Strong, who was appointed shortly afterward. The search was now on for a new professor and Ruth made it clear that she was a potential candidate, even though the Faculty of Political Science had never appointed a woman to a full professorship. Margaret Mead may have been taking the climate at Columbia into account when she herself did not consider Ruth a serious candidate, though she also, in fact, thought Ruth unsuitable. Ruth had been tired and unwell a good deal in 1936 and Margaret aired her concerns to Marie: "I sometimes wonder if I am responsible for urging her to take a more and more active role in anthropology and one not really congenial to her. . . . I never approved of her being head of the department, I always thought that was culturally and temperamentally too difficult for her and would only bring difficulties. But I think on the whole she really wants it now, and that takes its toll."

Margaret initially had hopes for Gregory at Columbia—Ruth had earlier suggested him—but he now expected to inherit the chair at Cambridge. In early 1936, Margaret supported Lloyd Warner from Yale, telling him "of course Ruth is definitely for you up to the ears" (MM, B1). Mead learned after Ruth's death that Howard Lee McBain, dean of the graduate school, had favored Benedict and had remarked that women chairmen being inevitable, Columbia ought to be first in this respect. Before he could execute his intention, he died of a heart attack in the spring of 1936.

Elsie Clews Parsons was hostile to Benedict's candidacy, writing in an unsent draft of a letter to Robert Lowie that Benedict, W. Lloyd Warner— trained by Kroeber and Lowie and influenced by Radcliffe-Brown—and Ralph Linton were in the running: "The Department is my immediate world in anthropology and I would regret being cut off from it in a Warner-Benedict plunge into the Radcliffe-Brown morass." As she understood it, Boas supported Benedict: "He has such a blind spot about people that he can't foresee a mess or see through designfulness."[14] Parsons may have been particularly annoyed that the work on the concordance of Southwest mythology, which had provided Benedict's first paid job in anthropology, had come to nought. Benedict seems not to have been fully committed to it, and during the 1930s she had passed it over to Erna Gunther, who refused to answer letters from Parsons concerning its whereabouts. Eventually it was given back to Benedict, now editor of the Folklore Society's publications, but considerable work remained to be done. A year later Parsons complained to Boas that it was an "outrageous mess" and could not be published in its present form, so it was dropped, Parsons's investment of two thousand dollars lost.[15] *Zuñi Mythology* was one publication from the project, but Parsons did not approve of the psychoanalytical tenor of Benedict's interpretations, much preferring Ruth Bunzel's Zuñi work.[16] Whether Parsons had any influence on the Columbia appointment is unclear.

In the event, Boas was not allowed to name his successor. Ralph Linton, a younger candidate whom Boas despised, was appointed, first as visiting professor but with the assurance that he could expect a permanent position. Years before, still in service during World War I, Linton had appeared at Columbia in military uniform to discuss graduate work and Boas had given him such a hostile reception that Linton changed his mind and went to Harvard.[17] Boas rated him "a mediocre man without any original ideas."[18] Initially, Ruth and Margaret were not against the imposingly masculine and somewhat chauvinist six-footer since he favoured the culture-and-personality approach, but by the time he appeared they had misgivings, fearing him unequal to the task. Ruth was uneasy about his anti-Semitism, and had once remarked in a letter to Margaret: "I wish that Linton didn't talk so much about the 'Jewish' ring in anthropology." Margaret now assured her that Linton might not be too bad, and if he "cooks his own goose you may be left in peaceful possession yet."

Linton's appointment was a horror for Ruth. Bad feeling arose almost immediately. Boas had no intention of surrendering his office, the biggest in the department and adjoining the secretary, with Benedict, acting chair, lodged in the second best room on the other side.[19] Linton, relegated to an office down the hall, was greeted by Boas with the words, "Of course, you know this is not what I wanted."[20] Ruth also could hardly have avoided smarting under the insult of being overlooked for the professorship, writing to Robert Lynd that she had been "disqualified because I'm a woman."[21] Linton found Benedict's manner to be "cool and unreceptive." As his biographers, one of whom was his wife, recalled, "Ruth Benedict had an irritating manner of regally dismissing the ideas and accomplishments of those whom she did not hold in high regard. She would not openly criticize, but with a smile or gesture indicate that she felt her adversary to be elementary or childish. Linton found such treatment infuriating and frustrating, and the relationship between the two colleagues developed into intellectual and personal hostility, sustained more in after years on his part than on hers."[22]

Linton's and Benedict's shared interest in psychological anthropology, which might have strengthened the department, made matters worse. Ruth could move nowhere without being in Linton's line of sight. She stopped going to departmental lunches and scaled down her participation in the psychoanalytical seminar that Abram Kardiner coordinated, missing out on potentially significant theoretical contributions to her work. Edward Sapir's quarrel with Margaret Mead had already caused an awkward rift among culture-and-personality anthropologists, and the rift between Linton and Benedict further weakened the school.[23]

Linton profited in one way from the alienation of Benedict. Margaret, assessing Linton as unproductive, advised Ruth to give him something to work on that would distract him. She willingly handed over the Southwest field materials her students had collected over the years so he could prepare them for publication.[24] She was also pleased when he became editor of the *American Anthropologist*. Despite these attempts at cooperation, hostilities were entrenched and quickly became obvious to students. Ruth wrote to Margaret, "The children [her graduate students] report odd conversations which they interpret as his trying to get them to report on favoritism in my administration of field funds etc." Margaret diagnosed the problem: "If only he doesn't get paranoid," she wrote, voicing a worry that proved justified, since Ruth reported back that Linton had berated a class because someone had stolen a book from his office, only to find that it had not disappeared at all.

Ruth told herself that these incidents were maybe molehills, not mountains, but Margaret's suspicions had been confirmed: "Of course Linton is paranoid, you know he's always been my type case of the paranoia which is due to being less good than the place which life has given one." Matters grew steadily worse. By the end of Linton's first year, Ruth predicted that "it is perfectly possible that I may have to wallop Linton hard in public someday." "He is a swine," she continued, in unusually strong language.

As the national political climate became chillier, Linton's tactics changed from annoying to sinister: he began a program of red-baiting, claiming to colleagues that he could name communists in his department. The students divided themselves up into "his and hers."[25] The acrimony can be gauged by remarks, such as Jules Henry's to Ruth, when he signed off a letter, "Love to everyone—and my usual dose of rat-poison for the fat boy with the watery eyes" (RFB, Box 29).

On the other hand, Benedict was not universally liked either. Nathalie Woodbury, an anthropologist who was a graduate student at Columbia in the late thirties, recalls that she was "vague," "ethereal," and "like dealing with plasma." Although her stammer was not bad, she was slow off the mark as a speaker, and that trait combined with her partial deafness and her habit of "looking past or through you" as if in a kind of absence, was "disconcerting to a younger person." This former student recalled Ruth as impractical, "unhelpful and rather irritating."[26]

To students, Ruth's feminism was notable, but her lesbianism was not openly talked about. According to Woodbury, there were "no whispers" in the corridors of Columbia, although she remembers at least one discussion with another graduate student about their shared sense that Benedict carried "an aura of lesbianism." Benedict's sexual orientation apparently was known to her colleagues, including Linton, but public visibility would have put her job at risk. It was rare then for professional women to reveal lesbianism; as Estelle Freedman has pointed out in her biography of

Miriam van Waters, "lesbian" was usually a term of opprobrium applied to black women or women in prison, unless it was used rebelliously by bohemians of Greenwich Village.[27]

With all of the burdens and disappointments of this period in Benedict's life—the wearisome administrative load, poor health, fatigue, Stanley's death, and the disappointment in Natalie—one might have expected a return of the same sort of psychological frailty that she had experienced in her twenties and thirties. But she now was secure in herself, having resolved her patterns of intimacy and the direction of her life. In adversity she was now calm and peaceful, with a serenity which struck others as detached, impractical, remote, or spiritual, depending on their own attitudes.

Perhaps the psychological explorations she was involved in during the thirties helped. Although never psychoanalyzed, she did write her own life history and was part of a group, led by the Jungian Bruno Klopfer, who studied Rorschach tests. The group included Esther Goldfrank, Ruth Bunzel, a psychiatrist specializing in adolescence named Carolyn Zachry, and Zachry's "close friend and housemate," Wilma Lloyd. Goldfrank recalled Ruth's descriptions of her Rorschach test results: "I gave only one answer to each card and each of them was a whole. Quite schizophrenic . . . Klopfer was amazed at my integrations of color and movement." A holistic response was particularly indicative of ambition, and in this context the terms *schizophrenic* referred to "the personality of an individual who has evolved a scheme of life or system that was so satisfying or compelling that there was no need to consider any elements beyond those already included."[28] This analysis of Ruth's personality clearly applies to the style of anthropological thinking she favored; to Goldfrank this anecdote suggests the reasons Ruth would never revise *Patterns*, despite her colleagues' increasing dissatisfaction about its emphasis on cultural ideals rather than cultural realities. "I'm so bored with Pueblos," she said to Goldfrank. There would be no revisiting her schema, not from an unwillingness to consider an alternative point of view—Benedict was nothing if not tolerant—but she had simply worked out that set of ideas to her satisfaction.

Ruth found it difficult to explain her internal landscape to anyone other than Margaret. Marie had noticed in early 1937, even before Linton's arrival and its stresses, that Ruth had put on weight, writing to Margaret that Ruth was looking beautiful, despite "not paying any special attention to clothes" and "wear[ing] a blue suit most of the time." Marie observed that Ruth was "at peace in a way that I have never known her to be, and talks little or not at all about herself." She had made a new circle of friends, including women who invited her to their country homes for weekends. Her students during this period were mainly young men, "her constituents," as Nat called them, who "poured out their love lives to her" and to whom she "gives and lends . . . money, to get married, or stay married, or get divorces, or have babies." Ruth told Marie she had found "a sense of peace,—a release from emotional tension of all kinds." No longer bothered by depression, "she thinks of herself as getting old, in a way, and happy over the fact that she is not involved in being in love. She wondered whether she would or could fall in love again, but said she didn't want to." Marie, inquisitive as usual, asked Ruth what her major pleasure was: the response was: "the students and their enthusiasm over their work."

Margaret quizzed Ruth about this unconvincing reply. Ruth said she had given Marie an off-hand explanation since "there is no way to make my inner life intelligible to Marie." The real situation, she explained to Margaret, was that "my inner core is all right" and "in spite of all my busyness I have constantly freer and freer access to my obsessional self—and happier access—and you are the only person in the world who knows or cherishes that side of me. It makes you seem very close to me, when other people who see quite a different person in me seem very remote. I don't have devils any more; it's hard to put in words how completely they're gone. You'll understand when nobody else would if I put it that I feel as if I lived in the country I despaired of for so long; none of the nagging things I have to do really touch me. I don't feel lonely either—not really, even with you away. It's like a little piece of eternal life, with all that's past and all that's present enormously real, and no desperateness about the present. . . . I suppose I've achieved identification with my father—or something. Anyway I like it and I think you would."

Perhaps it was Ruth who inspired Margaret's well-known catch phrase, "postmenopausal zest," referring to the renewed energy women often find in midlife.[29] Ruth's transformation seems to have occurred after menopause when she had relief from her fainting spells and wrote Margaret, "now I have my healthiest years ahead of me." Because her depressions had grown out of childhood temper tantrums and vomiting spells that were cyclical in nature, some sort of hormonal trigger may have been involved, though Ruth saw her troubles as psychological, resulting from a failure of spiritual discipline.

Ruth's spiritual qualities made a profound impression on one of her students. Abraham Maslow, later a founder of humanistic psychology, saw her as an example of what he would call "the self-actualizing personality"; Ruth was a "very, very wonderful" teacher, he wrote, a person "whom he loved, adored, and admired."[30] According to Maslow, self-actualizers are unconventional thinkers who do not necessarily present an unconventional face to the world. They gave an impression of serenity despite conflicts they have experienced, and their breadth of vision draws them to socially important work. Their occupations are characterized by intrinsic rather than status rewards and their views are democratic rather than authoritarian. They enjoy friends who can surprise them, though they are kind and patient with the admirers they attract. Sometimes they act ruthlessly in cutting themselves off from dishonest relationships. Self-actualizers appear self-contained, their detachment often interpreted as coldness, but they are capable of loving deeply. Sexual experiences are not casual or merely sensual to them, but enlivening. They have a mystical element in their make-up and are prone to what he called peak experiences. Maslow's portrait of the self-actualizer is, in most respects, an uncannily accurate portrait of Ruth.

It is interesting, then, to find in Margaret's correspondence after Ruth's death a disagreement with Maslow's categorizing: "Maslow's theories about her work I have always regarded as major misapprehensions: he speaks of her as a fully actualized person: actually she was a very deeply troubled one and her achievements were the fruits of tragedy rather than actualization in his sense" (MM, TR2). Erik Erikson concurred with Mead. He saw Ruth's psychological state as less robust, for she was "too young to be complete and detached, . . . deeply alone, [a friend] who had, in fact, stopped fighting loneliness. . . . There is tragedy here, we know."[31] One has to ask, however, whether Maslow's views are incompatible with Mead's and Erikson's. Maslow never denied the role of conflict in the history of the self-actualizer, and perhaps Mead, always threatened by Ruth's detachment, only meant to emphasize that Ruth's hard-won state of mind was not to be idealized. Whatever the verdict, Ruth truly experienced a midlife transformation. She had found a way of making peace with her two worlds, represented by her father and her mother.

Natalie Raymond was more cheerful during this time, too—"for no reason at all," Ruth told Margaret, Natalie was "not in the slough of despond." She decided to accompany Jeannette Mirsky, one of Ruth's students, on fieldwork in Guatemala. Ruth funded the trip, taking "a gambler's chance" on encouraging Nat in "the first thing in years that she had wanted to undertake."[32] They sailed just before Christmas 1937, but they proved to be an ill-matched couple who "depressed each other." Nat went off for four months, with just a horse, leading "a gypsy life" of sleeping in the hills, under trees or in a hut. According to Marie, Ruth "liked very much being on her own." On her return, Nat decided to write a guidebook to Guatemala and persuaded Ruth to go back with her for a summer vacation, after which Nat intended to stay on. Marie observed to Margaret, in a meaningful tone: "I am not sure but I think Nat uses the front room now, when she is in New York."

In June 1938, Nat drove Ruth through Guatemala. Ruth enjoyed the trip immensely, she wrote to Boas (FB, 3 July 1938). Patty Brisbane, Nat's friend, saved rent by living in Ruth's apartment while they were away. Nat stayed on in Guatemala as planned, delaying her return for months. When she did return to the United States she made a prolonged visit with her family in California. Unlike earlier and longed-for reunions, Ruth did not even record Nat's arrival in New York in her datebook. Their vacation, although pleasurable, had apparently marked the end of their domestic relationship. Only a year earlier Ruth had willed her personal property, including Shattuck Farm which she would inherit, to Natalie. The trust fund from Stanley, however, and any other funds were willed to "Margaret Mead Bateson," who was charged with overseeing their use for "the continuance of anthropological work in which I am interested" (RFB, Box 39).

Margaret and Gregory left Bali in March 1938, completely exhausted and having worked to the limit. Margaret had been suffering spells of toothache, malaria, and stomach complaints. They returned to New Guinea to re-study Gregory's Iatmul using photographic techniques. The Batesons were running short of money, but friends of Margaret's donated further field funds. Jane Belo, who was divorcing her husband, wanted to accompany them, and Gregory was strongly attracted to this exquisitely beautiful, sensitive, and mentally fragile woman, who, as a "remote and self-absorbed" easterner, certainly provided a contrast to Margaret.[33] The last thing Margaret must have wanted was another Sepik triangle. She told Ruth rather airily that though Jane "teased very hard to go to New Guinea . . . we haven't the time to take her on the trip really, and she would just be an extra responsibility."

The Mead-Batesons approached New Guinea with some trepidation as Rabaul, their point of entry, had been virtually destroyed in a volcanic eruption some months earlier. On the international scene, clouds of war were drawing over the West. In 1936, Margaret had sounded a note of discouragement: "Always the possibility of war and the possibility that we are collecting all this . . . for a world that will cease to care about slow and accurate research, a shadow behind all that we do . . . an individualistic gesture of stubbornness in the face of the facts." By the time they reached New Guinea, the worsening international situation, somber and difficult to interpret, was daily news to Americans, but as Ruth wrote: "We might all be halfway up the Sepik for all the ability we have to follow really what is going on."

Margaret and Gregory cheered up when they arrived in Tambunum; among this "swell people . . . it is rather like coming home." They were given a rousing welcome and Margaret was able to show proof of Gregory's shipboard Iatmul lessons when for the first time she arrived in a new culture with some linguistic proficiency: "We walked through the village, followed by troops of laughing, delighted, unfrightened children, while Gregory exchanged totemic quips with the old men, and I made a great hit by managing to say in Iatmul, to an old man, that I would not venture nearer the house tamberan because it belonged to the men, and I was a woman. He was so pleased he shouted it several times."

The work went well at first. Geoffrey Gorer had suggested that Gregory's *Naven* would have been improved if he had said more about homosexuality among the Iatmul, giving depth to his portrayal of the ritual homosexuality of the Naven ceremony. Margaret wrote to Ruth that, unlike the Balinese who willingly had sex with European men, regarding homosexual acts as unimportant, the Iatmul "talk sodomy, they act provocative sadistic gestures of both types, they show every sort of homosexual symptom—there are 14 regular verbal expressions for pederastic attack—and as nearly as we can find out—no pederasty at all. They take it all out in talk and symbolic gestures. . . ." Only a month later, though, Margaret had more information. The Iatmul enjoyed sex, she said, and "I have never had such blithely unworried informants. The more delicate parts of the homosexual stuff are coming out beautifully; everyone is willing to be active, but no one not the tiniest child to be passive."

Working in New Guinea always involved risk. Margaret arranged, through Ruth, a new will which left her assets to anthropological research. Ruth would be a trustee, for "you are the only person I can trust you know; everyone else is willing but they do such funny things. But sometimes it seems to me as if you ought to have had me for a child to deserve all the trouble I make you. Does that make sense?" Margaret and Gregory's isolation was underlined in their feeling that Ruth was "the only living person whom we feel would really know what we were doing. . . . Gregory thinks that three people in the world who know what the others are talking about isn't so bad for a ten year old approach, but I hate to see it hang by the slender threads of our three lives. . . . I hate this school label [with their emphasis on patterns, they had come to be known as the Configuration School], but I do admit, privately, that we are different, dont you?"

The joy of returning to Iatmul did not last, and in the six months of their stay, "what had seemed to be a possibly feverish dream in Bali came closer to being a nightmare on the Sepik river" (BW, 237). Gregory was ill with malaria and a skin infection much of the time, and the village was too absorbed with crocodile hunting to engage in their ceremonial life. The stress made Margaret insecure and querulous, and this showed in her relation to Ruth. If there were only three genuine configurationists in the whole world, it seemed a bit hard that Ruth communicated irregularly and seldom seemed to relish hard thinking: "You write so little about anthropological points, of theory or method, that its an act of faith to go on writing letters like this page—a quite vivid faith, well informed by memory of never failing exciting interest, but still—definitely faith."

With Marie writing of Ruth's peacefulness and withdrawal, Margaret wondered whether she was still important to Ruth. Her few letters were "all full of what other people are doing, and what you have done about my affairs—and God knows I give you enough things to bother with—and nothing, nothing about what you yourself are either doing, or feeling or thinking, or even reading. It doesn't exactly frighten me, it just makes me shiver temporarily; I feel deprived, and its like those weeks when Lydia was living in your apartment with all the babies and we never saw each other. Who or what is the Lydia in this case? You know there wasn't any way out of this trip for us. . . . Or is Nat's being away especially difficult?" Replies took so long to arrive that her next letters from Ruth caused her just as much dissatisfaction: "I don't suppose I should have started all that controversy, or potential controversy about letters, when I can't have an answer from you for months. . . . Maybe . . . I am merely at my old trick of what you call scene making, to make life more exciting. To say I dont think so doesn't mean much because I have often thought my fears or excitements were genuine when you thought they were—functional. I do hope it didn't bother you. I don't mean to bother you, darling. I just felt a little lonely."

Faced with silence, Margaret grew more and more upset: "The mail came. . . . I got twenty letters but none from you. It might just as well not have been a mail at all." Perhaps it was no help to her own peace of mind that she was studying temper tantrums in the children. Ruth began to figure in her dreams: "I dreamt of you in an odd new fashioned hat, a kind I'd never seen. . . . Everyone—you, Jane, Louise Bogan, were beautifully dressed and I felt very odd and grubby in field clothes and finally, at the end of the dream, it suddenly occurred to me that I could go and buy a new dress at once, one that would look like the others." Margaret interpreted: "It's funny how persistent that dream pattern is, whenever I am unhappy about you and think you are going away from me, you appear in an odd hat, all harking back to the day you came in your plumed picture hat to teach the Museum class and I was so terribly disappointed." She went on to dream, wishfully, that Ruth's letters were disguised, so that they only seemed to be from someone else but were really from Ruth: "Only of course they aren't—ever. . . . It looks as if all the weary hours I'd put into writing duty letters to Marie at times when I didn't want to were coming home to roost at last, for without her letters commenting on having seen you, on your plans . . . I should be so enshrouded in unreality and sick from anxiety that I doubt whether I should be able to work at all. Which is after all what we are here in this hot, crowded, uncomfortable, public way of living for."

Margaret reread *Patterns of Culture* to make up for the lack of letters, so that she could "hear the cadence of your sentences," and she also read *Swann's Way* "because I had such a vivid picture of your delight that time you read it over a weekend, the summer we spent on 124th Street, and it gave me a sense of being with you again, because I could be sure you had read just those words, all those words, in just that order." Uncharacteristically, she was stricken with self-doubt: "For ten years I have been on a sterile track in developing field methods which rely too much on my idiosyncratic abilities and interests. . . . The net result is a tremendous waste of time. . . . Our capacity to attract the type of skills which social work and Psychiatry attract seems to be nil. . . . I vary between wanting to wail, and bewail, or say with properly gritted teeth, its alright if you are bored with writing to me. . . . And as long as I am in doubt about the cause of it all, I tend to be optimistic, with of course attacks of dispair [sic] . . . I think it argues for a kind of forgetfulness of time, and a lack of urgency about our whole relationship which hasnt even caught your attention. That means I haven't done anything to seriously displease you. . . . It also argues that nothing else very drastic has happened in your life because whether you meant to tell me or not, you would be very careful not to seem other than usual. . . . To face the probability of your not even knowing what has happened of course is not easy for me. . . . I can't go back to sleep at all these days once I waken, I simply start to mill and mill."

She reached a crescendo, writing plaintively of the "growing feeling that I bore you, that I have had to stay away too long. Maybe the mechanics of psychic energy will work so that I will feel in my unconscious that if I invent methods of field work which are better, which will produce material which you can use, which your students can use, then I will be reinstated. If that should happen, I'd have a fine drive for the remaining ten weeks here. But in my heart I know well enough that while I may begin over again as an anthropologist, there is no such beginning over again with you if 'our cup is broken.' And the better part of wisdom is to stop this kind of writing from which no good can come. Marie says you are looking beautiful. I hope you are happy."

A couple of weeks later, suffering from a miserable cold, she told Ruth she had found "a good many snow white hairs, not grey, white," her discovery a reminder of the summer in Europe when Ruth felt she had been rejected by Margaret and her hair turned white prematurely. The signs of aging also reminded Margaret that she was increasingly unlikely to have children, which was very discouraging.

Ruth returned from Guatemala to a "feast" of Margaret's letters (the most challenging had not yet arrived) and "a beautiful silk scarf with . . .

heavenly off-reds." She waited until reaching the farm before she replied to Margaret in a leisurely manner. Some letters had been lost but, she admitted, her busyness had led her to concentrate on surface detail rather than "the things I'd have liked better to write about." As to her remoteness: "I'm so sorry you got to feeling from my letters that I was so far away and maybe inhabiting different spheres. . . . As for real distance between us, I know there's no need to be troubled." She reassured Margaret about the value of her work: "I know you long to work always with people better than you are, and it's hard to discover they are lacking. And it's a situation I've recognized for at least fifteen years—and given thanks all that time for the miracle of you being you."

When Ruth received Margaret's seriously distressed letters, she wrote more carefully, heading her reply "For M.M.," making sure that it was not for circulation, not even to Gregory: "Margaret, my darling, I wouldn't for anything have caused you that nightmare. I wonder if my last letter reassured you completely; I think it would. It should, darling. And I can add more of the like for we do not grow apart. If I do not write about us, it's only because I have such continued undeviating delight in you and there are no changes to record. I shouldn't leave out the reiteration, for reiterations help, but it's only because our love is so accepted a part of my life, something which doesn't change. . . . O darling, I do so long to talk with you and have you back. It will be such a delight. There isn't anything else like it, not with anybody else. . . . [My neglect] caused you a lot of pain. I'm miserable about it, darling." She ended the letter, "I love you darling, and I trust the permanence of our companionship as I do hardly anything else in the world. Be happy, my dear—and love me. Ruth"

Margaret was finally reassured: "I haven't been sure from one day to the next what I thought, some days I've thought that at the bottom of my heart everything was really alright . . . but others, the world has just been black and I have been sure that horrible unconscious forces were at work in you, even if you didn't know it. . . . I was in a sufficiently morbid state so that . . . it seemed that you thought my work was utterly worthless too, and that cast me further into the depths. . . ." Later she wrote, "Oh darling, you don't know what a difference it makes not to have a constant echoing misery at the back of my mind."

From New Guinea Margaret and Gregory made their way to Sydney, where they had to get used to living in walled houses. Jane Belo came down to meet them and they learned of unrest in Bali and elsewhere, which Margaret later described as a "witch hunt against homosexuals [breaking] out in the Pacific which echoed from Los Angeles to Singapore" (LF, 155).[34]

Their immediate concern was that Walter Spies had been arrested and Colin McPhee, Jane's former husband, had fled the country. Gregory and Margaret wanted to return briefly to Bali and Jane paid their steamer fares. As Margaret wrote to Marie, "It is absolutely necessary for us to go to Bali and see just how great the wreckage is from this clean up of inverts. . . . It probably means everyone we know leaving the island, and will make any future plans for work in Bali very different. . . . We wouldn't let Jane go back to a wrecked world alone." Margaret herself found the whole business "pretty sickening. Why men cant manage inversion except in terms of promiscuity and prostitution, is hard to understand. In a way I dont blame the Dutch; they are not attacking dignified personal relationships, but out and out promiscuity, and in many cases exploitation of the Balinese, who are merely gentle and compliant, not inverts."

Margaret once said, no doubt thinking of men like Geoffrey Gorer and Walter Spies, that homosexual men made the best companions in the world.[35] However, she believed that their tendency to avoid intimacy could have antisocial consequences, writing to Ruth that "one of the reasons that Bali has never become a colony like Tahiti is because all the people here are fleeing from human contact, are primarily interested in male homosexuality, which is not a community forming bond when all is said and done."

This edge of disapproval did not mean that she and Gregory failed to put their best efforts into securing Spies's release. Among her unpublished papers is a "Background Statement on Homosexuality," written by Mead with contributions from Bateson, propounding liberal views on homosexuality supported by anthropological evidence. "According to the findings of modern psychology," she said, "it is possible to say: all human beings are born with bisexual tendencies. . . . Furthermore homosexual interests are the normal accompaniment of early puberty in young people of both sexes in European-American cultures [and] the extent to which their homosexual tendencies are suppressed, relegated to early adolescence, or branded as anti-social is a function of the society in which they have been brought up" (MM, N30). Mead discusses different types of homosexuality, including congenital, situational, that which occurs as a result of dislike of the male role, and that which arises from neurosis. Walter Spies, Mead argued, belonged to the "rare" type of homosexual who is not in any way pathological, someone with a special artistic gift which he must preserve by keeping his individuality intact and who "merely wishes for casual, graceful, warm physical contacts with other individuals who are like himself," a role that Balinese youth are better suited to fulfill than European women.[36] It is fascinating to read Mead's document, with its context of special pleading on behalf of a friend, against the increasing illiberal interpretations of homosexuality she made during the 1940s and 1950s.

Around this time Margaret wrote to John Dollard that she was theorizing male homosexuality as a problem only in societies that strongly institutionalized aggression, such as Australia, "one of the most aggressive groups of humans going," who could hardly bear for a man to ask another man, " 'Do you like so and so?' . . . One doesn't *like a man.*" The Balinese, on the other hand, though not homosexual themselves, readily expressed "free physical companionship" and thus provided a "libidinal background of homosexuality," even of homosexual prostitution, which attracted the expatriate "inverts" (MM, N109).

Writing to Walter Spies's lawyer, Margaret marshalled the arguments in his defense: that he was not exploitative by nature, that he did not prefer the Balinese because they were of another race but "because this culture is congenial to him," and that "the number of his contacts is a point in his favor" because it meant that he was not possessive toward any of his companions; indeed he fostered their artistic gifts. Furthermore, he was not interested in children, though it was hard to judge the age of Balinese boys; their research had shown that young Balinese could not date past life events with any accuracy (MM, N30). Gregory wrote, too, saying, "My estimate of Walter's character would be 'a homosexual, but the sort of homosexual who is a man loving man,' " forming a very different picture from the "type of homosexual who loves little boys, [who is] generally either a frightened rabbit . . . or a bully, and the little boys are substitutes for women" (MM, N30).

The result of the Bali crisis was that Margaret and Gregory managed to impress officials with their own clean record, convincing them that Jane Belo was a bona fide researcher, even though the police arrested all her servants and questioned the thirty-four dancing girls in her village. Their valiant efforts did not save Spies, who remained in prison for three years before being killed in 1942 when the boat on which he was being shipped to Ceylon was torpedoed by the Japanese.

Edward Sapir suffered a heart attack in 1937 and his poor recovery, along with the threat of war, disrupted his plans to spend a sabbatical in China. He moved to New York City instead, where his wife, Jean, picked up the pieces of her social work career, expecting that she might become the breadwinner. Their marriage had been rocky at times, and Edward encouraged Jean to undergo analysis with Karen Horney, though the analysis was terminated before its completion because of Horney's discomfort at Jean's disclosure that she told Edward all about the sessions. Horney seemed afraid that Sapir might blame her if the analysis led to further marital woes; given her interest in psychological anthropology, she wanted to remain on friendly terms with him.[37]

Edward's closest friend during this time was Harry Stack Sullivan, who visited him daily. Ruth was on cordial terms with Jean Sapir and visited Edward on occasion. In January 1938, she remarked to Margaret, "Praise God, I've had easy and pleasant talks with him whenever I've seen him," but a year later she said: "I know of course that he is dying technically of an organic heart disease, but I can't get over the feeling that he is dying unnecessarily, that his hatreds have killed him. All the last times I've seen him he has poured vitriol continually upon the whole earth. And it isn't as if I felt that anyone or anything could have saved him."

Ruth knew Edward intimately, and though usually an astute observer, she seems not to have considered that Edward had been experiencing, as well as giving forth, hatred of a lethal kind. Anti-Semitism was rife at Yale; as a Jew he had not been allowed to join the Graduate Club and therefore was denied access to the most powerful networks at the university.[38] Although he was not a religious Jew, he delighted in studying Talmud, which he had done from the time he was a boy translating passages with his father and which helped to inspire his love of linguistics. At Yale, as if deliberately to snub the New England Brahmins, he assiduously collected books on Semitic languages. Anti-Semitism, both as a personal experience and as a rising force in world politics, concerned him increasingly. His son Michael, studying in Germany, sent home vivid descriptions of the persecution of Jews, while many of his colleagues at Yale considered Germany an ally. Along with Boas, Sapir became involved in the fight against racism on the home front, trying, with disappointing results, to rally anthropologists to the cause.

Edward's illness caused family and financial stress. Following his sabbatical, he dragged himself back to work against medical advice, but eventually he became too ill to work. His recommendations for a successor were ignored, a matter for further bitterness. Before he died, Sapir burned much of his personal correspondence, including Ruth's letters. The letters from Margaret quite possibly had been destroyed much earlier, just as Margaret had destroyed his (JH).

In early 1939, on board ship bound for the States after their three-year absence, Margaret heard the news of Edward Sapir's death. Ruth, who could not mourn him publicly as the family arrangements were private, wrote to Margaret, "I find it's easier to think of him dead than thinking of him as I had lately, eating his body and soul away. I can go back now to years and years ago." She seemed calm about the death of "one who had loved her canoe" (a phrase from one of her poems), a man whose friendship and unremitting support had literally saved her life at the time she was most paralyzed by depression. As when Stanley had died, Ruth's diary points to a reaction several days later, in this case "a sick headache." She later wrote a rather wooden obituary of Sapir in *American Anthropologist*.

Margaret wrote to Ruth: "I think in a way I was relieved to hear of Edward's death. It was better than these years of suffering, but oh such a waste. He was the best of his generation. . . . I dont suppose one can say he was entirely wasted; you and John and I owe far too much to him for that—although I suppose he never really counted us for gain." She had no inhibitions in checking out, through Ruth and John Dollard, whether Edward's death might mean a Yale position that Gregory could fill. She told Ruth she was glad to be out of the country so that there was no need to resist a temptation to go to the funeral.

Margaret's reaction to Edward's illness and death was conditioned by the fact that she had broken off relations with him more finally than Ruth had. Years later she remarked that if someone died to whom she had "a broken relationship" she would dream a reconciliation; perhaps Edward figured in such dreams. She had been sensitized to the possibility of harm to her reputation after his thinly veiled attack in "the sex problem" article, and in the last year of his life, when he was president of the American Anthropological Association and Margaret wanted to push through a proposal concerning child studies, she urged Ruth to "pick a moment when Edward isn't looking." Nevertheless, her response to his death displayed a level of callousness. In Bali she had corresponded regularly with John Dollard, whom Sapir found difficult and from Dollard she often received a different slant on events from Ruth's ("I think it would be useful if you heard John's versions of what goes on at Yale too," she wrote.)

Perhaps because her years of absence from the United States had rendered her insensitive to the seriousness of anti-Semitism, Margaret was dismissive of its effects on Edward.[39] She judged him a "snob" for having taken the Yale position and was unsympathetic to his rebuff by the Graduate Club, which she regarded as predictable. Her alliance with the WASPish Dollard also contributed to her misjudgment. Her later comment, that in the last years of Edward's life he did nothing but pile up Hebrew grammars in the bathroom and that he "died of corroding resentment," was not only inaccurate, but also insensitive to his well-founded feelings of betrayal.

Compare her attitude to that of Jean Sapir, who recalled Edward's final period, dogged by illness and fatigue: "He died with the feeling that he had an important point to make that he hadn't managed to get across. He gave up even hoping to get it all written, even before he accepted the fact that he was ill. His work on language was such a pleasure to him that he was able to remain 'busy' in that manner [in later years he returned to his earlier love of Indo-European languages], but he did deeply feel that he died without saying his full say!"[40]

Margaret eagerly looked forward to returning to New York, confident that she was still important to Ruth: "I am getting hungry for another letter from you, but just healthily hungry, not famished, or dying of thirst. In South Africa they soak people who come in thirst-struck." Ruth replied, "If you are starved for talk, I'm just as badly off. You'll be manna in the desert and I can hardly wait." For Margaret there were apprehensions: "In a way I dread coming back to civilization, especially to all the clothes and use of money and fuss, to long evenings of too much smoking and too much drinking, and to small minded politics and jealousies." Her plans were unclear, perhaps to remain in the United States for thirteen or fourteen years until Gregory inherited the Cambridge chair: "You and I could get a lot said in that time."

The reunion was carefully planned. After arrival on the West Coast ("at least the same continent that you are on, darling") she and Gregory made their way to Chicago, where Margaret was "heartbroken" that a pregnancy test proved negative, disappointment all the more distressing because she had suffered a particularly painful miscarriage on the final Bali trip. In fact she was pregnant, though she did not know it yet.

Marie awaited Margaret's return as eagerly as Ruth, if not more so. She was in a happy state, having a good job with a good salary ("I don't think of it as a JOB anymore; it is my WORK. I now have my WORK, just as you and Ruth have") and had found a wonderful furnished apartment. Showing extraordinary selflessness, she wanted to move into Christadora House so that Gregory and Margaret could have it. Marie had overcome her anxiety and insomnia, wondering to Margaret "whether I am going to be like you once said I might: an uninteresting dinner companion in my forties, having lost my neuroses." It was a coup that Margaret's first public airing would be at a conference Marie was involved in planning.

Margaret's first lecture in New York was scheduled for the morning of her arrival. Gregory remained in Philadelphia to get to know his in-laws. (Someone asked Margaret's father how he felt to have such a famous daughter; he replied, "How does it feel to own a Rembrandt?" [BW draft]). Margaret would have breakfast with Marie, lunch with her sister Elizabeth, check in at the museum in the afternoon, and then it was time for Ruth: "If you can arrange for us to have dinner and have that evening and night together . . . no one else need be told I am back until Monday."

Gregory, unlike Reo, was not possessive and seemed not to begrudge Margaret her intimacy with Ruth. Ruth and Gregory, said Mary Catherine Bateson, "were the two people [Margaret] loved most fully and abidingly."

She recounted that "after Margaret's death, I asked my father how he had felt about the idea of Margaret and Ruth as lovers, a relationship that had begun before Margaret and Gregory met, and continued into the years of their marriage. He spoke of Ruth as his senior, someone for whom he had great respect and always a sense of distance, and of her remote beauty. What came through quite clearly was a sense of the incongruity of any kind of jealousy or competition."[41] So when the two women met that night in late April 1939, there was no hindrance to their delight in the reunion.

# 13

## November Burning

MARGARET WOULD ALWAYS HAVE A GAP in her development, said a friend, because she had missed the Depression.[1] She and Gregory, occupied with their field research, were apolitical during the thirties. She wrote in a draft of *Blackberry Winter* that "the political upheaval of the Depression and later of the Spanish War went in a sense unnoticed. . . . Fascism, Communism, Nazism, Capitalism, from such a long standpoint, were perturbations, with which other people had to deal."[2] And Gregory was by temperament a natural skeptic, indifferent to the radical leftist views that were de rigueur among his colleagues at Cambridge before the war.[3]

Back in the United States Margaret became infected by the spirit of activism among her contemporaries. She joined the Committee for National Morale, a group of social scientists working to preserve democracy. Unlike her friend Léonie Adams, Mead joined forces with people who, as she put it, were not "caught up in the fashionable radicalism of the 1930s with its roseate views of the Soviet Union" and were not "stunned and confused" by the 1939 Soviet-German pact.[4] Margaret had not voted since 1924, yet less than four months after her return she wrote to Eleanor Roosevelt to offer a culture-and-personality analysis of Hitler which, if her husband would only act upon it, might "cut the Gordian knot of the present world crisis."[5]

Ruth's political activism developed more slowly. Not a joiner by inclination, she was mostly happy to support Boas who, in his mid–seventies, found his flagging energy rekindled by outrage over anti-Semitism at home and in Europe, threats to democracy in the United States, and the outbreak of the Spanish Civil War. A socialist and admirer of the Russian experiment, Boas nevertheless was quick to condemn lack of intellectual freedom in the Soviet Union. When Hitler came to power, he immediately began agitating, directing his efforts to undermining "the pseudo-scientific theory on which the anti-semitic propaganda is based."[6] The effects of this activity were international; his books were being removed from German university libraries.

From 1936 on, Ruth increasingly engaged in political causes, perhaps because Stanley's death had made it easier for her to use her name publically. She joined the Progressive Education Association whose Commission on Intercultural Education was dedicated to combating racial prejudice, and in 1937 she was a member of the Columbia University Faculty Committee for Aid to the Spanish People. Later she was the first secretary to the University Federation for Democracy and Intellectual Freedom. She helped Boas with his Committee for Austrian Relief, organized a petition condemning Nazi science, sought scholarships for refugee students, and publically condemned a suggestion that teachers denounce radicals in their midst. She joined the Descendants of the American Revolution, a liberal alternative to the Daughters of the American Revolution, of which her Norwich aunt was a proud member.

Boas, accustomed to receiving flak for his political stances, was not deterred by the atmosphere of red-baiting encouraged by the House Un-American Activities Committee. Walter Winchell, the newspaper columnist, called him "the principal commy" at Columbia. The University Federation for Democracy and Intellectual Freedom was attacked by John Dewey and Sidney Hook, anticommunist liberal intellectuals who published a report on "Stalinist Outposts" in the United States. Linton, of course, freely joined in the mud-slinging, making Ruth's position in the anthropology department all the more uncomfortable.

Ruth saw Margaret on the day she found out she was expecting a baby and they celebrated together. Fearing she was in danger of miscarrying, Gregory kept her housebound in Marie's apartment on West Twenty-second Street and Margaret took a leave of absence from the museum. Through May and June 1939, she met Ruth for lunches and dinners and one overnight stay. Their close companionship would not last, as Ruth had been planning her sabbatical in California and left New York at the end of June.

As her first venture into the field since Mescalero in 1931, Ruth supervised a trip to the Blackfoot and Blood in Montana and Alberta, Canada.[7] Accompanying her were her colleague, Esther Goldfrank, Abraham Maslow, Maslow's brother-in-law Oscar Lewis, then a graduate student (who after this trip published a study of the "manly-hearted woman"), Gitel Poznanski, a Greenwich Village blues singer turned anthropology student, and Poznanski's lover, painter Robert Steed. The trip was marred by several unfortunate incidents and caused Ruth temporarily to lose her newfound ability to rise above stress. After their arrival in Browning, Montana, Bob Steed was involved in a car accident in which his passenger, Jim Little Plume, was thrown from the vehicle and died in the hospital the next day.

Ruth, the expedition leader, dealt efficiently with the incident, her responsibility perhaps tempered by knowledge that the deceased had recently been released from prison after serving time for shooting seven neighbours and stabbing his wife. Some reparation, she wrote Boas, should be made to the family, who had been "kind and courteous beyond belief. . . . The car carried a limit of $10,000 per person of public indemnity. If they get it, it will make us mythical among these Indians" (FB, 12 July 1939).

After dealing with this misadventure, Ruth arrived at the field site "pale and preoccupied." After a few days of living in a shared tent, Esther Goldfrank recalled, Ruth "complained of a severe migraine. . . . For days, except for meals, short periods of consultation with one or another of us, and sporadic efforts to work on the book she was writing on race—a subject she found boring—she lay on the bed. At first I thought her malaise was due to menopause, but before the summer was over I came to understand that . . . from her earliest days withdrawal had been her not infrequent response to strain."[8] Goldfrank's perspective was confirmed by a former Columbia student, who later recalled that Benedict would "always go into a tizz when there was a crisis" and that as an administrator she was "just a blue-eyed disaster."[9]

A situation back in New York intruded unexpectedly, involving a tense, triangular predicament that had been developing among Ruth and Margaret's mutual friends David (Hannah Kahn), Jeannette Mirsky, and her husband, Arthur. During the time that Margaret was still in Bali and Jeannette and Natalie were in Guatemala, Arthur had begun an affair with David, one of the friends so aptly described by Léonie Adams as the "Oh-God-the-pain-girls." In the judgment of most who knew her, David had been behaving particularly badly of late, rejecting one suitor after another, reeling with self-pity over her responsibilities toward an ailing father, and drowning her sorrows in barbiturates. Ruth, though usually fond of David, wrote to Margaret that "the present moment is one of these recurring times when I long to the point of exasperation to be able to inject some guts into [her]" (MM, B14).

Ruth became doubly exasperated when Jeannette, finally being told that David and Arthur wanted to marry, refused to cooperate and proceeded to vent her anger on Ruth, whom she perceived as unfriendly to her plight. Ruth, in fact, was far from unfeeling; "I sympathize with any woman who is having problems with her husband," she wrote to Margaret. But she also knew that Jeannette had had her share of love affairs and believed that the only reason for her recalcitrance over the divorce was that "she had no man on the horizon." Marie reported to Margaret that "Ruth is thoroughly disgusted with Jeanette. She said she had never seen a face twisted with such hate and hardness. . . . I think, myself, she is dangerous and would stop at nothing" (MM, B14).

Now, with Margaret back in New York and Ruth in the field, Arthur plucked up enough courage to initiate divorce proceedings and also to travel thousands of miles to Montana to ask Ruth to testify about Jeannette's infidelities. Learning about Ruth's willingness to do so, Jeannette told Margaret angrily that she would retaliate by spreading word of Ruth's lesbianism, and Margaret, irate with Ruth for being so foolish and naive, wrote her a harsh letter. The letter itself has not been preserved; perhaps Ruth, or Margaret, or both thought it wise to destroy any evidence that might involve them in a lesbian scandal. Information about this episode comes from Esther Goldfrank, who wrote in her own memoir that Margaret's letter caused Ruth to take to bed for three days with another migraine. Later, Ruth told Esther that if called as a witness she " 'couldn't lie,' " but that she dreaded the danger of " 'my character impugned, my professional career endangered.' "[10]

Margaret probably felt Ruth should have learned from her extensive letter about the Bali troubles only a year before, when she had written about an Australian anthropologist, Ian Hogbin, who narrowly escaped dismissal after a malicious colleague "spread the word all over Sydney that [he] was a fairy." On Esther Goldfrank's return to New York, Margaret summoned her, interrogated her about the whole business, and summed up, "I can't understand Ruth."[11] By the time Ruth returned from her sabbatical, the divorce had been granted. But clearly this was an episode that left her emotionally shaken.

The most crushing event of the trip was the news from Brazil of the death of Ruth's student, Buell Quain. It was not his first time in the field, but in the rain forests of the Amazon, loneliness, illness (including a skin ailment resulting from syphilis), and anxiety that he might have been infected with leprosy unbalanced his mind so much that he took his own life. After receiving the cable bearing this news, Ruth received his suicide note, with a warning written across the top in capital letters, "Sterilize this letter."[12] Rumors spread at Columbia. Some thought he had been killed, and Margaret reported to Ruth that she was told he had deliberately infected himself with syphilis.

In his will Quain, who was from a wealthy family, left Ruth a legacy of thirty thousand dollars to use as she saw fit in the furtherance of anthropology. The Quain money further complicated tensions between Ruth and Ralph Linton, who tried to stop her access to other sources of funding, fobbing off approaches from Benedict's allies with the suggestion that they go to the Quain fund. That year he cut back Ruth Bunzel's extension courses; when she protested that she would not have enough to live on, he suggested she get hold of some of Quain's money.[13]

It must have been with relief that Ruth finished the field trip, earlier than planned: "I could do with someone besides my children at Browning," she told Margaret. Luther Cressman and his wife, Cecilia, were vacationing on the Pacific Coast; they offered their hospitality, and she stayed a night with them, reporting that Cecilia reminded her of Emily Mead but had "made her bed in Oregon" with "no restlessness in her adjustment." Ruth was amused that Luther referred to his wife as "Mrs. Cressman" and she always called him "my husband." Their child, a girl of ten named Elizabeth Priscilla, after Margaret's two sisters, was not "particularly attractive . . . and she wasn't born with charm, but she's intelligent and secure."[14] Luther, writing to Margaret after Ruth's death, recalled that at their meeting he had detected "a new element in [Ruth], a sense of bitterness and futility," which he put down to despondency about the rise of Nazism, but which may have resulted directly from the stressful time in the field (RFB, Box 14).

The next stop for Ruth was San Francisco, where by chance or design, Nat's friend Ruth Valentine was also on holiday—and also staying at the same house, belonging to a mutual friend. Ruth may not have known "Val" particularly well. Whether Val had once been Nat's lover will always be a matter of speculation, but several years before, when Val had visited Nat in New York, Ruth had hoped to be out of town. At the age of 48, Ruth Valentine was four years younger than Ruth Benedict and also a Vassar alumna. She had completed a doctorate with Edward Tolman at Berkeley in 1929 and became a clinical psychologist for the Los Angeles school system. Of her appearance, the only record to be found is that she had "piercing blue eyes."[15]

Ruth Benedict and Val shared a guest house, a peaceful place overlooking "the whole sweep of San Francisco bay." Ruth enjoyed meeting colleagues at Berkeley, including Erik Erikson; she found him "a delight," though he was unsure of the impression he had made, a common feeling among Ruth's acquaintances. After a satisfactory fortnight, in early September Ruth and her new companion drove down to Pasadena along the "magnificent" new Pacific Coast highway. There Ruth stayed at her sister's house, keeping her mother and young relations company while Margery and Bob toured Norway.

The relationship between Ruth and Val continued to develop in Pasadena. They suffered through a heat wave of temperatures rising as high as 107 degrees. They visited Nat's mother and stepfather and Margaret's youngest sister, Priscilla, who told Ruth she was undergoing analysis and did not want Margaret to know. On 21 September Ruth recorded in her datebook "Val's invitation to stay with her" and underlined the following day's entry, "Cancelled NY trip" (RFB, Box 32).

That Ruth would not return at the expected time came as a bombshell to Margaret. One day Ruth wrote from Margery's house complaining there was no one worth discussing the news of the world with and telling her, "I'm glad I'm going to be back soon"; the next she had canceled her ticket because Val wanted her to stay. A longer visit would be peaceful, Ruth argued; "Her house is empty all day while she's off on her job . . . and she's a comfortable person to be with." Nothing in Ruth's letters overtly indicated the development of a romance, but perhaps Margaret had a sixth sense because in a diary of her pregnancy she noted several homosexual dreams at exactly this time. One, she commented, was the first she had ever had about an "unidentified woman"; two other entries, the only dreams of that time, merely note cryptically, "h.s. dream" (MM, TR3).

Margaret had been banking on Ruth's return, Gregory having sailed for England to help with the war effort, leaving her behind in the second trimester of pregnancy. Three days before Gregory's departure, Margaret was still not sure if she would accompany him, but with some fortitude she bore the decision to remain. Gregory had said "leaving a baby behind is a mitigation of having to go into a war, and his feeling [is] that is a great comfort." Marie moved back to her apartment to be with Margaret and Ruth had promised to be in New York on 28 September—"If [Margaret] were still there [rather than in England] it would be one of those turns of dreadful events that still blow good to me."

Margaret's first response to Ruth was matter-of-fact; she would no doubt stay in Philadelphia with the family after the birth "as the simplest and least expensive way to live, not very exciting." Ruth suggested that she might be back after Christmas, though "all plans are subject to change." Margaret became petulant: "Ruth darling, well, after a couple of hours of futile tears and a sleepless night, I have got myself into the mood to call it 'bad luck' with at least fair grace. They could always keep the baby in the hospital until you came East, if anything happens to me. Perhaps if its a husky baby and I myself am reasonably husky, I could come up to the farm in the spring before going back to work." Ruth had agreed to be the child's guardian in the event of untoward circumstances, and clearly Margaret expected Ruth to stand in for Gregory in other ways as well. Indeed, a year or two before, Ruth had told her that among the Mohave, "when a mother dies, a childless near relative, or one past the menopause, usually the baby's grandmother, heats her breasts with hot stones and massages them" so as to suckle the infant. Moreover, "the female inverts insist on children too: the Mohave believe that with continued sexual intercourse the paternity of the unborn child changes up to six months. So female inverts marry pregnant women, and have children, thanks to this dogma."

Ruth responded with studied innocence: "I don't understand the sleepless night and the 'bad luck' solution. You expect the baby in January don't you? I'm sad every day that I'm so far away from you these days, but I don't know why you agreed with my first letter about change of plans so peacefully, and were upset by the second. Tell me and I'm sure I can make my plans better. . . . Write me what bothered you the night you cried." She reminded Margaret who, surprisingly, had never visited Ruth's farm, that it had no central heating and "Aunt Myra doesn't open the house till late April or May."

Margaret, growing suspicious, replied that she "was very upset by your first letter, but I succeeded in behaving. You didnt give a definite date, and I could pretend that you only meant to stay out there a month or so, even though fundamentally I believed the news was worse than that. . . . The baby is meant to be born about December 29th, and it did seem bad luck that you weren't going to be around. Then I think I was upset that you were in a sense making a negative choice, which isn't a point which would make any difference to you, but which, as you know, always does to me. The points in favor of California seemed to be that it wasn't New York. I knew quite articulately that if there were someone you terrifically wanted to be with in California, I'd have been sad and disappointed not to have you here, but I wouldn't have felt nearly as miserable. But to have you making a choice because New York just wouldn't be bearable . . . seemed to me horrible. I know what the points are of course (a) Nat's working out an adjustment for herself, independently of you; (b) no more close up dose of the A[rthur]J[eannette]D[avid] tangle, (c) none of the pressure of students to whom you have given more than you could spiritually stand and from whom you need a rest, and (d) no close-up reverberations of the mediocrities of the Columbia Department."

Margaret "daydreamed" that she and Ruth might perhaps go to New Haven together after the birth. It would be a good place to work, though "Malinowski's being there will considerably de-enhance [its] charms." She ended on a conciliatory note: "Darling, don't worry about my fits. . . . It's a logical solution of this year, and I'll be good really." Marie, of course, was delighted to have Margaret to herself, setting out to "grow" the baby in the manner of Arapesh husbands, feeding Margaret a special low-calorie diet supplemented by calcium and thyroid. Margaret later decided the diet was a mistake, although at the time she bloomed with the "mask of pregnancy."[16]

Ruth replied that her need for retreat—"I suppose I'd have made a good monk, or better yet a samurai"—was certainly a positive decision. Putting Margaret off the scent, she argued "for me it's quite as precious as finding 'someone I wanted terrifically to be with.' " Nevertheless, she said, she was enjoying an old friend, Betty Heron, and Ruth Tolman and Val: "Val is my principal recourse, and she's a good one." But all the same, "I feel all the time that I'm paying high for it by being away from you, darling. I feel very close to you."

Meanwhile, Margaret was trying to stop fits of crying, though "not crying means being considerably more disassociated than I have ever been before, but . . . the baby doesn't like fits of crying; they make it much more restless." And later, "I lead a kind of surface life, not giving my imagination much leeway these days to wish for Gregory or wish for you. Pregnancy seems to make possible a kind of superficiality. . . ."[17] Worse, it was rumored that Reo might turn up. Margaret inveigled the Columbia secretary into giving her his address and told Ruth to cable him, "Absolutely no funds or jobs available here. Advise against coming." She worried Reo might try to destroy her research material, and, remembering his violence at Tchambuli and her miscarriage, had a "morbid fear" that she would lose the baby if he showed up. Léonie Adams had just had a miscarriage: "it makes me feel greedy," she wrote to Ruth, "for she really needs a child more than I do."

Ruth did not think a cable to Reo would be effective. A couple of her letters had not got through to him, and he had written that she must have "gone over to the enemy." Margaret decided not to let Gregory know Reo might be in the vicinity—"no need to worry him endlessly." Gregory, in the meantime, was frustrated at trying to persuade anyone in Britain to let him put his social science skills to the aid of the war effort; academics were put to use in intelligence as spies. "Still going on rather unhappily here," he cabled.

As the likelihood of miscarriage grew less, Margaret took up a heavier workload, giving a series of lectures at Vassar and one at the museum. Leah Josephson Hanna, one of the Ash Can Cats, was in the audience, and according to Margaret's report to Ruth, she claimed that "[I] was devaluating my material by making it so pleasant and comprehensible, and nobody would ever think I was profound if I talked so simply and easily." None of the "enemy" came to hear Margaret and she was miffed that "everybody, just everybody" went to hear Cora Du Bois lecture in a dull manner for two hours, elaborating on minor details of land tenure, pig raising, and what people ate: "It's incredible to take up the time of grown up people listening to stuff that one ought to be able to summarize in the first five minutes."

Nevertheless, Margaret wondered whether "the really horrible state that anthropology is in is due to there being . . . women who are better than so many of the men."

When her sister arrived home, Ruth moved to Val's house where, she wrote to a friend, she could write in the sun, read in bed in the morning, and "indulge in my passion for one-thing-at-a-time" (RFB, Box 34). Following the familiar pattern surrounding major entries and exits in her life, in this safe place Ruth became ill, succumbing to a serious bout of pleurisy. Her mother came every day to nurse her, and only after some days was she able to dictate a note to Margaret. A few days later she and Val phoned New York, asking Nat to pass on to Margaret the news that she was recovering: "I hated not calling you instead, but Nat is very depressed at the moment since her job folded up and she's made no new adjustment." But "Val has been goodness itself and I'm not an imposition for having me here has got her past some bad times after her brother's death."

Marie and Ruth Bunzel were passing on their own anxiety about Ruth's health, but Ruth knew Margaret would remain sensible and dismiss their fears. Ruth's analysis was that because of Bunny's love for her, "she has fantasies about my being sick and at that moment she steps in and takes charge and all is well. . . . Marie of course is a different case; she has a vested interest in all lung troubles [a reference to Marie's tuberculosis] and this was enough to set off her whole complex of fears about them." Margaret, who had sent flowers, was not to worry: "I only wish I were where I could come in and visit all day long and put you to bed at night."

Margaret, of course, was not Ruth's only source of news about New York. Ruth Landes, a graduate student and now author of *The Ojibwa Women*, filed news of Nat. Benedict's remark about the lack of a "new adjustment" on Natalie's part, coupled with Margaret's earlier question about whether Ruth was finding her new status difficult, suggest that both women had found the breakup fraught. Nat seems to have initiated it, albeit in a passive manner, by staying away indefinitely. She may have found it demoralizing to live in the shadow of Ruth's disappointment, just as Ruth had found Stanley's disapproval undermining. But now the tables had been turned and Ruth was staying away indefinitely. Both Nat and Margaret knew that when she canceled her ticket. Ruth continued to pay the rent on her apartment, which Nat may have been using. Their finances were still intermingled as they shared a checking account and Nat's friend, Dutchie, was Ruth's lawyer.

Margaret, meantime, helping Ruth Landes with a paper on homosexuality, found Landes infuriating because she kept confusing active and passive male homosexuality, and what is more, acted neither like a lady nor an "ordinary academic female." She was as much trouble, Margaret told Ruth, as "all my protegés you've had to bother with."[18]

Bunny, another correspondent, was currently distressed by Linton's canceling payment for her extension courses, pleading with Ruth to come back and sort things out. Ruth told Margaret that Bunny "writes me that because I don't jump on the train and get into all this, my soul is poisoned and I've let her down (and I'm 'responsible' for the fact that this is the only job she's got). All this sounds crazy to me. I've got to keep my health and sanity and be alive and kicking long after Linton has hanged himself in his own rope." Bunny's "wild forebodings" about the state of affairs in the department did lead Ruth to write an "S.O.S." to Boas. Bunny had intimated that Ruth was to be "liquidated," and though Ruth assured Boas that "I just can't take this seriously," she still looked to her mentor for advice and reassurance: "I think of you every day, and I miss terribly the seeing of you that I've counted on for so many years. They wrote me not long ago that you were sick, and that made me feel doubly far away" (RFB, Box 103).

Boas replied calmly, suggesting that Bunny might be overreacting, but that even so, he did not approve of the present regime. He could do nothing, however: "I am there on sufferance only." The impending war worried him so much that events at Columbia seemed insignificant by comparison. As to concerns about his health, he was not so much ill as on the downward grade. "Well! Do not feel disturbed about me," he wrote Ruth. "I ought to be satisfied, even if my world ended today" (AW, 415–16).

That Boas accepted his decline with equanimity Ruth found hard to accept, replying: "Your physical weakness distresses me daily. I know what great reason you have to be satisfied with your life and your work—far greater than you would ever admit to yourself—but, for the rest of us, you set new goals every year in what one life can stand for and accomplish, and we would give anything in the world to see you strong and able to go on working as you always have. As for me, there has never been a time since I've known you that I have not thanked God all the time that you existed and that I knew you. I can't tell you what a place you fill in my life" (AW, 417).

Ruth eventually came clean to Margaret about herself and Val: "We've been comfortable together from the moment we saw each other. . . . She's usually not much of a talker, but we don't have difficulty about topics for conversation. I know she thinks God made me out of rare and special clay." Val was now ready to reshape her life, her brother's death finally having relieved her of responsibilities to a "disappointed and violent family." Quick to decide about her new loyalties, she made a new will almost immediately, leaving her money for Benedict to add to the Quain fund for the furtherance of anthropology.

Margaret had little time to absorb this news. At the Vassar lectures, the dean had anxiously hovered near the lectern lest the advanced state of Margaret's pregnancy lead to any embarrassing moments. On 7 December while working on the Balinese film material, Margaret was delighted to receive a cable from Gregory saying that he was coming home. The following evening she had dinner with her father and then went into labor. Her baby was born shortly after Ruth's letter was written.

Having observed childbirth and baby tending in so many cultures, Margaret had her own definite ideas on the matter. She was unwilling to submit to the barbaric practices of her peers who "for generations [had] been muffled in male myths instead of learning about a carefully observed actuality" (BW, 254). After careful consideration, she decided against giving birth in the squatting position, which would, in her culture, have seemed outrageous. Labor proceeded quickly, though it triggered a bout of malaria. At one point the process was slowed down while the woman filming the birth sent out for a new flash bulb. And on 8 December 1939, in the presence of her obstetrician, the nurses—who had been prepared with a film of a New Guinea birth—a child psychologist, and pediatrician, Dr. Benjamin Spock, Margaret became the mother of a healthy girl. She named her Mary Catherine Bateson, Mary from a family name on Gregory's side, and Catherine "after my lost little sister" and, no doubt, carrying resonance from someone else Margaret had loved, Katharine Rothenberger. The baby's name, Margaret would later admit, was a "heavy weight . . . compounded of . . . all the Katherines who preceded my daughter" and difficult to use in full (BW, 259). But now a mother, Margaret need no longer dream of lost or murdered babies. Her heterosexuality was secured.[19]

Ruth's reaction to Marie's cable was entirely generous. She wrote at once, "I never minded so much being so far away. I love you double, for I wonder if I don't love your baby as much as I love you." Her name "places her among the precious. . . . I can't think of any better name." She awaited with excitement each news bulletin: "If she's gaining an ounce a day since your milk came, my question about how good a cow you are is already answered." Her student, Ruth Landes, perhaps understood Benedict's feelings correctly when she congratulated her on the birth, with the comment: "Your family is increasing!" (RFB, Box 31).

Margaret and her baby came home to "Aunt Marie's" apartment, where baby "Chook" took up residence in a bureau drawer. Later mother and baby went home to Pennsylvania, where Margaret could live comfortably until she and Gregory found a place of their own: "I am taking life very quietly. I have an excellent little nurse, energetic and non-compulsive and pretty, and quite ready to disregard the doctor's orders." Margaret breast-fed the baby on demand and kept in good health, though troubled by nightmares, which she thought must have been caused by codeine. Ruth wrote that she was glad a physical cause had been found, for "my thoughts of you are so confident and peaceful that I'd feel a great chasm if your dreams had such a different affect."

Gregory, in England, jubilantly threw his pipe over the garden wall on hearing the news and immediately sent a telegram instructing Margaret not to christen the baby. Six weeks later, when he was welcomed back, "we let the nurse go and took care of her ourselves for a whole weekend. . . . [It was] the only time he took much physical care of her. But it was enough to establish a very close relationship" (BW, 263). Gregory was appalled by the Appalachian nurse's poor grammar and hired a trained English nurse who had to cope with the fact that Gregory and Margaret "planned to have photo floodlights in every room so that we could catch important moments in Cathy's life" (BW, 265).

By the time her sabbatical was over, Ruth had completed the book on race: "I feel I've done my GOOD WORKS and my Christian duty for the rest of my natural life and shan't ever have to again." Although Race: Science and Politics was conceived of as a popular book, a summary of scientific arguments and evidence rather than an original contribution to anthropology ("it's all old stuff really"), it is notable for introducing the term "racism" to the American public. Indeed, its original title had been "Race and Racism," but Margaret agreed with Ruth's publisher that "the word racism is not well known in the U.S." and on Ruth's behalf she accepted his alternative suggestion.

Ruth returned to New York in the middle of April. In California she had looked around for a position that would have allowed her to remain, but then it had been decided that Val would rent out her home in Pasadena and join Ruth in New York. Before leaving the West Coast, Ruth had met up with Reo Fortune, who was looking for summer work in a salmon canning factory. Despite his difficulties in finding a position, Ruth "was much reassured about his psyche; he was at his best, no chip on his shoulder, no exaggerated kicking at the pricks of his joblessness. . . . He was friendly in talking about everybody from Malinowski up and down." They stayed away from the topic of Margaret, though Ruth had written him about Catherine's birth.

Ruth remained only a few weeks in the city before going to Norwich for the summer with Ruth Bunzel. Bunny, she was relieved to report, was now "placid and undemanding . . . at her best." But hearing of Alexander

Goldenweiser's sudden death was saddening; he had been her first mentor in anthropology in the early days at the New School, though his own career had proved disappointing. Ruth probably shared Boas's sentiments: he wrote to her, "Isn't it sad to think of the life of a gifted man wasted on account of self-indulgence!"

Ruth Valentine arrived in Norwich with Ruth Tolman in late July, making three Ruths in all, four if Bunny was still in residence. Val had picked up a new car in Detroit, and at one point drove into Manhattan to visit Nat, perhaps to smooth out tensions that might have arisen over the new "adjustment." Having resigned from her position with the Los Angeles school system, Val found work with the New York City Community Mental Hygeine department, though she retained the Pasadena house. At the end of the summer, Benedict sorted through the old apartment while Nat set herself up on West Forty-seventh Street. Ruth rented for Val and herself an attractive apartment at 448 Central Park West that overlooked the park, was cool and airy in summer, and had a fireplace for winter.

Then it was into the fray at Columbia again. Margaret said of Ruth at this time, "She was wearied now not by the old tension between inner and outer life, but rather by an external fragmentation of time resulting from the situation of the moment, the pressure for action, the state of anthropology, the state of her own work. . . . She found herself once more in the old position of power without patronage" (AW, 350). Linton was as rivalrous as ever, Ruth had her many students and "numberless lame ducks," and to make matters worse, she was immediately embroiled in a controversy over an attack by President Butler on academic freedom of speech (AW, 350). Ruth and seven others from the Democracy and Intellectual Freedom committee wrote an open letter to the New York Times, and to their credit and his, he backed down.

With the United States likely to be at war, anthropologists began considering contributions they could make. An assistant undersecretary in the Department of Agriculture who admired Ruth's work interested her in the study of cultural aspects of nutrition, always a concern during wartime, given likely food shortages. Ruth was instrumental in setting up a Committee on Food Habits for the prestigious National Research Council, to meet in Washington.

When the Japanese bombed Pearl Harbor on 7 December 1940, Margaret, Ruth, and Larry Frank were at a conference; on hearing the news they realized that further decisions would need to be rapid. Gregory, Margaret, and Larry were already developing a voluntary organization to further anthropological work, the Council for Intercultural Relations which later became the Institute for Intercultural Studies. They invited Ruth to join as well, and Larry suggested that the Mead-Batesons should move into the Frank home at 72 Perry Street in Greenwich Village and also invited them to share summer quarters in New Hampshire. Ruth initiated an invitation for Margaret to become the first executive secretary of the Committee on Food Habits, a position that would mean a leave of absence from the museum to set up an office in Washington, returning to New York only at weekends.[20] The following day, 8 December, Congress declared war. It was Catherine's second birthday and a week before Margaret's fortieth—and Margaret still hoped for a second baby.

Margaret and Gregory settled in downstairs on Perry St. with Cathy, the nurse, the nurse's teenage daughter, and later two British teenagers who had been sent to America for the duration of the war. Upstairs were Larry Frank, his second wife, Mary, and their five children. This wartime arrangement would last for fifteen years. As Margaret's daughter explained later, the situation gave her mother a chance to use her imagination to construct a satisfying life, with a household and a working schedule that offered freedom and flexibility and allowed her to meet family needs and fulfill her civic duties. These domestic arrangements were also familiar to an anthropologist who studied societies in which extended families and cooperative work were the norm.

Mary Frank was the maternal center of the new household. Margaret, once asked if she was jealous of Mary who had displaced her, replied "that jealousy was culturally produced, an emotion she did not feel."[21] The American version of wifehood and motherhood had never been congenial to Margaret, though in her role as popular commentator she increasingly was striking a more conservative note which contrasted uneasily with her unique family and working arrangements. But the students at Smith College knew an odd couple when they saw one. Betty Friedan recalled that they referred to Mead and Bateson, who visited that year, as "God the Mother and Jesus Christ."[22]

Against this bustle of preparation for war Ruth gave Margaret a special gift—a handwritten and handbound book of her own poetry. The anthology, which Margaret published in her biography of Ruth, represented a final selection of Ruth's work. It was now over a decade since she had unsuccessfully submitted her manuscript for publication. The dedicatory verse, to Margaret ("Haws when they blossom . . .") was not new, having been composed in the twenties. Whether the secret delights that the poem summons up ("Still through their roots runs the most secret liquor") still formed an element in Margaret and Ruth's relationship after two decades is hard to guess. But in that summer of 1941, Ruth and Margaret stole some precious time together. With Margaret and her extended family ensconced in New Hampshire, Ruth booked herself into the nearby Asquam Inn on

Squam Lake, and the two friends spent four days together. Afterwards, Ruth wrote, "being with you at Holderness was all that counted in this last week. It was something to chalk up beside our week at Westport and our week at Mahopac. The miracle is that you could manage it so in the midst of all the claims on you this summer, and that these claims only made our being together the richer. I love you, darling, and that's for what you are. And by sheer good luck I get no end of joy out of what you *do*, and no end of stimulation out of what you *think*. They're all part of what you *are*, and I don't think of separating them, but some people I've loved don't give the other blessings too." The letter ends with affectionate greetings to Gregory and Catherine; Ruth Valentine is not mentioned. In fact, Val was virtually never mentioned in the few letters that passed between Ruth and Margaret in the period following Ruth's California year. As Margaret had said, Ruth compartmentalized people, partly to preserve her own integrity and partly, one has to suppose, to enable her to maintain a closeness to Margaret which could well have been threatening to, and threatened by, a domestic partner.

The summer interlude may have been the occasion of Ruth's presenting her poetry to Margaret, or perhaps the gift marked Margaret's fortieth birthday. Margaret, at forty, was a woman who appeared to be in command of her destiny, unhesitatingly shaping the circumstances of her life with a loyalty to her own needs unusual for a woman of her time. She broke the cultural mold where it suited her, maintained her unorthodox relationships with husband, daughter, and lovers, yet was careful to cherish the respectability needed for her public work. Her youthful confidence had not been dented, and to Marie she wrote, "I guess God meant me to be fat at forty, but my figure is becoming steadily more out of tune with my eleven year old manners."

Ruth had taken charge of her life in a quite different way, having overcome her psychic struggles to achieve a form of quietude which, on most occasions, enabled her to surmount everyday annoyances. She would never feel in control of her destiny in the way Margaret seemed to and Margaret was still her touchstone, her passport to serenity.

Early in 1942 Margaret began spending weekdays in Washington. She stayed at a friend's house there and Ruth would often join her for meetings. Margaret now acquired as a research assistant Rhoda Métraux, now married to another anthropologist, Alfred Métraux, but eventually to become Margaret's domestic companion. Gregory remained in New York until he joined the Office of Strategic Services, a posting that would take him for long periods into the Pacific and Asia working on techniques of psychological warfare. Geoffrey Gorer, also in Washington, was working in the Office of War Information, and when he moved to the British Embassy in 1943 he suggested Ruth as his replacement.[23] Ruth took an indefinite leave from Columbia, moving to Washington while Val remained in New York. Affectionate notes to and from Benedict's secretary at Columbia often mentioned "the girlfriend," indicating that the domestic set-up was well known to her colleagues. For example, her secretary wrote, "Darling, Just had a short conversation with your 'girl friend' and decided I had better write to you at once. . . . Your 'girl friend' says you are not getting fat on the job. You had better take a little care of yourself. . . ." And, "Your Valentine friend makes herself very scarce, of course I couldn't blame her much but I like to see her. . . . L[ove] & K[isses]" (RFB, Box 27).

Eventually Val shifted to Washington, too, becoming an associate psychologist for the U.S. Public Health Service. The pair lived in an apartment in the northwest sector; now Ruth was able to write to her secretary, "I and the girlfriend are well and often think of you" (RFB, Box 27). Natalie also obtained a Washington job, most likely recommended by Ruth, preparing a report for the quartermaster-general on rations for "primitive people." Later, Nat served in Germany as part of a unit providing theatrical entertainment to the troops.[24]

Ruth had a noisy office in Washington, but her deafness helped create a relatively peaceful space. Her first task was a culture-and-personality study of Thailand, then of several European countries, and finally of Japan. The Japanese work, of course, was the underpinning of her postwar classic, The Chrysanthemum and the Sword.

During Ruth's last winter at Columbia, Franz Boas died. Though his death had been long anticipated, he died suddenly on a bitterly cold winter's day in December 1942 during an anthropology luncheon. "A great giant of the forest felled," Ruth wrote to Margaret (FB, 30 Dec. 1931). Although some people dispute the version of the event told by Margaret and others, the story has Ruth sitting just beyond Boas at the speaker's table. Addressing the group, with a glass of wine in his hand, Boas is said to have announced, "I have a new theory about race"; he was immediately stricken there and then (AW, 355).

The death of one's mentor is both an incomparable loss and an occasion to move forward. The obituaries written by Ruth conveyed her admiration for "a great man" who "labored indefatigably" and with unquestioned integrity to make the world safe for difference. Even at age eighty-four, Ruth wrote in the Nation, Boas "had not sold out or stultified himself, or locked himself in a dogmatic cage" (AW, 422). Moreover, he had unwaveringly believed in Ruth and supported her, not as a faithful disciple but as a powerfully creative individual in her own right. She, in turn, had found herself able to love Boas as unreservedly as she loved the father of her childhood imagination.

For Margaret, the loss was less severe. Boas had been her teacher and her inspiration, but her relationship to him had never been personal; Ruth had usually been the go-between.

On Boas's death his mantle fell on Ruth's shoulders. Although she had vowed that writing *Race: Science and Politics* was the last of her good deeds, now she was committed to the war effort, which she saw as a fight for democracy and a future internationalism even as she was saddened by it. Nevertheless, an invitation to attend the launching of the naval vessel "Franz Boas" must have struck her as an ironic memorial, given Boas's pacifism (RFB, Box 105).

Ruth did not have an easy time obtaining security clearance. In 1942 the Dies committee named her Committee for Democracy and Intellectual Freedom a communist front. Later, a political furor broke out over the pamphlet, "The Races of Mankind," which she and her Columbia colleague Gene Weltfish put together one weekend in Washington. The authors saw it as a means of publicizing the ideas contained in Ruth's book on race, which emphasized that racial differences were only skin deep and that learning to live with cultural difference was a matter of being a good neighbour. "The Races of Mankind" was translated into many languages and distributed worldwide, particularly among the U.S. armed forces.[25]

During the war Gene Weltfish remained at Columbia, keeping the Boasian tradition alive. She was Jewish, an active feminist the same age as Margaret, and divorced from anthropologist Alexander Lesser. The success of "The Races of Mankind" would lead to further collaborations with Ruth, including consulting over an animated film, and writing a children's book, *In Henry's Backyard*. The latter had a uniquely Benedict touch, its main character, Henry, being possessed by the "green devils" of racist envy and fear, an image that paralleled the "blue devils" of depression that had once possessed Ruth.

Controversy over "The Races of Mankind" broke out in 1944 when an outraged congressman from Kentucky labeled it communist propaganda, since it included factual information demonstrating that northern blacks showed superior performance on intelligence tests to southern whites (stating this baldly was a "tactical error," according to Margaret).[26] The armed forces had the pamphlet recalled, and the fallout for Ruth was that she had to endure an FBI investigation, including a security conference in which she defended the absurd charge, quite possibly originating with Ralph Linton, that she had sent Buell Quain to South America to get killed so that she could get her hands on his money.

Benedict never obtained a top-level security clearance and for Weltfish the matter was even more serious. Her position at Columbia was untenured and now looked threatened. With uncharacteristically brash behavior, Ruth stormed into a closed board of trustees meeting and demanded that Weltfish's employment continue. A reprieve was granted, but the administration was clearly gunning for the younger woman. In the early 1950s she was investigated by Senator McCarthy's committee for her "subversive" pamphlet and her association with women's peace groups; as a consequence, her position was terminated, over the objections of her department. She had taught at Columbia for seventeen years. Benedict's and Weltfish's collaborative work is now regarded as a significant contribution from the social sciences to antiracism efforts.

During the war Margaret saw more of Ruth than of Gregory, who was not free to return to the United States until some time after the victory. Margaret did make one international journey, visiting England on behalf of the Office of War Information to investigate tensions that had arisen about relationships between the G.I.s and British girls which resulted, she believed, from cultural differences in courtship patterns. She also wrote *And Keep Your Powder Dry*, a surprisingly monocultural analysis of Americans, which she saw as a contribution to an understanding of America at war and an affirmation of democracy. This book was in the genre of American character studies which became popular around that time.[27]

Margaret was so busy that Christmas 1943, was the first time in two years that she spent three uninterrupted days with Cathy, now four years old. Often, during the Washington years, Margaret and Ruth would take the train together back to New York on weekends, especially before Val moved down there too. Marie had become indispensable in Catherine's upbringing; her letters to Margaret are full of practical details and have none of the obsessional misery that had often colored them in earlier times. Among other responsibilities, Marie was in charge of Cathy's clothes; as Margaret remarked phlegmatically, "I would have adored doing her clothes, but Marie cared about it more, so I let her do it."[28]

Although many aspects of her work were secret, Ruth was far from isolated in Washington as friends and colleagues streamed into town. Edward's old friend, Harry Stack Sullivan, now in Bethesda, invited her to lecture at his Washington School of Psychiatry; she also became an assistant editor of his journal, *Psychiatry*, which Edward Sapir had helped found. Ruth hoped to remain on good terms with Karen Horney, despite Sullivan's having supported Horney's former lover, Erich Fromm, when Horney expelled him from her psychoanalytical association after it passed regulations outlawing lay analysis. Erik Erikson was also in Washington and Benedict hired him as a project consultant.

Ruth's most absorbing project was her research on Japan. She interviewed all available Japanese, watched Japanese movies, and read everything she could lay her hands on about "the most alien enemy" the United States had done battle against.[29] She spoke out on the conditions of internment of Japanese "aliens," many of whom were in fact U.S. citizens, though she did not publically oppose the fact of their internment, a "disappointing blindness" according to her biographer, Margaret Caffrey, or perhaps a strategic exercise of caution.

Whether Ruth's war work had any influence on American policy is hard to assess. Social scientists were often dismissed as impractical idealists, and no doubt many of their reports were shelved. (Gregory Bateson, in his attempts at psychological warfare, once tried to enact a bizarre scheme involving parachuting the ashes of a dead airman into Japan in order to alarm the local populace; he actually incinerated a body for the purpose.) A significant question for strategists in the later days of the war was how much the Japanese would endure before they surrendered, since they were known for their extraordinary capacity for self-sacrifice in the service of their emperor. Ruth's position, which found general agreement, was that in the event of a surrender, the emperor should be spared, the course that was eventually taken.

There is no published record of whether Ruth's section at the Office of War Information played any role—either pro or con—in the decision to detonate the atomic bomb in 1945. It is surprising, though, that The Chrysanthemum and the Sword: Patterns of Japanese Culture, based on Benedict's war work, never once refers to the bomb. One has to wonder about the influence on Ruth's attitude of her acquaintance, via Natalie Raymond, with Robert Oppenheimer, "father of the bomb." Oppenheimer was hidden away at Los Alamos, New Mexico, for much of the war, though he did visit Washington from time to time. His involvement with the project was guided by a fear that the Nazis might develop atomic weaponry first, although the finishing touches on the bomb were carried out after the fall of Nazi Germany. Ruth had even closer personal ties to Oppenheimer's friend, Richard Tolman. His wife was one of Ruth Valentine's closest friends and the Tolmans spent the latter part of the war years in Washington; she worked at the Office of War Information at one point and he was vice chairman of the National Defense Research Committee. As scientific advisor to Gen. Leslie R. Groves, the head of the Manhattan Project, Tolman was closely linked with policy issues surrounding the development of the bomb.[30]

Like many intellectuals, Margaret was horrified that the bomb was actually used. She described her reaction to Hiroshima and Nagasaki as being so extreme that she tore up the manuscript of her sequel to *And Keep Your Powder Dry* in the belief that atomic warfare had projected the world into an entirely new age.[31] Ruth, in contrast, wrote to Margaret only a few weeks after the bomb was dropped that she was annoyed at being prevented from an assignment to work on "Likert's Japanese bombing survey" because of the "blanket rule that no women can go over on that survey. . . . Why didn't I transvestite when I was young?" (MM, TR1). Years later Margaret implied that she disapproved of Ruth's attitude, writing that "the contemporary reader [of *The Chrysanthemum and the Sword*] is immediately struck by the absence of any reference to the atomic bomb and the Japanese response to the catastrophe. In 1946, the significance of the impact of Hiroshima on Japanese thinking had not yet penetrated American consciousness."[32] Elsewhere, Mead suggested that the social scientists who worked on the war effort were sometimes nationalistic, sometimes naive, and sometimes injurious to the cultures that they studied. Psychological warfare, Gregory's field, "rebounded on those who perpetuated it," and the secrecy requirements of war work, she argued, were inimical to the scientific spirit.[33]

Ruth's reason for failing to address the question of the bomb in her book was surely strategic. She wished to focus on how an anthropologist approached the understanding of Japanese culture during wartime, and moreover, she had a political purpose. As she explained to Margaret at the time, "protests against our 'soft' peace [i.e. the American occupation] will continue" (MM, TR1). Ruth praised General MacArthur's strategies of occupation and he, in turn, admired her work. That she said nothing of the bomb gave her leeway to support judicious strategies of occupation at a time when many Americans called for revenge. Perhaps her true attitudes were shown elsewhere, for in 1946 she gave a favorable review to John Hersey's *Hiroshima*, the book about the impact of the bomb which galvanized the American public. As Ruth put it, "The matter at issue has become [for Americans] scenes of the burned and wounded staggering endlessly along the roads, of living burial under fallen timbers and rubble, of vomit and suppuration and lingering death. . . . [*Hiroshima*] is written with complete simplicity, and the calmness of the narrative throws into relief the nightmare magnitude of the destructive power the brains of man have brought into being."[34]

The war ended, and as Margaret cynically put it, "the social scientists . . . took their marbles and went home" (BW draft). Ruth and Val were in California during part of 1946. Ruth's mother, living with Margery, was still alive, though beginning to show signs of senility. Aunt Myra had died in 1945, leaving Ruth the farm at Norwich. Margery wondered if Ruth planned to retire there, but Ruth said that she might "spend her sunset years" in California (RFB, Box 106). Margery, who deeply admired her sister for all she had done, was thrilled. Approaching sixty, she felt that the two of them were closer than at any other time in their life.

While in California in 1946, Ruth completed the manuscript of *The Chrysanthemum and the Sword*, her "crowning achievement" and one of the first anthropological descriptions of a national culture. In this book, her personal favorite, she showed her literary talents to best effect. Clifford Geertz aptly described Benedict's accomplishment as resting on her "powerful expository style at once spare, assured, lapidary and above all resolute: definite views, definitely expressed." The book became (and still is) widely known in Japan, as well as the United States, where it was an immediate success. Its innovative exploration of Japanese shame versus American guilt as social control mechanisms, a contrast that developed out of earlier work with Margaret in the cooperation-competition project, evoked some criticism but mostly widespread enthusiasm. And in Ruth's delightful account of Japanese childhood, the psychoanalytical interests of Margaret and others in their circle such as Erik Erikson and Geoffrey Gorer also show their influence.[35]

Clifford Geertz, in perhaps the most profound assessment of Benedict as a writer, points out that the hallmark of her writing lies in its continual development of what he calls the "Us/Not us" motif. Comparisons between the social arrangements of other cultures and our own pervade her texts, and she works these contrasts with ingenuity, her tone of Swiftian irony put to serious purpose. This repetitive use of cultural contrast, Geertz continues, "is what so divides Benedict's professional readers into those who regard her work as magisterial and those who find it monomaniacal. It is also what brought her such a popular audience. Unlike Mead, who achieved a somewhat similar result with a loose-limbed, improvisational style, saying seventeen things at once and marvelously adaptable to the passing thought . . . Benedict found herself a public by sticking determinedly to the point."[36]

Ruth's return to Columbia in the fall of 1946 was made more pleasant by the fact that Ralph Linton had left for Yale. Julian Steward was now head of the department, and while they were not simpatico, Ruth found him easier than his predecessor. But the students had changed, too, with veterans swelling the department's numbers and bringing with them attitudes and values Ruth saw as sexist and materialist. She complained to a friend that the place was turning into a factory. As before, she had vigorous detractors and staunch admirers, one of whom, Sidney Mintz, turned toward anthropology when he first heard Ruth lecture. Describing the scene, he recalled: "Benedict stood before us, tall, spare, seeming rather distant, her voice startlingly low and slightly hoarse, plainly dressed, her silver hair short and severe, what I judged to be her shyness heightened by the contrast between the penetration of her ideas and the somewhat absent gaze with which she regarded us."[37]

Margaret's adjustment to postwar life was not easy. She picked up the threads readily enough at the Museum of Natural History, where her office was becoming more and more like a headquarters of Margaret Mead, Inc. But in relation to Gregory she found herself in the same position as other wartime wives, with a stranger returning to their midst. Gregory's wartime experiences had changed him, and the contrasts which had made them, in Margaret's view, a perfect intellectual partnership, now seemed to elicit in Gregory a need for self-protection and withdrawal. Students of the time recalled a Gregory Bateson lecture series at the New School where Margaret plumped herself in the center of the front row, interjecting and correcting with such frequency that before long she had taken over the class. Others remembered the startling look of the couple in the street, Margaret bustling ahead, gesticulating energetically and talking animatedly, while Gregory loped along behind, his natural easy-goingness sometimes strained. Margaret assessed Gregory as having an extraordinary low level of physical energy; Gregory thought that Margaret was "almost a principle of pure energy. I couldn't keep up and she couldn't stop."[38]

The best thing about marriage, Margaret once said, was that it provided a chance to finish conversations. Her conversations with Ruth, equally valued, had so often been interrupted by the interminably slow mail. Gregory, it seems, was beginning to feel that the conversations were a little one-way, and he did not have to look far for consolation. American women, as with Australians in the past, found him devastatingly attractive. His shyness, awkwardness, and lack of aggression, combined with his upper-class English intellectual manner, acted like a magnet. Margaret continued to insist that jealousy was a culturally produced emotion unknown to her—and she herself had not let marriage narrow her own range of attachments. Notably, her intimacy with Ruth flourished, as did the myriad friendships which Reo Fortune had once found difficult; fortunately, Gregory was the soul of tolerance.

But the marriage was floundering and Margaret persuaded Gregory to go into analysis with the Jungian psychoanalyst, Elizabeth Hellersberg, who was immediately charmed by him. It was not long before Gregory and his analyst were off on a vacation together. As Margaret put it, "Gregory threw Elizabeth into such a bad panic that the rest of us all had to spend our time rescuing her."[39] In 1947 Bateson was a visiting professor at Harvard where his personal charisma overcame his appalling lecture style. He had an extraordinary impact on his students and spent much of the year socializing, suggesting to all and sundry that they undergo analysis.

Although Margaret would not undergo analysis herself, her interest in personality testing led her to graphology analysis and Rorschach testing. On occasion she and Gregory consulted the Jungian analyst Gotthard Booth, who seems to have functioned as their marriage counselor. Their interest in dream interpretation continued, Gregory, around this time, dreaming of Margaret as a mother rat pulling her babies back into the nest whenever they tried to escape.

On his return from Harvard, Gregory became involved in a love affair with a dancer and took up residence with her on Staten Island. Margaret tried to be cheerful, but it was clear to her friends that she was distressed. Her handwriting analysis for 1946 showed a "severe emotional upset," and a 1947 specimen showed that she was living her life in a "kind of somnambulistic state," coping on the surface but isolated and "deeply schizoid" (MM, Q35). She no doubt confided in Ruth, writing in September 1947 from a Texas hotel, "I tried to telephone you before I left to say that I think I've now got body mind and spirit reasonably in line again—at any rate, the words which are running through my head are not, 'Lift up your heart as any cup, And drink it desolate'" [from the poem Ruth had written to her before the long ago Samoan trip]. She ended, "You looked beautiful at the Easter party. I love you, Margaret" (MM, TR1).

The ending of the marriage was not Margaret's decision. This was a first; she was the one who had moved on from her "student" marriage to Luther Cressman, she had decided that pursuing a relationship with Edward Sapir would endanger her future career, and she had lost patience with Reo over his jealousy and possessiveness. It was also she who had moved on from Katharine Rothenberger. The emotional ins and outs of relationships in the days of the Ash Can Cats days were quite tangled, but Margaret had allowed none to interfere with her planned marriage to Luther. Marie was always kept under control, and it was only Ruth who had sustained an intimacy which always proved nourishing and never hampering. So it was unfamiliar and not easy to be left—and there was the matter of Cathy, too. Margaret later recalled, "I was beginning to get a taste of what it would be like to be a divorced mother, with a child to bring up" (BW draft).

The personal distress she was experiencing around this time in no way hindered Margaret from her usual pronouncements on life. In 1946 she had been invited to California to give a series of lectures on the psychology of sex; out of these came her next book, *Male and Female*, which was drafted during 1948, though not published until 1949. Erik Erikson's work, she recalled, inspired this book, which would not have been written while she was with Gregory since sex was not a subject of scholarly interest to him. Larry Frank commented, "with the warmth and care that never left his voice: 'Each to his own therapy' " (BW draft).

Critics usually turn to *Male and Female* when they wish to put a dent in Mead's feminist reputation, and it is true that the chilly climate of the post-war era led to Margaret's more conservative pronouncements here about men and women, gender, the family, and sexuality. Regarding the latter, her description of "the natural springing potency of men and slower-flowering responsiveness of women" is one example of such tradition-alism.[40] Her personal situation also may have been behind some changes of attitude. Since *Sex and Temperament*, the thirties classic, she had become a mother, and the recent separation from Gregory no doubt lent an edge to her writing. When the Kinsey report appeared in 1948, she was scathing about it, arguing that its focus on counting sexual "outlets" confused sex with excretion and overglorified "simple copulation."[41]

Homosexuality is also dealt with more conservatively than in her previous books. She did note with concern a general upswing in intolerance, but she also implied that homosexuality, a state arising from too rigid sex role expectations of boys and girls, was something to be socially engineered out of existence. The swinging twenties flavor of *Coming of Age in Samoa*, in which homosexual practices had been described as a delightful interlude, was far in the past.[42]

In the ultraconservative decade of the 1950s, Margaret still saw her own culture as one of many possible arrangements, but she seemed less interested in radical change in the positions of men and women. She had begun to step into the role of "Mother of America," as *Time* magazine was later to call her, and during this period her promotion of liberal causes, such as opposition to atomic warfare, was perhaps tempered by political caution.[43] Following an investigation in which she falsely declared that "I have never known anyone whom I know to be a Communist, as a friend" (MM, Q35), Margaret kept her "top security clearance" during the fifties.[44] The security clearance issue, in itself, may have been the reason for down-playing any suggestion of involvement with homosexuality.

Ruth never obtained a full security clearance, but her work on Japan meant she was in good standing in some quarters of the military. She had enjoyed the war work immensely, and on returning to Columbia she did not wish to continue specializing in Native American cultures. Her lack of field experience also may have counted against her, since she had taught a generation of students who had gone into the field. Through her Washington connections she explored research funding possibilities and in 1946 was able to report a triumph. Margaret recalled a party in Greenwich Village, where

Ruth, "unaccountably gay" and with "a twinkle in her eye," flabbergasted her friends by telling them that she knew where she could get a hundred thousand dollars in research monies; "mischievously" she would disclose nothing further (AW, 433).

The source of the funding turned out to be the Office of Naval Research; the project came to be known as "Research in Contemporary Cultures" (R.C.C.).[45] In designing it, Ruth worked closely with Margaret to set up a structure that would facilitate a large number of anthropologists and graduate students working on thematically and methodologically linked projects. The structure was nonhierarchical, Margaret was pleased to report, and "everything we had learned about interdisciplinary research, about organizing teams . . . was to be used. All the gifted people who had somehow managed in wartime but who did not fit into the peacetime mold—the aberrant, the unsystematic, the people with work habits too irregular ever to hold regular jobs—all of them were woven together into a fabric of research" (AW, 434).

The research was administratively centered in Ruth's office at Columbia and Margaret's office at the museum, but as it began to grow and sprawl at a rapid rate, their apartments were taken over. Team members included Rhoda Métraux and Ruth Bunzel, and eventually 120 people of sixteen nationalities were working on seven national cultures in a massive project, the usefulness of which is still debated among anthropologists.[46] The budget over the four-year period of the project stretched to $250,000—and it still was not enough. Some members worked voluntarily or for little pay and Ruth Valentine took an administrative position to remove pressure from Ruth, who was looking increasingly tired and drawn.

Margaret and Ruth continued to find time for each other, but the "evenings in which we used to discuss poetry and the novelistic aspects of real life were now filled with petty details."[47] There were regular visits to Perry Street on Thursdays, where "Aunt Ruth" and Margaret enjoyed Cathy on her nanny's afternoon off; and one evening in May 1948 Margaret and Ruth went to The New School to hear their old friend Louise Bogan read poetry in the company of Robert Lowell, Marianne Moore, and Allen Tate. Léonie Adams and her husband, Bill Troy, were also there. Writing to a friend, Louise described the scene: "O yes, Margaret Mead and Ruth Benedict in the front row. I hadn't seen them in years. Ruth looking old and beautiful; Margaret as 'earth-bound' as ever. Such celebrities, yet!"[48]

That same month Ruth heard the news that, after all these years, she was to be made a full professor at Columbia. Sex discrimination was still alive and well at Columbia, and rumor had it that the presence of Benedict had prevented anthropology from being included in the Faculty of Political Sciences because of opposition to the presence of women at faculty lunches, where business was done. As Sidney Mintz noted, years later Benedict was the only woman who was seen as noteworthy enough to have her picture hung in Fayerweather Hall at Columbia. That same year she received the Achievement Award of the American Association of University Women, and in 1947 she became president of the American Anthropological Association.

In the summer of 1948 Ruth traveled to Europe. She had not gone in 1945, when the Office of War Information was keen to send her to Germany where her race pamphlet was being used in the deNazification program. But high blood pressure and a return of fainting spells suggested a heart problem, though she made light of these symptoms and was annoyed when she failed to get a medical clearance. The army doctor had said she was "organically sound," she told Margaret, but "as a woman over 45" (she was then 59) he doubted her stamina (MM, TR1).

But now, in 1948, there was another chance, under the auspices of the contemporary cultures project, with an invitation from UNESCO. Ruth looked frail before she left, strained by the complex nature of her large project. It has been suggested that Ruth's relationship with Val was under threat at this time, although the available evidence is contradictory. During the summer before the European trip, she and Val made a visit to California and Val stayed on to help Ruth Tolman care for her husband, Richard, who was dying of cancer. In a letter from Ruth's sister, Margery Freeman, to Margaret Mead, she reported that Val had said she was "weighing Pasadena against N.Y. very seriously [but] had decided to return to Ruth and the project, or as she put it, to 'the old gal—the famous anthropologist.' " And Margery wrote to Ruth, perhaps with a touch of diplomacy, "I know she *wanted* most to be with you, but I was afraid her inordinate sense of duty might make her feel that her *duty* was to stay by Ruth T," who would face a new life alone (RFB, Box 39).

In the event, Ruth Benedict may have needed her partner every bit as much as Ruth Tolman did. In California, Erik Erikson had made a line drawing of Benedict; he later told Margaret that "he felt as if he were drawing the face of a very old woman, on the verge of death," even though she was only sixty-one. Despite the fatigue, she appeared to be very calm and "to ask whether she was happy in any conversational sense would have seemed incongruous" (AW, 436).

Ruth returned by plane from California to New York on 16 July 1948, to leave for Europe the following Monday. She had managed to give a critical reading to the manuscript of *Male and Female*. Margaret was concerned about her friend, persuading her to visit a doctor. Ruth obliged but was determined not to give up her trip. A worker from the project was assigned to see her to the plane; in part of their last conversation, Ruth told this young woman that she was suffering from insomnia, but that it did not bother her; in fact, she valued it as it was during sleepless nights long ago that she had written her poetry.[49]

The European trip lasted six weeks. Ruth enjoyed the UNESCO seminar in Czechoslovakia where Harry Stack Sullivan was also present. From there she wrote to Margaret, now in England for a different conference, that she had found her trip comfortable, the country beautiful, and the seminar "a mixed bag." News of the world was "practically nonexistent," but she had been so busy that she had hardly "a chance to catch my breath." She ended, "All my love, darling, and more power to you for the Congress. As ever, my dear, Ruth." Then a footnote, "Later. Your note just came. I'm glad England is so full of affection. Be happy, darling" (MM, TR1).

When Ruth appeared at her next conference, an international anthropological gathering in Brussels, colleagues reported that she was suffering from exhaustion. On her return to New York City—Val was still in Pasadena where Richard Tolman had just died—Margaret caught up with her. Ruth hardly had time to tell her about the European trip before, two days after her return, she suffered a coronary thrombosis. She was taken to Marie's apartment, then Margaret got her to a doctor; from there she was admitted to the hospital. The heart problem was identified and she was told to spend her time resting. She apparently "smiled peacefully and said, 'My friends will take care of everything'" (AW, 438). Margaret immediately wired Ruth Valentine, whose fear of flying led to her reply, "Leaving on Union Pacific Train City of Los Angeles this afternoon from Pasadena due Chicago Wednesday morning New York Thursday morning Will phone you from Chicago Please tell Marie" (RFB, Box 106). Natalie Raymond was cabled and so was Jean Sapir, according to Margaret's notebook (MM, A1).

During Ruth's final illness, which lasted five days, Margaret kept a vigil at her bedside, aided by other close friends, undoubtedly including Marie. Margaret later commented that Ruth never spoke of work and they did not bother her with the details of the R.C.C. administration. She "put all her effort into staying quietly alive until Ruth Valentine got back from California." When Val finally arrived, they spent several hours in the afternoon talking together. That same evening, 17 September 1948, Ruth died. Margaret was at her bedside. At the moment of her death she looked "magnificent, almost supernatural, like a figure in the ceiling of the sistine chapel. . . . with her hair white and her life over," as if she were "ninety years of age" (BW draft). It was "as if the wisdom and suffering of several hundred years was momentarily expressed in a face which, for that instant, seemed more than life-sized" (AW, 438).

# 14

## At Ending

THE NIGHT BEFORE THE FUNERAL Margaret took her daughter to view Ruth, who "had always felt so strongly about the beauty of the dead." Margaret agreed, believing that viewing the body gave Cathy "a protection which few children have today, in an acceptance that death is a part of life" (AW,438). Mary Catherine Bateson recalled Ruth as "archetypically beautiful and cold, her large luminous eyes closed, her white hair perfectly sculptured."[1]

At the funeral, which was held in the University Chapel at Columbia, Margaret "wept fiercely."[2] She was supported by friends who were concerned about the effects of this devastating loss following so closely upon her separation from Gregory. Afterward Marie Eichelberger and Isabel Carter, a Washington friend, went back to Margaret's Perry Street home. Margaret, who had an interest in the paranormal, recalled that while they were at the dinner table a cord holding a great gilded mirror on the wall snapped and the mirror fell, coming to rest precariously on the edge of the mantelpiece among the Balinese carvings. It hovered, but did not break.[3]

Margaret was treated by many, not entirely without justification, as Ruth's principal mourner. Ruth Valentine had a more obvious claim as Ruth's lover, partner, household companion, executive secretary of her contemporary cultures project, and the executor and principal beneficiary of her will. No doubt Val also received support, but her commitment to secrecy meant that letters of condolence she received have not been saved. None of the letters to Margaret seem to have referred to Val, even in passing (RFB, Box 106). To one correspondent who asked for a family address Margaret sent that of Ruth's sister, Margery Freeman.

Margaret had phoned Margery in Pasadena immediately after the death, describing Ruth as "lying there so utterly peaceful and serene, preparing herself for eternity." Margery, in turn, wrote Margaret a warm letter, telling her that "one of the deepest satisfactions of [Ruth's] life has been the privilege of stirring up your interest [in anthropology] and then watching you carry the torch into fields where she could never go." Margaret must have already decided to write a book about Ruth—perhaps she had even discussed it with her during those last days—as Margery's condolence letter refers to the project (RFB, Box 106).

Luther Cressman wrote to Margaret, describing Ruth as "the most deeply vital, gentle, tolerant and civilized person I have known." Helen Lynd, the sociologist, recalled her striking beauty and the deep rose dress she used to wear. One of the Ash Can Cats, Eleanor Phillips, told Margaret that Ruth was "an inextricable part of events and emotions that left their impress forever, but are now of the past. But I know what a constantly living and loving past she remained in your life." Pelham Kortheuer (now Stapelfeldt), who had been talking with Léonie Adams, expressed the feelings of Margaret's friends succinctly: "What must it mean to you—this last blow?" (RFB, Box 106).

Ruth's death was widely noted, though of course the public recognition did not do justice to her private life. In the *New York Times* obituary only her marriage was mentioned. Colleagues were stunned by the loss, and Margaret recalled that on the contemporary cultures project "each member . . . interpreted Ruth's death . . . in their own local cultural terms; dreamt of their mothers appearing to them, or of refusing Ruth water" (BW draft). The only sour note came from Ralph Linton, who showed his deep-rooted enmity by complaining that Ruth could not even die of a woman's disease. Sidney Mintz, a student of Benedict's, tells the extraordinary story of Linton's showing off a leather pouch from the Tanala and boasting that he had used its occult powers to kill Benedict.[4]

Some months later a memorial gathering was held where friends and colleagues, who included Erik Erikson, Cora Du Bois, Alfred Kroeber, and Margaret, spoke of Ruth's life and work. Kroeber recalled Ruth as "completely fine-grained, surcharged with feeling, yet irrevocably tolerant. Reserved as a person, restrained in expression, yet sympathetic and kindly, she was civilized utterly. . . ." Cora Du Bois observed that for Ruth, "achievement was a means of self-expression, and not a weapon of self-assertion." Erik Erikson recalled meeting Ruth in 1948 when she was "not vitally healthy any more." He said of her: "Here was a friend, who was deeply alone, who had, in fact, stopped fighting loneliness. She had begun to befriend death, without in any way inviting it or being demanding of it. Here, then, was a consciously aging woman, who looked as much like a young girl, as she looked like a man, without being in the least juvenile or mannish. . . . There is tragedy here, we know. Ruth was too young to be complete and detached."[5]

Margaret's tribute to the woman whose friendship over "quarter of a century has covered my whole professional life" was restrained, focusing on Ruth's quest to resolve lifelong feelings of alienation. By studying cultural difference Ruth had managed to achieve the "selfless hope [of] those who found themselves strangers among their own people, that others of their kind might somewhere, sometime, be at home." In Ruth's work (as in her life, so the subtext read), "the deviant ceased to be either a tragic or merely pathetic figure and became more and more a measuring device against which the pattern itself could be understood."[6] Margaret closed her eulogy with a reading of Benedict's "Eucharist," the poem of spiritual yearning whose title calls up their long-shared "bread and wine" metaphor. Perhaps it is reasonable to suggest that the multilayered meanings of this poem may include reference to Margaret's "earth-bound" refusal to go "storm-driven down the dark," which had always formed an uneasy strand of their friendship:

> Light the more given is the more denied.
> Though you go seeking by the naked seas,
> Each cliff etched visible and all the waves
> Pluming themselves with sunlight, of this pride
> Light makes her sophistries.
>
> You are not like to find her, being fed
> Always with that she shines on. Only those,
> Storm-driven down the dark, see light arise,
> Her body broken for their rainbow bread
> At late and shipwrecked close.[7]

Years later Margaret remarked, "When people die, I have no sense that I have lost them. I mean, too bad they aren't here. . . . I would love to hear Ruth's laugh when I told her something absolutely ridiculous that has happened this week. . . . I thought [what] I might do was try to write a letter to Ruth about . . . things that are happening now that we hadn't thought possible. . . . I've played with the idea, but I do it in my mind, so [I imagine] how Ruth would laugh at this. And how mother would feel about that. They are all part of my life; I haven't lost them. I've lost the pleasure of their immediate company" (JH).

Margaret grieved, but it was in her nature to move on. A month later she was writing the preface to *Male and Female* at a friend's house in Connecticut. She took a Rorschach test around this time which showed her alone, without any emotional support. Discussing it later, Margaret recalled that she was still not "conscious of the load that had descended on me with Ruth's death. It was still too close. I was still concerned with the personal issues and not with the fact that I was going to have this responsibility for all these people and all this work." Inheriting leadership of the contemporary cultures project, Margaret said that she had had to take "Ruth's place in anthropology" and that it was "peculiarly lonely" to have lost the one person who had read everything she had written (MM, Q35).

Still, Margaret successfully sustained Ruth in her imagination, having had practice from many separations. She once observed that when she dreamed of Ruth, her image was not of the emotionally detached woman of the later years, nor the shy, distracted woman of the early days, but as Ruth looked after 1926 when her hair had turned white and was cut "like a helmet on her head, and she looked very beautiful" (JH).

As Ruth's beloved friend, Margaret wrote an obituary for *American Anthropologist.* As her literary executor, she made decisions about publications and storing of her papers, which went to Vassar. As her future biographer, she undertook the massive task of preparation for *An Anthropologist at Work,* assembling all Ruth's papers and correspondence as well as her own. Although the book would not be published until 1957, preparations began right away; Mary Catherine Bateson recalls that Ruth's papers were spread over Marie Eichelberger's apartment for much of her childhood. Rhoda Métraux was enlisted to type out much of the earlier handwritten correspondence, including the Sapir-Benedict letters. Margaret had once conceived of the book as a collection of Ruth's unpublished papers, but now she thought of it as a four-way conversation between Ruth, Franz Boas, Edward Sapir, and herself. Interestingly, Margaret once told Esther Goldfrank that "there was much she learned about [Ruth] only after her death."[8]

As she wrote the biographical chapters—and interspersed them with Ruth's papers, poetry, and letters—Margaret was faced with a dilemma. What should she say about her relationship with Ruth and Ruth's relationships with other women, particularly Natalie Raymond and Ruth Valentine? In the late fifties, with McCarthyism at its peak, acknowledgment of a lesbian relationship between Margaret and Ruth would have been unthinkable. On the other hand, Margaret did not want to dishonor her friend by downplaying significant parts of her life, nor did she want to dishonor herself by underestimating her importance to Ruth. These things were hidden, not just from the public, but also many in her own circle. Her daughter, Mary Catherine Bateson, said later that probably only Marie Eichelberger was "privy to all the complexities of her double relationships, without judgment, without prurience, and without jealousy."[9]

The result was a calculated risk. Though she felt the necessity of taking "the ordinary sad precautions of the twentieth century," a strategy she said Ruth had found difficult (BW draft). Margaret found it even harder to convince Ruth's partners that even slight risks of lesbian exposure were justified. Natalie Raymond and Ruth Valentine appeared panic-stricken at the thought. Val must have helped sort through Benedict's papers, but no correspondence between herself and Ruth or Natalie Raymond and Ruth seems to have been preserved. When Margaret wrote to her about "the book of Ruth," Val replied that she "was not only surprised but considerably startled to learn that there would be any reference to me in the book." She understood it to be about Ruth's development as an anthropologist. "I am not so stupid as to think that an anthropologist develops in an interpersonal vacuum," she remarked, but argued she had had no influence on Ruth's anthropology. Ruth had made a tremendous impact on Val's attitude to life, but "if you are going to bring in all persons influenced by Ruth, you'll have a list as long as the Manhattan phone book" (MM, Q23).

After this letter Val spoke with Natalie Raymond, who was in Palos Verdes visiting her stepfather. Val then wrote to Margaret, saying Nat "feels even more strongly than I do that no personal reference to her or to me should be made in your book. And I feel very strongly!" She argued that Ruth "is entitled to some private life" apart from her public persona and "she many times made that very clear and explicit to me." She went on:

> Therefor[e], if you include Nat's and my purely personal association with Ruth, I think that you will be doing violence to Ruth's private life—invading it in an inexcusable manner. As I wrote you, I just cant see what Nat and I have to do with Ruth as an anthropologist. Ruth, as a person, was a "lady" too. And I like the (partial) definition of a lady as one who "has a private life."
>
> Now, if you interpret this letter as a sort of ultimatum, you are entirely correct!
>
> Dont let your "runaway typewriter" lead you into realms which—so far as I am concerned—are tabu" (MM, Q23).

Margaret, meantime, had replied reassuringly that she was not going to write at any length about Ruth's life outside anthropology but wanted to have "some purely formal statements about companionship. . . . I don't think anyone who has followed the book through and read the poems with feeling, could bear to feel that she was alone at the end of her life" (MM, Q23). But after Val's "ultimatum" she replied, "My intention had been to treat both you and Nat with simplicity and without fuss or underlining of any sort, as the most effective sort of privacy which could be offered. I happen to be as interested in protecting Ruth as either one of you" (MM, Q23). Moreover, since Val had played an important role in the contemporary cultures project, omitting her entirely from the book would "certainly defeat your purpose of protecting Ruth's private life rather heavily, because I do mean to discuss RCC and certainly everyone connected with it will wonder why your name is left out." She told Val that she could have been as "mad as a hornet" at her letter, but was more interested in sorting out some amicable compromise.

Val replied placatingly that there had been a failure of communication; Margaret should use her own judgment: "I know that I do over-react in the matter of 'privacy.' In this respect I always remember one of Ruth's favorite daydreams—you know the one—in which she was in a monastic cell from which she could look out, but the world could not look in" (MM, Q23).

She went on, "Now, dear Margaret, forgiving me my trespasses, let me say that I had no intention of letting flow any 'spate of accusations' against you. If you want to be 'mad as a hornet,' well be so (that is often enjoyable!). Although you and I are very very different persons, we have to meet on some common ground for Ruth's sake."

Margaret was relieved. "I think probably what upset me was an echo of Nat's voice in your second letter," she wrote. "I do tend to react with irritation sometimes to her points, which I always get second hand, because you know I don't really know her at all. I've only seen her with other people, and then not much" (MM, Q23). In the event, Ruth Valentine was mentioned briefly in An Anthropologist at Work as sharing an apartment with Ruth. Natalie Raymond was not mentioned at all, though in one letter she appears as N——. One can only speculate about what Mead herself suppressed before handing the Benedict papers over to Vassar, and a number of less than kind remarks have been made implying that Mead, as the guardian of Benedict's memory, was selective, indeed self-serving.[10]

Fifteen years later, Margaret wrote her own autobiography, Blackberry Winter, drafting it while she was based in Pere in the Admiralty Islands, the site of her happiest fieldwork with Reo Fortune and a place to which she returned, taking younger anthropologists. Admired by a generation of readers for its emphasis on Margaret's women friends, Blackberry Winter sadly undervalues Ruth's importance.[11]

Margaret does say that "by electing anthropology as a career, I was also electing a closer relationship to Ruth, a friendship that lasted until her death in 1948. When I was away, she took on my varied responsibilities for other people; when she was away, I took on hers. We read and re-read each other's work; wrote poems in answer to poems, shared our hopes and worries about Boas, about Sapir, about anthropology, and in later years about the world. When she died, I had read everything she had ever written, and she had read everything I had ever written. No one else had, and no one else has" (BW, 113). This is a fitting tribute, but Ruth is not honored with the detailed attention Margaret's husbands receive. It is therefore interesting that Margaret found herself unable to continue writing past 1948 when her relationships with Gregory and Ruth ended and she felt very alone. She wrapped the book up with an account of being a grandmother and promised a sequel—which was never written.

Margaret returned to her role as Ruth's biographer in 1974, when she interwove a new series of biographical chapters into a collection of Ruth's papers appearing in a Columbia University series of "Leaders of Modern Anthropology."

The outlines of Margaret's later career are well known. She became the popular face of anthropology, a woman in public life who insistently explained Americans to themselves and contrasted them with others (Ruth's "Us/Not-Us" technique, to use Clifford Geertz's phrase). She was a world celebrity, with her distinctive red cape and forked cane, and she epitomized the modernist era with its commitment to social progress and liberation from the past.[12] Though the years after Ruth's death are not the subject of this book, it is tempting to steal a glance at Margaret and Ruth's circle in the later years and their continuing efforts to create satisfying patterns of work, love, and friendship.

Margaret, of course, always based herself at the American Museum of Natural History. Despite public recognition, she was not as successful in terms of her career as might have been expected. She was not promoted to full curator until 1964, did not serve as president of the American Anthropological Association until 1960, and resented the fact that despite her many honorary academic awards, Columbia never offered her anything more than an adjunct professorship.[13] Among her peers, it must be said, Mead did not have the reputation of a team player. She set her own agendas and utilized people where she could. Some were devoted to her, some feared her sharp tongue, and some resented her public profile. As an "elder statescreature" among the anthropologists, her role varied from the embarrassing to the inspiring.[14]

A grandmotherly figure to women's liberationists, Mead sometimes chafed at this position as she still regarded feminism with some disdain, relating it to her mother's generation. However, she was well aware of the forces that restricted women. "American men," she told James Baldwin while reminiscing about the opposition to women professors at Columbia, "have been taught that the point of being a man is that you're not a woman."[15] Jane Howard reports that Mead said in 1976, "We women are doing pretty well. . . . We're almost back to where we were in the twenties."[16] "The word out on the streets" though, a younger anthropologist recalled, was that Mead was not always supportive toward women.[17]

And what of her attitudes toward homosexuality and lesbianism? Though the 1960s and 1970s provided a more tolerant atmosphere than the

1950s, Mead continued to guard her reputation. A graduate student once asked her in public about Benedict's lesbianism and the nature of her own relationship with Benedict, only to be rebuffed, albeit graciously.[18] Lesbian women who knew Mead in the 1950s felt that she was uncomfortable with openly gay people.[19]

However, she did make liberal pronouncements about homosexuality from time to time. To the Washington Press Club Margaret once said that she thought "rigid heterosexuality is a perversion of nature."[20] In her *Redbook* column she wrote on the topic of bisexuality: "We shall not really succeed in discarding the straitjacket of our cultural beliefs about sexual choice if we fail to come to terms with the well-documented, normal human capacity to love members of both sexes."[21] Bisexuality, she argued, was common among those to whom "the cultivation of individuality has been a central value." When a cousin asked what she thought of homosexuals, Margaret replied that "they make the best companions in the world." And she once argued that an ideal society would consist of people who were homosexual in their youth, again in old age, and heterosexual in the middle of their lives," drawing unstated parallels with her own life.[22]

In this life the two strands of loving women and men continued to run together. Mary Catherine Bateson wrote, "Sometimes . . . I simply want to laugh aloud at Margaret's refusal of all forced choices. She kept Ruth's photograph on the mantel and Gregory's on her bureau. . . . She moved generously through a diversity of relationships, wounded and surprised when others responded with jealousy, and trusting to warmth and zest to make it right."[23] Margaret emphatically refused to be labeled, rejecting fixed categories of sexual orientation. She kept the nature of her relationship with Ruth from her daughter, but emphasized that love need not be exclusive: "She said to me as a child, 'You may someday find yourself feeling that you are in love with two people and think that that is impossible. If two people are really different you can indeed be in love with both.' "[24]

Margaret's intimates in later life included Marie Eichelberger, who continued to perform homemaking, secretarial, and maternal tasks for the friend to whom she had devoted her life. Of the men, Larry Frank remained close, as did Geoffrey Gorer, the gay friend with whom she shared gourmet meals and European holidays and whom she once considered marrying, perhaps for reasons of companionship and respectability. Later she had a male lover whom she met occasionally over a long period of time, but she was very secretive about his identity.

Her closest companion over the last third of her life was the younger anthropologist she had met during the war years, Rhoda Métraux, whom she lived with from 1955 until her death. Mead initially rented a floor of the apartment where Rhoda lived with her son and moved in with her teenage daughter, but she later purchased an apartment in the Beresford on Central Park West for the two women to share. It was known to some of their intimates that Mead and Métraux were lovers, although this may not have been a feature of their relationship across its whole span. In some ways it was a relationship primarily devoted to Mead's work. Intellectually, the two women were well suited. Métraux collaborated professionally with Mead, writing drafts of many of her popular articles, editing her work, and contributing loyally to her various enterprises. Once again, Mead's affections were not exclusive and the relationship was said to be a turbulent one. Rhoda was apparently jealous of some of Mead's associates, which may have contributed to their notorious quarrels. It remains for a future biographer to assess the role of this relationship in Mead's life; certainly, Mead shared her life with Métraux for longer than with anyone else. It also has to be said that Métraux, in her role as editor, sometimes acted as a censor, and quite a few of Mead's reminiscences for *Blackberry Winter* were excised at the hand of Métraux.[25] The younger generation in Mead's close circles included, of course, her daughter, Mary Catherine Bateson, and later a granddaughter. Jean Houston became a trusted friend in later years. Mead's own family thinned out with her mother's death in 1950, followed by her father in 1956. Her sister Priscilla committed suicide in 1959, her brother Richard died in 1975, and she was outlived only by Elizabeth.

Of Margaret's former husbands, Luther Cressman led a quiet life in Oregon, distinguished by his notable archeological discovery of the earliest dated artifact in the Americas, a nine thousand-year-old pair of sandals. Reo Fortune married his first love, Eileen Pope, and landed a job at Cambridge, where he owned a house he named *Bonde Mteko*. He occasionally contacted Margaret and remained on her Christmas list. After reading *Blackberry Winter* he wrote that he had "some bones to pick" over her account of the New Guinea triangle: "I don't know that you knew at last who you were" (MM, 1204). He died in 1979 after falling down the stairs in his college library.

After his separation from Margaret, Gregory Bateson had moved to California, where he initiated a divorce, married Betty Summer, and set up a conventional household, in marked contrast to the Perry Street ménage. They had a son, then twins who died soon after birth. This marriage deteriorated, Mary Catherine Bateson relating that the decline reflected his "darkly complicated feelings about women" and his dislike of "Momism."[26] He married a third time in 1960 and had one more child. Margaret continued to feel strongly bonded to him, explaining the connection as arising from their joint parental role (JH). Gregory became something of a cult figure in the sixties, his work appealing particularly to the younger generation.

Margaret kept in touch with the Ash Can Cats throughout her life; in fact, she remained in contact with nearly everyone who crossed her path. Léonie Adams's stature as a poet grew. She must have taken pleasure in sharing a Bollingen Prize with Louise Bogan, though she was never as well known as her friend. She recalled, as an elderly woman, hearing Margaret's "televised voice through an open door as she walk[ed] home from church along the quiet Sunday streets of a small town" (BW, 289).

Margaret had little to do with Ruth's former partners, though she did hear from them on matters connected with Ruth, as the earlier correspondence demonstrates. Ruth Valentine returned home to Pasadena after Benedict's death and went into private practice as a psychologist. She formed a close relationship with another woman, Gloria Gartz, who shared her home until she died in 1963 at age seventy-one. In her will she left the house and personal effects to her "friend" Gloria (MM, Q23). Val, with an estate of $370,000, was quite a wealthy woman, probably partly through the inheritance from Ruth, but she did not live lavishly, though she owned a Mercedes Benz. In her will she made bequests to a number of charities and gifts to friends, including five thousand dollars to Marie Eichelberger. The copyright income from Ruth's books was turned over to the Institute for Intercultural Studies. She left ten thousand dollars to Natalie Raymond and twenty thousand dollars to Margaret Mead and, had Gloria Gartz predeceased her, Nat would have inherited Val's house as well.[27]

Natalie Raymond traveled to Portugal after the war on a relief project organized by the Unitarians; she may well have been there when Ruth died. Margaret contacted her concerning the death (MM, L29). During the early sixties Natalie lived in Brooklyn and worked at the Vanguard Press where she made good friends, one of whom wrote, "I am sure she saw herself as a lesbian which was well known among her friends and colleagues . . . [although] we were more like characters in an Edith Wharton novel than those of today who tell and talk of everything. . . . She told me she had lived with Ruth Benedict in a manner or context which indicated to me that it was a lesbian relationship and which I felt was what she wanted me to understand."[28]

Natalie was "bright and funny."[29] In later years she moved back to the West Coast, ending her days near Carmel as a freelance writer, with a close woman friend who was probably her partner. Ruth's sister, Margery Freeman, also retired to Carmel. She and Natalie occasionally met and Margery was with Natalie when she died in the hospital after a heart attack in 1975, age 71. The news was passed to Margaret via Marie Eichelberger (MM, TR1); Gloria Gartz, Val's friend, also wrote to her (MM, Q23).

Louise Bogan, once a friend to both women, although she had been fonder of Ruth than Margaret, became recognized as one of the most significant American poets of the century. Women continued to fall for her, as May Sarton did in the fifties, and she continued to kindly rebuff admirers.[30] Ruth Bunzel, another friend in common, who had once loved Ruth Benedict, in later years shared her life with a woman partner, continuing to live in Greenwich Village and keeping up her active contributions to anthropology.[31]

Margaret worked energetically into old age at the task of fashioning American culture closer to her heart's desire.[32] In her mid–seventies she was diagnosed with pancreatic cancer but resisted the illness until the last possible moment. Shortly before her death in 1978 she awoke in distress, telling a friend who was at her hospital bed that "dead people," her mother, her father, and Ruth Benedict were there, trying to take her with them; she yelled at them to go away because she was not ready.[33]

Margaret Mead and Ruth Benedict have together left an enduring legacy to anthropology, the social sciences, and twentieth century thought. They shaped their lives with creativity and intelligence, making room for love, friendship, and anthropology. They sought equality for themselves and others in the spheres of gender, ethnicity, and sexuality. Both molded by, shaping, and resisting the imperatives of the twentieth century, they desired a world in which men and women could work together professionally, enjoy friendships with each other, and create family lives that did not sacrifice women's talents and abilities. Both women also experienced passionate love between women, valued women's friendship, and created kinship-like communities of women which sustained their work. A passage Ruth once wrote perhaps serves best as an epitaph for these two extraordinary women: "For what is the meaning of life except that by the discipline of thought and emotion, by living life to its fullest, we shall make of it always a more flexible instrument, accepting new relativities, divesting ourselves of traditional absolutes."[34]

# NOTES

## Introduction

1  Louise Bogan's description of Mead as "earthbound" is from *What the Woman Lived*, ed. Ruth Limmer, 261; the other quotation is from Caffrey's title, *Ruth Benedict: Stranger in This Land*.

2  From Rich, "Twenty-One Love Poems," in *The Fact of a Doorframe*.

3  George Stocking, "The Ethnographic Sensibility of the 1920s," in *The Ethnographer's Magic*, 282.

4  Benedict, *Race: Science and Politics*.

5  "Margaret Mead Today: Mother to the World," *Time*, 21 March 1969, 74–75.

6  Edward Said and various postmodernist writers have elaborated on this point. Edward Said, *Orientalism* (Harmondsworth: Penguin Books, 1985).

7  For an excellent account of progressive intellectual women of their day, see Rosenberg, *Beyond Separate Spheres*.

8  Mead, *Blackberry Winter*, 113.

9  Bateson, *With a Daughter's Eye*, 125.

10  Beauvoir, *Adieux*, 1.

11  *An Anthropologist at Work*, ed. Mead; Mead, *Ruth Benedict*; Mead, *BW*; Bateson, *With a Daughter's Eye*.

12  Howard, *Margaret Mead*; Modell, *Ruth Benedict*; Caffrey, *Ruth Benedict*. Only Bateson and Caffrey speak of the friendship as lesbian, though Howard refers to Benedict as a lesbian. Modell merely hints at such an interpretation. Darnell, *Edward Sapir*, has also proved an excellent source of biographical information.

13  Key sources in lesbian studies, women's studies, and feminist psychology include Rosenberg, *Beyond Separate Spheres*; Faderman, *Odd Girls and Twilight Lovers*; Miller, *Out of the Past*; Duberman et al., *Hidden from History*; Smith-Rosenberg, *Disorderly Conduct*; Solomon, *In the Company of Educated Women*; Brown and Gilligan, *Meeting at the Crossroads*.

14  "The Female World of Love and Ritual: Relations between Women in Nineteenth-Century America," in Smith-Rosenberg, *Disorderly Conduct*, 53–76. Detailed historical work on women's friendships in the twentieth-century period is yet to come, but work in women's studies on women's friendships today is helpful, nevertheless. See, for example, Raymond, *A Passion for Friends*.

15  Freeman. *Margaret Mead and Samoa*. When the book was reissued in Australia a decade later, it was given a new title to draw attention to the controversy: *Margaret Mead and the Heretic*.

16 Elizabeth Hardwick, interview in *Writers at Work: the Paris Review Interviews* 7, ed. Plimpton (New York, Penguin Books, 1988).

## The Punk

1  Mead, *Anthropologist at Work*, 4. Other descriptions by Mead of this meeting are in *Ruth Benedict*, BW, and JH.

2  Wanda Franken Neff, *We Sing Diana*, cited in Miller, *Out of the Past*, 61.

3  See also draft versions of BW, MM Papers; "Margaret Mead," in *A History of Psychology in Autobiography*, ed. Lindzey; JH; Bateson, *With a Daughter's Eye*; Howard, *Margaret Mead*. The issue of autobiography as a defense of self is also discussed in Jelinek, *The Tradition of Women's Autobiography*.

4  Heilbrun, *Writing a Woman's Life*; Heilbrun, "Margaret Mead and the Question of Woman's Biography" in *Hamlet's Mother and Other Women*. Bateson's *Composing a Life* is also of interest in relation to this topic.

5  The work of progressive women social scientists who graduated from the University of Chicago in the same era as Emily Fogg Mead is described fully in Fitzpatrick, *Endless Crusade*.

6  "Margaret Mead," in *History of Psychology in Autobiography*, ed. Lindzey, 301.

7  Ibid., 305.

8  Ibid., 298.

9  Brown and Gilligan, *Meeting at the Crossroads*, 2, 3. Other useful sources are Miller, *Toward a New Psychology of Women*, and *Women's Growth in Connection*, ed. Jordan et al.

10 "Margaret Mead," in *History of Psychology in Autobiography*, ed. Lindzey, 300.

11 Ibid., 308.

12 Howard, *Margaret Mead*, 32, quoting Mead's 1913 diary, MM.

13 Brown and Gilligan, *Meeting at the Crossroads*, 53.

14 "Margaret Mead," in *History of Psychology in Autobiography*, ed. Lindzey, 308.

15 See Solomon, *In the Company of Educated Women*.

16 Quoted in Howard, *Margaret Mead*, 38.

17 Mary Catherine Bateson, telephone interview by author, 9 November 1994.

18 Solomon, *In the Company of Educated Women*, 98.

19 Alfred C. Kinsey et al., "Homosexual Responses and Contacts," chap. 11 in *Sexual Behavior in the Human Female*, (Philadelphia: Saunders, 1948).

20 Faderman, *Odd Girls and Twilight Lovers*, 63. For more on Katharine Bement Davis, see Fitzpatrick, *Endless Crusade*.

21 Faderman, *Odd Girls and Twilight Lovers*, 31.

22 Ibid., 51.

23 Ibid., 30.

24 Howard, *Margaret Mead*.

25 Ibid., 40.

26 For information on the college population of this time see Solomon, *In the Company of Educated Women*.

27 Alison Lurie, *The Language of Clothes*, quoted in Howard, *Margaret Mead*, 41.

28 Howard, *Margaret Mead*, 44, 45.

29 Caffrey, *Stranger in This Land*, 190.

30 Howard, *Margaret Mead*, 48.

31 Ibid., 47.

32  See Cook, *Eleanor Roosevelt*, vol. 1, 1884–1933, 294.

33  Howard, *Margaret Mead*, 50.

34  Ibid.

35  For discussions of heterosexuality and homosexuality during this era, see especially Faderman, *Odd Girls and Twilight Lovers*, Caroll Smith-Rosenberg, "Discourses of Sexuality and Subjectivity: the New Woman, 1870–1936" in *Hidden from History: Reclaiming the Gay and Lesbian Past*, ed. Duberman, Vicinus, and Chauncey; and Miller, *Out of the Past*.

36  Cook, "Women Alone Stir My Imagination."

37  Howard, *Margaret Mead*, 50, 44.

38  Bateson, *With a Daughter's Eye*, 24.


## 2. Two Worlds

1   Cited in Modell, *Patterns of a Life*, 145.

2   Mead, *Ruth Benedict*, 3.

3   Modell, *Patterns of a Life*, 212.

4   Miller, *Out of the Past*, 60.

5   The story of Ruth's love for Naomi is, of course, one of the most poignant accounts of love between women in the Old Testament, and the story of Job and his tribulations has an unerring pull for the melancholy.

6   From a 1918 article Benedict wrote for the *Vassar Quarterly*, cited in Caffrey, *Stranger in This Land*, 34.

7   Brown and Gilligan, *Meeting at the Crossroads*.

8   For more about Mabel Dodge Luhan, see Faderman, *Odd Girls and Twilight Lovers*, and Eric Homberger, "John Reed, Mabel Dodge and Sexual Politics in New York," in Mulvey and Simons, *New York: City as Text*.

9   Caffrey, *Stranger in this Land*, has been particularly helpful for information about Vassar College, Benedict's time there, and contemporary debates about education for girls.

10  In the "Story of My Life" (*AW*, 109), Benedict refers to a girl she knew when she was fourteen who was "one of the first of those people who have been romantically devoted to me."

11  Caffrey, *Stranger in This Land*, 63.

12  Pater is quoted in Caffrey, *Stranger in this Land*, 52.

13  For more information about Benedict's social work "career," see Modell, *Patterns of a Life*, and Caffrey, *Stranger in This Land*.

14  See Richard Handler, "Vigorous Male and Aspiring Female: Poetry, Personality and Culture in Edward Sapir and Ruth Benedict," in Stocking, *Malinowski, Rivers, Benedict and Others: Essays in Culture and Personality*, 129.

15  See Tomalin, *The Life and Death of Mary Wollstonecraft*; Marie Mitchell Olesen Urbanski, "Margaret Fuller: Feminist Writer and Revolutionary"; and Liz Stanley, "Olive Schreiner: New Women, Free Women, All Women," in Spender, *Feminist Theorists*.

16  Modell, *Patterns of a Life*, 97.

17  Bernard, *Academic Women*, 24.

18  Modell, *Patterns of a Life*, 98–99.

19  Mead, *Ruth Benedict*, 18.

20  For information on Elsie Clews Parsons, see Zumwalt, *Wealth and Rebellion*, which provides a more detailed account than a previous biography, and Hare, *A Woman's Quest*

*for Science.* Desley Deacon's splendid and particularly sympathetic *Elsie Clews Parsons: Inventing Modern Life* arrived too late to inform this account of Parsons.

## 3. Companions in Harness

1 This quotation from Rossiter, *Women Scientists in America,* 129, applies equally to women in nonscience professions. See also Rosenberg, *Beyond Separate Spheres,* and Fitzpatrick, *Endless Crusade* for information about women social scientists; for information about women anthropologists, see Nancy Parezo, "Conclusions: The Beginning of the Quest" in *Hidden Scholars: Women Anthropologists and the Native Southwest, 1880–1980,* ed. Parezo. Further information on professional women and the feminist movement during this period can be found in Cott, *The Grounding of Modern Feminism* and Matthews, *The Rise of Public Woman.* Rosenberg, *Divided Lives,* is a useful overview of the historical background to women's lives.

2 Bender, *New York Intellect,* is a useful source on the relationship of Columbia University to the city. For a picture of the city itself and its intellectual life in this period, see Douglas, *Terrible Honesty: Mongrel Manhattan in the 1920s.*

3 An especially insightful essay on Boas is George W. Stocking Jr., "Anthropology as Kulturkampf: Science and Politics in the Career of Franz Boas," in *The Ethnographer's Magic and Other Essays in the History of Anthropology;* Other works consulted include Hyatt, *Franz Boas, Social Activist;* Voget, *A History of Ethnology;* Darnell, *Edward Sapir;* Virginia Yans-McLaughlin, "Science, Democracy, and Ethics: Mobilizing Culture and Personality for World War 11" in *Malinowski, Rivers, Benedict and Others,* ed. Stocking; E. Torrey, *Freudian Fraud;* and biographical works on Mead and Benedict.

4 Yans-McLaughlin, "Science, Democracy, and Ethics," 186.

5 Darnell, *Edward Sapir,* 9.

6 Caffrey, *Stranger in this Land,* 99.

7 On the role of Elsie Clews Parsons at Columbia see Louise Lamphere, "Feminist Anthropology: the Legacy of Elsie Clews Parsons" in *Women Writing Culture,* ed. Behar and Gordon; Zumwalt, *Wealth and Rebellion;* Hare, *A Woman's Quest for Science;* Deacon, *Elsie Clews Parsons.*

8 Cole, " 'One Does Not Get As Much From the Girls,' " 5.

9 Parezo, "Conclusion: The Beginning of the Quest," in *Hidden Scholars* refers to Columbia as welcoming to women; this discussion is further informed by Rosenberg, *Beyond Separate Spheres,* and Solomon, *In the Company of Educated Women.*

10 Rosenberg, *Beyond Separate Spheres,* 239.

11 Rossiter, in *Women Scientists in America,* examined all biographies in this comprehensive biographical dictionary but warns that criteria for being listed there have excluded some women scientists.

12 Rosenberg, *Beyond Separate Spheres.*

13 Parezo, "Conclusion," in *Hidden Scholars,* 352.

14 George W. Stocking Jr., "Ideas and Institutions in American Anthropology: Thoughts Toward a History of the Interwar Years" in *The Ethnographer's Magic,* 125.

15 Voget, *A History of Ethnology.*

16 Benedict, *Patterns of Culture,* 21–22.

17 Deacon, *Elsie Clews Parsons,* 258, provides information which makes it clear that if anything, Reichard had the stronger claim on the position.

18 Work on the concordance was tedious, and the task was passed over some years later to a

person who was never to complete it, much to Parsons's frustration. See Zumwalt, *Wealth and Rebellion*.

19  Caffrey, *Stranger in This Land*, 112.

20  Goldfrank, *Notes on an Undirected Life*, 35.

21  Arthur P. Noyes and Lawrence C. Kolb, *Modern Clinical Psychiatry* (Philadelphia: W. B. Saunders, 1963), 84.

22  Originally published in *Palms* 3, no. 6 (1926): 164; reprinted in *AW*, 487.

23  The best source of information about Edward Sapir is Darnell's biography, *Edward Sapir*.

24  See Phillips-Jones, *Mentors and Protegés*, for a discussion of the typical stages of a mentoring relationship.

25  See Rosenberg, *Beyond Separate Spheres*.

26  "Margaret Mead" in *History of Psychology in Autobiography*, ed. Lindzey, 311.

## 4. I Shall Lie Once With Beauty Breast to Breast

1  Mead, *Sex and Temperament in Three Primitive Societies*, 300.

2  Bateson, *With a Daughter's Eye*.

3  Bateson, telephone interview by author, November 1994.

4  Mead's thesis research is mentioned in Hamilton Cravens, *The Triumph of Evolution*, 235. The book provides the broader context for the debate.

5  Jane Dunn, *A Very Close Conspiracy: Vanessa Bell and Virginia Woolf* (London: Jonathan Cape, 1990).

6  Miller, *Out of the Past*.

7  With what may have been a meaningful mistake, Luther also recalled that they visited Ruth and Stanley Benedict on their honeymoon. Other evidence suggests that this visit occurred later, shortly before Margaret left for Samoa.

8  Howard, *Margaret Mead*, 62.

9  For more about Ellis's influence, see Chesler, *Woman of Valor*; Mead's reference was perhaps to this passage from Ellis's *The Art of Love* (cited in Edward M. Brecher, *The Sex Researchers* [London: Panther, 1972], 70): "She is, on the physical side, inevitably the instrument of love; it must be his hand and his bow which evoke the music."

10  Mead, *Male and Female*, 23.

11  See Christina Simmons, "Modern Sexuality and the Myth of Victorian Repression," in *Gender and American History Since 1890*, ed. Melosh.

12  Solomon, *In the Company of Educated Women*, 138.

13  For more information on Bogan, see Frank, *Louise Bogan*; Bogan, *What the Woman Lived*, ed. Limmer; Bogan, *Journey Round My Room*, ed. Limmer.

14  Wilson, *The Fifties*, 519.

15  Bogan, *What the Woman Lived*, 144.

16  Bogan, *What the Woman Lived*, 26.

17  Frank, *Louise Bogan*, 63.

18  Bogan, *The Blue Estuaries: Poems: 1923–1968* (New York: Noonday Press, 1968).

19  Virginia Yans, conversation with author, New York City, October, 1996; she had this story from an interview she conducted with Luther Cressman. It was unclear to her whether Luther knew about Margaret's lesbian attachments.

20  Mead, *Ruth Benedict*, 6.

21  Years later Margaret's sister Priscilla committed suicide and Margaret was the one who found her.

22  Mead, *Ruth Benedict*, 10.

23  Frank, *Louise Bogan*, 55.

24  Modell, *Patterns of a Life*, 15.

25  Bateson, *With a Daughter's Eye*, 125.

26  Originally published in *Palms* 3, no. 6 (1926):167; reprinted in *AW*, 486.

27  Houston, *The Search for the Beloved*, 122–23.

28  Jean Houston, telephone conversation with author, November 1994.

29  Modell, *Patterns of a Life*, 148.

30  Kammen, in *Mystic Chords of Memory*, 389, refers to Benedict's work in the context of "Puritan-bashing" of the 1920s.

31  "Our Task is Laughter," originally published in *Palms* 3, no. 6 (1926): 168; reprinted in *AW*, 167–68.

32  "For the Hour After Love," *AW*, 480.

33  See "Withdrawal," *AW*, 482; "Moth Wing," *AW*, 488; and "Burial," *AW*, 483.

34  *Palms* 3, no. 7 (1926): 166; the version quoted is from *AW*, 167–68.

35  Quoted in Modell, *Patterns of a Life*, 156.

36  *Palms* 3, no. 6 (1926): 166; reprinted in *AW*, 170.

37  *Palms* 3, no. 6 (1926): 169; reprinted in *AW*, 486.

38  *New Republic*, 19 October 1932, 255; reprinted in *AW*, 89.

## 5. I Hear the Wind at Your Heart

1  Mead, *Letters from the Field 1925–1975*, 8.

2  See, for example, Crunden, *From Self to Society*; Kammen, *Mystic Chords of Memory*; Richard Handler, "Vigorous Male and Aspiring Female: Poetry, Personality and Culture in Edward Sapir and Ruth Benedict," *Malinowski, Rivers, Benedict and Others: Essays in Culture and Personality*, ed. Stocking; George Stocking, "The Ethnographic Sensibility of the 1920s and the Dualism of the Anthropological Tradition," in *The Ethnographer's Magic*; White, *Social Thought in America: the Revolt Against Formalism*; Rosenberg, *Beyond Separate Spheres*.

3  Handler, "Vigorous Male and Aspiring Female," 138.

4  The exchange of letters between Sapir and Benedict which are referred to in the discussion that follows took place from the spring of 1924 until the end of the year, unless otherwise indicated. A typescript version made for Mead's *Anthropologist at Work* is in the Sapir family papers (SF).

5  Modell, in *Patterns of a Life*, argues that Benedict, in her frequent use of water imagery, was inclined to portray heterosexuality as out of control (e.g., the imagery of "floodtide") and love between women as quieter and more self-contained, as in the imagery of still pools. My interpretation differs.

6  For a discussion of homoeroticism in women's writing, see Joanna Russ, "To Write 'Like a Woman': Transformations of Identity in the Work of Willa Cather," in *Historical, Literary and Erotic Aspects of Lesbianism*, ed. Kehoe.

7  Perry, *Psychiatrist of America: The Life of Harry Stack Sullivan*, 249.

8  See Stocking, "Ethnographic Sensibility of the 1920s."

9  The following sources provided information on the Southwest and the fieldwork of Parsons, Bunzel, and Benedict: *Hidden Scholars*, ed. Parezo; Zumwalt, *Wealth and Rebellion*; David M. Fawcett and Teri McLuhan, "Ruth Leah Bunzel," in *Women Anthropologists: Selected Biographies*; ed. Gacs et al.; Ruth Bunzel and Charles Wagley, videotaped interview, 1983 Smithsonian Institution Human Archives collection; Margaret Ann Hardin, "Zuñi Potters and 'The Pueblo Potter:' The Contributions of Ruth Bunzel," in *Hidden Scholars*,

ed. Parezo; Barbara A. Babcock, " 'Not in the Absolute Singular:' Re-reading Ruth Benedict," in *Women Writing Culture*, ed. Behar and Gordon; Caffrey, *Stranger in This Land*;
Modell, *Patterns of a Life*; Deacon, *Elsie Clews Parsons*.

10  Stocking, "Ethnographic Sensibility of the 1920s," 291.

11  Mabel Dodge Luhan quoted in Zumwalt, *Wealth and Rebellion*, 239–40; D. H. Lawrence
quoted in Stocking, "Ethnographic Sensibility of the 1920s," 291.

12  Zumwalt, *Wealth and Rebellion*, 180.

13  Ibid., 248.

14  Ruth Bunzel quoted in Hardin, "Zuñi Potters and 'The Pueblo Potter,' " in *Hidden Scholars*,
ed. Parezo, 260.

15  Ibid, 261.

16  Ruth Bunzel quoted in Caffrey, *Stranger in This Land*, 262.

17  See Darnell, *Edward Sapir*, 173; Zuñi is reproduced in AW, 88..

18  Alfred Kroeber quoted in Babcock, " 'Not in the Absolute Singular,' " 112.

19  Benedict, *Zuñi Mythology*, cited in Babcock, " 'Not in the Absolute Singular,' " 113.

20  Ruth Bunzel quoted in Modell, *Patterns of a Life*, 175.

21  Ruth Bunzel and Charles Wagley, videotaped interview. See note 9 above.

22  Benedict, *Patterns of Culture*, 42–43.

23  Ruth Benedict, entries on "Folklore" and "Magic," *Encyclopedia of the Social Sciences*, 1933,
cited in Babcock, " 'Not in the Absolute Singular,' " 112, 113.

24  Quoted in Howard, *Margaret Mead*, 66.

25  Howard, *Margaret Mead*, 72.

26  Extraordinarily, the sexologist Havelock Ellis, whom Margaret admired, once said that
homosexuals favored the color green, whereas heterosexuals preferred blue and red.
Ellis also made a distinction between "true" inverts and women who were not con-
genitally inverted but who could "develop the germs of it" in a "spurious imitation"
perhaps inspired by a "crush" on or a "seduction" by a woman with a "congenital
anomaly." Such anomalies occurred "with special frequency in women of high intelligence, who voluntarily or involuntarily, influence others." Cited in Neil Miller, *Out of the
Past*, 20.

27  Bogan to Benedict, 1 July 1925, Louise Bogan Papers, Box 10, Amherst College Archives
and Special Collections.

28  Howard, *Margaret Mead*, 67, and Darnell, *Edward Sapir*, 183–88.

29  This comment about Ruth's worst day would have appeared puzzling without an explanation of the emotional involvement between the two women; the remark was omitted
from the published version of *Blackberry Winter*.

30  In the earlier *Anthropologist at Work*, Mead does give the correct details of the journey in an
endnote, 552.

31  Bateson, *With a Daughter's Eye*, 125. Another version of this story, from someone who
knew Sapir, suggests that Mead and Benedict plotted about which one of them was to
seduce him. This sounds unlikely, though, and perhaps the original source was Sapir
himself, who may have suffered from wounded pride. To make matters more difficult,
we have no way of knowing that Benedict and Sapir were not lovers. Some passages seem
to have been excised from the copies of Sapir's letters to Benedict which Mead had typed
when she was preparing *An Anthropologist at Work*. I have not managed to establish the
whereabouts of the originals. My best guess is that, although Benedict was romantically
attracted to Sapir, their friendship did not lead to an affair.

32  The reference to the Phi Beta Kappa key is in BW, 158. My guess is that it was Benedict's,
as elsewhere Mead mentions that early on she lost Luther's key (BW draft).

## 6. In Coral Oceans Lovelier than Any Still Midnight

1   Mead, LF, 19. Other sources consulted on Mead in Samoa are BW; Howard, *Margaret Mead*; Freeman, *Margaret Mead and Samoa* (recently republished with a new preface as *Margaret Mead and the Heretic*); Holmes, *Quest for the Real Samoa*; and Orans, *Not Even Wrong*. Mead's original fieldwork materials in the Margaret Mead Papers were also consulted, as were her field bulletins and other correspondence from the period.

2   Freeman, *Margaret Mead and Samoa*, 66.

3   Margaret Mead, "Field Work in the Pacific Islands, 1925–1967" in *Women in the Field: Anthropological Experiences*, ed. Peggy Golde, 325.

4   The Samoan letters between Margaret Mead and Ruth Benedict are held by Mead's daughter, Mary Catherine Bateson; extracts were published in Mead, *An Anthropologist at Work* (AW). Jean Houston has read the letters from Benedict to Mead and described them as love letters (phone interview with the author, November, 1994).

5   Bogan to Benedict, 25 August 1925, Louise Bogan Papers, Box 10, Amherst College Archives and Special Collections.

6   Frank Heimans, *Margaret Mead and Samoa* (Sydney: Cinetel Productions, 1988), film.

7   Boas to Parsons, quoted in Zumwalt, *Wealth and Rebellion*, 162.

8   Freeman, *Margaret Mead and Samoa* (reprinted as *Margaret Mead and the Heretic*); Freeman, "Fa'apua'a Fa'amu and Margaret Mead," *American Anthropologist* 91, no. 4 (1989), 1017–22; Frank Heimans, *Margaret Mead and Samoa*.

9   See Derek Freeman, interview by Nikki Barrowclough, "Sex, Lies and Anthropology," *The Australian*, 9 March 1996; ironically Boas, too, was censured for criticizing anthropologists following World War I.

10  Bradd Shore, interview by Phil Donahue, the "Phil Donahue Show," 1982, transcript 03183, Multimedia Program Productions.

11  David Williamson, *The Heretic*.

12  Derek Freeman, interview by Jane Howard, 1983, Jane Howard Papers.

13  Freeman, interview with Barrowclough, "Sex, Lies and Anthropology."

14  Freeman, interview by Howard.

15  Freeman, interview by Barrowclough, "Sex, Lies and Anthropology." There is a similar report in Holmes, *The Quest for the Real Samoa*. Ironically, when Freeman met Mead in Australia (and Mead was well aware of his criticisms, for they had been circulated for many years) he made a blunder. In the Barrowclough interview he says self-critically that when Mead asked him in a public setting why he had not left his thesis out for her to look at overnight, he replied, "Because I was afraid you might ask me to stay the night."

16  Quoted by anonymous informant, interview with author, Amherst, Massachusetts, December 1994.

17  Mead, "Field Work in the Pacific Islands, 1925–1967," in *Women in the Field*, ed. Golde, 322.

18  Howard, *Margaret Mead*, 85–86; Holmes, *Quest for the Real Samoa*, 8–9. Mead once commented, "where men may chafe under continence enforced by the exigencies of field work, what women miss deeply are strong personal relationships and tenderness" (Mead, "Field Work in the Pacific Islands," 323). One anthropologist told Jane Howard that "We were always leaping to her defense if she was accused of dallying with the natives. . . . She was the original prude" (Howard). However, Derek Freeman apparently has sworn testimony from a Samoan man that he had an affair with Mead during her stay there. This may be correct, though given that Freeman points to the pleasure Samoans have sometimes taken in "recreational lying," the veracity of the secondhand testimony

is difficult to assess. This affair is recreated in David Williamson's play, "The Heretic," and Freeman's first public reference to the sworn testimony was made on the "Brian Edwards Show," New Zealand National Radio, 28 February 1998.

19 I am grateful to Serge Tcherkezoff for a greater understanding of sexual terms in the Samoan language. See Serge Tcherkezoff, "Beyond the Mead-Freeman Controversy: Translating Sex and Gender Between Samoan and Western Cultures" (paper presented at the University of Waikato, Hamilton, New Zealand, 16 August 1996).

20 Also see Orans, *Not Even Wrong*, esp. 50–54.

21 Quoted in Howard, *Margaret Mead*, 83.

22 Margaret's claim that the girls of Ta'u spoke only Samoan has been disputed. She can certainly be taken to task for claiming, in *Coming of Age in Samoa*, that "there were no young people on the island who spoke English" (262), when, as Orans points out, her field notes indicate that several of her female adolescents had some facility and so did some of the young men and adults. Orans argues that Mead probably obtained most of her interview material from young girls using English, secondhand informants, or an interpreter. He makes this inference because her notes are mainly in English, whereas many other of her field materials are transcribed directly in Samoan. I believe this is an unwarranted assumption, given various comments of Mead's, such as those in her letters to Boas. Clearly, she did use her admittedly imperfect Samoan in conversation with her young friends, which is confirmed by the numerous letters from them to her, written to her in Samoan (MM, N2).

As to the time Mead spent on her investigation, there appears to be some confusion about the date of Mead's departure from Samoa. In *Blackberry Winter* she says she left in June, but the evidence suggests that she left Ta'u in mid–April and Pago Pago at the end of April or early May. In *Coming of Age* Mead gives confusing and inconsistent information about her stay. In the acknowledgments she thanks the Holts for giving her a home for four months; she later refers to nine months spent in Samoa (10), and the reader could be forgiven for imagining that she was referring to fieldwork on Ta'u, since she is writing about the collecting of data on the girls there. In an appendix (260) she states that she spent six months in Ta'u. It seems most likely that she spent a little over five months in Ta'u and possibly only four months with the Holts, since she visited villages and at one point went to neighboring islands. Mead's plans for leaving Ta'u were unclear at the beginning of her stay and any slight errors in her dating are understandable. Undoubtedly, Mead was sensitive about the length of time she spent on the field trip, because she had heard that while she was in Samoa Malinowski in the U.S. "had gone out of his way to tell everyone that my field trip to Samoa would come to nothing, that nine months was too short a time to accomplish any serious research, and that I probably would not even learn the language" (BW, 160). Mead thought that Sapir may have put Malinowski up to this (JH).

23 Tcherkezoff, "Beyond the Mead-Freeman Controversy."

24 As an aside, Edward Sapir, through the well-known Sapir-Whorf hypothesis, is associated with the opposite view, that language constitutes experience, in other words, that the power of naming permits or prohibits the experience of phenomena. Interestingly, in one of the two extant letters from Sapir to Mead, he refers to some assertion she had made about *tabula rasa*, the idea that children arrive into the world as blank slates ready to be written on by experience. Sapir goes on to joke, "Of course you are right about tabula rasa and the rest of it. 'Experience' is mostly imagination anyway, as Ruth can tell you" (MM, Q11).

25 Fa'apua'a's remarks were translated from Samoan and appear in Freeman, "Fa'apua'a

Fa'amu and Margaret Mead," 1020. A filmed version of extracts from the interview can be found in the Heimans Film, *Margaret Mead and Samoa*.

26  Heimans, *Margaret Mead and Samoa*.

27  See Lola Romanucci-Ross, "Telling Tales of the South Pacific," in *Anthropological Poetics*, ed. Ivan Brady (Savage, Md: Rowman and Littlefield, 1991).

28  Orans, *Not Even Wrong*.


## 7. Never Break a Date with a Girl for a Man?

1  Background material on Reo Fortune and his family is derived largely from BW; Howard, *Margaret Mead*; and family correspondence in the Reo Fortune Papers.

2  Information on Malinowski from Stocking, *The Ethnographer's Magic*; Powdermaker, *Stranger and Friend*; Kuper, *Anthropology and Anthropologists*.

3  Stocking, "Maclay, Kubary, Malinowski: Archetypes from the Dreamtime of Anthropology," in *The Ethnographer's Magic*, 271.

4  Powdermaker, *Stranger and Friend*, 35; Lutkehaus, " 'She Was Very Cambridge.' "

5  Bronislaw Malinowski, *A Diary in the Strict Sense of the Term* (New York: Harcourt Brace & World, 1967); Margaret Mead defended him, saying, "the tendency to blow off steam and condemn everyone roundly in private is a good safety valve and not a suitable topic for moralistic recriminations" ("Field Work in the Pacific Islands, 1925–1967," in *Women in the Field*, ed. Golde, 324.)

6  Howard, *Margaret Mead*, 98.

7  Fortune, *The Mind in Sleep*, 79–80; a set of earlier interpretations of this dream by Reo is in Box 18, RF Papers and include marginal notes such as "not taking hasty action" and "not censoring me."

8  Mead, "Bisexuality: What's it All About?", Redbook, January 1975, 29–31.

9  Bogan to Benedict, 16 Dec. 1926, Louise Bogan Papers, Box 10, Folder 21, Amherst College Archives and Special Collections.

10  Quoted in Howard, *Margaret Mead*, 100.

11  Mead, *Ruth Benedict*, 34.


## 8. The Deviant and the Normal

1  See Belenky et al., *Women's Ways of Knowing*. Women's collaborative work in relationships has recently been explored in Chadwick and de Courtivron, *Significant Others*, and Mead's daughter, Mary Catherine Bateson, covers similar territory in her classic, *Composing a Life*.

2  See Anne Higonnet, "Myths of Creation: Camille Claudel and Auguste Rodin," in *Significant Others*, ed. Chadwick and de Courtivon. Janet Malcolm, *The Silent Woman: Sylvia Plath and Ted Hughes* (London: Picador, 1994), acidly demonstrates the dangers of biography. Bair's wonderful biography, *Simone de Beauvoir*, considers the element of propaganda Beauvoir introduced into her accounts of her relationship with Sartre.

3  There is useful material in Steiner, *Notebooks of the Mind*.

4  Ruth Benedict remembered the brilliance of Sapir's courses in the obituary she wrote for *American Anthropologist*. For an account of these influences, see Barnouw, *Culture and Personality*.

5  See Torgovnick, *Gone Primitive*.

6  See Rossiter, *Women Scientists in America*.

7  Natalie Woodbury and Richard Woodbury, interview with author, Amherst, Mass., November 1996.

8   A version of this poem was published in Poetry 35, no. 5 (1930), 253.

9   It has already been argued that Derek Freeman is wrong in claiming that Mead's views on Samoan sexuality resulted from her being hoaxed. Nevertheless, the validity of Mead's portrait of Samoa remains a matter of contention. Before Freeman introduced the hoax claim, the so-called Mead-Freeman debate revolved around questions of accuracy. Was Mead correct in showing Samoa as a carefree, sensual society relatively free of conflict, where adolescence was smooth and untroubled and adolescent girls sexually uninhibited? Forests of paper have probably been devoted to this academic and popular debate.

Before Freeman's attack, Mead's work was spoken of disdainfully by Sapir, who had ulterior motives, and at times by Malinowski, who tended to disparage anyone he considered a threat. Some anthropologists criticized Mead's ethnographic assertions less than her writing style (Nancy C. Lutkehaus, "Margaret Mead and the 'Rustling-of-the-Wind-in-the-Palm-Trees School' of Ethnographic Writing," in Women Writing Culture, ed. Behar and Gordon). Mead, uneasy with the early reception of her work, once commented to Gregory Bateson that though she was "hyper sensitive" to any suggestion of flaws, she could understand his point that some of her anecdotes had "a fictional air" because of "my telling whole events without placing myself somewhere—in a canoe, listening from my house, etc." (MM, B14) Indeed, the opening chapter of Coming of Age is a composite, novelistic portrait of village life, not a true record of an actual day in Samoa.

Martin Orans, a recent Mead scholar, has pointed out that in assessing her work one should bear in mind the "cognitive slippage" that clouds the issue. First, the public image of Mead's work is an oversimplification—Coming of Age is caricatured more often than it is actually read. Then Mead's conclusions are sometimes belied by the details of her book. She describes jealousy and violence, punishments for losing virginity, the value put on the taupou's virginity, and many other points that contrast uneasily with her general conclusions about sexual freedom and ease of transition through adolescence. Nor does the book itself do justice to the complexity of Mead's field materials; here, Martin Orans's close examination of the field materials has been most useful. Finally, there is the extent to which Mead's Samoan experience may have been influenced by her own preconceptions (Orans, Not Even Wrong).

It could be argued that it is not possible to make an authoritative assessment of Coming of Age—nor, probably, of any of the classic works of anthropology. Lowell Holmes carried out a restudy on Ta'u some thirty years after Mead and concluded that her "methodological skills were exceptionally good for one of her age and experience" and that she was "essentially correct in her characterization and conclusions about coming of age in Samoa" (Quest for the Real Samoa, 173), even though he found numerous minor errors, took issue with some of her interpretations, and argued that she overgeneralized. Both Holmes and Orans suggest that Mead did not benefit from her association with Ruth Benedict who encouraged generalization in her attempts to fit whole cultures under the rubric of particular patterns. Orans, like Holmes, finds that Mead's conclusions go further than her data, but on the whole he does not fault the latter. The argument about overgeneralizing probably holds, though placing the blame on Benedict may arise from a misunderstanding of her interpretive approach. Throughout her work Mead was fond of making "points," as she used to call her insights. This feature is probably endemic to any attempt to characterize cultures and similar criticisms could be made of other classic works.

Another point often raised, with some validity, is that Mead, as a woman, probably elicited different responses from her informants than a man would have done. Freeman's experience of Samoa was largely in the company of high-status adult men. The question of whether Ta'u in the 1920s might have differed in some respects from the rest of Samoa, and whether Samoa as a whole has changed radically since the 1920s, has also been thoroughly debated. Also, it has been argued, no doubt justly, that sexism played a role in Mead's being singled out for attack. Would the work of any anthropologist of her era fare any better under such careful reexamination? Certainly, where restudies have been done (and they have been few and far between), original studies have been found wanting; this reflects problems with anthropological methods rather than careless researchers (see Stocking, *The Ethnographer's Magic*).

Perhaps the most underrepresented in the whole debate have been Samoan voices, especially those of Samoan women. Fa'apua'a Fa'amu has been quoted, but suspicion remains that her testimony was motivated by factors other than questions of scientific accuracy. But certainly Samoans are usually conscious of the restrictions placed on young women, both today and in the past. A New Zealand Samoan, Anne-Marie Tupuola, who has researched contemporary sexual attitudes without particular reference to Margaret Mead, tells us that premarital sex is frowned on and male relatives often discipline female sexuality. Moreover, making pronouncements about women in Samoan culture is traditionally the preserve of older women; for a younger woman to do so could be a violation of cultural codes ("Learning Sexuality: Young Samoan Women," *Women's Studies Journal* 12, no. 2 (1996), 60–75). Perhaps the last word should go to Sia Figiel, a young Samoan novelist who recently published her view of growing up in Samoa in *Where We Once Belonged*, a book full of verve and humor, which includes the following passage on the Mead-Freeman controversy:

"How did the palagi woman [Mead] know that we do 'it' a lot?"

"You do 'it' a lot, not we," said Moa to Lili.

"Malo Moa!" I laughed.

"And what about the palagi man [Freeman]" I asked. "What about him? How does he know that we . . . I mean, that people like Lili *don't* do it a lot? Ha!"

"I wouldn't know," said Moa. "Maybe he was talking to someone like Fauakafe, who'll be a spinster for the already rest of her life . . . or to some matai, like your father, who are too embarrassed to tell palagis where their hundreds of children come from" (204).

Mead was not a "bad scientist," and *Coming of Age in Samoa* can still lay claim to the status of a classic, albeit a flawed one. The discipline of cultural anthropology remains robust and so must Mead's reputation. In a postmodern age, there should be no difficulty in acknowledging that personal and cultural biases inevitably permeate scientific investigation. Fraud or incompetence is a different matter, and Mead was guilty of neither.

10  Douglas, *Terrible Honesty*.

11  Haddon cited in Nancy Lutkehaus, "Margaret Mead and the 'Rustling-of-the-Wind-in-the-Palm-Trees-School.' "

12  Such men are known as *fa'afafine*, which loosely translates as transsexual, a term well known to those familiar with Samoan life but not used by Mead.

13  According to Wendy Cowling, (conversation with author, May 1994), modern commentators disagree with Mead on this point.

14  Interestingly, Suzanne Raitt (*Vita and Virginia*) says that the island figures as "a crucial image for lesbian writing after Sappho" (95) and refers to Vita Sackville-West's *Challenge*, a novel of the '20s, which declares: "An island! and that had slipped the leash of continents, forsworn solidarity, cut adrift from security and prudence!"

15  Limmer, *What the Woman Lived*, 35.

16  Cited in Howard, *Margaret Mead*, 360–61.

17  Chesler, *Woman of Valor*, 421.

18 Howard, *Margaret Mead*, 102.

19 In a footnote in *AW* (563), Mead says that in 1941 Benedict made a selection of her poetry which she wrote out by hand and gave to Mead. It is not entirely clear whether Benedict intended the dedication, with its accompanying poem, "Haws when they blossom," to be published.

20 Howard, *Margaret Mead*, 108.

21 Wanda Fraiken Neff, *We Sing Diana*, quoted in Caffrey, *Ruth Benedict*, 191. Mead may have known Wanda Fraiken Neff at Barnard, since there is a reference in one of her dream interpretations to "Miss Fraiken, the domesticated intellectual female" (MM, A21). Other sources for gay and lesbian culture are: George Chauncey, *Gay New York*; Lillian Faderman, "Love Between Women in 1928," in *Odd Girls and Twilight Lovers*; Miller, *Out of the Past*.

22 Bateson, *With A Daughter's Eye*, 124. Margaret Mead was not entirely receptive to her daughter's confidences: "That night . . . she disconcerted me by turning from my confidences about tenderness and exploration to a discussion of what it would have meant for her professional life if I had been involved in a scandal" (124).

23 Léonie Adams, "Those Not Elect," in *The Things that Matter*, ed. J. Neuberger, 252.

24 Cited in Caffrey, *Stranger in This Land*, 201.

25 Howard, *Margaret Mead*, 104.

26 Ibid., 50.

## 9. *Strange Untraveled Lands*

1 Romanucci-Ross, *Mead's Other Manus*, x.

2 Powdermaker, *Stranger and Friend*, 41–43.

3 Howard, *Margaret Mead*, 107.

4 Quoted in Limmer, *What the Woman Lived*, 37.

5 Barbara Babcock, "Not in the Absolute Singular," in *Women Writing Culture*, ed. Behar and Gordon, dates the theoretical beginnings of the personality and culture school to a 1927 paper of Sapir's.

6 Sapir, "Observations on the Sex Problem."

7 Ibid.; Quotations from *American Journal of Psychiatry*, 527, 522–23.

8 Ibid., 523.

9 Ibid., 528. Sapir obviously believed in the age-old cure for the intellectual woman. He once wrote to a graduate student that Elsie Clews Parsons "needs psychoanalysis. . . . You might solve her difficulties by having intercourse with her. Her interest in 'science' is some kind of erotic mechanism" (cited in Desley Deacon, *Elsie Clews Parsons*, 260).

10 Ibid., 529.

11 Ibid., 533.

12 Of course Benedict's letters have not survived, so what she said to Edward can only be inferred from his reply to her, which in turn is a typed version with excisions from the originals, which cannot be located. It is hard to believe that Sullivan would have been altogether pleased with Edward's paper, since he was homosexual himself. See Perry, *Psychiatrist of America*, and Michael Allen, "Sullivan's Closet: A Reappraisal of Harry Stack Sullivan's Life and His Pioneering Role in American Psychiatry," *Journal of Homosexuality* 29, no. 1 (1995): 1–18. Edward's close friendship with Sullivan is discussed in a later chapter.

13 Quoted in Howard, *Margaret Mead*, 105.

14 Ibid., 105.

15 Quoted in Limmer, *What the Woman Lived*, 37.

16 Quoted in Frank, *Louise Bogan*, 131. The phrase is from the poem, "Solitary Observations Brought Back From a Sojourn in Hell," *Poems and New Poems* (New York: Charles Scribner's Sons, 1941).

17 A number of Fortune's dreams were recorded in *The Mind in Sleep*.

18 Ruth's datebooks for this time are scattered with references to "MM lunch" and "MM eve" (RFB, Box 42).

19 Mead, *Growing Up in New Guinea*, 164.

20 Faderman, *Odd Girls and Twilight Lovers*, 88.

21 Information about Léonie Adams and Edmund Wilson from Jeffrey Meyers, *Edmund Wilson*.

22 Mead, in discussing the separation, remarked somewhat disingenuously (in a footnote) that Ruth never married again (*AW*, 557).

23 When Mead was putting together *An Anthropologist at Work*, she wrote to Ruth Valentine, Ruth Benedict's partner at the time of her death, that Tom was the only person who had "mattered" to Ruth who would not be mentioned, since he had not made anything of himself as a writer and most references seemed to reflect badly on him (MM Papers, Q23).

24 Quoted in Deacon, *Elsie Clews Parsons*, 277.

## 10. Witch Fires at Morning

1 Deacon, *Elsie Clews Parsons*, 258–272, discusses these issues at length; Kroeber quoted in Deacon, 262.

2 Ibid., 263, 264.

3 Ibid., 269.

4 Caffrey, *Stranger in the Land* and Modell, *Patterns of a Life* describe Benedict and the Southwest laboratory. See also George Stocking, "The Santa Fe Style in American Anthropology: Regional Interest, Academic Initiative, and Philanthropic Policy in the First Two Decades of the Laboratory of Anthropology," *Journal of the History of the Behavioral Sciences* 18 (1982): 3–19.

5 Information on Natalie Raymond has been difficult to locate. Sources include interviews and correspondence with two friends from New York days, Ralph Paterline and Evelyn Shritt; a death certificate and will from Monterey County; letters of Benedict to Mead, Eichelberger to Mead, and Ruth Tolman to Benedict, as well as other correspondence in the RFB and MM papers. *Robert Oppenheimer*, ed. Smith and Weiner contains several letters from Oppenheimer to Raymond. Oppenheimer's various biographers have little or nothing to say about Raymond. No photograph of Natalie Raymond could be located. For information on Richard Tolman, see his entry in *Biographical Memoirs of the National Academy of Science*; and for Ruth Valentine, her entry in *Membership Directory* (Washington, D.C.: American Psychological Association, 1948).

6 For information on Robert Oppenheimer, see Stern and Green, *Oppenheimer Case*.

7 Evelyn Shritt, interview with author, New York City, October 1996.

8 Quoted in Smith and Weiner, *Robert Oppenheimer*, 143.

9 See Nancy J. Parezo, "Conclusion: The Beginning of the Quest," in *Hidden Scholars*, ed. Parezo, 334–368.

10 Mead later referred to Schmerler as an "unpleasant Jewish woman" (MM, B14).

11 Quoted in Howard, *Margaret Mead*, 129.

12 Howard, *Margaret Mead*, 129.

13 Stella Gibbons, *Cold Comfort Farm* (1932; reprint, Harmondsworth: Penguin Books, 1938).

14 Ann McLean, interview with author, Wellington, New Zealand, June 1995.

15 Chauncey, *Gay New York*, reports on this survey.

16 Later Margaret Mead denied she had ever known communists. Speaking of Ruth Benedict in 1957, she made what may well have been a veiled reference to Léonie: "If she had ever had a friend who became a Communist, she would have shrugged her shoulders as she had done when close friends turned to Christian Science or Anglo-Catholicism or psychoanalysis" (AW,349). But when she was investigated in the 1950s Mead wrote that she never knew a communist.

17 Wilson, *The Sixties*, cited in Meyers, *Edmund Wilson*, 105.

18 Quoted in Limmer, *What the Woman Lived*, 127.

19 Mead, "Ruth Fulton Benedict," 461.

20 "Anthropology and the Abnormal," 279.

21 Nathalie Woodbury, interview with author, Amherst, Mass., November 1996.

22 Benedict, "Edward Sapir," 473.

23 Handler, "Vigorous Male and Aspiring Female," 147.

24 Caffrey, *Stranger in this Land*, 205.

25 Mead, *Sex and Temperament*, 216.

26 Nancy McDowell, *The Mundugumor*. Another kinship error made by Mead in her work on Samoa led the anthropologist Ralph Piddington to postulate an entirely imaginary prehistoric culture in order to account for the phenomenon that Mead had reported mistakenly. This point was made in discussion following a lecture by Serge Tcherkezoff, University of Waikato, August 1966.

## 11. Points of the Compass

1 Howard, *Margaret Mead and BW* provide the best accounts of events in New Guinea. Only a proportion of the letters between Mead and Benedict from this period are currently available.

2 Howard, *Margaret Mead*, 154.

3 Stocking, *The Ethnographer's Magic*, 34; Mead, *Coming of Age in Samoa*, 8.

4 Charles Seligman, quoted in Stocking, *The Ethnographer's Magic*, 30.

5 Mead, "Field Work in the Pacific Islands," 328.

6 Jean Houston, telephone interview with author, November 1994.

7 Quoted in Howard, *Margaret Mead*, 160.

8 Ibid., 159.

9 Gregory Bateson, *Naven*, cited in the Virginia Yans film, *Margaret Mead: An Observer Observed*.

10 In *With a Daughter's Eye* Mary Catherine Bateson transposes east for west, arguing that Mead's theory, given in a more expanded version in the draft of *Blackberry Winter*, is unintelligible because she changed her way of organizing the diagrams halfway through the writing.

11 Bateson, *With a Daughter's Eye*, 136.

12 Ibid., 133–35, 140.

13 Howard, *Margaret Mead*, 151, citing a 1937 letter in the Malinowski Archive, London.

14 Quoted in Howard, *Margaret Mead*, 160.

15 Bateson, *With a Daughter's Eye*, 135.

16 Sidney W. Mintz, "Ruth Benedict," in *Totems and Teachers*, ed. Sydel Silverman, 156.

17 At some stage, probably later, Natalie inherited ten thousand dollars. She decided to apprentice herself to a stockbroker for a year and increased her capital tenfold (Evelyn Shritt, interview with author, New York City, October 1996).

18 Ralph B. Paterline, letter to author, 31 December 1995.

19 Bateson, *With a Daughter's Eye*, 140.

20 Howard, *Margaret Mead*, 167.

21 Quoted in Smith and Weiner, *Robert Oppenheimer*, 172.

22 Quoted in Modell, *Patterns of a Life*, 212.

23 Benedict, *Patterns of Culture*, 33.

24 Stocking, *The Ethnographer's Magic*, is a useful source for this period.

25 Mead, in *Ruth Fulton Benedict: A Memorial*, 25, 26.

26 Howard, *Margaret Mead*, 176.

27 See Perry, *Psychiatrist of America*; and Allen, "Sullivan's Closet."

28 Quoted in Perry, *Psychiatrist of America*, 339.

29 Rosenberg, *Beyond Separate Spheres*, 237. Gewertz, "The Tchambuli View of Persons," cites examples of the representation of *Sex and Temperament* in textbooks.

30 For example, see Hsu, "Margaret Mead and Psychological Anthropology."

31 See McDowell, "Oceanic Ethnography" and *Mundugumor* for an assessment of Mead's fieldwork.

32 Deborah Gewertz ("Tchambuli View of Persons") criticizes Mead for overworking comparisons with westerners; see also Gewertz, *Sepik River Societies*, for more on Mead and Tchambuli.

33 McDowell, *Mundugumor*, 293, quoting Mead's later fieldwork student Ted Schwartz.

34 *Sex and Temperament*, 256.

35 Contemporary queer theory takes us full circle, this time deliberately blurring the sex/gender distinction which had become an important concept in the human sciences since the 1960s. See for example, Judith Butler's gender-as-performance theory in *Gender Trouble*.

36 See Faderman, *Odd Girls and Twilight Lovers*; Chauncy, "From Sexual Inversion to Homosexuality"; Chauncey, *Gay New York*; D'Emilio and Freedman, *Intimate Matters*.

37 McDowell, *Mundugumor*.

38 Cited in Howard, *Margaret Mead*, 169.

39 Cited in Howard, *Margaret Mead*, 169.

40 Cited in Howard, *Margaret Mead*, 170.

41 Fortune's notes and annotated copy of *Patterns of Culture* are in the RFF Papers.

42 Reo Fortune, letter to the editor, *Man* 64 (May/June 1964).

43 Copies of the manuscripts are in the FB papers.

44 From an untitled manuscript among the Fortune correspondence, FB Papers.

45 Jock Phillips, *A Man's Country?*, is an excellent account of masculinity in New Zealand.

46 Ann Chowning, telephone conversation with author, January 1995, referring to a member of the Fortune family.

47 RFB Papers, Box 37; reprinted in *AW*, 97–112.

48 "Anthropology and the Humanities," *AW*, 469.

## 12. *Is Our Cup Broken?*

1 Howard, *Margaret Mead*, 187 says it was Ruth Benedict who took Mead to Harlem, citing BW, 229, which only says "a friend." Presumably Howard had some additional source of information.

2 Unless otherwise noted, all letters cited in chapter 12 are located in Box B14, MM Papers.

3 Cited in Lipset, *Gregory Bateson*, 150–51.

4 Mead, "Memories of Walter Spies" (1965), cited in James A. Boon, "Between-the-Wars Bali: Rereading the Relics," in *Malinowski, Rivers, Benedict and Others*, ed. Stocking, 234.

5   Bateson, *With a Daughter's Eye*, 166.

6   Ibid., 137.

7   See Lipset, *Gregory Bateson*, for more on Bateson's anthropology.

8   Ray Birdwhistell, quoted in Bateson, *With a Daughter's Eye*, 113.

9   These events were noted in Benedict's datebooks RFB, Box 42.

10  Cited in Smith and Weiner, *Robert Oppenheimer*, 191.

11  Benedict did in fact save some correspondence with Stanley Benedict; early letters are cited in *AW*.

12  Resumés are in RFB, Box 39.

13  An anthropologist who once consulted regularly with Mead at the Museum of Natural History told me she found Mead so intimidating that she used to swallow a tranquilizer before the regular visits to discuss her work; Jean Houston described Mead as having "freedom from load," meaning that she did not hold on to negative feelings (Jean Houston, telephone interview with author, November 1994).

14  Cited in Zumwalt, *Wealth and Rebellion*, 163–64.

15  See Zumwalt, *Wealth and Rebellion*, 216.

16  See Deacon, *Elsie Clews Parsons*, 278.

17  For a full account of this episode, see William C. Manson, "Abram Kardiner and the Neo-Freudian Alternative in Culture and Personality," in *Malinowski, Rivers, Benedict and Others*, ed. Stocking, 73–94.

18  Quoted in Caffrey, *Stranger in This Land*, 277.

19  The situation was described in a videotaped interview with Ruth Bunzel and Charles Wagley, 1983, Smithsonian Institution Human Archives collection.

20  Quoted in Linton and Wagley, *Ralph Linton*, 48.

21  Cited in Modell, *Patterns of a Life*, 256.

22  Linton and Wagley, *Ralph Linton*, 48.

23  Manson, "Abram Kardiner and the Neo-Freudian Alternative in Culture and Personality," in *Malinowski, Rivers, Benedict and Others*, ed. Stocking, provides an analysis of the ways in which neglecting Kardiner proved detrimental to Benedict's and Mead's later work on national character.

24  Hence Barbara Babcock's suggestion that Linton appropriated Benedict's work in his *Acculturation in Seven American Indian Tribes*; see " 'Not in the Absolute Singular:' Re-reading Ruth Benedict," in *Women Writing Culture*, ed. Behar and Gordon, 116.

25  See Goldfrank, *Notes on an Undirected Life*, 110.

26  Nathalie Woodbury, interview with author, Amherst, Mass., November 1996.

27  Freedman, *Maternal Justice*.

28  Goldfrank, *Notes on an Undirected Life*, 126.

29  Apparently she first used the term on the "Dick Cavett Show" in 1978 (Yans-McLaughlin, *Margaret Mead: An Observer Observed*).

30  Quoted in Caffrey, *Stranger in This Land*, 255.

31  Erikson, *Ruth Fulton Benedict*, 16.

32  Quoted in Caffrey, *Stranger in This Land*, 300.

33  Bateson, *With a Daughter's Eye*, 78.

34  This reason for returning to Bali was not mentioned in *BW*.

35  Howard, *Margaret Mead*, 367.

36  See also Mead, *Male and Female*, chapter 13.

37  Darnell, *Edward Sapir*, 408.

38  See Dan Oren, *Joining the Club: A History of Jews and Yale* (New Haven: Yale University Press, 1985) for details about anti-Semitism at Yale; for further information about social sci-

ences at Yale see J. G. Morawski, "Organizing Knowledge and Behavior at Yale's Institute of Human Relations, *Isis* 77 (1986): 219–42.

39  Another comment of Mead's shows her attitude in the face of discrimination. Given the difficult job situation for graduates, she suggested to Ruth that "I think it would be a fair go to unofficially discourage unpleasant Jews more than unpleasant Gentiles, because they are bound to have twice as hard a time getting jobs. The same thing of course holds of unpleasant women, and unpleasant Jewish women—like Schmerler [the young woman murdered by the Apache], just shouldn't be let in at all." Ruth replied that it had been the Jewish students among the recent crop who had got the jobs. (MM, B14).

40  Quoted by Phillip Sapir, interview with author, Bethesda, Md., October 1996.

41  Bateson, *With a Daughter's Eye*, 117–18. Bateson now believes that Margaret and Ruth's physical relationship may not have continued into their later years (telephone interview with author, November 1994), but the record of their occasional arrangements to spend nights together may suggest otherwise. However, there is no suggestion in later years of an emotional investment in the physical side of the relationship. What transpired there will most likely never be known.

## 13. November Burning

1  The friend was Louise Rosenblatt, whose comment was quoted by Mead to Benedict in a 1938 letter (MM, B14). Unless otherwise noted, all letters cited in chapter 13 are located in Box B14, MM Papers.

2  BW draft, quoted in Yans-McLaughlin, "Science, Democracy, and Ethics: Mobilizing Culture and Personality for World War II," in *Malinowski, Rivers, Benedict and Others*, ed. Stocking, 193.

3  See Lipset, *Gregory Bateson*.

4  Mead, introduction to *And Keep Your Powder Dry* (1967 edition), xxvi.

5  Quoted in Yans-McLaughlin, "Science Democracy and Ethics," in *Malinowski, Rivers, Benedict and Others*, ed. Stocking, 194.

6  A press release from the Benedict archives at Vassar, apparently prepared by Ruth, refers to Boas's attacking the Harvard physical anthropologist Earnest Hooton, who had declared that national intelligence was declining and advocated a sterilization of "ineffectual breeders" as a solution. Boas's debunking of Hooton's arguments reads as if it were written yesterday, rather than sixty years ago, making clear how entrenched is this form of prejudice ("Boas Challenges Biological Purge," *New York Times*, 31 March 1937 [RFB, Box 108]).

7  In addition to the Benedict biographies, sources for this expedition include Goldfrank, *Notes on an Undirected Life*; Stocking, "The Ethnographic Sensibility of the 1920s and the Dualism of the Anthropological Tradition," in *The Ethnographer's Magic*; Gloria Levitas, "Esther Goldfrank," in *Women Anthropologists*, ed. Gacs et al. Lewis's study of the "manly-hearted woman" is referred to in the Stocking essay, 322.

8  Goldfrank, *Notes on an Undirected Life*, 134.

9  Nathalie Woodbury, interview with author, Amherst, Mass. November 1996.

10  Goldfrank, *Notes on an Undirected Life*, 134ff., describes Ruth's reactions to Mead's letter; Howard, in *Margaret Mead*, makes it clear that Margaret was anxious about the possibilities of a lesbian scandal.

11  Quoted in Goldfrank, *Notes on an Undirected Life*, 134.

12  Cited in Caffrey, *Stranger in This Land*, 274.

13 The Buell Quain affair is discussed in Caffrey, *Stranger in This Land*; Benedict to Boas, 5 November 1939 (FB); Mead to Benedict, 1 December 1939 (MM, B14); *AW*, 353–54.

14 The naming of Luther's daughter is reported in JH.

15 Sources on Ruth Valentine, in addition to the Mead-Benedict correspondence and the Benedict biographies, include the 1948 and 1963 American Psychological Association directories, and Smith and Weiner, *Robert Oppenheimer*; some of her correspondence is in RFB, Box 35.

16 *BW*, 250.

17 It is interesting that nowhere in Mead's account of pregnancy and childbirth in *BW* does she mention Benedict.

18 Landes, a Jewish woman, was one of Benedict's many protégées. She had difficulty in obtaining employment after completing her Ph.D. and Benedict wrote many letters of recommendation for her (see Landes-Benedict correspondence, RFB, Box 31). She carried out field work in Brazil in the late 1930s, studying cults and homosexuality in collaboration with her lover, a Brazilian journalist. The work that Mead so disdained was later published as *The City of Women* (1947) to a mixed reception. Benedict found her a job during the war, but afterward Landes was subjected, for apparently political reasons, to a campaign of allegations that she had prostituted herself in Brazil. As a result she was blacklisted and did not obtain an academic position until 1965, in her late fifties. See George Park and Alice Park, "Ruth Schlossberg Landes," in *Women Anthropologists*, ed. Ute Gacs et al.; Sally Cole, "Ruth Landes and the Early Ethnography of Race and Gender, in *Women Writing Culture*, ed. Behar and Gordon.

19 Though in later years this continued to be a theme of her dreams, which she interpreted as standing for something she had left undone; see Jean Houston's memoir, *A Mythic Life*.

20 Margaret Rossiter, in *Women Scientists in America*, suggests that this was "a rather odd assignment for one of the world's experts on the Pacific Islands" (3).

21 Bateson, *With a Daughter's Eye*, 38.

22 Quoted in Howard, *Margaret Mead*, 226.

23 See Louise E. Hoffman, "American Psychologists and Wartime Research on Germany," *American Psychologist* 47 (1992): 264–73.

24 Information on Natalie Raymond is from MM, B15; correspondence is in RFB (Box 39) and from a series of letters between Raymond and Robert Oppenheimer from the 1950s (Robert Oppenheimer Papers, Library of Congress).

25 See Takaki, *A Different Mirror*.

26 Quoted in Caffrey, *Stranger in This Land*, 297. Information on Weltfish is available in Silverman, *Totems and Teachers* and Ruth E. Pathé, "Gene Weltfish," *Women Anthropologists*, ed. Gacs et al. Mead, chairing an anthropology meeting around this time, showed that she was not keen to rock the boat when she called Elsie Clews Parsons out of order when the latter tried to put forth a remit arguing for racial integration in the armed forces (Goldfrank, *Notes from an Undirected Life*).

27 See Graebner, *The Age of Doubt*, 76.

28 Quoted in Howard, *Margaret Mead*, 244.

29 Benedict, *The Chrysanthemum and the Sword*, 1.

30 For information about Ruth Tolman, see Rossiter, *Women Scientists in America*. An unidentified newspaper clipping, "Dr. Tolman, Famous Atomic Scientist Dies," was appended to a letter Margery Freeman sent to Ruth in September 1948 (RFB, Box 39).

31 Mead, introduction *And Keep Your Powder Dry* (1967 edition), xii.

32 Mead, *Ruth Benedict*, 64. In contradiction to her stance, Paul Boyer argues that within days

of Hiroshima all the main themes of atomic warfare discourse were publicly aired (*By the Bomb's Early Light*).

33 For an extended discussion, see Yans-McLaughlin, "Science, Democracy and Ethics," *Malinowski, Rivers, Benedict and Others*, ed. Stocking.

34 Ruth Benedict, "The Past and the Future: Hiroshima, by John Hersey," *Nation*, 1946, 656.

35 See Sidney W. Mintz, "Ruth Benedict," in *Totems and Teachers*, ed. Silverman, 154. For Japanese and American responses to the book, see Joy Hendry, "The Chrysanthemum Continues to Flower: Ruth Benedict and Some Perils of Popular Anthropology," in *Popularizing Anthropology*, ed. MacClancy and McDonaugh.

36 Clifford Geertz, *Works and Lives*, 111.

37 Mintz, "Ruth Benedict," 156.

38 Quoted in Howard, *Margaret Mead*, 253.

39 Ibid., 259.

40 Mead, *Male and Female*, 29; *Male and Female* was exposed as insufficiently feminist by Betty Friedan in her 1963 bestseller, *The Feminine Mystique*. William S. Graebner, in *The Age of Doubt*, sees its discussion of "momism" as a response to the identity crisis in American males produced by the "new and overbearing" woman of the 1940s (74).

41 Quoted in Howard, *Margaret Mead*, 288, Benedict also disliked the Kinsey report, which she reviewed on its publication, for its emphasis on statistical facts at the expense of cultural understanding: "The Kinsey Report," *Saturday Review of Literature* 30 (1948): 34–35.

42 For the chilly climate toward lesbians in the postwar period, see Donna Penn, "The Meanings of Lesbianism in Post-War America, in *Gender and American History*, ed. Melosh.

43 Rhoda Métraux refers to the importance of Mead's security clearance in "The Study of Culture at a Distance."

44 Léonie Adams apparently was involved with the Communists in the 1930s; see *What the Woman Lived*, ed. Limmer. Franz Boas, too, was certainly sympathetic to the Communist Party, as Goldfrank, in *Notes on an Undirected Life*, points out.

45 For a description of R.C.C., see the Benedict biographies and Métraux, "The Study of Culture at a Distance."

46 For a critical view, see Manson, "Abram Kardiner and the Neo-Freudian Alternative" in *Malinowski, Rivers, Benedict and Others*, ed. Stocking.

47 Mead, *Ruth Benedict*, 74.

48 Limmer, *What the Woman Lived*, 261. In 1955 Bogan wrote to May Sarton (who had also been rejected by Bogan in her desire for an "amitié amoureuse") that Margaret looked "exactly the same" as she had done thirty years before, and that between her and Louise there was "a sort of chemical kind of non-attraction. . . . She is so sure of everything, and has that daring career among the New Guinea natives to prove her mettle (but I still think she is a popularizer and not a really dedicated scientist)" (Limmer, 293).

49 Howard, *Margaret Mead*, 281.

## 14. An Ending

1 Bateson, *With a Daughter's Eye*, 211.

2 Howard, *Margaret Mead*, 281.

3 This episode was mentioned in BW draft and JH; Mead argued that paranormal phenomena were culturally influenced, that the British saw ghosts and Americans suffered from poltergeists. When her mother died a few years later, Margaret, before receiving the call from her father, suddenly felt a sense of disintegration (JH).

4 Mintz, "Ruth Benedict," in *Totems and Teachers*, ed. Silverman, 161.

5 *Ruth Fulton Benedict: A Memorial*, 5, 16.

6 Ibid., 25–26.

7 The full text of "Eucharist," in Benedict's handwriting, forms the frontispiece for *An Anthropologist at Work*.

8 Goldfrank, *Notes on an Undirected Life*, 40; this was probably the basis of Margaret's remark that Ruth kept people in separate rooms.

9 Bateson, *With a Daughter's Eye*, 123. Marie once wrote to Margaret that if Margaret "predeceased" her, "no biographer is going to get any verbal material out of me. Although I don't know everything about you, I probably know more than any living person." Eichelberger seems to have remained true to her word (MM, TR1).

10 For example, Babcock, "Not in the Absolute Singular," in *Women Writing Culture*, ed. Behar and Gordon, suggests she distorted aspects of Benedict's writing; Geertz, in *Works and Lives* calls her the "proprietor" of Benedict's life.

11 Rhoda Métraux edited Margaret's drafts to produce a manuscript around half the original size; the drafts are in the MM Papers and have been frequently referred to in this book (as BW draft).

12 Lola Romanucci-Ross makes this point in "Telling Tales of the South Pacific," in *Anthropological Poetics*, ed. Brady, 59.

13 It seems that she was offered the chair at Barnard's anthropology department after Gladys Reichard's death, which she declined (anonymous informant).

14 Torgovnick, *Gone Primitive*, 242.

15 Baldwin and Mead, *A Rap on Race*, 107.

16 Howard, *Margaret Mead*, 362.

17 Deborah Gewertz, interview with author, Amherst, Mass., December 1994.

18 Howard, *Margaret Mead*, 367.

19 Ibid.

20 Quoted in Harold North, *Memoirs of a Bastard Angel* (London: Bloomsbury, 1994), x.

21 Mead, "Bisexuality," 31.

22 Quoted in Howard, *Margaret Mead*, 367.

23 Bateson, *With a Daughter's Eye*, 126.

24 Ibid., 121.

25 Information about the relationship between Mead and Métraux came from an informant who wished to remain anonymous; Howard, *Margaret Mead*, deals with its more public side; and there is further information in the Howard collection. Métraux, still living at the time of writing, also played a major role in the archiving of the Mead Papers at the Library of Congress.

26 Bateson, *With a Daughter's Eye*, 59.

27 The provisions of the will lend further credibility to the idea that perhaps Val had an earlier romantic link with Natalie; or perhaps she felt that both Natalie and Margaret should benefit from what had been Ruth's money.

28 Ralph Paterline, letter to the author, 25 April 1996.

29 Evelyn Shritt, interview by author, New York City, October 1996.

30 See Frank, *Louise Bogan*.

31 See Hardin, "Zuñi Potters" *Hidden Scholars*, ed. Parezo.

32 "Fashioning culture closer to her heart's desire" is a paraphrase of Mead's words at Ruth's memorial service, *Ruth Fulton Benedict*, 26.

33 Houston, *A Mythic Life*.

34 From the 1929 essay "The Science of Custom," quoted in Babcock, "Not in the Absolute Singular," *Women Writing Culture*, ed. Behar and Gordon, 123.

# BIBLIOGRAPHY

Adams, Léonie. *Those Not Elect*. New York: Robert McBride, 1925.

——. *High Falcon and Other Poems*. New York: John Day, 1929.

Allen, Michael. "Sullivan's Closet: A Reappraisal of Harry Stack Sullivan's Life and His Pioneering Role in American Psychiatry," *Journal of Homosexuality* 29 (1995): 1–18.

Babcock, Barbara A., and Nancy J. Parezo. *Daughters of the Desert: Women Anthropologists and the Native Southwest, 1880–1980: An Illustrated Catalogue*. Albuquerque, N.M.: University of New Mexico Press, 1988.

Bair, Deirdre. *Simone de Beauvoir: A Life of Freedom*. London: Vintage, 1991.

Baldwin, James and Margaret Mead. *A Rap on Race*. London: Corgi, 1972.

Barnouw, Victor. *Culture and Personality*. Homewood, Ill.: Dorsey Press, 1973.

Bateson, Gregory. *Naven: A Survey of the Problems Suggested by a Composite Picture of the Culture of a New Guinea Tribe Drawn from Three Points of View*. Cambridge: Cambridge University Press, 1936.

Bateson, Mary Catherine. *Composing a Life*. New York: Penguin Books, 1990.

——. *With a Daughter's Eye: A Memoir of Margaret Mead and Gregory Bateson*. New York: William Morrow, 1984.

Beauvoir, Simone de. *Adieux: A Farewell to Sartre*. London: Deutsch, 1984.

Behar, Ruth, and Deborah A. Gordon, eds. *Women Writing Culture*. Berkeley: University of California Press, 1995.

Belenky, Mary Field, Blythe McVicker Clinchy, Nancy Rule Goldberger, and Jill Mattuck Tarule. *Women's Ways of Knowing: The Development of Self, Voice, and Mind*. New York: Basic Books, 1987.

Bender, Thomas. *New York Intellect: A History of the Intellectual Life in New York City from 1750 to the Beginnings of Our Own Time*. Baltimore: Johns Hopkins University Press, 1987.

Benedict, Ruth F. *An Anthropologist at Work: Writings of Ruth Benedict*. Edited by Margaret Mead. Boston: Houghton Mifflin, 1959.

——. "Anthropology and the Abnormal." *Journal of General Psychology*, 10 no. 2 (1934): 59–82.

——. "Anthropology and the Humanities." *American Anthropologist* 50 (1948): 585–93.

——. *The Chrysanthemum and the Sword: Patterns of Japanese Culture*. Boston: Houghton Mifflin, 1946.

——. "Configurations of Culture in North America." *American Anthropologist* 34 (1932): 1–27.

——. "Edward Sapir." *American Anthropologist* 41 (1939): 465–77.

——. *Patterns of Culture*. London: Routledge Kegan Paul, 1934; 2nd. ed., 1935.

——. Papers. Vassar College Library, Poughkeepsie, N.Y.

——. *Race: Science and Politics*. New York: Modern Age, 1940.

——. Review of *Hiroshima* by John Hersey. *The Nation*, 163 (1946): 656–58.

——. *Tales of the Cochiti Indians*. Bureau of American Ethnology, Bulletin 98. Washington, D.C.: Smithsonian Institution, 1931.

——. "The Vision in Plains Culture," *American Anthropologist* 24 (1922): 1–23.

——. *Zuñi Mythology*. 2 vols. New York: Columbia University Press, 1935.

Bernard, Jessie. *Academic Women*. State College, Penn.: Pennsylvania State University Press, 1964.

Boas, Franz. *General Anthropology*. Boston: D.C. Heath, 1938.

Bogan, Louise. *The Blue Estuaries: Poems, 1923–58*. New York: Noonday Press, 1968.

——. *Journey Around My Room: The Autobiography of Louise Bogan*. Edited by Ruth Limmer. New York: Viking Press, 1980.

——. *Papers*. Amherst College Library, Amherst, Mass.

——. *What the Woman Lived: Selected Letters of Louise Bogan 1920–1970*. Edited and with an introduction by Ruth Limmer. New York: Harcourt Brace Jovanovich, 1973.

Boyer, Paul. *By the Bomb's Early Light: American Thought and Culture at the Dawn of the Atomic Age*. Chapel Hill: University of North Carolina Press, 1985.

Brady, Ivan, ed. *Anthropological Poetics*. Savage, Md.: Rowman & Littlefield, 1991.

Brown, Lyn Mikel and Carol Gilligan. *Meeting at the Crossroads: Women's Psychology and Girl's Development*. Cambridge, Mass.: Harvard University Press, 1992.

Bunzel, Ruth. *The Pueblo Potter: A Study of Creative Imagination in Primitive Art*. 1929. Reprint, New York: Dover Publications, 1972.

Butler, Judith. *Gender Trouble: Feminism and the Subversion of Identity*. New York: Routledge, 1990.

Caffrey, Margaret M. *Ruth Benedict: Stranger in This Land*. Austin: University of Texas Press, 1989.

Chadwick, Whitney and Isabelle de Courtivron. *Significant Others: Creativity and Intimate Partnership*. London: Thames and Hudson, 1993.

Chauncey, George. "From Sexual Inversion to Homosexuality: Medicine and the Changing Conception of Female Deviance." *Salmagundi* 58 (1982–3): 114–46.

——. *Gay New York: Gender, Urban Culture, and the Making of the Gay Male World 1890–1940*. New York: Basic Books, 1994.

Chesler, Ellen. *Woman of Valor: Margaret Sanger and the Birth Control Movement in America*. New York: Simon & Schuster, 1992.

Cole, Douglas. " 'One Does Not Get As Much From the Girls': Franz Boas and Women Students." *History of Anthropology Newsletter* 19, no. 2 (1992): 3–5.

Cook, Blanche Wiesen. "Women Alone Stir My Imagination." *Signs* 4 (1978): 718–39.

——. *Eleanor Roosevelt, Volume One 1884–1933*. New York: Viking Penguin, 1992.

Cott, Nancy M. *The Grounding of Modern Feminism*. New Haven: Yale University Press, 1987.

Cravens, Hamilton. *The Triumph of Evolution: American Scientists and the Heredity-Environment Controversy, 1900–1941*. Philadelphia: University of Pennsylvania Press, 1978.

Cressman, Luther. *A Golden Journey: Memoirs of an Archaeologist*. Salt Lake City: University of Utah Press, 1988.

Crunden, Robert M. *From Self to Society 1919–1941*. Englewood Cliffs, N.J.: Prentice-Hall, 1972.

Darnell, Regna. *Edward Sapir: Linguist, Anthropologist, Humanist*. Berkeley: University of California Press, 1990.

Deacon, Desley. *Elsie Clews Parsons: Inventing Modern Life*. Chicago: University of Chicago Press, 1997.

D'Emilio, John and Estelle B. Freedman. *Intimate Matters: A History of Sexuality in America*. New York: Harper & Row, 1988.

Dimitroff, Gail Ruth. *Guiding Spirits: An Inquiry into the Nature of the Bond Between Ruth Benedict and*

*Margaret Mead.* Ph.D. diss., United States International University, 1983. Ann Arbor, Mich.: University Microfilms, 1983.

Douglas, Ann. *Terrible Honesty: Mongrel Manhattan in the 1920s.* New York: Farrar, Straus & Giroux, 1995.

Duberman, Martin Bauml, Martha Vicinus, and George Chauncey, Jr. *Hidden from History: Reclaiming the Gay and Lesbian Past.* London, Penguin Books, 1991.

Faderman, Lillian. *Odd Girls and Twilight Lovers: A History of Lesbian Life in Twentieth-Century America.* New York: Penguin Books, 1991.

——. *Surpassing the Love of Men: Romantic Friendship and Love Between Women from the Renaissance to the Present.* London: The Women's Press, 1985.

Figiel, Sia. *Where We Once Belonged.* Auckland: Pasifika Press, 1996.

Fitzpatrick, Ellen. *Endless Crusade: Women Social Scientists and Progressive Reform.* New York: Oxford University Press, 1990.

Fortune, Reo F. "Arapesh Warfare." *American Anthropologist* 41 (1939): 22–41.

——. *Manus Religion.* Philadelphia: American Philosophical Society, 1935.

——. *The Mind in Sleep.* London: Kegan Paul, Trench, Trubner, 1927.

——. *Papers.* Alexander Turnbull Library, Wellington, New Zealand.

——. *Sorcerers of Dobu: the Social Anthropology of the Dobu Islanders of the Western Pacific.* New York: Dutton, 1932.

Frank, Elizabeth. *Louise Bogan: A Portrait.* New York: Alfred A. Knopf, 1985.

Freedman, Estelle B. *Maternal Justice: Miriam van Waters and the Female Reform Tradition.* Chicago: University of Chicago Press, 1996.

Freeman, Derek. "Fa'apua'a Fa'amu and Margaret Mead." *American Anthropologist* 91 (1989): 1017–22.

——. *Margaret Mead and Samoa: The Making and Unmaking of an Anthropological Myth.* Harvard: Harvard University Press, 1983. Reprint, with a new introduction by Derek Freeman, *Margaret Mead and the Heretic.* Sydney: Penguin Books, 1996.

Friedan, Betty. *The Feminine Mystique.* New York: Dell, 1963.

Gacs, Ute, Aisa Khan, Jerrie McIntyre, and Ruth Weinberg. *Women Anthropologists: A Biographical Dictionary.* Westport, Conn.: Greenwood Press, 1988.

Geertz, Clifford. *Works and Lives: the Anthropologist as Author.* Cambridge, Mass.: Polity Press, 1988.

Gewertz, Deborah B. *Sepik River Societies: A Historical Ethnography of the Chambri and their Neighbours.* New Haven: Yale University Press, 1983.

——. "The Tchambuli View of Persons: A Critique of Individualism in the Works of Mead and Chodorow." *American Anthropologist* 86 (1984): 615–29.

Golde, Peggy, ed. *Women in the Field: Anthropological Experiences.* Chicago: Aldine, 1970.

Goldfrank, Esther. *Notes on an Undirected Life: As One Anthropologist Tells It.* New York: Queens College Press, 1978.

Graebner, William S. *The Age of Doubt: American Thought and Culture in the 1940s.* Boston: Twayne, 1991.

Hare, Peter H. *A Woman's Quest for Science: Portrait of Elsie Clews Parsons.* Buffalo, N.Y.: Prometheus Books, 1985.

Heilbrun, Carolyn. *Hamlet's Mother and Other Women.* New York: Columbia University Press, 1990.

——. *Writing a Woman's Life.* New York: Norton, 1988.

Holmes, Lowell D. *Quest for the Real Samoa: the Mead/Freeman Controversy and Beyond.* South Hadley, Mass.: Bergin & Garvey, 1987.

Horney, Karen. *The Neurotic Personality of Our Time*. New York: International Universities Press, 1937.

Houston, Jean. *A Mythic Life: Learning to Live Our Greater Story*. New York: Harper Collins, 1996.

——. *The Search for the Beloved: Journeys in Mythology and Sacred Psychology*. Los Angeles: Jeremy P. Tarcher, 1987.

Howard, Jane. *Margaret Mead: A Life*. New York: Simon and Schuster, 1984.

——. Papers. Columbia University Library, New York, N.Y.

Hsu, Francis L.K. "Margaret Mead and Psychological Anthropology," *American Anthropologist* 82 (1980): 349–53.

Hyatt, Marshall. *Franz Boas: Social Activist: The Dynamics of Ethnicity*. New York: Greenwood Press, 1990.

Jelinek, Estelle C. *The Tradition of Women's Autobiography: From Antiquity to the Present*. Boston: Twayne, 1986.

Jordan, Judith V., Alexandra G. Kaplan, Jean Baker Miller, Irene P. Stiver, and Janet L. Surrey eds. *Women's Growth in Connection: Writings from the Stone Center*. New York: Guilford Press, 1991.

Kammen, Michael. *Mystic Chords of Memory: The Transformation of Tradition in American Culture*. New York: Vintage Books, 1993.

Kehoe, Monika, ed. *Historical, Literary and Erotic Aspects of Lesbianism*. New York: Harrington Park Press, 1986.

Kuper, Adam. *Anthropology and Anthropologists: The Modern British School*. London: Routledge & Kegan Paul, 1983.

Limmer, Ruth, ed. *Journey Around My Room: the Autobiography of Louise Bogan*. New York: Viking Press, 1980.

Limmer, Ruth, ed. *What the Woman Lived: Selected Letters of Louise Bogan 1920–1970*. New York: Harcourt Brace Jovanovich, 1973.

Linton, Adeline and Charles Wagley. *Ralph Linton*. New York: Columbia University Press, 1971.

Lipset, David. *Gregory Bateson: the Legacy of a Scientist*. New York: Prentice-Hall, 1980.

Lutkehaus, Nancy. "'She Was Very Cambridge': Camilla Wedgwood and the History of Women in British Social Anthropology." *American Ethnologist* 13, no. 4 (1986): 776–97.

MacClancy, Jeremy and Chris McDonagh. *Popularizing Anthropology*. London: Routledge, 1996.

McDowell, Nancy. *The Mundugumor: From the Fieldnotes of Margaret Mead and Reo Fortune*. Washington, D.C.: Smithsonian Institution, 1991.

——. "The Oceanic Ethnography of Margaret Mead." *American Anthropologist* 82 (1980): 278–303.

Marsh, Jan. *Bloomsbury Women: Distinct Figures in Life and Art*. London: Pavilion Books, 1995.

Matthews, Glenna. *The Rise of Public Woman: Woman's Power and Woman's Place in the United States 1630–1970*. New York: Oxford University Press, 1992.

Mead, Margaret. *An Anthropologist at Work: Writings of Ruth Benedict*. Boston: Houghton Mifflin, 1959.

——. *And Keep Your Powder Dry: An Anthropologist Looks at the American Character*. 1942. Reprint, London: Roland Whiting & Wheaton, 1967.

——. "Bisexuality: what's it all about?" *Redbook*, January 1975, 29–31.

——. *Blackberry Winter: My Earlier Years*. New York: William Morrow, 1972; Pocket Books, 1975.

——. *Coming of Age in Samoa: a Psychological Study of Primitive Youth for Western Civilisation*. New York: William Morrow, 1975 (originally published 1928).

——. *Cooperation and Competition Among Primitive Peoples*. 1937. Reprint, Boston: Beacon Press, 1961.

——. "Field Work in the Pacific Islands." In *Women in the Field: Anthropological Experiences*. Edited by Peggy Golde. Chicago: Aldine, 1970.

——. *Growing Up in New Guinea: A Comparative Study of Primitive Education*. 1930. Reprint, Morrow Quill, 1975.

——. *Letters from the Field 1925–1975*. New York, Harper & Row, 1977.

——. *Male and Female: A Study of the Sexes in a Changing World*. 1949. Reprint, Harmondsworth: Penguin Books, 1962.

——. Papers. Library of Congress, Washington, D.C.

——. *Ruth Benedict*. New York: Columbia University Press, 1974.

——. "Ruth Fulton Benedict, 1887–1948," *American Anthropologist* 51 (1949): 457–62.

——. "Margaret Mead." In *A History of Psychology in Autobiography*, vol. 4, edited by Gardner Lindzey. New York: Prentice-Hall, 1974.

——. *Sex and Temperament in Three Primitive Societies*, 1935. Reprint, New York: Morrow Quill, 1963.

——. *Social Organization of Manua*. Honolulu: Bernice P. Bishop Museum, 1930.

Melosh, Barbara, ed. *Gender and American History Since 1890*. London: Routledge, 1993.

Métraux, Rhoda. "The Study of Culture at a Distance: A Prototype." *American Anthropologist* 82 (1980): 362–73.

Meyers, Jeffrey. *Edmund Wilson: A Biography*. New York: Houghton Mifflin, 1995.

Miller, Jean Baker. *Toward a New Psychology of Women*. Harmondsworth, Middlesex: Penguin Books, 1991.

Miller, Neil. *Out of the Past: Gay and Lesbian History from 1869 to the Present*. New York: Vintage, 1995.

Modell, Judith Schachter. *Ruth Benedict: Patterns of a Life*. Philadelphia: University of Pennsylvania Press, 1983.

Mulvey, Christopher, and John Simons. *New York: City as Text*. London: MacMillan, 1990.

Neuberger, Julia, ed. *The Things that Matter: An Anthology of Women's Spiritual Poetry*. London: Kyle Cathie, 1992.

Oppenheimer, J. Robert. *Robert Oppenheimer: Letters and Recollections*. Edited by Alice Kimball Smith and Charles Weiner. Cambridge, Mass.: Harvard University Press, 1980.

Orans, Martin. *Not Even Wrong: Margaret Mead, Derek Freeman and the Samoans*. Novato: California, Chandler and Sharp, 1996.

Parezo, Nancy J., ed. *Hidden Scholars: Women Anthropologists and the Native American Southwest*. Albuquerque: University of New Mexico Press, 1993.

Perry, Helen Swick. *Psychiatrist of America: The Life of Harry Stack Sullivan*. Cambridge, Mass.: Belknap, 1982.

Phillips, Jock. *A Man's Country? The Image of the Pakeha Male: A History*. Auckland: Penguin Books, 1996.

Phillips-Jones, Linda Lee. *Mentors and Protegés*. New York: Arbor House, 1982.

Powdermaker, Hortense. *Stranger and Friend: The Way of an Anthropologist*. New York: Norton, 1966.

Raitt, Suzanne. *Vita and Virginia: the Work and Friendship of V. Sackville-West and Virginia Woolf*. Oxford, Clarendon Press, 1993.

Raymond, Janice. *A Passion for Friends: Toward a Philosophy of Female Affection*. London: Women's Press, 1986.

Rich, Adrienne. *The Fact of a Doorframe: Poems Selected and New 1950–1984*. New York: Norton, 1984.

Roberts, Priscilla. *Female Mentor Relationships*. Ph.D. diss., Wright Institute, 1987.

Romanucci-Ross, Lola. *Mead's Other Manus: Phenomenology of the Encounter.* South Hadley, Mass.: Bergin & Garvey, 1985.

Rosenberg, Rosalind. *Beyond Separate Spheres: Intellectual Roots of Modern Feminism.* New Haven: Yale University Press, 1982.

——. *Divided Lives: American Women in the Twentieth Century.* New York: Farrar, Straus & Giroux, 1992.

Rossiter, Margaret W. *Women Scientists in America: Before Affirmative Action 1940–1972.* Baltimore: Johns Hopkins University Press, 1995.

Rossiter, Margaret W. *Women Scientists in America: Struggles and Strategies to 1940.* Baltimore: Johns Hopkins University Press, 1982.

*Ruth Fulton Benedict: A Memorial.* Wenner-Gren Foundation for Anthropological Research. Viking Fund, 1949.

Sahli, Nancy. "Smashing: Women's Relationships Before the Fall." *Chrysalis* 8 (1979): 152–162.

Sapir, Edward. "Observations on the Sex Problem in America." *American Journal of Psychiatry* 8 (1928): 519–34. Reprinted in *American Mercury* 16 (1929): 413–420.

——. Papers. Private Collection.

——. "The Unconscious Patterning of Behavior in Society." In *The Unconscious: A Symposium,* edited by E. S. Dummer. New York: Alfred A. Knopf, 1927.

Silverman, Sydel, ed. *Totems and Teachers: Perspectives on the History of Anthropology.* New York: Columbia University Press, 1981.

Smith-Rosenberg, Carroll. *Disorderly Conduct: Visions of Gender in Victorian America.* New York: Oxford University Press, 1985.

Solomon, Barbara Miller. *In the Company of Educated Women: A History of Women and Higher Education in America.* New Haven: Yale University Press, 1985.

Spender, Dale, ed. *Feminist Theorists.* London: The Women's Press, 1983.

Steiner, Vera-John. *Notebooks of the Mind: Explorations of Thinking.* New York: Harper and Row, 1987.

Stern, Philip M. and Harold P. Green. *The Oppenheimer Case: Security on Trial.* London: Rupert Hart-Davis, 1971.

Stocking, George W. Jr. *The Ethnographer's Magic and Other Essays in the History of Anthropology.* Madison: University of Wisconsin Press, 1992.

——. ed. *Bones, Bodies, Behavior: Essays on Biological Anthropology.* Madison: University of Wisconsin Press, 1988.

——. ed. *Malinowski, Rivers, Benedict and Others: Essays in Culture and Personality.* Madison: University of Wisconsin Press, 1986.

Takaki, Ronald. *A Different Mirror: A History of Multicultural America.* New York: Little, Brown, 1993.

Tomalin, Claire. *The Life and Death of Mary Wollstonecraft.* Harmondsworth, Middlesex: Penguin Books, 1977.

Torgovnick, Marianna. *Gone Primitive: Savage Intellects, Modern Lives.* Chicago: University of Chicago Press, 1990.

Torrey, E. Fuller. *Freudian Fraud: the Malignant Effect of Freud's Theory on American Thought and Culture.* New York: Harper Collins, 1992.

Viking Fund. *Ruth Fulton Benedict: A Memorial,* New York, 1949.

Voget, Fred W. *A History of Ethnology.* New York: Holt, Rinehart & Winston, 1975.

White, Morton. *Social Thought in America: the Revolt Against Formalism.* Boston: Beacon Press, 1957.

Williamson, David. *The Heretic: Based on the Life of Derek Freeman.* Melbourne: Penguin Books, 1996.

Wilson, Edmund. *The Fifties: From Notebooks and Diaries of the Period*. New York: Farrar, Straus and Giroux, 1986.

——. *The Twenties: From Notebooks and Diaries of the Period*. New York: Farrar, Straus and Giroux, 1975.

Yans-McLaughlin, Virginia. *Margaret Mead: An Observer Observed*. Produced and directed by Alan Berliner, 1996.

Zumwalt, Rosemary Lévy. *Wealth and Rebellion: Elsie Clews Parsons, Anthropologist and Folklorist*. Urbana: University of Illinois Press, 1992.

# INDEX

Benedict, Ruth Fulton (*cont.*)
74, 165, 179, 190, 231, 283, 289–90;
childhood of, 34–40; early career of,
43–49, 61–62; at Columbia University,
52, 53, 60–62, 74, 110, 134, 139, 168,
178–79, 200, 226, 250, 256–57, 297–
99; death of, 301–4; health of, 10, 38,
50–52, 117, 168, 212, 252–53, 259, 261,
282, 289, 300; inner life of, 34–38, 40–
41, 44–47, 50, 64–65, 68, 86, 158–59,
179, 181–82, 260–62, 301; and *Journal
of American Folklore*, 74; lesbianism of,
75, 87–89, 92–96, 240, 252, 259–60,
277, 313 n. 12, 330 n. 10; marriages
of, 46–50, 51, 52, 63–65, 86, 90, 117,
197–98, 199; at New School for Social
Research, 52–53, 60, 286; personality
of, 33–34, 87, 260–62; political activities of, 274–75; pseudonyms, use of,
85, 100, 122, 134, 212; and Research in
Contemporary Cultures project, 297–
98; and Southwest Concordance project, 62–63, 139, 257; and UNESCO,
299–300; at Vassar College, 41–43; war
work of, 289, 291–93

fieldwork of: Apache, 202–5; Blackfoot
and Blood, 275–76; Cochiti, 108–9,
177; Pima, 177–78, 183; Serrano, 61; in
Southwest, 101, 102–10, 177; Zuñi,
102–8, 178

and Margaret Mead: early relationship of,
9–10, 33, 68–74, 81–82, 85–87, 90–
93, 94, 96, 102, 113–14, 117, 121–25,
138, 155–58, 160–63, 165, 169–70,
319 n. 29; sexual relationship, 1–7, 75–
77, 92, 93–96; Grand Canyon pact,
124–25, 158, 319 n. 31; loving friendship, 228, 264–67, 272–73, 279, 287–
88, 298; collaborative partnership,
164–66, 207–8, 216, 235; correspondence, 106, 131–33, 156, 205, 210, 211,
221, 226, 252, 254–56, 264–67, 277,
279–82, 283, 320 n. 4

writings of: "Anthropology and the
Abnormal," 213–14, 235; *The Chrysan-
themum and the Sword*, 3, 236, 289, 292,
293, 294; "Configurations of Culture in
North America," 215; diary, 129–29;
*Patterns of Culture*, 3, 61, 178, 214–17,

222, 229, 230–33, 260, 266; poetry, 51,
65, 85, 87–89, 90–91, 94–96, 98–100,
113–14, 131–32, 139, 159–60, 179–80,
185, 287; on psychological types in the
Southwest, 190; *Race: Science and Politics*,
276, 285, 290; "The Story of My Life,"
34, 35, 47, 244, 260; *Tales of the Cochiti
Indians*, 109, 139; unfinished essays, 89–
90; "The Vision in Plains Culture," 33;
*Zuñi Mythology*, 106, 109, 139, 229, 257

*See also* Boas, Franz; Eichelberger, Marie;
Raymond, Natalie; Reichard, Gladys;
Sapir, Edward; Valentine, Ruth ("Val")

Benedict, Stanley, 46–52, 63–65, 77, 79, 86,
90, 110, 117, 134, 139, 156, 182, 194,
197–99, 253–54

Bernard, Jessie, 41, 51

bisexuality, 31, 76, 158, 243, 308

*Blackberry Winter* (Mead), 4, 10–11, 23, 27, 29,
68, 111, 183, 184, 244, 274, 306–7, 309

Blackfoot and Blood, 275–76

Bloomfield, Leonard, 67

Bloomfield, Marie, 10, 33, 67–68, 82, 89

Blumensohn, Jules. *See* Henry, Jules

Boas, Franz: and anthropology, 55–58, 108,
165; fieldwork of, 9; and RFB, 9, 53,
60–61, 74, 165, 179, 190, 231, 283,
289–90; and Ruth Bunzel, 105; family
misfortunes of, 118, 190; and Alexander
Goldenweiser, 286; illness of, 190; and
Ralph Linton, 258; and MM, 69–70,
77, 111–12, 120, 121, 127, 129, 165, 170,
171, 173, 255, 304; political activities
of, 274–75, 332 n. 44; retirement and
death, 226, 250, 256, 289–90; and
Henrietta Schmerler, 205–6; as
teacher, 71; and women, 58–60

Bogan, Louise: and Léonie Adams, 82, 84,
138, 166, 181, 212, 298, 310; and RFB, 87,
139–40, 156, 159, 174, 177, 182, 298; and
MM, 1, 87, 114, 126, 194, 265, 298; marriages of, 83, 133; mental breakdown,
194–95; as poet, 82–83, 310, 311

Booth, Gotthard, 296

"Boston marriage," 42. *See also* collaborative
friendships; mentoring relationships;
romantic friendships between women

Bourdet, Edouard, 158, 180

Bradley, Albert and Undine, 139, 203, 278

New School for Social Research, 52–53, 55, 60, 286

Newton, Lee, 31, 78

"New Women," 54, 140

Nietzsche, Friedrich, 42, 178

normality. *See* deviance and normality

Ogburn, William Fielding, 70, 74, 81, 82, 175, 176

O'Keefe, Georgia, 103

Omaha, 196–97

*Omaha Secret Societies* (Fortune), 197

Opler, Morris, 204

Oppenheimer, Robert, 203–4, 205, 229, 252, 292

Orans, Martin, 147, 236, 321 n. 22, 323 n. 9

Orton, Anna B., 47

Parsons, Elsie Clews: and RFB, 52–53, 62–63, 139, 141, 190, 257; at Columbia, 74; and female anthropologists, 201–2; fieldwork methods of, 104–5, 107; and Alexander Goldenweiser, 110; as mentor and patron of anthropologists, 58; as protégée of Boas, 58; and racism, 231 n. 26; Sapir's view of, 325 n. 9; and Southwest Concordance project, 62–63, 139, 257; views on choice of Boas's successor, 257

*Patterns of Culture* (Benedict) 3, 61, 178, 214–17, 222, 229, 230–33, 260, 266

Phillips, Eleanor, 160, 302

Piddington, Ralph, 327 n. 26

Pima, 177–78, 183

Plath, Sylvia, 164

Plume, Jim Little, 276

Pope, Eileen, 255, 256, 309

Powdermaker, Hortense, 152

Poznanski, Gitel, 275

Progressive Education Association, 275

*Psychiatry*, 291

psychoanalysis, 17, 27, 233–35, 239, 253, 294, 295. *See also* Freud, Sigmund

*The Pueblo Potter* (Bunzel), 106, 215

Purari, 240–41

Quain, Buell, 235, 277–78, 290

Quintana, Santiago, 109

*Race: Science and Politics* (Benedict), 276, 285, 290

"Races of Mankind" (Benedict and Weltfish), 290

racism, 56, 69, 77, 276, 285, 290. *See also* anti-Semitism

Radcliffe-Brown, A. R., 176, 186–87, 221, 226–27, 231, 240, 241, 242, 257

Radin, Paul, 137

Raymond, Natalie, 140, 204, 227, 230, 251–52, 262–63, 276, 278, 282, 286, 289, 310–11; 327 n. 17; and RFB, 139–40, 203–5, 210–13, 227, 245, 249–53, 282, 300, 304–6, 310; lesbianism of, 204, 205, 304–6, 310; and MM, 228; and Robert Oppenheimer, 203–4, 229, 292

Reichard, Gladys, 62, 73, 77, 160, 161, 168, 183, 196, 200, 202, 205, 206, 233

Research in Contemporary Cultures (R.C.C.) project, 297–98

Rich, Adrienne, 2

Rivers, W. H., 221

Rodin, Auguste, 164

romantic friendships between women, 6, 24–25, 32, 42. *See also* collaborative friendships; mentoring relationships

Romanucci-Ross, Lola, 186

Roosevelt, Eleanor, 274

Rorschach testing, 260, 296, 303

Rosenblatt, Louise, 28, 82, 114, 153, 156, 180, 181, 274, 330 n. 1

Rossiter, Margaret, 59

Rosten, Priscilla Mead (MM's sister), 16, 175, 279, 309, 317 n. 21

Rothenberger, Katharine, 23–26, 27, 73, 84, 153, 157, 284, 296

Sackville-West, Vita, 164, 324 n. 14

Samoa, 126–30, 135–37, 140–47, 323 n. 9, 327 n. 26

Sanger, Margaret, 176

Sapir, Edward: and "culture and personality" school of anthropology, 109–10, 165, 178, 258, 325 n. 5; career of, 118, 211–12, 227, 325 n. 9; death of, 269–72; and feminism, 121; and MM, 100–102, 110–11, 112–13, 115, 116, 118–22, 135–36, 140, 151, 165, 193, 270–71,

Victoria University College, 149
"The Vision in Plains Culture" (Benedict), 33

Waddington, C. H., 229
Walton, Edna Lou, 176
Warner, W. Lloyd, 257
*The Waves* (Woolf), 214
*We Sing Diana* (Neff), 180–81
Wedgwood, Camilla, 152
Wellesley College, 11, 22
*The Well of Loneliness* (Hall), 180
Weltfish, Gene, 290–91
*Where We Once Belonged* (Figiel), 324 n. 9
Whitman, Walt, 42
Williamson, David, 143, 321 n. 18
Wilson, Edmund, 83, 84, 196, 212
Winchell, Walter, 275

Wissler, Clark, 166, 190
Wolfson, Rose, 85
Wollstonecraft, Mary, 43, 48–49, 156
women: in anthropology, 58–60, 119, 166, 201–2, 205–7, 226, 232–33, 299, 307; in higher education, 27, 54, 59; in science, 42, 59, 166, 232, 298–99
women's suffrage, 42–43, 46, 78, 164
Woodbury, Nathalie, 259
Woolf, Virginia, *The Waves*, 214

Yale University, 211–12

Zachry, Carolyn, 233, 260
Zuñi, 102–8, 129, 178, 257
Zuñi, Flora, 106, 107
*Zuñi Mythology* (Benedict), 106, 109, 139, 229, 257

Hilary Lapsley teaches women's and gender studies
and psychology at the University of Waikato,
Hamilton, New Zealand.